THE
SILENCED
THEATRE

Marketa Goetz-Stankiewicz

THE SILENCED THEATRE: Czech playwrights without a stage

UNIVERSITY OF TORONTO PRESS

Toronto Buffalo London

© University of Toronto Press 1979
Toronto Buffalo London
Printed in Canada

Library of Congress Cataloging in Publication Data

Goetz-Stankiewicz, Marketa.
The silenced theatre.
Bibliography: p.
Includes index.
1. Czech drama – 20th century – History and
criticism. 2. Dramatists, Czech – 20th century
– Biography. I. Title.
PG5009.G6   792'.09437   79-13423
ISBN 0-8020-5426-9

TO MY MOTHER
AND THE MEMORY OF MY FATHER

Contents

Preface

In several ways this book does less than its title promises; in other ways it tries to do more. Although a considerable number of the plays discussed in this volume have been translated into English (as well as German and French), I felt that in order to familiarize the reader with the material, I had to give some idea of the content of the plays. To those who know the plays I apologize for discussion of plots. This is by no means a systematic survey of modern Czech theatre, or even a complete study of the playwrights I have chosen. There are other playwrights who could have provided additional interesting material. Indeed the disturbing thought that I am not doing justice to much good writing has pursued me throughout my work. However, the line had to be drawn somewhere. I have shaped my argument around those playwrights and plays which I found most significant in regard to the particular quality of the genius of Czech writers; and I have tried to shed light on those areas that reflect the close relationship of the spirit of modern theatre in Czechoslovakia to theatre in the Western world.

Throughout my work I have been conscious of moving in the vaguely defined area where politics and the humanities meet. I wanted to write a book about the theatre but I constantly ran into political questions, matters of ideology, social criticism, censorship, and philosophical questions, such as freedom of choice, ethical judgments, and the nature of truth.

Gradually I found I was assessing the literary works of a group of writers over a twenty-year period which encompassed three phases of what is officially called a 'Socialist society': the recovery from the personality cult of Stalinism in the late fifties; the gradual coming of the political thaw which culminated in the Prague Spring of 1968 with its by now famous phrase 'Socialism with a human face,' coined by the then party leader Alexander Dubček, and its almost incredible outburst of artistic creativity; and the renewed tightening of controls after the occupation of Czechoslovakia by Soviet troops in August 1968 which has turned the most western of Slavic countries into a fortress of orthodox Communism and has submitted almost all the writers discussed in this book to various kinds of persecution.

Seen from the point of view of literature, a graph of the twenty years under discussion would show an abrupt change of direction: in the first ten years, literature was on the rise, acquiring constantly more freedom of expression and developing with increased momentum into a veritable renascence movement of amazing artistic vitality. Then, on the high point of creativity, the Damocles sword of Soviet occupation indeed fell and, after a period of stunned silence, there began a new literary movement, carried out by the same and new writers – but underground. The plays dated after 1969 therefore – and more than half of the ones discussed in this book are among them – have virtually all been brought out of Czechoslovakia by some means or other in typescript and were published abroad, more often than not in translation. In Czechoslovakia itself they circulate underground, together with prose and poetry, read to shreds by hundreds within months, retyped by loyal hands, nicknamed *Edice Petlice** the Czech equivalent of *samizdat*.

And so, like the characters in Ivan Klíma's play *Games*, I found myself treading on political ground where I thought I was merely on a theatre-stage. Inevitably it became one of my aims to try to transmit this singular experience to the reader.

M.G.-S.
University of British Columbia
July 1978

---

* Rendered into English it means something like 'series under lock and key.' According to lists published in *Svědectví*, ten of the works discussed in this book are circulating under official *Edice Petlice* numbers. The full library of the underground editions includes by now more than a hundred numbered typescripts.

Acknowledgments

I would like to acknowledge my gratitude to a number of people, though I cannot mention all by name. I am particularly indebted to Professor Josef Škvorecký for invaluable advice and encouraging support throughout my work. My colleague Dr Peter Stenberg was a constant source of help and read critically most of the manuscript. I am also grateful to Professor Milan Dimić of the University of Alberta for his support. Mr Eric Spiess of the Bärenreiter-Verlag in Kassel, and Mr Klaus Juncker of the Rowohlt Theater-Verlag in Hamburg, helped me generously by making information and typescripts of new plays available to me.

My thanks for help at the University of British Columbia also go to Ms Margaret Friesen, Head of Interlibrary Loan, and her staff, and to Ms Anne Yandle, Head of Special Collections, and her staff. I wish to thank Ms Beryl Morphet for her assistance during various stages of the manuscript, Ms Evelyn Cobley for typing in various languages, and Ms Elizabeth Spence for her careful typing of the index. From my husband, W.J. Stankiewicz, I have learned much more about reasoning than he realizes.

I would like to acknowledge with gratitude permission to use material which has appeared before. An abbreviated version of chapter 1 appeared in *Survey* 1/2 (1975) 85–100, and appears here with the permission of the editor. Chapter 3 is an expanded and revised version of the article 'Pavel Kohout: the Barometer of Czechoslovakia's Theatre' which appeared in *Modern Drama* 20 (1977) 251–62. Integrated into this study at various points is material used in a paper I gave at the meetings of the Philological Association of the Pacific Coast in November 1971, printed in *Pacific Coast Philology* 7 (1972) 54–64.

I gratefully acknowledge a leave fellowship and a research grant from the Canada Council and financial aid from the University Committee on Research, University of British Columbia.

This book has been published with the help of a grant from the Canadian Federation for the Humanities, using funds provided by the Social Sciences and Humanities Research Council of Canada, and a grant to University of Toronto Press from the Andrew W. Mellon Foundation.

Pavel Kohout

Václav Havel

Milan Kundera

Ivan Klíma with his wife

Pavel Landovský and Václav Havel

Milan Uhde

Pavel Landovský in *The Cherry Orchard*, Činoherní Klub, Prague, 1973/74

Josef Topol's *Cat on the Rails*, University of Toronto, 1974

David Harford

Václav Havel's *Vernissage*, with Joachim Bissmeier, Sebastian Fischer, and Sonja Sutter: première at the Akademietheater des Burgtheaters in Vienna on 9 October 1976
Elisabeth Hauptmann

Vernissage, with Irmhild Wagner, Horst Reichel, and Horst Naumann, Munich 1977

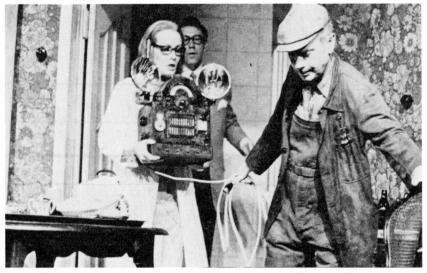

Václav Havel's *The Increased Difficulty of Concentration* Berlin 1968

Première of Havel's *The Conspirators* Baden-Baden 1974 Tschira

Johannes Schauer as Sládek in the première of Havel's *Audience*
Vienna 1976

Horst Naumann and Horst Reichel in *Audience* Munich 1977

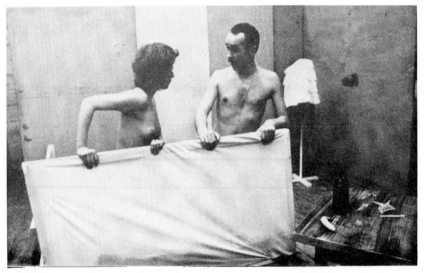

Première of Pavel Kohout's *Fire in the Basement* Ingolstadt 1974   Roman Weiss

Jan Grossman's 1967 staging of *The Trial* at Theatre On the Balustrade

Maria Schell as Tatyana and Laurence Luckinbill as Kerzhentsev in Pavel Kohout's
Poor Murderer at the Ethel Barrymore Theatre on Broadway in October
1976; Luckinbill was also co-translator of the play.

Kohout's production of *Macbeth* in a Prague apartment in 1978. Pavel Kohout
(left) directed. Pavel Landovský (centre) and the great Czech actess Vlasta
Chrámostová (second from right) played lead roles; neither has appeared on a
'legal' stage for years. V. Třešňák (with guitar) wrote musical accompaniment
and, with Kohout and his daughter Tereza (right), played all the other roles.
This production inspired Tom Stoppard's *Cahoot's Macbeth*.

THE
SILENCED
THEATRE

Introduction

If life cannot be destroyed for good, neither then can history be entirely brought to a halt. A secret streamlet trickles on beneath the heavy crust of inertia and pseudo-events, slowly and inconspicuously undercutting it. It may be a long process, but one day it has to happen: the crust can no longer hold and starts to crack.

VÁCLAV HAVEL 'An Open Letter from Prague' 1975

Czechoslovakia is a country of paradoxes: it lies at the crossroads of Europe where East and West meet – but also part. It has an ancient history; the Kingdom of Bohemia 'on the roof of Europe' has been coveted by rulers for centuries and there is a good deal of truth in the saying that 'he who rules over Bohemia rules over Europe.' Yet Czechoslovakia's history as an independent nation lasted only for a brief twenty-one years – hardly enough time for an individual to achieve maturity, let alone an entire people. Its national anthem, singularly peaceful and unpolitical, dwells on the beauty of the hills and valleys of home; yet these hills and valleys have been overrun by alien armies three times during the last thirty years. Czechoslovakia is known to the world as the small country with the long name, the land that makes fine crystal and pretty toys and brews good beer. But Czechoslovakia is also, to name only a few examples, the home country of one of the most outstanding figures of the Reformation (Jan Amos Comenius); it has given the world great composers (Smetana, Dvořák, Janáček, Martinů); it has played an important part in launching modern linguistics; and it has won a disproportionate number of prizes at international film festivals.[1]

'Czechoslovakians' – Czechs and Slovaks – are not easily identifiable outside their own country. This is partly due to the reticence of the citizen of a small country; partly because of the cosmopolitan air which seems to come from their deep collective awareness that they have always been centre stage when the European theatre of war and politics carried out its great conflicts over the past hundreds of years. Yet their attachment to their land is deep and lasting. It is not particularly enlightening to speculate whether this dual nature of the nation is historically conditioned. Nevertheless it might be worthwhile to remind ourselves that for centuries they have had 'foreigners' inhabiting, working in, or ruling their country. They got used to the world moving in on them. They got used to remaining quietly rooted in their own culture while they had to cope with changing regimes, changing 'official' languages, armies coming and going and coming again.

The history of the Czech theatre,[2] like that of the people themselves, has had this dual nature, being strongly localized on the one hand and international on the other. Born during the Czechs' struggle against oppression in the late eighteenth century, the theatre was initially a means for expressing strong national convictions. But its further development was hampered by political, economic, and social factors. The development of Czech culture was repeatedly interrupted by violent historical changes and upheavals and survived a series of crises only because of the unfailing creative spirit of the rural population.

By the fourteenth century, in early liturgical plays, the theatrical and comic genius of the Czech people was apparent. For example, an anonymous author extracted an unimportant scene from a Latin religious play, The Three Marys, and expanded it into a spirited comedy called The Quack written in the lively Czech vernacular of the fourteenth century. After the Hussite Wars of the late sixteenth century, Czech folk plays became increasingly secularized and, although of little interest today, they pay witness to the colourfulness of the Czech language and the theatrical resourcefulness of its writers. After the Battle of the White Mountain (1620) and the Thirty Years' War, the Czech nation was reduced to its lowest cultural level. Recovery was very slow.

More than a century and a half later, in 1788, one of the nation's most honest spokesmen and patriots, the scholar Josef Dobrovský, made the sad prediction that in the course of the next fifty years the last remnants of Czech individuality would be drowned in the sea of German culture. So general was the feeling of resignation that there was considerable excitement in Prague in 1771 when people discovered that a municipal theatre in Prague was going to stage a play in the Czech language. For the first time in Czech theatrical history a play in the language of the people reached the august stage of an 'official' theatre.[3] If we add that the play was actually performed by German actors who did not know how to pronounce Czech, we realize that Czech culture was in an 'absurd' state long before this word was sanctioned by literary critics. Nevertheless, these curious performances mark the beginning of the modern Czech theatre. A few years later two theatres in Prague staged plays in the Czech language. Czech translations of Shakespeare became great successes in an independent Czech theatre, 'The Royal Imperial Patriotic Theatre,' nicknamed *The Shanty*.[4] Joseph II, the Holy Roman Emperor, greatly beloved and respected by the Czech people, officially sanctioned these patriotic endeavours to further the rise of local culture. Of course by now it was quite late. The literature of the rest of Western Europe had begun to flourish much earlier.

At the end of the eighteenth century a remarkable original dramatization of a legendary tale based on eleventh-century Czech history – the story of Oldřich and Božena – became a focal point for the growing patriotic consciousness. Oldřich was a ruling Czech prince who took a simple peasant girl as his wife. Under the guise of writing a historical play the author formulated entirely new views about the beneficial influences of a wise and just ruler who is in contact with the people and is aware of their problems. It is typical of the constant harassment of Czech culture that almost 200 years later, in 1967, another Czech writer – the poet František Hrubín – chose the same historical material to tell his people that they ought to remember that the great moments of their past came from quiet wisdom and rational peacefulness rather than from the victories and conquests which were constantly sought by neighboring nations. And again this writer had to disguise his message as a remote historical play in order to make it acceptable to the censors. Both performances, that of the eighteenth and that of the twentieth century, were great successes. The earlier version even became something of a cause célèbre. Simple country folk, ignorant of other languages than their own, who had moved to Prague as a result of the abolition of serfdom, made an enthusiastic audience, grateful for being able to see a play that they could understand. They were the first dedicated patrons of the new Czech theatre.[5]

With the achievement of national independence in 1918, vigorous Czech and Slovak theatres became national institutions. Now the theatre culture could expand and flourish freely. Translations of foreign authors were produced at the national theatres; opera, in which the Czech musical genius excelled, was integrated into the programs; a talented new generation of stage designers began to do highly original work. World theatre opened up to Czechoslovakia and Czechoslovakia opened up to world theatre. It is here that one encounters figures like Karel Čapek (1890–1938) whose works have made their way into the ranks of world literature. In his prophetic play *RUR* (1920) he not only coined the expression 'robot' or human machine with all its explosive connotations which have become even more dynamic since the appearance of computers, but he also wrote the brilliant novel *War with the Newts* (1935) which anticipates Orwell, and wrote (with his brother Joseph) *The Insect Play* (1921), which took the world by storm and was produced with great success in London (1923) after its world première in New York (1922).[6]

There is a saying in what used to be a bilingual part of Bohemia that if a son is born to a German mother and Czech father (or Czech mother and German father) you just have to watch his behaviour when he sees the light of his first day and you will be able to foretell his future. If he starts kicking he will be a German – and a soldier; if he starts crying, he will be a Czech – and a musician. This piece of folk wisdom is obviously simplistic (and could be interpreted as slighting either the Czechs or the Germans, depending on who tells it to whom, and when) but it is nevertheless interesting for its suggestion that a Czech is identifiable by his early dedication to the art of music, and hence to performance, to the theatre. Indeed, the Czechoslovak nation is a nation of the theatre par excellence.

A few facts must suffice: Consider the extraordinary phenomenon of Czech amateur theatre groups which were much more influential in the forming of modern professional theatre than those of any other European culture. The paradoxical fact is that the unpropitious historical circumstances – the prolonged suppression of the Czech language as a medium for official forms of art and other communications – resulted in the exact opposite of what had been intended. In areas where the Czech-speaking population was concentrated, amateur theatre groups flourished, and their productions, conducted exclusively in the Czech language, became an important source of culture for the population.[7] There were all kinds of theatrical centres in the mid-Bohemian plains as well as the encircling mountain ranges where popular plays were staged and villagers watched their friends and relatives perform on stage.

It was, as we know, only at the end of the eighteenth century that we have the first signs of professionalism in the Czech theatre. However, even then plays in the Czech language were performed only in cities like Prague, Brno, and Olomouc and the population of small towns and rural districts rarely managed to see any of these performances. It was the amateur stages that kept alive the tradition of theatre in the Czech language. Glancing at the historical material one finds surprising facts: for example, during the 1830s and 1840s, amateur groups played in 130 Bohemian and Moravian towns. Even local Czech authors' plays which are now part of classical Czech literature had their premières in smaller towns in amateur theatres. The official theatre in Prague did not favour local playwrights.

An even more surprising fact is that as late as the 1880s amateur theatres were responsible for introducing to the Czech stage what were then 'avant-garde' authors – for example, Ibsen and Hauptmann. Even in the twentieth century, when professional theatres in Czechoslovakia thrived in cities and small towns alike, the activity of amateur theatres continued as lively as ever. Between the First and Second World Wars almost all new plays by contemporary authors were performed by amateur groups. In the mid-sixties Prague alone had sixty amateur theatre groups; in 1971 we find there were 1535 amateur ensembles in Czechoslovakia. Moreover the citizens themselves frequently financed the construction of buildings which would house amateur groups; in the nineteenth century there were fifteen such subsidized theatres built, in the twentieth century, eighteen.

The amateur theatres, in addition to demonstrating the sheer enthusiasm of the population for theatrical activity, had a profound effect on the shaping of Czech national culture. An ensemble consisting, say, of the physician, the barber, the school teacher, the mayor's daughter, the cobbler's brother, the lawyer's and the butcher's wives, and the priest's sister will have a much stronger influence on moulding the cultural awareness of the village than a professional theatre group could ever have. The actors are an integral part of the life of the community; they study their parts at breakfast, discuss the intonation with their families, the meaning of a line with their neighbours, their costume with the mailman; the staging of a play becomes an event in which the whole community becomes involved.

In one of the most beautiful buildings in Prague, the National Theatre, on the embankment of the Vltava from where one has the most famous view of the Hradčany Castle, we find an inscription on an arch above the stage: 'To the Nation by the Nation.' This building, *Národní divadlo*, has not ceased to be a symbol of national pride despite the violent political changes it has witnessed and the restrictions and orders with which it has had to comply. Constructed during the 1860s, the theatre was built from funds raised throughout the country and its symbolic value for the nation is one of cultural identity and national independence. Yet, ironically, the plays performed on its magnificent stage have often been out of harmony with the spirit in which the theatre was conceived: for a time it was a stronghold of imitation of the Paris and London theatre scene; during times of occupation it housed 'safe' classics or non-committal comedies. However, the Czechs have learned to live with ironic situations.

It must be noted in all fairness that until now Czech and Slovak literatures have made their marks on the international literary scene only at rare occasions. The fact that writers wrote in languages which are spoken by fewer than fifteen million people (ten million speaking Czech; five million the closely related Slovak) has, of course, something to do with this. But this is a large question and touches on the complex problem of the vicissitudes of cultural interchanges. It takes more learning than I have at my disposal to attempt to tackle such a problem. All that I can say here is that the plays discussed in this volume, representing the output of just over a dozen writers and a time span of about two decades, stand up extremely well in a match with the best plays written during the same period in Western countries. Written in a variety of brilliant dramatic styles they reflect our world in all its confusion of values: its mixture of cruelty and resignation, hope and cynicism; its nervous realism and anxious groping for metaphysics; its laughter for fear of crying; its frantic attempt to make sense of nonsense by making nonsense of sense.

By now we have realized the truly paradoxical nature of much of Czechoslovakia's life and culture. Here comes another significant paradox: Franz Kafka and Jaroslav Hašek, two great writers whose writings are deeply rooted in Czech culture and who have had a profound effect on contemporary Czechoslovak literature, have been called 'the outsiders'[8] of Czechoslovak literature. Kafka did not write in Czech; Hašek was an embarrassment to Czech literary authorities. Kafka wanted his writings to be burned after his death, works so mysterious that volumes have been written in an attempt to find the key; Hašek published his great novel as an entertaining serial in a Prague newspaper.

Kafka became one of the towering figures in twentieth century literature after his death; yet he is not as a rule thought of as a Czech writer because he wrote in German. Hašek's *Good Soldier Švejk*[9] has become popular throughout the Western world as the naïve fool who always gets by somehow, the simpleton who always has just enough luck, the thick-skulled fellow who always survives with his sly sense of humour. Švejk is probably better known as a general image of man than as the character of a Czech novel, so that Czechoslovak literature gets less credit from its most famous literary character than might be expected.

These two so drastically different, internationally acclaimed writers emerged at the same time (both were born in 1883) from largely the same environment (although, of course, I am not discounting the influence of Kafka's Jewish religious background on his writings). They grew up under the same peculiar social and political developments – developments which within their lifetimes brought about an independent Czechoslovakia from the old province of the Austro-Hungarian Empire. Would it perhaps be possible to trace certain intrinsic qualities from these two great 'outsiders' of Czechoslovak literature to that literature itself and regard their writings as keys to that particular consciousness of the human being which is reflected in the works of the playwrights we will be discussing?

W.H. Auden is quoted as having said about Kafka that he came nearest to 'bearing the same kind of relation to our age as Dante, Shakespeare and Goethe bore to theirs.'[10] Or, as the anonymous saying goes: 'Everyone has his Kafka.' Perhaps it is a typical sign of our times that one of the most universal writers changes his identity with the beholder; in other words, he exemplifies the deep-seated relativism of our age. Or, to rethink the proposition from another aspect, it is significant that our age takes so much interest in a writer whose variable meaning presents a constant challenge to our intellectual sensibilities, a writer whose work was described by Camus as 'steeped in a vast hope'[11] and by Edmund Wilson as 'the half expressed gasp of a self-doubting soul trampled under.'[12] Everyone, indeed, has his own Kafka.

The case of the Czechoslovaks' Kafka is particularly complicated because he came from among them. He was born in Prague and spent almost all of his life there, yet was not a Czech; he described Prague with the sure instinct of deep familiarity, yet he did so in a language that was not Czech; foremost representative and an outsider at the same time, his very situation as a writer forms a strange parallel to the ambiguous homelessness of his heroes. Kafka was born a citizen of the Austro-Hungarian Empire and died a citizen of the Czechoslovak Republic. He was surrounded by an active literary scene but his relationship to it was arranged and regulated by his friends. He lived at the focal point of great historical changes but his work shows no trace of this fact, and his personal attitude seems to have been that of a distant, unconcerned observer. On 2 August 1914, for example, he wrote in his diary: 'Germany declared war on Russia – afternoon to swimming pool.'[13] Milena Jesenská, the woman to whom Kafka wrote his magnificent letters (later published), wrote in a Czech newspaper an obituary on Kafka that began: 'The day before yesterday, Dr. Franz Kafka, a German writer who lived in Prague, died in the Kierling sanatorium near Klosterneuburg near Vienna.'[14] She could have written equally well 'A

Czech citizen who wrote in German,' or 'A German who lived and wrote in Czechoslovakia.' Each statement would have been equally correct and equally incorrect. Somehow the only fact that remains is that Kafka was a writer and lived in Prague; everything else seems incidental.

The Czech translation of *The Castle* appeared in 1935 in a surrealist series published by the Society of the Plastic Arts Manes in Prague. On the cover was a surrealist photomontage by a contemporary artist.[15] The label of surrealism stuck well as – regrettably – most labels do. As late as 1948 a Prague writer of the same background as Kafka called him 'a great surrealist before surrealism.'[16] But on the whole the Czech reaction to the first translation into Czech of what I think to be Kafka's greatest novel was very slight. The foremost Czech critic of the time, F.X. Šalda, off-handedly mentioned Kafka in a contemporary review as a German writer who had had some impact in France. Apart from two or three reviews and some agitation among young writers and artists who seemed to feel a spiritual affinity with the novel, scholars and commentators (including the German literary circles in Prague) remained silent. During the German occupation Kafka's work was ostracized once again from the official literary scene. Regarded as dangerous and disruptive during the period of Stalinism, he was once again sentenced to silence and oblivion.

On 14 December 1963 the Prague literary journal *Literární noviny* announced the production of an American play with a strange title: *Kdopak by se Kafky bál?* (*Who would be afraid of Kafka?*) When Western sources realized that Edward Albee's *Who's Afraid of Virginia Woolf?* had been translated in this way, they expressed amusement about the awkward way the Czechoslovaks had rendered Albee's suggestive English title. However, the translator of Albee's play, the poet and artist Jiří Kolář, knew precisely what he was doing.

Virginia Woolf was at the time practically unknown in Czechoslovakia,[17] equally unknown or forgotten was the Walt Disney song 'Who's afraid of the Big Bad Wolf?' A literal translation of Albee's title would therefore not produce any associations. The name Kafka, however, would substitute for it extremely well. Both writers, Kafka and Woolf, are regarded as difficult, obscure, incomprehensible to many readers.

There is in addition another, more concealed connotation which suggests how perfect the rendering was. Kafka (which means 'jackdaw' in Czech) had become much more threatening than a black bird with an unpleasant croak; his literary image was indeed something like a big bad wolf, vicious and perverted, dangerous to the obedient herd of the general population. During periods of political thaw, all kinds of allegedly dangerous creatures are given a second look. And so in the 1960s the eternal outsider was finally taken (though again only for a brief period) to the bosom of his own country.[18]

In May 1963 an official Kafka Conference was organized on the property of the Czech Academy of Sciences, the Liblice Castle near Prague, where approximately one hundred scholars and writers, including many foreigners, spent several days discussing the writings of Franz Kafka. We have space here to delineate only one of the key ideas which emerged from this conference but it is one that should help crystallize the differences between Western and Eastern European understanding of literature. Interpretations of Kafka in the West stress above all his 'timeless' aspects, the workings of man's consciousness, his primeval sense of guilt, his isolation and distorted sense of reality. Eastern Europeans tend to underline the 'topicality' of Kafka for this age and its problems. The Polish critic Jan Kott finds that Kafka expresses the nightmares of our age through the relentless present tense of a dream that cannot escape into the past or the future. In Kafka's world there exists only the here and now and his heroes 'are constantly in the cruel present.' Erotic dreams, Kott argues, are probably the same in all epochs; 'but each epoch has its own particular bad dream.'[19] The critic, perhaps unconsciously, makes the attempt to span the differences between the Western Kafka as the definer of man's timeless spirit – a sort of latter-day Pascal without god – and the Eastern European Kafka as the definer of man *today* – a sort of mystical George Orwell.

One of the Western participants at the Liblice conference called Kafka 'the poet of absurd responsibility,' and speculated that 'perhaps what makes all Kafka characters so tragic is that they go through the world with an immense burden of responsibility on their shoulders.'[20] One cannot help detecting a logical hitch in this statement. 'Absurd responsibility' does not necessarily go together with being 'tragic.' Is there not rather something comic about a character who has taken on more than he can handle?

One can see a comic aspect in Hamlet, who inflates his paternally imposed duty to get rid of the usurper to the throne and claims he must set things right in the whole world, whereupon he logically curses the day of his birth because the job is simply too much for him. When Kafka's Josef K. with grim eagerness takes it upon himself to find out what justice means, he simply takes on too much. When the naïve Man from the Country launches into the gigantic debate with the powerful Gatekeeper who is guarding the dwelling of the Law, he is also reaching beyond his abilities. It is the dogged insistence and tireless energy to find out what they have decided to find out that gives them a comic dimenison – the aspect of the man who does not recognize himself for what he really is, and hence tries to do things he cannot seriously expect to accomplish.

Perhaps it would have taken a Czech director to do justice to yet a third treatment of Kafka's work that came out of Czechoslovakia. In 1974, ten years after Ivan Klíma had written his version of *The Castle*, he and Pavel Kohout dramatized Kafka's first full length novel *Der Verschollene* (The One Who Was Never Heard of Again) which was published after Kafka's death under the probably not too happily chosen title *America*. This is, in a way, the most 'dramatic' of Kafka's works. (It did not need to be translated back into German because the authors had worked with the novel's text itself which they merely cut and arranged for the stage.) The adaptation was staged in March 1978 in Krefeld, Germany, by a director[21] who conceived it as an exaggerated satire to be played like a kind of musical comedy.[22] This is surely against the very spirit of the dramatization which should derive its dramatic tension as well as its comedy from its psychological and social realism. In 1973, Antonin J. Liehm, reassessing what had happened to the image of Kafka in Czechoslovakia a decade after the Liblice Conference, wrote that Kafka 'has again become literature ... has ceased to be a *res politica*.'[23] Klíma and Kohout remind us once again that the horizon of human consciousness, so radically expanded by Kafka's writings, can never again be shrunk to its former dimensions. Or, as Dürrenmatt – another contemporary writer preoccupied with the nature of guilt and justice whom Klíma considered a kindred spirit – put it: 'Whatever has been thought once can never be taken back.'[24]

However, the dramatic story of Karl Rossmann, the boy who was seduced by a maid and consequently shipped to America, where he stumbles and is pushed from one dependent guilt-inducing relationship to another, until he is either destroyed or saved – Kafka does not tell us which – is, of course, today not allowed to be told on a Prague stage. The question 'Kdopak by se Kafky bál?' – Who would be afraid of Kafka? – has, regrettably, become a forbidden enquiry.

Jan Grossman, who was responsible for the most successful stage version of Kafka's *The Trial* (which opened at the Theatre on the Balustrade in May 1966) and also directed Ivan Klíma's *The Castle*, and who would most likely have staged an equally good production of *America* if he had been given the chance, wrote a significant essay on Kafka which deserves to be known in the West. Interpreters of Kafka, Grossman argues, have encouraged us to read the author above all with whatever solemn depth of thought we are capable of – the deeper the better. Perhaps Grossman would be amused to hear that Albert Einstein, when he was lent one of Kafka's books, returned it with the comment: 'I couldn't read it, the human mind isn't complicated enough.'[25] Perhaps Einstein would have needed

Grossman to introduce him to Kafka. At any rate, if Einstein had read Erich Heller's essay on Kafka written in 1959, perhaps only a few years after Einstein borrowed the book from his friend (who, by the way, was Thomas Mann) he would have read the following: 'It was a curse, and not a word of light which called the universe of Kafka's novel into existence. The very clay from which it was made bore the imprint of a malediction before the creator had touched it.'[26] This is Kafka, the cursed. Now let us see Kafka, the clown.

Jan Grossman shows us[27] how the hero of *The Trial*, Josef K., self-confident and indignant about not being treated as he might expect in his official position, gradually becomes more and more subservient, and finally goes as far as to put on his Sunday best for an interrogation that takes place in the next room. This in itself is as amusing as any shift in social roles and behaviour, but Kafka, Grossman argues, is after yet another laugh. The Sunday suit suddenly inspires K. with a victorious thought: the guard forgot to make him take a bath – so he got the better of them, after all! This comic proposition resembles the point of the clown who, when they take away his violin, calmly continues fiddling away on a broomstick, as if he had not noticed anything. It shows the clown's simple-mindedness but also his victory. He may have lost his violin but if he chooses not to consider it a loss, he has not suffered a defeat. In the clown's world it is he who makes the laws and if he decides that the broomstick is as good as a violin, then that's fine.

The other 'unkafkaesque' quality that Grossman points out is Kafka's theatricality. This should not be confused with the dramatic tension (Will K. manage to see a certain official? Will we find out who his helpers really are?). Kafka's theatricality lies in the dialogue that arises between the reader and the text. His novels 'practically count on these forms of dialogue.'[28] Although critics in the West have perceived Kafka's dramatic quality as well as his humour – which has commonly been called 'black' since this term became current – no one in the West has called him anything like 'the one Magnus parens' of the Theatre of the Absurd, who actually created in his prose writings a new 'theatrical technique.'[29] And here we have already arrived in Švejk's world. Jaroslav Hašek, too, counted on a dialogue arising between the reader and the text – a dialogue on which Pavel Kohout based the stage version of *Švejk* which played to sold out houses in Hamburg in 1967.

If Kafka criticism encompasses thousands of pages, Hašek criticism could be collected in a volume or two. This does not mean that he was not controversial. From the moment that Hašek's novel appeared in serial form in a Prague paper in 1921, attitudes to *The Good Soldier Švejk* fluctuated between high praise and sharp attack.[30] It was not surprising that the Czech literary avant-garde of the early twenties, conscious of their new national independence, and concerned with the general cultural questions of literature, did not show much enthusiasm about Švejk. However, people read and enjoyed the novel. Švejk's popularity raised questions about whether the hero did not mock certain national ideals, ridicule the army, and altogether reflect qualities unworthy of representing the Czech character. Even the President of the Republic entered into the discussion and Švejk became both a cause célèbre and a bête noire. However – and we see it much more clearly with fifty years hindsight – Švejk has stood the test of time by radiating a wealth of meaning that transcends the shifts of circumstances. In the course of its relatively brief life span, the novel has changed its topical meaning no less than four times.

It had been written as a satire of Austrian rule and as such had had a moral and positive meaning as a reflection of Czech nationalism; as soon as the Czechoslovak Republic was established, however, Švejk's behaviour, regarded from a different point of view, was criticized by official sources as immoral and nihilistic. Less than two decades later, in 1939, when Czechoslovakia was occupied by the forces of Nazi Germany, Švejk regained his national honour by demonstrating how a little man can survive within a huge alien machinery and, by playing the fool, managing to put up resistance while going about his own business. The Germans, grasping the subversive nature of the work, banned it. It is this particular example of the changing faces of *Švejk* that Brecht used in his adaptation of the novel for the stage in 1943; Brecht's Švejk is an anti-fascist. More recently the timeless figure of Švejk has caused yet another political stir. High officials of Czechoslovak culture began to be disturbed when spoken and written quotes from the novel began to appear in inappropriate places. Again Hašek's immortal character, with his deadpan assertion of human nature, has caused discomfort in circles which try to deny it or at least try to mould it into a system.

Are the two writers really very different or do they merely reflect two different points of view of the same thing – one comic and the other tragic? Or are we again too literal-minded if we attempt to apply these terms to both writers? Do they not rather represent the mingling of both? Karel Kosík has told us that 'one posits the negative, the other the positive scale of humanism.' In a more accessible way Kosík argues that 'the only dignity Kafka's man can find is in interpreting the world he has been sentenced to live in'; Hašek, in contrast, shows us that 'man is irreducible to an object, he is more than a system.'[31]

To make the argument more concrete: Imagine good Švejk before the Entrance to the Law described in Kafka's parable. When told by the Gatekeeper that he could not be admitted just then, Švejk would ply the guardian of the Law with stories of countless other people, entering or not entering other gates. He would drown the awesome and open question about the accessibility of the Law with motley details about concrete forms of life. The intense effort with which Kafka's Man from the Country formulates his questions to gain some insight into the inner regions of the higher law of life would, in Švejk's case, be changed to a heap of information and advice to the Gatekeeper about what happens to all sorts of people when they try to get into all sorts of entrances. Kafka's heroes are all concerned with giant question marks. Švejk's favorite punctuation is the exclamation mark or the self-assured full stop.

Lest this comparison seem far-fetched, let us recall two other scenes from these authors. On his way to the front, Josef Švejk gets left behind at a railway station. After downing a considerable number of beers at the station restaurant, he is arrested by a sergeant-major who has discovered that Švejk has no documents. Although the Good Soldier rightly claims to be the orderly of Lieutenant Lukáš who has already left on the train to the front, Švejk cannot prove his identity because he has nothing on paper. He is promptly arrested and taken to the station army-headquarters. We know there is another literary character who is caught without documents in a pub and, although he has not been drinking, is in a similarly dazed state because he has been fast asleep. It is K., the hero of Kafka's *The Castle* who, upon his arrival, is asked by the authorities to produce a residence permit which he does not have. The similarity of the two basic situations is surprising. Naturally, the ways in which the two characters deal with their predicaments are drastically different. Švejk showers the investigating officers with irrelevant information until they let him go, just to get rid of him. And Švejk is glad to go. K., on the other hand, obstinately stays on and tries – in vain, as we know – for the next three hundred pages to procure, in one way or another, the necessary documentation to gain legal entrance to the Castle.

With these two diametrically opposed and yet strangely related patron saints, Kafka and Hašek, at its gates, Czech theatre launched into its most recent and extraordinary renaissance which is the subject of this book. The tension between Kafka's characters with their intensely single minded search for the truth and Švejk's equally single-minded readiness to ignore the nature of the truth and 'carry on regardless,' is close to the heartbeat of the new Czech plays.[32] Kafka's characters take the nature of truth seriously, Švejk does not. Kafka's characters believe life must be truth, Švejk believes life is life and whatever they call the truth has little to do with it. Both writers are intensely concrete and theatrical in their work; both explore and question the nature of laughter; both, as it were, are aware that many of life's most serious moments contain a farcical element and that life's farce is often deadly serious. This is the stuff of which the new Czech theatre is made.

Responses: East and West

The Theatre on the Balustrade does not stage absurd plays because it wants to imitate Western fashions but because it is again concerned with an approach to reality.   JAN GROSSMAN in an interview, September 1968

I RESPONSES: EAST

In 1964/65 the Slovak theatre journal *Slovenské Divadlo* published in three instalments a long review article on Martin Esslin's *The Theatre of the Absurd*. What is significant about the article, apart from the fact that it welcomes the 'tragic humanism' of the Theatre of the Absurd, which represents 'the antipode of superficial and false optimism,'[1] is that it readily accepts the new literary label 'absurd' and uses it as a tool for analysis. Before we try to throw some light on the Czechoslovak encounter with the plays within this debatable dramatic category, it might be useful to recall the remarks of the man who initiated the general usage of the term.

In the 'Preface to the Second Edition' of *The Theatre of the Absurd*, Esslin finds that his title, originally conceived as a 'working hypothesis,'[2] has become not only a catch-phrase in its own right but has also engendered a number of other catch-phrases of a similar nature. It is one of the ironies of definition that what has happened here to the name illustrates unwittingly its substance. A phrase which was thought of tentatively, in order to indicate an area of concern, has promptly been cast into an absolute category, thereby justifying the creation of other, similar categories. Is this not an absurd situation per se? Whether we choose to call it absurd or not, it is one of those instances where a mechanistic, literal interpretation of a speculation has resulted in the formulation of a complex model of an apparently existing order, certain sections of which have become the concern of certain people who then proliferate this order by creating further sections. One could, for example, easily imagine a university committee investigating the feasibility of new courses to be offered, dealing in all seriousness with five new courses, offered by the Department of, say, Dramatic World Literature, which would propose to study individually the Theatre of Revolt, Cruelty, Fact, Paradox, and the Antitheatre. We will find later that Václav Havel, who is discussed in the second chapter, has built his plays – already well known in the West – around this very idea: the 'absurd' power of language as the precision tool but also the great mystifier of human intellect.

However, what concerns us at this moment is the fact that, when the plays of Ionesco, Genet, Beckett, and others reached Czechoslovakia, they arrived there under the package-description of the 'Theatre of the Absurd.' Whatever our own attitude to the term, we should remember that Czechoslovaks were acquainted with it even before they had the opportunity to read and see the plays concerned. Perhaps this is why something truly 'absurd' happened when the Theatre of the Absurd finally arrived in Czechoslovakia – with a delay of about fifteen years – during the mid-sixties.

The prime example of theatrical originality of the fifties was received in Prague as a historical curiosity. The avant-garde playwright who would be expected to shock a conformist audience was given a red-carpet treatment. The Prague critic Sergej Machonin who reviewed Beckett's *Waiting for Godot* and Ionesco's *The Bald Soprano* and *The Lesson* – which had their first performances in Prague at the Theatre on the Balustrade – actually wrote: 'Finally we will take a look at it [the Theatre of the Absurd] and see for ourselves *what it really was*.'[3] The 1959 Congress of the International Theatre Institute had reported on the opening address given by the foremost playwright of the Absurd under the heading 'Eugène Ionesco opens fire.'[4] In 1965 the ammunition seemed to have been discharged and a Czech critic could calmly shelve it with theatrical history and refer to it in the past tense.

And so it may be said that Eastern Europeans saw the plays of the Absurd not as avant-garde events that smashed traditions but as literary museum pieces. Having made their youthful, revolutionary splash in the past the plays by now had reached middle-aged respectability, had their places in theatrical source-books, and were listed in the subject catalogues of university libraries. It is difficult to sustain a revolutionary posture when you are an accepted member of a revered élite. This was the problem of the 'Theatre of the Absurd' when it arrived in Czechoslovakia.

The term itself had filtered into Eastern Europe through the cracks in the wall of Stalinism during the fifties and, as communication between Czechoslovakia and the West began to increase during the early sixties, all kinds of information about a new kind of theatre were eagerly absorbed by the theatre-loving population. In this way Czechoslovaks lived with a 'myth' of the Theatre of the Absurd until their first encounter with the prototype of the genre when Jan Grossman, then leading the dramatic ensemble of the Theatre on the Balustrade, put on his own adaptation of Alfred Jarry's *Ubu Roi*. The production was a huge success and, despite the displeasure expressed by the authorities, it had almost 500 performances in Prague and was performed at several drama festivals outside Czechoslovakia.

Ubu Roi, however, is a more 'open' work than the plays of, say, Ionesco and Beckett, and the stage-success of Grossman's version was no real indication of the general critical reaction to what we call the Theatre of the Absurd. When the latter became available, Czechoslovaks had to find their bearings. In the words of the writer Ivan Klíma: 'When Dürrenmatt, Beckett and Ionesco appeared on the Czech stage almost overnight, I found myself in a situation similar to Tarzan who has been put in a seat in the Paris Opera.'[5] However, the puzzlement was of short duration and soon Czechoslovaks came to two important realizations: first, that they understood this kind of theatre in a different way than did people in the West; secondly, that they had possessed an Absurd Theatre of their own without having known it.

Sergej Machonin seems to be aware of the complex nature of this reaction. In his review of an edition of plays by Beckett and Ionesco he tries to reduce the reverence-before-the-classic attitude by overstressing to the point of distortion the programmatic aspect of the Western Theatre of the Absurd. 'Fifteen years ago,' he writes, this theatre 'went to war against all theatre of the past in order to laugh at it, sneer at it, set it on fire, and sweep it away with anger and contempt.' But in the very same article he proceeds to take the Theatre of the Absurd very seriously indeed and expresses concern for its audience who sit there shivering and laughing simultaneously while absorbing the message that 'it is futile to try to make any effort at all because nothing makes sense.'[6] We know the attacks that have been launched against the Theatre of the Absurd by prominent Marxist critics who deny its value because it 'does not seek the reason for man's deformation in history ... and ... takes pleasure in assuming that mankind is in its final stages.'[7]

Despite the apparent similarity of the feelings that underlie these remarks by a Czech and a German critic, there is a considerable difference between them. The latter critic argues from a definite ideological point of view; the former from a politically neutral humanist attitude. From Machonin's lengthy remarks, let us consider the following: 'It is impossible to accept [these plays] as great works of art which would be relevant in people's lives for the discovery of their identity and imaginative search for the purpose in life ... People in the audience do not voluntarily give up their lives, though they are so often absurd, insoluble and difficult.'[8] Beneath the more obvious reasons for the mixed feelings of this Czech critic there is a resistance (healthy, perhaps?) against the secret moralistic attitude of the plays which, in the words of another Czech critic, 'is basically not comical ... on the contrary, the comic element appears here as if closed off in parenthesis.'[9]

It is a pity that the Czechs did not have the opportunity to follow the by now famous controversy between Kenneth Tynan, drama critic of the London *Observer*, and Eugène Ionesco on the role of the modern playwright. Had they done so they might have had an easier time with the enigmatic obscurity of his plays. When reviewing a London production of Ionesco's *The Chairs* and *The Lesson* in 1958, Tynan expresses a strong warning about the playwright's 'bleak new world' which, if 'held up for general emulation,' might banish from the theatre of the future 'faith in logic and belief in man.'[10] Tynan might have learned as much from the Czechoslovak reaction to Ionesco (which took place about seven years later) as the Czechs might have learned from him: they would have found in him the defender of the humanism they cherished so anxiously because it was threatened in their society; he, on the other hand, would have been reassured that faith in logic and belief in man are not lost as easily as he feared.

Nine years after his controversy with Ionesco, Tynan had the opportunity to observe Czechoslovak theatre first hand. In an essay he wrote after his visit there in 1967, the critic discusses plays by Havel, Topol, Klíma, and others, all of whom figure in our study under the heading of playwrights of the Absurd. Although Tynan – perhaps remembering his joust with the prototype of a dramatist of the Absurd – carefully and wisely avoids the term itself, he nevertheless offers, perhaps unconsciously, a definition of the Czechoslovak version of Absurd Theatre. In his discussion of Klíma's adaptation of *The Trial* and Havel's *The Memorandum* Tynan speculates on the hero's guilt in accepting an absurd situation rather than resisting it. The audience, Tynan argues, is made to 'query the hero's culpability.'[11] This point could serve as an orientation sign for our discussion, indicating the deep-seated difference between East European and Western plays of the Absurd. The former consist of an earnest search for the hidden moment at which reasoning becomes absurd, the latter – be they the plays of Ionesco, Genet, Beckett, Albee, or Pinter – illustrate the conviction that this moment can never be found.

When Ionesco's *The Bald Soprano* was produced in Prague in 1965 it was put on not as a bombshell of avant-garde theatre but rather as a classic, and with the intention of finding out whether the work would yield new 'unforeseen meanings.'[12] Whether the latter has happened must be left unanswered, since the Czechoslovak theatre did not have the opportunity to stage the several productions of the play which it requires to bring out hidden possibilities of interpretation. Still what we do find is rather interesting.

We know that *The Bald Soprano* contains several scenes in which the characters – middle class couples with stereotyped reactions to everything – hold conversations that consist entirely of clichés. Western critics have found them to be the funniest scenes of the play. Well aware of Ionesco's 'image' as a satirist of mechanized society, the Czech director was trying to go one better than the playwright to make sure the audience got the message. He made the characters move about the stage with mechanized movements and speak their clichés in monotonous voices. The Czech audience failed to be amused. What they would have found funny is 'the tension between inner mechanization and lively presentation,' i.e., stupid clichés said with a matter-of-fact naturalness. But 'if a puppet speaks like a puppet it is neither absurd nor funny.'[13]

Here we have another example of the Eastern European mentality resisting a deeply serious, didactic approach to the potentially comic problem of standardization – an approach that has been prevalent in most critical discussions of Ionesco in the West. Perhaps the playwright himself, who told us that *The Bald Soprano* was 'something like a *tragedy of the language*,'[14] is partly responsible for most of those brooding comments of Western Literary critics about language as 'the death of all communication.'[15] And actually the critics are right. The problem is as serious as Ionesco implied. But there precisely *is* the rub. In a country such as Czechoslovakia, where individual happiness is not sold on every poster and bar of soap, the writer has the urge to provide the spark of humor that, no matter what his critical target is, has a liberating effect on reader or audience. An interesting case in point is Ionesco himself whose relatively cool reception in Czechoslovakia was due to what was felt to be his lack of a sense of humor.

Perhaps it is significant that the play in which Ionesco used a really humorous absurd image in order to make a sociological point was the play that was most appreciated by both the Czechoslovak audience and the critics. *Rhinoceros*, produced in Prague in 1966, had various repercussions. Compared with some reactions of Western critics Czech reactions reveal basic differences in attitude – but not where one might expect them. Like all outstanding plays it radiates different shades of meaning, depending on the background of the audience. The play is about a small provincial town that is awakened from its placid slumber by the appearance of a rhinoceros; soon the inhabitants find they have much in common with the thick-skinned, brutal creature and begin to change – social élite, clergy, civil service and all – into rhinoceros. At the end the play's hero Berenger is left as the only human being in a world of animalistic grunts.

We see the varied possibilities of interpretation. In Germany, for example, the audience immediately related the play to its own experience with Hitler: the arguments given to justify doing what everyone else was doing; the power of conformism that does not enquire into the nature of what it is comforming to. To the German audience the play was a clear analogy to National Socialism and was staged entirely without irony as a 'naked tragedy, without concessions.'[16] Jean-Louis Barrault, on the other hand, following his own particular genius as well as a certain tradition in French theatre that goes back to Molière's *Le Misanthrope*, directed the play in Paris (with himself in the main role) as a 'tragic farce.'[17]

In North America something entirely different happened: Ionesco, who in 1961 attended a dress rehearsal of *Rhinoceros* in New York, was perturbed about being interpreted in a manner directly contrary to his intentions. Berenger, the meek, drifting anti-hero of the play, was turned into a 'sort of lucid intellectual, hard, a kind of unvanquished revolutionary who knew exactly what he was doing.'[18] Obviously the American production treated conformism as something contemptible and ridiculous. (Ionesco himself was surprised to find all American critics agreeing that the play was very funny.) The sinister element got lost entirely.

At first glance this might seem to contradict my previous argument about humour in the Theatre of the Absurd, but on closer inspection it appears as merely another facet of the same problem. Conformism was represented (as indeed it still is in North America) as something mediocre, petty bourgeois, and unworthy of the brave new world of the young individualist who is not going to be submerged in the swamp of mediocrity. Ionesco's main point, 'the mental transformation of a whole collective' where 'old values are degraded, overthrown, other values come into being and impose themselves'[19] was completely inverted. The fact that the critics stressed the comic aspect of the play was the result of a deadly serious, almost moralistic attitude to the problem of mediocrity.

Czech sources regarded Berenger as anything but a tough uncompromising individualist. Rather they found the character lacking in even a trace of heroism or hardness of mind. The fact that Berenger does not change into a rhinoceros like all the others was explained by the simple fact that he is all too human: 'His humanity is not programmatic but natural.'[20] To become a greedy, snorting animal would have violated Berenger's nature. His fellow men, on the other hand, lacking certain human qualities, had in their make-up 'certain inhuman traits or at least possibilities'[21] which made them undergo the change. This kind of interpretation suggests two things: Eastern Europeans still seem to believe in the good potential of human nature (and this in a different sense than Marxist determinism); and, as a consequence of this attitude, write a different kind of Theatre of the Absurd that is more value-laden and less relativistic than that of the West.

A clear example of this difference is a discussion of *Rhinoceros* by a foremost Western critic of the Theatre of the Absurd, Martin Esslin, who is also – perhaps not all too happily, as we have seen – responsible for the term itself. To him Berenger's 'final defiant expression of faith in humanity is merely the expression of the fox's contempt for the grapes he could not have,' and the play therefore conveys 'the absurdity of defiance as much as the absurdity of conformism ... for now that being a rhino is normal, to be human is a monstrosity.'[22] This seems to me an example of the deep-seated relativism of Western critics. By denying that there is a certain point at which a situation becomes absurd, Esslin denies absurdity as such. If the absurdity of becoming a rhinoceros ceases to be an absurdity once it has been done by a sufficient number of people, then either everything is absurd or nothing is. This relativistic thinking has not borne fruit in Eastern Europe. Unheroic and ridiculous – but by no means 'absurd' – Berenger is regarded as the typical, average 'little man,' who sees no other way out but to 'face an undignified situation without giving two hoots about his own dignity.'[23]

In Ionesco's collected comments *Notes et Contre-notes*, which have never been published in Czechoslovakia, the playwright argues that 'it is the human condition that governs the social condition and not vice versa.'[24] Eastern Europeans are bound to react to such a comment, depending on their political convictions, either with ideological indignation or a wistful smile. Those belonging to the latter group may find his preceding comment much more meaningful: 'The authentic human community is extra-social ... [and] reveals itself in our common anguish, our desires, the secret nostalgias felt by us all.'[25] It is the strong sense of this kind of community that prevents the Czechoslovak Theatre of the Absurd from losing sight of the point at which absurdity starts, and thus making all values relative.

By the time the Czechoslovaks got a chance to review a performance of Genet, they had found their own way of looking at the masterpieces of the Theatre of the Absurd: they concentrated on the formal aspects. The obsessive universe of Genet 'where sexuality and power balance and devour each other'[26] became a welcome field of theatrical experimentation. After all, little Czechoslovakia has a surprising number of outstanding designers and directors some of whom have achieved international renown.

In his review of a Prague production of *The Maids* in 1967, the critic Zdeněk Hořínek approached the play as a kind of rhythmical composition. The action, he felt, was not sufficiently rhythmically structured, the director was overly concerned with emotions rather than with 'meanings, relationships and thoughts.'[27] Although the critic uses the words 'meaning' and 'thought,' he obviously stresses the *formal* aspect, and the 'existential' problems analysed by Sartre in his famous discussion of the play (which must have crossed the Czechoslovak borders in some form or other) are hardly touched upon.

A year later the same critic approached the 'existential' aspects. But if we expect an echo of Western essays on *The Maids* that speak of 'the ritual of wish-fulfilment,'[28] the 'demonstration of nonbeing in being,'[29] or the 'change of consciousness after the murder'[30] we are disappointed. What we read is this: 'Genet's cramped world and Genet's cruel theatre have one important fault – the humor is missing. Genet takes the world and himself in it ... too seriously. That is why he is unjust, dogmatic, and arrogant. That is why he is incapable of sympathy and humility. That is why he is a pamphletist rather than a judge. That is why he cannot escape the captivity of his psychic trauma.'[31]

Those who have contemplated – sadly or sceptically – Genet's grim determination to see only evil, hear only evil, speak only evil, may feel that the critic has a good point. It should be added, however, that the fact that Czechoslovaks preferred their Genet on the stage rather than in their philosophical library does not mean that they were not eager to read him. The Czech translations of *The Balcony* and *The Blacks*, published in an edition of 1300 copies in 1967, disappeared literally on the day of publication.

It could be said that the Czechoslovak attitude to Beckett forms a sort of parallel to the political thaw. It is one of the ironies of the fluctuating tension between literature and life that the liberalization of a regime has a rather paradoxical effect on the creative work of the authors writing under it; they will want to write not about the joys of a newly found freedom of expression but about the darker aspects of life – futility and death.[32] This discovery casts a peculiar light on an aspect of the problem of censorship that has hardly received any notice: if artists are told to write about life only, they will want to write about death; if they are told to write about the accomplishment of tasks, they will want to say that there is nothing to be done. For years Czechoslovak writers had been constrained to write in an 'ideologically sound' and optimistic vein, pointing to a bright future in the perfect classless society. Now suddenly they came face to face with Samuel Beckett, the most sombre of the writers of the Absurd.

The freer the Czechoslovaks became from the political pressures of systematized thinking, the more they liked Beckett. The less they had to worry about the daily problems of doing anything ideologically 'wrong' and getting into trouble, the more they responded to Beckett's arid speculations on futility and death. 'Absurd'? Perhaps, but real.

Take some samples of reactions to Beckett's writings. In 1963 the Slovak theatre journal *Slovenské divadlo* cautiously introduced the first translation of *Krapp's Last Tape* as an interesting but slightly rotten fruit: Beckett was a great poet expressing the 'apocalyptic feelings' of an individual emerging from a society 'the values of which have been crumbling for a long time.'[33] Only a few months later the Czech theatre journal *Divadlo* printed an article that said the same play, despite its brevity and plotlessness, represented the 'whole curve of events of a long, stretched-out human life.'[34] A year and a half later, in the spring of 1965, the critic Hořínek called Beckett 'one of the greatest analysts of the crisis of modern man;'[35] and – we must remember that during that period things were developing with unprecedented, almost feverish rapidity – only another five months later we actually read about the impossibility of assessing Beckett with a Marxist evaluation. A Marxist critic, defining the difference between Marxist thinking and Beckett's conclusions, nevertheless admits 'the impossibility of erasing the phenomenon Beckett from our cultural subconscious.'[36]

On the whole we are bound to be struck by the strong Czechoslovak awareness of the analytical component in Beckett's works (which has been given a rather low priority in Western commentaries). One critic, for example, finds that *Texts for Nothing* are 'by no means gloomily hopeless' because they are 'passionately analytical.' The same attitude is apparent in Hořínek's stressing 'the strict order of thought and structure [which] is precisely balanced by emotionally urgent rhetoric ...'[37] This sharp recognition that the great poet is also a great analyst is refreshing indeed, coming from an area that had been isolated for so long from the great documents of the occidental imagination. But it is also gratifying for another reason: Czechoslovaks discovered their own spiritual kinship with these documents. By that time both Havel's dramatic analyses of the absurdity of language and Topol's plays about man's isolation and the futility of endeavour had been performed at different theatres. Moreover Beckett's aphorisms are distinctly, even surprisingly comparable to the verses of Vladimír Holan, the greatest living Czech poet.[38]

When *Waiting for Godot* was performed for the last time at Bratislava's *Divadlo na korze* in 1969, the production proved how deeply that Slovak production had grasped the essential Beckett. The first half of the performance was sheer slapstick comedy. It seemed as if the audience were being told: 'Look, we have become used to living absurdly during those last seventeen years since *Waiting for Godot* was written. Let's just use it as a libretto for unlimited fun, let's make it a hilarious comedy about today's man.' However, as the play proceeded, it became more and more melancholy and the spectre of hopelessness loomed across the fun with increasing urgency. The 'hope' that Godot would arrive and do away with all the misery began imperceptibly to change its nature until a disturbing realization dawned on the audience: Godot was only an excuse for the two tramps to stay together. 'They had become Godot for each other. Only they did not know it.'[39]

A final observation: Despite the disguising filter of translations there did not seem to be the slightest doubt that Beckett was a greater writer than the other playwrights of the Absurd. The reason for this clear-cut judgment was that he was instantly recognized as an outstanding poet. As one critic put it, sardonically referring to the relative unavailability of Beckett's work in contrast to Ionesco's: 'If I consider side by side the undernourished, emaciated torso of Samuel Beckett and pudgy Ionesco, weighing almost three hundred pages, I feel a little sad.'[40]

One day Josef Švejk, the good soldier, who at the time was Lieutenant Lukaš's orderly, found himself in a delicate situation. A young lady with various claims on the lieutenant's attentions arrived for what seemed to be an emergency call and the dutiful orderly had to cope with the demanding visitor in his master's absence. Slowly Švejk assessed the difficulties of the situation and finally decided that the best thing to do was to forget what he thought he knew about the lady and acquaint himself with her on his own terms. Consequently things worked out to the complete satisfaction of everyone: Švejk, the lieutenant and the lady in question.

There is something about this frivolous incident that reminds one of the far from frivolous encounter of the Czechoslovaks with Bertolt Brecht. But first of all we must remember that this encounter was in a way more complex than that of Brecht with other Eastern European countries. One of the reasons was that it came relatively late. When, in late summer 1957, the theatre journal *Divadlo* dedicated almost a whole issue to an introduction of Brecht, most other Eastern European countries had already made his acquaintance. Moscow audiences had seen Helene Weigel in *Mother Courage* that same spring;[41] the Belgrade Dramatic Theatre had produced its first Brecht play three years earlier;[42] Warsaw theatre-goers were treated to two appearances of the Berlin Ensemble (in 1952 and 1954).[43] By the time *Divadlo* came out with its Brecht issue, and the Berlin Ensemble had appeared in Prague in 1958,[44] Brecht's image had filtered into Czechoslovakia through the intangible network of the literary and theatre worlds.

His ship, it seemed, was sailing under a puzzling flag: it was impossible to say whether it was the emblem of a political classicist or the banner of an avant-garde revolutionary artist. The Czechoslovaks (scholars, critics, audiences) had scrutinized the ship from afar. Though a few may have remembered enough of the occasional pre-war productions of, say, *The Three Penny Opera*, and others had seen the stark *The Guns of Mrs. Carrar*, this did little to reduce the general puzzlement over what Brecht was all about. In this way Brecht's plays (much like the plays of the Theatre of the Absurd half a dozen years later) had to cope on every level with people who harboured some kind of image of them which did more to obstruct than to open up communication.

So much for the premises; now we must go to the solution which could be called Švejkian (with the understanding that we regard the term as highly as Brecht himself did). The basic problem was how to introduce Brecht's plays without getting too entangled in the other two areas of his work: his political attitude and his dramatic theories. For once the Czechoslovaks were lucky. An eloquent spokesman straightened out the problem for them before they had fully realized its nature. In a series of essays published in the influential journal *Divadlo* Jan Grossman argued that Brecht, the theorist, had been overstressed at the expense of Brecht, the poet. Today most critics have come to similar conclusions, but Grossman's late-fifties criticism shows insight as well as foresight.

Rather than stressing the normative aspects of Brecht's thought, Grossman writes about the playwright's 'aesthetic opinions, studies ... analyses of working methods in constant process of change, modification and adjustment.'[45] It is obvious that an author who was said to have such fluid and adjustable theories appealed to minds which had been exposed to models of unquestionable 'truth' for a decade. And so the questions that excited the Poles – Did Brecht prove that a Marxist writer need not write in a Socialist-Realist style? Or did the fact that Brecht did not write in a Socialist-Realist style prove that he was not a true Marxist? – took on an air of irrelevance in Czechoslovakia. Theatres all over the country staged Brecht plays, until in the sixties critics began to worry that the theatre had been seized by a sort of 'Brechtomania,'[46] because everyone played Brecht without any particular regard for what he was supposed to be about.

One other point is worth emphasizing. Brecht's epic theatre, with its particular way of addressing the audience, was less of a novelty on the Czechoslovak stage than might be expected. The latter was not a stranger to the lively nineteenth-century tradition of the Viennese stage with its Volkstheater which played to sold out houses in the suburbs of Vienna. In the farcical parodies made world-famous by Johann Nestroy (1801–1862) the audience was frequently directly addressed during the play and took an active, responsible part in the performance – just what Brecht advocates throughout his writings. Moreover, Czech theatre has its own strong tradition of the truly histrionic aspect of theatre.

During the thirties, two outstanding actors founded what became known as *The Liberated Theatre*. They were Jiří Voskovec and Jan Werich[47] who created their own librettos for brilliant sketches and comedies (often improvised) which were the delight of the sophisticated Prague audiences in the tense years preceding the Second World War. Voskovec and Werich – known all over the country as 'V + W' – returned to the stage its original function of theatricality, playing, acting, and showmanship that openly counted on the reaction of the audience. Music, dances, 'funny dialogue,' and sundry other scenes à la music hall made these performances lively, highly contemporary events. The theatre became again a contemporary institution, where new thought and entertainment were generated by the electrifying, ever renewable contact between actors and audience. This, it is worth recollecting, was exactly what Brecht meant when he said that he wanted his theatre to recreate the atmosphere of an athletic stadium or a boxing ring.[48]

And so Brecht's work was peculiarly suited to the Czechoslovak stage less for its social outlook than for its sheer theatricality. A Czech production of, say, *The Good Woman of Setzuan* might have surprised Brecht had he lived a few years longer and gone to Prague to see his own play performed, as Sartre and Dürrenmatt did theirs.

One of Dürrenmatt's grotesque tragicomedies (which George Wellwarth designates as belonging to the Theatre of the Absurd, while Martin Esslin does not) was performed at Prague's National Theatre, which, even in the days of the thaw, was not exactly a place for theatrical experimentation. Nevertheless the Swiss writer's work proved to be very exciting for the Czechs. His social ideas (his most famous play can, and has been interpreted as a full scale attack on 'capitalism'), his tension-loaded closeness to Bertolt Brecht, and his brilliant essays on the problems of the contemporary playwright are the subject of numerous essays in Czechoslovak literary journals. Indeed Dürrenmatt seems to be the only contemporary Western writer who has provoked something like a polemical exchange in print between two critics in Czechoslovakia;[49] and moreover he is most frequently compared with Czech writers (like Karel Čapek or Ludvík Aškenazy).[50] It is noteworthy that the influential critic Hořínek makes a crystal-clear distinction (too clear for those who know Dürrenmatt well) between him and the writers of the Absurd, by pointing out that Dürrenmatt's work was not as hopeless as theirs and that the cause of the defeat of his heroes was to be found not in the uselessness of action itself but rather in their 'wrong tactics.'[51]

When the playwright passed through Prague on his way from the Soviet Union in 1964, he gave a long interview to the lively literary weekly *Literární noviny*.[52] With his well-known humor and mixture of common sense and intellectual playfulness Dürrenmatt answered nine questions like 'What is your relationship to dialectics?' or 'Are you ... an optimist with regard to the world situation?' It would be regarded as self-defeating to ask Genet or Beckett such questions. Dürrenmatt, on the stage and in the flesh, seemed to be less elusive, less foreign perhaps. Although Czech critics noticed his 'total lack of trust in humanity as a whole,'[53] they nevertheless saw him wrestle with concrete problems that seemed to have a more direct relationship to their lives.

On the whole it could be said that Czechoslovakia's reaction to Dürrenmatt's work does not differ greatly from that of the West. Czechs and

Slovaks share our amusement about the playwright's 'clever relativization of historical certainties,'[54] when Romulus, a Roman emperor and hero of the past, is revealed as a chicken breeder with good intentions that make a mess of everything. Yet the particular gusto with which an audience in Czechoslovakia responds to Dürrenmatt's ironic perspective on an awesome historical figure cannot be matched by the Westerner, unused to historical hero worship en masse.

The case of Harold Pinter is revealing because Czech and Slovak productions and criticism seem to make light of those mysterious regions – stressed by both Western productions and commentators – that loom beneath the realistic texture of Pinter's everyday, colloquial language. The Czechoslovaks prefer to have their Pinter a realist – and it seems to work. In his comment on *The Caretaker*, produced in Prague in 1965, Sergej Machonin, though aware that the characters 'try to realize their most elementary ideas of human existence,'[55] stresses the *reality* of the alienation between them. Moreover *The Homecoming*, staged in Bratislava in 1969, was conceived as a completely realistic play.

Those who have read Martin Esslin's book on Pinter will be aware of his imaginative interpretation of the play's action as 'projection of archetypal fears and wishes.'[56] One character especially has triggered various archetypal interpretations among Western critics. This is Ruth, the son's wife, who arrives with her husband from America in the all-male household of his family, and stays there in the combined role of a kind of Mother-Mistress-Whore figure, personifying the fulfilment of archetypal wishes. In the Slovak première of *The Homecoming*, Teddy, Ruth's husband, who returns to America at the end, was seen as the main character, representing a sort of prodigal son who finds himself 'a stranger'[57] in his own home because his values have changed. How different this approach to the play is becomes apparent when we remind ourselves that Western sources tend to regard Teddy as the stuffy professor-conformist who goes back to his useless research and arid lecturing when he feels that his mask of respectability is beginning to peel off, as his wife prepares cheerfully to share bed and breakfast with anyone who will pay. But perhaps this difference in interpretation reveals less about Czechoslovaks than it does about the nature of Pinter's work itself which, like a magic mirror, enables everyone to find their own image in its depth.

Much more could be said about the way other English and American drama affected Czech and Slovak audiences and criticism. Exploring their

reactions, we find interesting insights into every new author: their awareness that O'Neill, despite his grand gestures, has to be staged with stress on
the intimate aspects of his plays; their fascinated recognition of the power
of bad faith portrayed by Arthur Miller in the character of Willie Lohman;
their conviction that Tennessee Williams was primarily an actors' playwright; their discovery that Paul Claudel's work was not narrowly dogmatic but rather 'wonderfully free;' the half-amused impression that Edward
Bond's fear of being suspected of being a middle class writer is a new
version of the emperor's new clothes.[58] However, we will single out only
two more writers, both French and famous, but very different in substance:
Sartre and Camus.

When Czech theatres began producing Sartre's plays in 1963 they knew
that they were faced with a complex problem. Not only did they lack a
repertoire of predecessors for his kind of quasi-philosophical theatre, but
they also realized that the very subjects of Sartre's plays – the activist-
idealist and the use of violence, the imposition of a sense of guilt as a power
instrument – were extremely 'hot' themes for a nation which was just
beginning to scan an opening horizon after being hemmed in by orthodox
ideology for half a generation. When Sartre reached Czechoslovakia, he
had long been discussed in the West as dramatist, novelist, philosopher,
literary politician. The inconsistencies of his dramatic theorizing had been
pointed out; the ambiguities of his philosophico-political standpoint had
been analysed; it had become obvious that his pithy formulations, which he
meant to be keys for his own philosophy, had also become 'slogans for
fools.'[59] All in all it is not unfair to say that the West had learned to take
their Sartre with a pinch of salt.
    People in Czechoslovakia had not had the opportunity to develop this
philosophic distance. They took their Sartre straight and – on the basis of
the first, rather staggering impact which resulted when *The Prisoners of
Altona* and *The Devil and the Good Lord* were performed in 1963 and 1964 –
they considered him a dramatist who brought into the theatre great
'philosophical problems ... in their state of birth, in an unsolved, dialectic
struggle,' and thought that he was therefore 'the creator of truly
philosophical drama.'[60] This accounts for the fact that the Czechs, very
much aware of the literary value of the new plays that were reaching them
at the time from the West, were initially not particularly sensitive to the
dramatic weaknesses of Sartre's theatre. They were so excited by *what* it
had to say that they did not find much to criticize in *how* it was saying it.

This is also the reason why the Czechs' and Slovaks' first reaction to Sartre's plays was less ambiguous than their reaction to the dramatists of the Absurd.

The intellectual climate in Czechoslovakia of the mid-sixties was one of renewed belief in human dignity together with the excitement of enjoying a growing freedom of artistic expression. All this created an atmosphere drastically different from the brutality of Genet's bordellos, the paralysing uselessness of Ionesco's rows of empty chairs, or even the agonized wait under Beckett's one and only tree (although there, at least, there was something to laugh at!). The philosophical speculations of Sartre seemed to be much more relevant to people's main concerns.

However, within a period of three or four years a surprising change occurred. At the risk of oversimplifying a complex issue we might say that Czechoslovak attitudes to Sartre and Beckett were related to each other like two ends of a see-saw. As Beckett went up, Sartre went down. In 1962 an edition of five of Sartre's plays was hailed by critics as a major literary event, and their excitement was only dampened by their regret that the selection failed to include the drama *The Flies*. This play's themes of the rejection of public exhibitions of guilt and the stress on individual freedom were, of course, highly topical and exciting.

Three years later we find a very different attitude to Sartre: 'Sartre is a writer-philosopher or a philosophizing writer – which apparently does not make the philosopher thrive and certainly harms the writer – but Beckett is always exclusively a great dramatic poet.'[61] If we overlook the fact that the critic, wanting to make a certain distinction, obviously over-simplifies the issue, we realize that there is more to this change in attitude than is apparent from a flippant turn of phrase. Is it that a poète engagé had less and less to say to a society that was trying to get away from imposed engagement and find its own form of involvement in general questions?

Perhaps it was also felt that under certain circumstances Sartre's political theories had a hollow ring, as when *Dirty Hands* was produced in Prague in the autumn of 1968, a short time after the Warsaw Pact troops had occupied Czechoslovakia. It was a problematic time to bring before an audience a play which deals with the conflict between a decisive political activist and an emotional humanist intellectual. The Czech audience responded with unexpected irony. Quite contrary to the author's intentions they treated *Dirty Hands* as if it were an 'absurd' play, and laughed during the anything-but-funny ending[62] – a reaction which, as a reviewer explains, was due to their realization that Sartre had not only posed an incomplete political question but had also failed to provide a dramatic solution.

During the same time another of Sartre's plays was running in Prague. *The Flies* had its première at the Komorní Theatre while *Dirty Hands* was still running at the E.F. Burian Theatre. The author himself attended the première and the weekly papers ran a large photograph of Sartre on the stage, a bouquet of roses in hand, thanking the audience for their ovation. The see-saw had moved again: the political events of August 1968 had made Sartre's theatre more exciting again for Czechoslovaks. As the awareness of the changed political situation forced itself on everyone, as the occupation raised anxious questions regarding individual freedom in everyone's mind, *The Flies* became a highly topical play. The author wanted to show man's abandonment in a godless world but the work had also been read as a resistance play. The questions of the assertion of man's own morality and his freedom and rejection of guilt are always as close to religion (or the rejection of religion) as they are to politics. The emotions of the audience, cheering the playwright, are echoed in the lengthy review of the play entitled 'The Freedom of Man among People': 'There will never be enough of these works which give strength to people who live in fear and anxiety, and therefore always tend to hide in something that is outside themselves, to create or accept any kind of myth, only if it relieves us even for a while from the responsibility of our own existence.'[63] It is clear that Sartre is approached here not so much as a writer but rather as a man who has used the word 'freedom' loudly at a time when everyone feared to lose it.

There remains Albert Camus, the writer who tried to give the concept of the Absurd a philosophical basis. The forceful and elegant way in which he formulated what he took to be the essence of the Absurd had its impact on the Czechoslovak literary scene although it seems that he puzzled even the best minds. On the whole the Czech and Slovak attitude to Camus is of a two-pronged nature which reflects upon the writer himself. Above all the critics seem to be worried about his sense of values. Again, as in the case of the playwrights of the Absurd, people's somehow deep-rooted resistance to a complete denial of values seems to obstruct their way to Camus. Sometimes they even try to prove that Camus did in fact defend values. This is so in the case of Machonin who reviewed *Caligula* when it was produced in 1965. Although the playwright, Machonin argues, does not offer any positive solutions in the play itself, he does tell us that 'it is self-destructive to try to realize a project ... at the price of wilful destruction and ruin of values. The greatest and most beautiful dream is senseless if it is achieved by means of tyranny and murder, force and the denial of the human being.'[64] At other times, as in the case of *The Misunderstand-*

ing which ran at the Liberec theatre in northern Bohemia in the spring of 1969, another reviewer discovered a contradiction[65] between the basic philosophical idea – the human being's absolute isolation, expressed by the character of Martha who has been described by Western sources as representing 'the anger of an absurd hero'[66] – and the figure of the Mother who laconically decides to die when discovering that the stranger whom she has killed is her own son. The loss of her only certainty, the mother's love for her child, destroys her. The critic's discovery of the playwright's inconsistency is as noteworthy as the decision of the director of the Liberec production largely to ignore Martha as the spokesman for the philosophy of the Absurd and to centre the whole play around the theme of motherhood. Both show that Camus as philosopher proved too fuzzy; it seemed better to stay with Camus, the literary man.

Furthermore we have the Czech philosopher-critic Oleg Sus who, trying to clarify the concept of the Absurd for the Czech reader, finds that 'absolute, existential absurdity honorably holds watch over the boundary line of *in extremis.*' This is rather a resourceful way of putting it. But later in his essay Sus reveals his doubts about 'Camus's conception of permanent revolt giving value to man's existence.' He considers it 'upright and honouring to the author [but] neither binding nor logical ... If everything in life is absurd, can nonsense be recognized at all? Is it *comparable* to anything, measurable? In the night of absurdity all cats are absurd ... How can absurdity occur without a contrasting background, without its opposite, a non-absurd world (never mind whether imagined or real ...)?'[67] Thus, by means of a logical argument, Sus punches holes in Camus's theories, and philosophically, he punches them well. Yet somehow they miss their aim because Camus must not be approached as a systematic philosopher. He was not what he wanted to be – the founder of a system of twentieth-century thought – but a poet who, with all the inconsistencies and intellectual blunders that go with a great spiritual effort, tried to wrench from the incomprehensible world some way of coping with it – like Beckett or Kafka rather than Heidegger or Jaspers.

There is one aspect of the impact of the Theatre of the Absurd in Eastern Europe that must not go unmentioned. It is an unforeseen result of a combination of circumstances and may be particularly interesting for that very reason. Plays, which no longer talk *about* the absurdity of man's existence but illustrate it with concrete examples, seem to change their nature with the social climate of an audience in another country and yield multiple meanings which the author might not have foreseen. They become something like fables – though without a moral structure – applicable to a variety of basic situations. The old writers of moral fables were well aware of this curious expansion of meaning. So was Freud, though from a more 'scientific' point of view.

What happened to the absurd play in the 1960s in Eastern Europe was something like a large scale, magnified illustration of Freud's example of unconscious humour – a form of communication not intended by the author. In his treatise *Der Witz* Freud describes the workings of the unconscious joke, a message that affects the audience in a way the author had never intended. Freud illustrates it, as always, with an example from the life of one of his patients: Two children, a boy and a girl, entertain their relatives by performing a little play they thought up: the boy acts a husband returning from the wars after a long absence, and regales his wife (the girl) with stories about his heroic deeds. She counters this by informing him that during the time he fought the battles she had been preparing a surprise for his homecoming. Pointing to twelve dolls neatly lined up in the background, she explains that she has made all these beautiful children for him to enjoy after his return. Freud tells us that when the whole family burst out laughing, the children, confused and hurt, refused to continue with their play and withdrew, obviously disturbed by the strange reaction to their performance.[68]

Something similar happened to the playwrights of the Absurd who, trying to write plays that would 'openly oppose realism, and tacitly reality itself,'[69] suddenly found that their works contained political messages when performed in a different social atmosphere. Take Ionesco's *The Lesson*, in which an authoritarian professor drains his pupil of natural responses and vitality to the point where he kills her. It is obvious that a nation that had to accept a certain form of 'the truth' for some time would react to this play with the excitement that comes from the awareness of how it related to their own lives. The absurd situation has become real in a different context. It even works with some of the great ambiguous classical plays. Molière's *Le Misanthrope*, for example, a work that presents us with a model of a loner (a seventeenth-century version of Camus' absurd hero in *The Stranger*) who opts out of society in the name of the honesty of his convictions, experienced a similar fate. When the play was performed in the late sixties, the audience in Prague, reacted so strongly that the authorities decided to close the play down.[70]

Despite or, more likely, *because* of its atmosphere of noncommittal mystery, the Theatre of the Absurd became charged with politically electrifying meaning. Of course this aspect of the performances was not discussed in print but remained the open secret of the dialogue between the stage and the audience, fleetingly recreated with every performance.

And so Czechoslovakia's short acquaintance with the Theatre of the Absurd was a strangely mixed experience that appears in the country's literary journals and papers of the sixties like the diary of a great spiritual adventure. Whatever the details of the encounter, the basic impact it left on Czechoslovakia was the realization that contemporary theatre had the 'responsibility to express judgements,' that it had to 'perform an act of recognition, no aspect of which could be kept silent.'[71] The fact that this eagerness to perform or share this act of recognition has ceased to have an outlet is an absurd epilogue to the story of the Theatre of the Absurd in Czechoslovakia.

II RESPONSES: WEST

Four days after the opening performance of Václav Havel's absurd play *The Memorandum* at the Theatre on the Balustrade in Prague, a Czech reviewer made the following comment on the play: 'The mechanism of cowardice, power and indifference – all this, although doubtless it is absurd, is only to a very small degree a product of the absurd imagination of the playwright.'[72] A short time later a German critic in the influential *Frankfurter Allgemeine Zeitung* expanded on that very point by arguing that in *The Memorandum* forms of 'absurd and realistic theatre ... can hardly be distinguished ... [and] turn out to be opposite sides of the same coin.'[73] Both critics are trying to make the same point: namely that an absurd situation on an Eastern European stage has a realistic impact on the audience. This is true enough, but the idea has been overused by Western critics who have availed themselves of this realization (with greater or lesser discretion) as a master key to the interpretation of the plays from Eastern Europe.

The idea is expressed in many variations. A few months after the above comments, Martin Esslin, in an article significantly entitled 'Political Theatre – absurd,' took the thought an important step further. He pointed out the particular ability of 'absurdist' writing 'to treat concrete – and political issues with such a high degree of generalization that audiences with entirely different backgrounds can understand them similarly and relate them to themselves.[74] By the time Esslin published the second expanded edition of his *Theatre of the Absurd* in 1969, he introduced the section on Eastern Europe as follows: 'In the early nineteen-fifties, at the time of the controversy between Kenneth Tynan and Ionesco, it appeared as though the Theatre of the Absurd – introspective, oblivious of social problems and their remedies – was the very antithesis of the political theatre as preached by Brecht and his followers, or by the official arbiters of the arts in the Soviet Union and her bloc. It is one of the ironies of the cultural history of our times that, after the thaw had set in in Eastern Europe, it was precisely the theatre of Ionesco which provided the model for an extremely vigorous and barbed kind of political theatre in some of the countries concerned.'[75]

This idea was surely exciting, possibly for two reasons: firstly, it provided an unexpectedly topical aspect for the much-discussed, enigmatic qualities of the Western Theatre of the Absurd; secondly, it seemed to open up an access route to the mystery of Eastern European contemporary culture, isolated from the West since virtually the beginning of the Second World War. It was exhilarating to realize that, for example, the prime play of existential anguish, *Waiting for Godot*, suddenly appeared in another social context as a topical political comment on the never-never-land of a future perfect society, when all hardships and wants of the present would be gone. It was equally stimulating to speculate on the magic power of a message that is not clearly expressed but clearly understood – thus creating between the artist and his public a hidden but very strong form of communication that is largely unknown (because, luckily, hardly needed) in the West.

Playwrights, directors, and designers, who had to cope with the amorphous power of censorship for many years and for whom the truth was the sweetest of forbidden fruits, were, of course, aware of the electrifying power of the sub rosa statement, and naturally they used it. Under the guise of nonsense – or absurdity – using the ancient prerogative of the fool to say what others must conceal, they felt free to address themselves to their audiences who responded readily and delightedly to anything that could be taken as a reference to the current situation – no matter whether it was in actual words, gestures, or a special feature of the stage set. This common ground on which the playwright, director, designer and actor met the audience – was a very fruitful context in which to make theatre. It was this context which – during the nineteen sixties and ending in 1968 – also had an important and singular influence on literary criticism. The reviews and commentaries published in literary journals like *Literární noviny*, *Host do domu*, *Divadlo*, *Plamen*, etc. (all of which are extinct now) played a particularly important and formative role. It was up to the critic to tune the audience's already responsive ears to the finer points of political and philosophical implications in the plays they were seeing on their numerous and lively stages – plays local and foreign alike. Thus the Czech and Slovak literary critics found themselves in an unexpectedly vital position: they had the responsible task of moulding their readers' perceptions and relating ideas presented on the stage to the mood of urgent enquiry experienced by a people who had been intellectually and culturally isolated in the political fortress of Stalinism. To explore more fully the creative interpretive work of the best of these critics would make a fascinating study of a period when literary criticism was not on the periphery but in the focal centre of the cultural life of a nation.

When Kenneth Tynan commented on his visit to Prague in 1967, he remarked that it was virtually impossible for a Czech artist to make a statement that had no political resonance. 'No matter how remote a playwright's symbols and metaphors may be, the audience translates them into terms of practical politics and current events.'[76] Sometimes this eagerness to grasp hidden meanings had little to do with the artistic impact of a play. Take the example of Shaw's *Saint Joan* which was staged in Prague in 1966. When in the *Epilogue* of the play the heroine returns as a serene ghost in order to see how things are going in the world a quarter of a century after having been burned to death, the Earl of Warwick greets her with a Shavian: 'Madam: my congratulations on your rehabilitation. I feel I owe you an apology.'[77] At this the Prague audience began to clap and cheer so that the end of the play was drowned out by the noise. They had heard a highly topical line, the political meaning of which was clear to the point that some members of the audience might actually have experienced the situation personally or in their immediate families. The word 'rehabilitation,' used playfully by Shaw in his ironic attack on the flexible policy of the Catholic church, was suddenly charged with electrifying meaning. After all, Rudolf Slánský, who had been a top man in the Czechoslovak Communist Party, had fallen into disgrace during Stalinism and had been executed after a show trial in 1951, was declared innocent of all major crimes in 1962 and officially 'rehabilitated.' Another later example of a similar kind is, amazingly enough, Edward Albee's play *A Delicate Balance* – reviewed in New York as 'dissecting the agony of fear and emptiness'[78] – which was one of three plays[79] withdrawn from performance in Prague in early 1970. The reason was, in Albee's case, the topical impact of a single sentence which, in the words of the Czech authorities, caused among the audience' reactions that were contrary to the idea and the spirit of the plays.'[80] This 'undesirable' response occurs when a meddling couple that have overstayed their welcome answers the question whether they have come to stay forever with a deadpan: 'If need be.'[81] The biting double irony of this odd example of censorship is that theoretically the authorities were right:

Surely this reaction was 'contrary to the idea' of the play, and Albee never dreamt of the political colouring these words would take on before an audience that had witnessed the events of August 1968 a year and a half earlier.

And so we have crossed the threshold of another 'absurd' situation concerning the Theatre of the Absurd in Czechoslovakia. The eager responsiveness of the audience, ordinarily a delight to anyone who has anything to do with the theatre, may not have had the best effect on Western opinions of recent Czech plays whether critics call them absurd or not. During the sixties, as more and more people travelled across the border, critics and commentators returned from Prague, ready to publish enthusiastic essays about the lively atmosphere of Czechoslovak theatres and the astuteness of the audience in catching topical nuances and political allusions. Add this information to the contemporary Western eagerness to make everything 'relevant,' and you have created an image of Czech theatre that may be exciting, but not quite for the right reasons.

The issue of relevance might be best illustrated by the case of Václav Havel who in general discussions of contemporary theatre is usually mentioned as a representative of absurd drama in Czechoslovakia. It is fair to say that most critics and scholars, eager to point out Havel's incontestable political relevance, have tended to shortchange the wider implications of his plays and pay insufficient attention to his artistic qualities. Even those who seem aware of the universal appeal of his work have – quite understandably – been side-tracked by the surprisingly original way in which he expresses his criticism of a systematized society, so that they have spent their energies on the political (though Havel might call it antipolitical) aspects of his writings. Even when they touch on the general meaning of Havel's work, speaking of the 'universality of his metaphors,' his exploration of 'the devaluation of language,' calling one of his plays 'a type of absurd ritual in which the act of being and non-being is commemorated,' or pointing out that his plays, though 'inspired by life in Czechoslovakia ... just as clearly relate to any technocratic society,'[82] none has really tried to formulate the relevance of Havel's work for a Western democracy.[83]

A related case is that of Ivan Klíma whose play *The Castle* – certainly not among the best of his dramatic works – has been receiving more than its share of attention because it seemed to politicize Kafka and was interpreted as criticizing the hierarchy of a people's democracy.[84] Klíma's later plays received much less attention abroad. Whether this 'political' image is partly the reason why the works of the most poetic Czech playwright, Josef

Topol, whose work is remarkably difficult by to translate, have not yet made the impact abroad which they deserve – Topol and politics mix as poorly as Beckett and politics – is a fruitless speculation.

Another case is that of Pavel Kohout, the only Czech writer who has been produced on Broadway. Kohout stirred considerable interest in Germany when his exchange of open letters with Günter Grass developed into a polemical debate which appeared in the German weekly *Die Zeit* in 1967. The critics who commented on the numerous productions of Kohout's plays in Germany, though aware of political implications, seemed to be concerned with primarily discussing the author's brilliant histrionics. Perhaps it is Kohout's remarkable combination of being in one way a writer of a typically Czech cast – his comic genius flashes in the most serious situations – and in another way a writer capable of a great variety of styles that gives him a mercurial image as a writer whose unpredictable succession of works has puzzled critics as much as it has pleased audiences.

It might be of interest here to scan some reviews of a recent première of a Czech play in Germany, namely Pavel Landovský's *Closed for Disinfection*.[85] Most critics stress the fact that the play comes 'from another world,' that it shows 'the inhumanity of dictatorship' that the Western spectator may not even be able to grasp 'the macabre nature of Landovský's humour.'[86] These critics obviously and rather sadly regard the play exclusively under what I would call the light of political relevance. It must be admitted that in certain ways they are right. The playwright does indeed give us an image of a totalitarian utopia which comes precariously close to the situation he knows at home. Yet, the meanings of this and other Czech plays are partially lost if they are reduced to local circumstances. Some commentators are beginning to notice this. They mention the 'Orwellian nature' of the play, its actuality in the face of 'Western data centres storing information on individuals,' its 'oppressive nature which goes under one's skin because it is dangerous to be a witness'[87] to what is happening there.

These remarks are definite signs that the 'political' image of the Czech theatre is waning and the international or supra-national nature of the plays is emerging. This would be very much in accord with the intentions of the playwrights who, since the late fifties, have consistently tried to write the opposite of political, namely anti-political theater – even if, in the last analysis, it becomes, in a wider sense, political again. After a decade of ideologization of drama, when plays had to be written to reflect the dictates of Socialist Realism – a form of 'applied art' in order to foster ideology – the stage, young writers felt, was again to exist for its own sake, and theatre was to be made for theatre's sake, as a protest against the ideologization of art. This protest, because of its very antipolitical attitude, was actually a political gesture – but only to Czechoslovaks. Once a play has left the system against which it strove, it ought to be given a chance to be considered out of context. Perhaps our awareness of this context is still – and is likely to be for some time – too strong to permit us to free ourselves from it. Indeed, that would not do full justice to the playwrights either. Havel reformulates for us the old truth that 'the extraordinarily intense relationship which the theatre has and has always had with political reality is not a fortuitous one, but has its natural roots in the structure of the theatre as an art form. Its essential need for *topicality* (in the broadest sense of the term) must necessarily lead to its essential *politicality* (again in the broadest and deepest meaning of the word).'[88] The asides in brackets are so important that Havel stresses them once more when he expresses his own conviction as a dramatic author that 'the best theatre is and always has been political. Political, I repeat, in the *broadest and truly serious sense of the term* ... as something which has the innate characteristic that it is not indifferent to the fate of the human *polis*, that it has a live, committed and penetrative relationship with the social reality of its country and its time and that it attains its "timelessness" and "universal" understanding through its concrete knowledge of its place and its time ... The theatre can depict politics precisely because it has no political aim. For this reason it seems to me that all ideas of a so-called "political theatre" are mistaken.'[89] Perhaps one ought to give some thought to what Havel means by the *broadest and truly serious sense of the term* 'political.' It might help one realize that the non-political politicality (or political non-politicality – whichever way we choose to take it) of modern Czech theatre has much in store for us.

On the whole much Western interest in Czech theatre has centered on such outstanding figures as set-designer Josef Svoboda,[90] whose work – he has designed nearly four hundred productions for Czechoslovak and foreign stages, and was responsible for the famed Czechoslovak pavilions at the Brussels and Montreal World's Fairs – has been applauded throughout the West. Also director Otomar Krejča's work[91] including the renowned stagings of *Hamlet*, *Romeo and Juliet* and Chekhov's *Three Sisters* – has caused much commentary and admiration. So have, on a more popular level, the technical innovations of the Black Theatre and the Laterna Magica which have become major theatrical tourist attractions in Prague because their appeal does not depend on language. In fact, Brockett and Findlay's recent *History of European and American Theatre since 1870* mentions Czechoslovakia's influence on international theatre as stemming 'primarily from technology and design.'[92] In a way Brockett and Findlay are right. A Westerner interested in theatre is more likely to know the name of Svoboda than the names of Havel and Klíma. And, to be sure, the brilliant designer has made a great impact on contemporary theatre. Yet the above entry in the history of theatre surely only gives an added impetus to the necessity of recognizing in the context of today's international theatre the importance of Czechoslovak drama during the anni mirabili of the nineteen sixties.

2
Václav Havel

What power – what group – finds it eternally necessary to make people as character-
less and submissive as possible? ... Why must peoples' support be won only at the
price of their moral devastation?   LUDVÍK VACULÍK

When Tom Stoppard, the well-known British playwright of Czech birth,
had completed *Jumpers*[1] which opened in London in February 1972 and
became an immediate international success, nine years had passed since
Václav Havel had written *The Increased Difficulty of Concentration* which
anticipated Stoppard's play in several ways. The heros of both plays are
scholars (Stoppard's is a moral philosopher, Havel's a social scientist) who
are trying to define – in hilarious, utterly confused lectures and dictations
which provide much amusement for the audience – the existence of moral
absolutes and the essence of man. In both cases, however, these valiant, if
grotesque, attempts are thwarted because the thinkers are constantly interrupted by the mad ways of the surrounding world. When the plays end,
their heros are not one iota closer to either the nature of morality or the
nature of man.

Although their characters have similar problems on stage, the authors
themselves have been leading – particularly during recent years – drastically different lives. Since early 1977, when he was arrested and imprisoned
as one of the three spokesmen for Charter 77,[2] Václav Havel's name has
been appearing in the Western press with increasing frequency. In 1978,
when Tom Stoppard dedicated his television play *Professional Foul* to
Václav Havel, the latter moved as it were officially into the consciousness
of Western writers. 'I had ill-formed and unformed thoughts of writing
about Czechoslovakia for a year or two,' Stoppard writes in the spring of
1977 in his introduction to *Professional Foul*. 'Moreover, I had been

strongly drawn to the work and personality of the arrested playwright Václav Havel. Thus it would be natural to expect that the setting and subject matter of *Professional Foul* declared themselves as soon as the Charter story broke ...'[3]

The play is a very witty work about a British academic, Professor Anderson, who is flying to Prague to attend the 'Colloquium Philosophicum Prague 77,' an international conference of scholars. He is scheduled to give a lecture on the topic 'Ethical Fact in Ethical Fiction' and also attend a football match – both, obviously, completely unpolitical activities. However, during his visit in Prague, Anderson is inevitably drawn into a political situation. A former student of his, Pavel Hollar, who is now reduced to cleaning lavatories at a bus station, appears in his hotel room and asks him to smuggle out a thesis arguing that the ethics of the state must be based on the fundamental ethics of the individual. Anderson, well-versed in ethical problems in fiction, finds himself in a very real ethical dilemma: after all, as a guest of the government he felt he could not, with a clean conscience, smuggle out what that state considered to be subversive literature. However, in the end Anderson performs an action which could or could not be considered ethical, depending on the circumstances: he puts Hollar's thesis into the briefcase of an unsuspecting colleague who unwittingly carries it out of the country. 'Ethics,' Anderson concludes when informing his stunned colleague of the latter's unconscious act of political smuggling, when their plane has left Czechoslovakia far below and behind, 'is a very complicated business.'[4]

When Top Stoppard created the figure of Pavel Hollar, he obviously thought of Václav Havel, although he was aware that Havel 'would be the first to object that in mentioning his name only, I am putting undue emphasis on his part in the Czechoslovakian human rights movement. Others have gone to gaol and many more have been victimized. This is true. But I have in mind not just the Chartist but the author of *The Garden Party*, *The Memorandum*, *The Audience* and other plays. It is to a fellow writer that I dedicate *Professional Foul* in admiration.'[5]

A short time after writing these words Stoppard went to Czechoslovakia in June 1977 (for the first time since he had left it as a small child thirty eight years ago) in order to meet Václav Havel.[6] They met in Havel's converted farmhouse for a few intense hours – two outstanding writers, born within a few months of each other in the same small country, whom life had led such drastically different ways. The two men knew they were kindred spirits and knew they were trying to do basically the same thing: to show in their creative medium what they conceived to be the truth about our age and its people lost in the network of vast societies. But only one of them is allowed to speak, to have his plays produced, to see international audiences respond to his humour, his thought, his brilliant histrionics. The other one is isolated from any stage, any audience; he has to let his plays, like bottles on the ocean, be carried to foreign shores. This is an incredible contrast in fates between writers who have such similar views of the world.

In an essay contributed to the *Times Literary Supplement* in 1967 Václav Havel makes the comment that theatre 'attains immortality only through its topicality. It can only achieve lasting value by the profundity of its topical value.'[7] Nine years later, in an author's comment published in the first edition of his suppressed plays, Havel makes the same point but modifies it this time with a sad undertone because it is no longer possible to attain that concrete realization of his plays on a Czech stage. He tells us that 'I must lean on something I know, on the concrete background of my life, and only by means of that authenticity can I – perhaps – give account of the times ... I must open myself much more fully to what was missing in the poetic structure of my older plays, to what I would call the *existential dimension of the world.*'[8]

In approaching Havel's brilliant and startling plays it might be useful to become aware of how the main theme of his work, which had been formulated as 'the relationship between man and the system'[9] in 1968, expanded and deepened to what the author himself calls the 'existential dimension of the world.' Perhaps the development Havel has undergone in his relatively brief career as a dramatist can be followed best by starting with a simple proposition: that social systems make their – more or less pronounced – demands to organize individual man into a system, in order to achieve certain – more or less laudable – aims which in turn are to serve the interests of man. Already we see a suggestion of a vicious circle in the argument: man is an organism, the system functions as a mechanism; one must subdue the other or be subdued. Around these tensions Václav Havel builds his unique, grimly comic theatre.

Since the mid-sixties, when his first two plays were translated into English and German, Havel – together with the Polish writer Slawomir Mrożek – has become known in the West as the prime example of the Theatre of the Absurd in Eastern Europe. Havel's actual connection with the playwrights of the Absurd is that he read them, loved them, and most likely derived some ideas from them. Nevertheless, the absurdity of his own plays is highly original and of a different brand than that of Ionesco, Genet or Adamov. Havel's theatre explores language as the primary agent in man's absurd situation.[10] The real hero of his plays is the mechanistic phrase, uttered from habit, repeated with parrot-like readiness, which decides people's actions, composes events, and creates its own absurd reality. At the outset of our first chapter, while reflecting on the highly problematic nature of the very term 'Theatre of the Absurd,' we considered the way a mere working definition, conceived for the sake of clarity, can create an absolute order which proliferates itself with surprising reproductive powers. It is precisely this type of situation that makes up the core of Havel's theatre: an exploration of the tremendous power of the word or phrase which becomes the unquestioned property of all, prevents anyone from thinking, and is the prime enemy of common sense and reason.

Critics and commentators never fail to mention the inherent 'logic' of Havel's writings. Jan Grossman was the first to apply the word[11] to Havel's works and it has been mentioned in variations ever since. One has indeed the feeling that events in Havel's plays follow each other with inevitable logical causality. Its particular quality, however, needs some consideration. Havel's plays work with the causality of mechanism. His is a unique combination of logical thinking and the inevitability of a mechanism set in motion. Take an electric carrot-slicer. It will go on cutting as long as it receives an object of a certain shape – that of a carrot. It will go on slicing, irrespective of any other considerations. We are reminded of one of Charlie Chaplin's most brilliant scenes when he is working on an assembly line and, by failing to react predictably, upsets the smoothly running mechanism of the whole establishment. Here we have the stuff Havel's plays are made of: the insoluble tension between the individual who knows that a carrot is a carrot for reasons other than its shape alone, and the system which identifies a carrot as a carrot solely by a mechanical reaction, leading, more often than not, to a logical disaster.

Ionesco, too, was concerned with this problem. Take, for example, the male characters in *The Bald Soprano*. When it occurs repeatedly that there is no-one at the door after the doorbell has been ringing, they base their speculations on logical theory: 'When one hears the doorbell ring, that means someone is at the door ringing to have the door opened.' The female characters, however, base their reasoning on the logic of experience: 'That is true in theory. But in reality things happen differently ... Experience teaches us that when one hears the doorbell ring it is because there is never anyone there.'[12] Both lines of reasoning, since made without the 'logic' of common sense, are proved wrong; and Ionesco leaves it at that.

Another case in point is the conversation in Beckett's *Waiting for Godot* in which Vladimir and Estragon are discussing the possibility of hanging themselves. Estragon, having warmed up to the idea, wants quick action:

ESTRAGON Let's hand ourselves immediately!
VLADIMIR From a bough? *they go towards the tree* I wouldn't trust it.
ESTRAGON We can always try.
VLADIMIR Go ahead.
ESTRAGON After you.
VLADIMIR No, no, you first.
ESTRAGON Why me?
VLADIMIR You're lighter than I am.
ESTRAGON Just so!
VLADIMIR I don't understand.
ESTRAGON Use your intelligence, can't you?
    Vladimir uses his intelligence
VLADIMIR *finally* I remain in the dark.
ESTRAGON This is how it is. *he reflects* The bough ... the bough ... *angrily* Use your
    head, can't you?
VLADIMIR You're my only hope.
ESTRAGON *with effort* Gogo light – bough not break – Gogo dead. Didi heavy –
    bough break – Didi alone. Whereas –
VLADIMIR I hadn't thought of that.[13]

Vladimir hoped to convince Estragon with a logical argument: Estragon was lighter. Estragon proceeds to reveal the fallaciousness of this reasoning by another type of logic. Each reasons to his own advantage; the situation dictates their reasoning. Vladimir's logic says the lighter man should try first because the bough should undergo the easier test first and, having passed it, could be submitted to the more difficult test. Estragon's logic says if the bough passed the difficult test first, logically it would also bear up under easier tests. Vladimir has based his logic on testing the branch as such, Estragon on its performing the required function. This double display of reasoning, however, is proved irrelevant a moment later when the two realize that actually they have no idea as to who is heavier. 'There is an even chance. Or nearly.' Estragon muses.

As in Ionesco's play, the chain of reasoning is proved useless because the premise is wrong or unknown. This deep mistrust of human reason permeates the absurd theatre of Western countries – it is obvious in the plays, say, of Harold Pinter or Wolfgang Hildesheimer. But Havel's case is different. He takes a seemingly rational subject (the creation of a new way of communication, a man's adaptation to his new job, the difficulties encountered in sociological experimentation, opposition to poor leadership) and analyses its consequences with minute logic. Regarded on the surface the absurd has no place at all in Havel's work. But then, in the fashion of some Surrealist painters, he injects into this perfectly sane situation one absurd element which inverts the whole meaning and stands it on its head. As in our examples from Ionesco and Beckett, human reasoning is again proved irrational. However, with Havel the point at which the 'reversal into absurdity' takes place is identifiable: it is the moment when the project in a man's mind – an idea, let us say – can create a mechanism which, once it begins to function, adapts everything to its function and makes it part of the mechanism. The theme of mechanization in Havel's plays is the search for that concealed point at which reasoning becomes absurd. The same theme in the Western branch of absurd theatre revolves around the claim that this point can never be found.

Martin Esslin has pointed out that it is a fusion of the worlds of Franz Kafka and Jaroslav Hašek – metaphysical anguish and low-life clowning – both peculiarly rooted in Czech tradition, which we find in Havel's plays.[14] This combination is obviously reminiscent of Beckett's plays, yet any comparison is very tenuous. The latter writes in a language that seems to be transparent and makes us realize the superficiality of all dialogue; the conversations of Beckett's characters seem like fences put up to designate some kind of – perhaps arbitrary – order in the vast spaces of the unknowable. Havel sets up his language as a barrier to knowing and realizing anything at all. Where Beckett questions without an answer, Havel answers without a question.

The stage settings in Havel's plays resemble each other. On the one hand they remind us of Kafka's oppressive houses with no way out; on the other hand they bring to mind Beckett's bare stage, where a leafless tree, a chair, handbag or step-ladder each takes on a vast importance beyond its actual usage and becomes a sign indicating the nature of the characters' lives. The most distinguishing mark of Havel's stage is a kind of standardized neutrality: the characters move about in the aridity of functional rooms and offices.

But even the private homes in Havel's plays are deprived of any touch of a homey atmosphere. They are like cells in a beehive where everything (even a gothic madonna in a window-recess) must be 'just the way it was planned,'[15] where certain things are expected to take place at certain times, and events are regulated by frozen habits which seem to have acquired an uncanny inevitability in the characters' minds. Lunch and dinner have become facts of life like birth and death – events which we all share and which provide the only certain ground of communication between the characters. The effect of this rigid patterning on the audience is paralyzing in its inevitability. When we hear Mrs Huml in *The Increased Difficulty of Concentration* rummaging backstage in the kitchen and drawing her husband's attention to the pot of beef he is to heat for his lunch, we have visions of thousands of similar pots of beef, thousands of similar husbands putting them on thousands of similar stoves.

The first production of *The Memorandum* at Prague's Theatre On the Balustrade under the direction of Jan Grossman was designed to bring out the standardized barrenness of Havel's world by reducing the visual aspect of the performance to the same collective cliché which makes up the texture of the whole dialogue. The stage set included an empty can front stage into which water kept dropping constantly and with deadening monotony. In almost unbearable contrast with it were loud, bouncy, optimistic snatches of music – a symphony orchestra blaring out some terrible mixture of Lohengrin and Nabucco[16] – the agitated bursts of laughter from the audience providing a kind of counterpoint, recreated with varying patterns during each performance. The numerous filing cabinets on stage turned out to contain nothing but the clerks' knives, forks, and spoons, wrapped in plastic bags, and taken out and replaced again with metronomic precision, according to the daily ritual of going to lunch. Special fire-extinguishers which go with the office of director, indicating his stature like a coat of arms, were set up and removed according to who occupied the director's desk: fire-extinguishers remain the same, directors are interchangeable. This prominence given to physical details on stage (as well as in the dialogue, as we will see later) maps out the area in which Havel's characters move. It is limited on one side by the sterile, fixed phrases of abstract language (be it of a politico-bureaucratic, proverbio-folksy, or private-emotional nature), and on the other side by physiological needs like eating, dressing, combing one's hair, and going to the bathroom. The stage instructions for the director's secretary Hana in *The Memorandum*, for example, read as follows: 'Hana hangs her coat on a coat-rack, sits down at typist's desk, takes a mirror and comb out of her bag, props mirror against typewriter and begins to comb her hair. Combing her hair will be her chief activity throughout the play. She will interrupt it only when absolutely necessary.'[17] When we have seen the play we realize that these instances of absolute necessity occur only when she runs out to get milk, rolls, or peanuts.

Another example is the Chief Censor Aram in *The Conspirators*. During the first and the last scene of the play when most of the characters are assembled on the stage, Aram consumes sandwiches with the punctual monotony of an egg-timer. Whenever the conversation stalls, he leans over to the hostess and utters a soft 'may I?' pointing to the sandwich plate on the table. Having received her mechanical response, 'of course,' Aram, according to stage instructions repeated six times during these two scenes, 'takes a sandwich and eats it hungrily, then wipes his hands on his handkerchief.'[18] The mechanistic predictability of man counterpoints the action like an electric instrument paying a certain tune at a set time.

Another point to consider is the naturalistic precision with which the playwright in his stage instructions to *The Increased Difficulty of Concentration* indicates what is eaten for lunch or dinner in the Humls' house and how it is served: on the tray there are 'two plates with steaming stew, a pot of mustard, a basket with bread, glasses, beer, knives and forks.'[19] Sometimes the tray is brought in by Vlasta, Huml's wife, at other times by Renata, Huml's mistress. The two are interchangeable like the directors in *The Memorandum*, but the lunch, like the fire extinguisher, remains the same. We are reminded of a scene in Dürrenmatt's 'absurd' play *An Angel Comes to Babylon* in which outside the king's palace there is a huge royal statue with an exchangeable head.[20] Every time one king is replaced by another, only the statue's head is changed and the state saves great expense in material and labour. Matter has taken over man's existence. Man himself has become exchangeable like a part of a machine.

A Czech critic said of Havel that when watching his plays one has the impression of listening to conversations between two rather primitive cybernetic machines which have at their disposal only a very limited range of answers to a very limited range of questions. In Havel's first full-length play, *The Garden Party*, we are even made the witnesses of the schooling process of such a machine, a young man named Hugo Pludek. In the course of the action he rises from being a monosyllabic, chess-playing son of an obscure middle-class family to the honourable position of heading a newly established ministerial commission which is to solve the political impasse in society (we never find out which society nor which political system – and it does not matter in the least). On closer inspection it appears that the impasse is a strange one indeed: the difficulty turns out to be a linguistic one; it is language that has created an acute political problem. How does Havel go about putting such intangible and undramatic material on the stage? He builds his play quite logically around one point of language and leads his audience on an extremely comic four-act exploration of the power of language itself. At one moment words seem to provide the only logical element on stage, at the next moment they create complete confusion. The audience, unable to stop laughing, is taken through bounds and leaps of reasoning, across swamps of phraseology, as it watches sense turn into nonsense and nonsense into sense.

The Garden Party is about the bureaucratic ordering of life – public and private. The setting is a utopian (though thoroughly Czech) society. Its various organizational organs must have identifiable labels and there must be order in every sphere. Under no circumstances may there occur any confusion between, say, the 'Secretariat of Humour' and the 'Ideological Regulation Commission.'[21] That might result in a confusion between an idea and humour, and that would never do. This is where the social system represented in *The Garden Party* gets into trouble. The government has made the decision to initiate some form of liberalization, the first step of which is to liquidate the Ministry of Liquidation. Expressed in words, the issue seems simply a matter of bad stylistics, and if we substitute the words 'close down' for 'liquidate' we have solved the problem and can proceed. But in Havel's world language is taken seriously and above all, literally. If it says 'liquidate,' it means it! But since liquidation is a measure that can only be performed by the appropriate body, which in this case is the Ministry of Liquidation, the politico-linguistic deadlock is already upon us.

This deadlock turns out to be the springboard for the central character's rising political career. By adapting himself with supreme linguistic agility to the ways of the officials in the bureaucratic structure he attains one prominent position after another. The whole play consists of a biting and very amusing demonstration of how he succeeds on the basis of linguistic talents alone. In the first act Hugo Pludek says very little indeed. Except for one or two monosyllabic comments on his chess game, his conversation is limited to variations of 'just fine, Ma,' and 'pretty bad, Dad.' Only toward the end of the act does he give an indication of his budding talents, by quoting one of his father's twisted proverbs: 'if we don't realize in time the historical role of the middle classes, the Japs, who don't need the middle classes, will come, remove them from history, and send them to Japan.'[22] Grammatically the statement is correct: the conditional if-clause is duly followed by the main clause, the relative clause describing the antecedent subject is in place, and the predicate consists of three verbs, one of them intransitive, the other two transitive, following each other properly according to the chronological order of the events. Hugo's statement gets an A plus in grammar, but in logic it gets an F for Failed. Havel has prepared the ground for the rest of the play. The combination of good grammar and suitable vocabulary irrespective of sense turns out to be the key to social success.

In the second act Hugo has gone out into the world to utilize his talents. Under pressure from his parents who are worried about his career, he attends a garden party at the Ministry of Liquidation in order to make useful connections. Beginning cautiously with the meaningless proverbs he had learned from his father (an example: 'lentils are lentils and rats are rats') he becomes increasingly sure of his linguistic powers. By keeping his eyes and ears open and committing to memory the impressive phrases of two secretaries, he soon commands a truly striking repertory of expressions that vary from hazy tautologies like 'lyrico-epical verses,' to false scientific language like 'the chemification of liquidation practice.'[23] Hugo scores his first socio-political victory by defeating a high official in a battle of rhetoric in which the weapons are phrases – repeated, inverted, declined, distorted, yet unassailable in their ready-to-use compactness. At the end Hugo has landed a new job in the Ministry and we know that he is on the road to a brilliant career.

In the third act, which takes place in one of the offices of the Ministry of Inauguration, the linguistic deadlock between inauguration and liquidation is reduced ad absurdum in a series of official discussions, and the mechanistic logic of the author's dead-pan humour is bound to delight audiences East and West. Eastern European audiences, trained in the simplified logic of popularized synthetic dialectics, roll with laughter because they recognize how close such scenes are to their daily experience. Hugo Pludek has now succeeded in the system. High-handedly he bestows clichés of friendliness on the official whose favours he had courted in the previous act. At the end he is even honoured as having been the only one to prevent the terrible mistake of wanting to liquidate an institution that was in charge of liquidation.

The fourth act takes us back to the Pludeks' household where telegrams are delivered, congratulating Hugo in turn on having been appointed chief official of Liquidation, then of Inauguration, and finally heading the illustrious 'Central Commission for Inauguration and Liquidation.' Now Hugo's bureaucratic personality takes over completely. He is so depersonalized that he refers to himself in the third person singular – he has lost his 'I,' his self. Moulded by the system into a standardized form, he is also the co-creator of this form. The circle is closed: man invents a system that in turn shapes him. Toward the end of the play Havel – following Shaw's advice to tell the audience what you have done after you have done it – illustrates his main point once more in concrete terms: Confused by the phrase-spouting official in whom he fails to recognize his son, Hugo's father asks him who he really is. Hugo responds with a long, extremely funny speech, explaining the difficulties, nay the impossibility of answering such a naive inquiry: 'Me? You mean who am I? Now look here, I don't like this one-sided way of putting questions, I really don't! You think one can ask in this simplifying way? ... Truth is just as complicated and multiform as everything else in the world ... and we all are a little bit what we were yesterday and a little bit what we are today; and also a little bit we are not these things. Anyway, we are all a little bit all the time and all the time we are not a little bit ... some only are, some are only, and some are only not so that none of us entirely is and at the same time each one of us is not entirely ...'[24] Although this can be taken as a parody of Engels' explanation of motion in terms of the dialectic law of contradiction, it is primarily an example of statements nullifying themselves, of circular logic run wild. What remains is not meaning but an exercise in grammatical construction. This is Havel's main concern: the power of language as a perpetuator of systems, a tool to influence man's mind and therefore one of the strongest (though secret) weapons of any system that wants to mould him to become a well-functioning part of a system rather than a free spirit – unpredictable, erring, imaginative, mysterious in his tireless search for the truth.

The Memorandum,[25] although again highly amusing, is an even more relentless exploration of language as a tool of power. The subject is grimmer than that of *The Garden Party*, not only because the hero's absorption into the system is represented not as a career but as a matter of survival, but also because Havel has by now mastered the art of placing the action against a background of 'real' life in an office hardly distinguishable, as a Czech critic says, 'from the office where we were yesterday.'[26] The setting is deceptively naturalistic and only some time after the opening of the curtain does the audience begin to adjust to the fact that only the surface looks normal, everything else is absurd! Or does this realization itself make it realistic in the deeper sense of the word? It seems that this secret tie –almost complicity – between the absurd and real emerges in the works of many of the best modern writers. Jan Grossman calls it 'trying to render reality more concretely and more intensely.'[27]

In *The Memorandum* Havel has shifted the whole action into one of those huge bureaucratic establishments on the periphery of which part of the action of *The Garden Party* took place. It is a world where complex hierarchies wield power, where coffee-breaks and lunch-hours regulate the office work. The whole play is like an extended parody of Parkinson's Law (in itself an excellent description of an absurd situation): Work expands to fill the time available for its completion. In order to make procedures and official communications allegedly more precise (while actually complicating everything *ad infinitum*), a new synthetic language, called Ptydepe, has been invented. Ptydepe, regarded as a sacred text by those who have not learned it, and used with reverence by those who have, is regarded as the utopian solution to all problems because it 'guarantees ... [the] truly humanistic function'[28] of language. In reality, however, it becomes a symptom of the establishment itself – useless, existing for its own sake, proliferating fake values and hollow communication – a monstrous offspring of bureaucracy for its own sake.

The Memorandum consists of twelve scenes. The place of action is, in turn, the Director's Office, the Ptydepe Classroom, and the Secretariat of the Translation Centre. This pattern is repeated four times, thus indicating the mechanical nature of the events. Into this closed four-sided structure which seems like a square link in an endless chain, Havel builds his play. Director Josef Gross, an innocuous official who has been functioning for years in his assigned slot, has one morning a kafkaesque experience. He does not wake up as a giant beetle, as does one of Kafka's characters, but he suddenly feels himself similarly alienated from his habitual existence. On his desk he finds an official memorandum of the type he has found a thousand times before, but this time it is written in an incomprehensible language!

This is the kind of situation which the playwright himself has defined as absurd. 'The feeling of absurdity,' Havel writes in his essay 'The Anatomy of the Gag,' '*results from estrangement* ... [the person] no longer sees the appearances of the world in their traditional function ...' By means of examples that vary from Tolstoy to Chaplin the author explains that the first phase of a gag merely states the situation. It is the second phase that '*alienates the first phase* and reveals its absurdity, thus being the "subject" of alienation. It is the active force which brings absurdity into the gag; it turns into nonsense that which made sense before, it denies the given situation, reverses and negates it.' This is precisely what happens to the hero of Havel's play. To find a message on your desk is nothing strange, but not to be able to decipher it means that what had made sense before does so no longer. 'How is it,' argues Havel in his essay, 'that prior to the alienation the given reality did not seem absurd to us? For a simple reason: sense is outlived by the illusion of sense; the sense of the past emerges; what is at work here is persistence, automatism.'[29]

Recovering from the shock of finding himself in this absurd situation, Josef Gross is informed by his secretary that the memorandum is composed in the new official synthetic language Ptydepe which was introduced into the official procedures without Gross's knowledge. The absurd incident thus seems to have a rational explanation, but only for a non-thinking bureaucrat whose mechanical reaction to the new way of communication is simply that he shrugs his shoulders and gets down to his copy of *Ptydepe for Beginners*.

On another level, that of an outside observer – in this case the audience – the whole proposition reveals itself as absurd. It soon becomes clear that the new language is infinitely more cumbersome and complex than the old 'natural' language it is replacing. Gross, however, well-trained in the ways of bureaucracy, is on the inside of the situation. Unaware of its absurdity – his moment of alienation, his discovery of the memo, has gone by unused – he immediately gets busy and makes several unsuccessful attempts to have the memorandum translated. Now he finds himself in a truly absurd situation: he has become a stranger in his own office (where clerks break into Ptydepe conversations at the drop of a hat), just as Kafka's Gregor Samsa became a helpless, mute beetle in his own home. Ptydepe has taken over; an expert on Ptydepe usage, a Ptydomet, has been hired; Gross's deputy, Baláš, takes over the director's desk; in the Ptydepe-classes Gross cannot remember a single word while others rattle off vocabulary and get an A plus. Gradually Gross loses all official power and Baláš and his followers threaten to reveal some minor instances of his having side-stepped bureaucratic procedures. In this way Gross moves from one demotion to another.

By the half-way mark of the play the hero's fortunes have reached their lowest point. In the second half we are shown his gradual recovery and renewed rise to the position of director. Just as his downfall had been paralleled by the relentless rise of Ptydepe, his ascent now takes place against the background of Ptydepe's dwindling fortunes. As things get more hectic and the opportunists try to switch sides again, Gross finally finds out the content of the fateful memorandum. The person who translates it for him is the secretary Marie, the only person in the establishment who seems to have preserved some non-mechanized human qualities like sympathy and kindness. What Gross finds out sounds like a parody on the Gatekeeper's message in Kafka's *The Trial*[30] – it renders all preceding efforts of the receiver of the message totally futile. The memorandum informs Gross that he has been exonerated from his minor failings and praises his steadfast opposition to the 'confused, unrealistic and anti-human'[31] elements of Ptydepe, recommending at the same time that he be ruthless in purging his office of any further subversive activities of this sort.

Now Gross is given the opportunity he had yearned for when his fortunes were low: to be able to start all over again and do things differently. But in the last moment Havel crushes our hopes. The symmetry of the play suddenly reveals itself not as reflecting the rise of goodness and fall of evil, as it had seemed to, but rather as a constant, rigidly mechanized process. The theme of mechanical adjustment which was treated with bright exuberance in *The Garden Party* is struck here on a more sinister level. Against his better convictions and allegedly humanistic ideals, Gross succumbs in turn to the absurd order of the Ptydepe movement, to the empty slogans, promises, and flattery of the opportunists, and finally to the new but equally absurd order of a new synthetic language, Chorukor, introduced at the end of the play.

Havel has made his point. Gross becomes a tool in the hands of those who keep functioning unperturbed in the name of new slogans. Like Brecht's Mother Courage they do not care under whose flag they do business, so long as the business flourishes. The spark of Gross' insight into the absurd nature of his mechanized existence that might have flared up when he discovered the incomprehensible message has been extinguished for good. His final phrase-ridden speech to Marie, who is fired as a consequence of her act of loyalty in translating the memorandum, shows that he will never be capable of experiencing that revealing moment of alienation which, Havel tells us, makes a man recognize the absurdity of his being tied to a mechanized process. Gross has become part of the process.

In his next play, *The Increased Difficulty of Concentration*, Havel again manages to amuse us while he unfolds before our eyes one of the grave problems of our century. The cooler critical reception abroad is likely due to Havel's rather misleading 'image' as critic of social circumstances in Czechoslovakia. Faced with this new play in which the playwright takes on contemporary society in general, Western criticism until quite recently has tiptoed cautiously around the play, without a sign of having recognized its genius.[32] In *Increased Difficulty of Concentration* Havel reduces his setting even further and focuses on a small unit in society, a simple household. This, as we know, has been done by Ionesco, Pinter, Albee, Genet, and others. But Havel goes about it in a new way and the result is not only highly entertaining but also very disturbing. One Czech critic, realizing the universal nature of the play more clearly than Western critics, warned that it should not be regarded as merely a further comment on local social

problems but that it reflected 'the problems of modern technical civilization.'[33] Here Havel has shown more than ever that he is a writer of world
stature.

The hero is, as defined in the play itself, 'a condensed model of human
individuality.'[34] Anyone who opens a book on behaviouralistic psychology
becomes aware of the numerous variations of such terminology, used in all
seriousness and with the disarming conviction of 'scientific' accuracy.

Now let us see what Havel does with this theme. The action takes place
in the house of Eduard Huml, a scholarly writer working for the humanist
section of the National Research Council. Huml is in the process of composing a radio talk for the 'Third Programme' of the BBC, which he keeps
dictating throughout the play to his young secretary who comes to the
house.[35] The rest of the time this 'condensed model of human individuality'
is occupied in trying to keep some kind of balance between the demands of
Vlasta, his wife, and his lady friend, Renata, who keeps coming for lunch
and other less innocuous activities, romping about in Mrs Huml's
dressing-gown while the latter is busy at her job as manageress of a toy
shop. Each woman feels that Huml ought to be hers alone, each plies him
with demands to free himself from the other. Vlasta wants him to break off
his relationship with Renata, while Renata wants him to get a divorce and
marry her.

Huml is obviously unable to do either and lives an exhausting, tenuous
existence under mounting pressure from both ladies. This pressure, however, is constantly interrupted – hence eased – by the various demands of
daily life: helping Vlasta to get ready for work, warming up lunch in the
kitchen, putting on the coffee-pot, having to dress and undress, bringing
coats or hanging them up, and so forth. Convenient interruptions of embarrassing questions, these daily chores become a sort of haven for Huml, to
which he turns like a predictable mechanism when things get too uncomfortable. As the play proceeds, the pressure of the ladies' demands is
lessened by another pressure, mounting imperceptibly before the audience's eyes and revealing itself as much more dangerous and destructive:
the pressure of repetition. Here Havel is master of his trade. He succeeds in
creating a kind of tightening-grip effect that shows the impossibility of
Huml's ever escaping the treadmill of his existence. The women echo each
other more and more in their demands and reactions. As they begin to
sound the same, Huml reacts to both with exactly the same answers. The
effect is strong. As amusement changes to dismay, the audience witnesses
how characters become interchangeable, how a basic human situation
becomes mechanized and duplicated.

In addition to these interlocked vicious circles there are two other areas in Huml's life which at first seem to provide him with the possibility of breaking out of his rut but, as the play proceeds, turn out to be variations on the same theme. There is first of all Huml's *magnum opus*, a treatise on man's happiness. Will he sublimate his practical frustrations with his theoretical speculations? Not very likely. When he gives us a sample of his philosophizing, we soon discover that his arguments have the same shape as his actions. They are like snakes biting their own tails. Huml's definition of value, for example, which begins with the pseudo-analytical statement: 'By a value we mean that which satisfies some human need – semicolon,' continues with the most banal truism: 'We distinguish material values ... from spiritual values ... full stop. Various people have at various times and in various circumstances various needs.'[36] The second reason for the failure of Huml's work to keep him 'human' is that his dictation sessions are counterpointed not only by coffee-breaks but also by his attempts to make love to his secretary. She, in turn, controls her properly righteous indignation, and has such experience in regaining her secretarial calm that this situation, too, has the desperate air of perpetuation about it. So much for Huml's professional career.

What remains is to consider him as a member of society. In this respect Havel, laughing grimly, shows us his hero only in the robot-like proportions of socio-behaviouralistic research. While harassed by all the other complications, Huml finds that he has been selected as a random sample of behaviour patterns, to be tested by a research team which promptly arrives at his house with a computer called endearingly PUZUK. The machine, though cared for and pampered like a moody child (it is in turn warmed and cooled, cleaned, and allowed to take a rest), is obviously totally useless. As PUZUK becomes more and more humanized in its sensitivity and unpredictability, Huml gets impatient, which in turn upsets Dr Balcárková, a member of the research team. As Huml pats her back to calm her down, he suddenly finds himself involved in a passionate embrace, and the next thing he knows is that she has established herself as a new woman in his life by the disastrous question: 'May I ring you tomorrow? Will you have some time for me?'[37] The play ends as it began, with Mrs Huml bringing in supper on a tray and asking the by now time-honoured question: 'Well then?' – meaning 'Did you get rid of her yet?'

The particular originality of the play lies in the playwright's having shuffled the events in Huml's life, like a pack of playing cards and interchanged their chronological order. In a comment for the director of the play Havel says that the play is not 'a jumbled up representation of a logical event, on the contrary, rather the logical event is ... merely a jumbled up, and therefore distorting representation of the play as such.'[38] The result is surprising. It appears clearly that the logical sequence does not matter at all. To show the workings of causality becomes superfluous because the entire web of situations – private, scientific-professional, meditative – is based on stereotypes. Again, as in Havel's earlier plays, language reveals its mechanizing power with frightening obviousness. Each thought and each emotion that is expressed is dictated by stereotyped language. The hollow ring of duplicated words pervades the whole play.

It is in this play that Havel has mastered the task of revealing language as a killer of intellect and feeling. Man is no longer the victim of the system as shown implicitly in *The Garden Party* and explicitly in *The Memorandum*. Rather man perpetuates the system by modelling his own life on it, and he depends on it as his stronghold. At first he fails to recognize that it is also his prison and tries to escape from this anonymous monster that schematizes his daily life and mechanizes his emotions. But the way he goes about escaping shows that the harm has been done: Huml wants to escape not by breaking but by doubling the system, and he thus creates a new mechanism which, far from destroying the old one, neatly fits into the spinning cogs. By necessity Huml himself becomes doubly mechanical and begins to repeat his own responses with machine-like exactitude. The events on stage appear as in a broken and endlessly repeated mirror-reflection and as the play proceeds, we feel an increasing certainty about being able to predict with machine-like precision the actions and reactions of the individual characters.

Imperceptibly the playwright makes us adopt the position of PUZUK, the computer, which registers a sample of individual behaviour. And as the machine seems to become more and more humanized, unsure of itself, unpredictable, and finally having something like a nervous breakdown, the audience becomes more and more certain of the predictability of events. The 'representative sample of individual behaviour patterns' has turned out to be such a stereotype that it can be registered by a stereotyped reaction. Havel has achieved a surprising tour de force. By making the audience adopt an almost automatic reaction to the characters on stage, he has shown that the tendency to mechanize the process of living resides secretly within the individual character and is therefore both more intangible and more dangerous than we take it to be.

If *The Increased Difficulty of Concentration* explores man's notorious tendency to mechanize his life and thus reduce it to the primitive level of adapting to and functioning in a certain environment, Havel's next play, *The Conspirators*, is a test of what happens when this idea is applied to a political situation. *The Conspirators*, finished in 1970, is a merry-go-round of political power. The play is constructed with mathematical precision. In fifteen scenes which follow one another like hammer blows, the struggle for political power unfolds with the inevitability of a mechanism set in motion. What sets it in motion is man's greed for power which, when rigidified and mechanized by a social system, becomes a sine qua non of his life. He tries to attain it by any means and his claims about high ideals – the common good, the nation's welfare, freedom from oppression – are merely cover-ups for his ruthless struggle to get where he wants to be. All in all this is not a highly original theme: from *Macbeth* to Büchner's *Danton's Death* and Brecht's *The Rise of Arturo Ui* man's craving for political power has proved to be among playwrights' main sources of inspiration.

However, Havel's signature on the play is unmistakable. Reduced to the bare essentials, the struggle for power of four 'public figures' (the chief prosecutor and the heads of the police, the military, and culture) is stylized into a grotesque circular dance of greed and deceit in which moves are as predictable as the periodical return of, say, the fiery white horse or the leaping lion on a moving merry-go-round. The central mechanism (provided in this case by the system) has taken over and the characters seized by its rhythm not only succumb to it but, as it were, propel its motion into greater smoothness by their own weight (the make-up of their characters – in turn formed by the system).

By saying that *The Conspirators* is about the struggle for power, we have indicated the inner meaning of the play. On the surface – as far as the characters themselves are concerned – it is a play about revolution. Again, as in Havel's other plays, it is revolution studied in a test tube. Not for one instant does the action even remotely approach a concrete problem. It remains suspended in the thin air of theoretical abstractions, and in the lengthy discussions 'freedom' and 'political oppression,' 'democracy' and the 'evils of anarchy,' 'unifying action' and 'reactionary groups' remain linguistic labels which have never been exposed to a real situation. The revolution never gets beyond the language lab. Havel's pen is getting sharper, his wit is getting more sinister. The mood of *The Conspirators* is dark indeed.

The theme of revolution is developed in several very intricate ways. At the risk of oversimplification I might suggest three ways. First of all, there is the official Revolution. It is in the title, after all, and the audience is not permitted to forget it for long. People greet each other with 'Long live the Revolution!' and there are numerous references to the great revolutionary victory which was achieved when the nation was freed from the bloody dictatorship of Olah whose past regime of terror is amply referred to in 'official' discussions. So much for the 'official' Revolution.

But there are two other forms of revolution in the play – unofficial, but much more significant than the well-advertised, institutionalized national Revolution of the past. In the first and the last scenes – the only ones that take place in a private house and not in offices – we are permitted to glance beyond the isolated world of political bureaucracy. What we learn in the first scene is coloured by hope. In the town, students demonstrate, demanding the release of an allegedly subversive political prisoner, whose harmless character (he reads philosophy, and lives a quiet life with his cat) is illustrated at various points during the play. The 'revolutionary' spirit of the demonstration grows out of a belief in justice and the dignity of the individual.

But when we are given our second glance at the outside world in the last scene, we rapidly lose what we gained in the beginning, the reassuring sense of the people's search for truth which seemed to reassert itself under any conditions. In the last moments of the play we hear that Concord Square has now become the scene for an agitated mob clamouring for the return of dictator Olah and setting up gallows for the present government. The fact that the newly formed Revolutionary Committee (consisting of our friends, the chiefs of the temporal authorities) is a step ahead of the population – they have already decided to appoint Olah their leader – does not lighten the grim picture we get of the will of the people.

At a third level of the play revolution is synonymous with greed for power. This version of revolution fills the action of the play. The struggle concerns the position of the leader of the new Revolutionary Committee and takes place primarily between Chief Prosecutor Dykl and Chief of Police Moher. Each proclaims himself in turn the new leader, as he convinces other possible contestants of his opponent's unsuitability for the job. In the course of a series of (very amusing) discussions in which everyone argues a point in order to achieve an aim that has nothing whatsoever to do with that point, the desired job swings back and forth like a pendulum at regular intervals (Dykl seems to have gained it in scenes IV and IX, Moher in scenes VIII and XII). In the meantime the job is offered as a decoy to the other two contestants in the game, the Commander-in-Chief of the Armed Forces (a sports-minded simpleton whose muscles are no real competition for his intellect – he has to take a quick swim in order to perform in the bedroom), and the Chief Censor (a voracious, vulgar nincompoop who starts to think only when he can denounce someone).

There is a woman in the game too, the widow Helga, well known to all in every sense of the word. Clearly favouring the man with the job, she manipulates and changes her position with great agility according to who has the most chance of becoming the boss. In the course of the play she ushers the Commander-in-Chief into her bedroom, establishes herself in the Chief Prosecutor's opinion as 'the only person who really understands me!'[39] and romps about the stage in an orgiastic flagellation-game with the Chief of Police.

We may remember that in Arthur Schnitzler's at first notorious, later famous play, *Der Reigen*, the game of sexual greed is presented as a closed circle. One partner keeps changing until the last partner couples with the first and the dance of desire can start all over again. Havel's dance of power also has a circular structure, inevitably and yet imperceptibly moving back to the beginning. The image of the exiled dictator Olah undergoes a gradual and disturbing change. In the first half of the play Olah and the '-ism' he stands for is a synonym for everything that is antisocial and destructive. As the play continues, however, Olah is mentioned less and less frequently. Since by now we know that in Havel's world things are the more important the less frequently they are mentioned, we develop an increasing sense of the return of terror, the reappearance of Olah. At the beginning of the play he had been thought safely dead; toward the end he is reported to have made an appearance in Monte Carlo.

In the last scene, when all the power seekers are assembled at Helga's house (as they were in the first scene), by now aware of the fact that no one will let anyone else assume power, the Chief of Police launches into a speech of circular logic which inevitably closes the vicious circle: 'my friends, let us finally stop beating about the bush! After all, we all know that one man exists who is able to establish order here, to return the nation to the path of disciplined work for its native country and thus secure true freedom and a truly democratic future! ... is it his fault that he governed just at a time which made it impossible for him to complete the task for which he is naturally predetermined? ... Seriously, my friends: if we do not want the leadership qualities of this man to be misused to the detriment of the people, why could we not at the same time use them for the benefit of the people? ...'[40] The silence of his listeners is interrupted by the maid who announces a telephone call from Monte Carlo. As the curtain falls, Moher walks resolutely to the telephone to invite tyranny to assume the leadership of the New Revolution.

The bleakness of Havel's vision is hardly tempered by the sympathetic figure of Alfred Stein, the political prisoner and adjustable scapegoat, who in the course of the play is tortured and brainwashed into making two diametrically opposed admissions of guilt. Moments before the fateful telephone call from Monte Carlo, the message is brought that Stein has hanged himself in his prison cell. The one character who had made some attempt to distinguish between a lie and the truth prefers to be absent, and the dance of power continues uninterrupted by anyone handicapped with a sense of ethics.

In a revealing comment on his 'forbidden' works, Havel tells us that *The Conspirators*, his first play written after he had been severed from any contact with the stage, suffered from having been conceived during a period of bitter struggle against a feeling of 'lack of air and senselessness.' He feels the play is 'lifeless, over-organized, bloodless, lacking humour as well as mystery ... a cake which has been left in the oven too long and is completely dried out.'[41] This stern judgment, though not really doing justice to the challenging play, is interesting because Havel thinks he wrote it in too abstract and too consciously 'universal' a manner, rather than writing it in the way he felt he should, namely 'as if my plays could be performed even here, and to address my concrete countrymen in their concrete world.'[42] Once this realization had become clear to him he seemed to be able to overcome the critical hiatus. In his next plays he does just that.

One of the paradoxes of Havel's career as a dramatist is that his next play, *The Beggar's Opera*, was actually written in response to a demand. Some time earlier, during a period when it still seemed remotely possible that such a play could be performed on an official Czech stage, one of the Prague theatres asked Havel to write a new version of Gay's classic. Havel tells us that he wrote the play with joy and ease – a considerable difference from his labours over *The Conspirators*. Some hope of seeing the play actually staged, coupled with admiration and love for Gay's original work, made it a pleasure for Havel to work with the text, and the final result was 'a play that is alive.'[43] It is interesting that *The Beggar's Opera* has not been very successful abroad.[44] Havel himself ascribes this regrettable fact to the Western cult of Brecht and the subsequent reluctance of Western theatres to stage a play based on a theme 'that had been touched by the great B.B.'[45] Whether this assessment is valid or not is a moot point. At any rate the response is regrettable because Havel's play is an important and thoroughly delightful work. Moreover, Brecht's play is doubtless a product of the 1920s and it is largely the lasting impact of Weill's magnificent music that keeps it as fresh as it is today. Havel's work is a play for the last quarter of the twentieth century. It is bound to be recognized as such sooner or later.

Let me recapitulate very briefly the content of Gay's play: Macheath, a gallant highwayman, has secretly married Polly, shopkeeper Peachum's daughter. Peachum, backed by his wife, opposes the relationship. He finds Polly useful in his shop and wants to keep her there; moreover he dislikes and fears Macheath as a formidable business competitor. Peachum denounces Macheath to the police. Macheath goes to prison but is freed by Lucy, the daughter of the chief of the prison. Not being able to stay away from the brothel where he is a favourite customer, Macheath is arrested again and saved from the gallows only by the intervention of the Player who claims that 'an Opera must end happily' and 'comply with the taste of the town.'[46] Instead of being hanged, Macheath whirls off with Polly and the others in a merry dance. And so *The Beggar's Opera* ends with a jolly tune, instead of representing 'a most excellent Moral,' namely 'that the lower Sort of People have their Vices in a degree as well as the Rich: And that they are punished for them.'[47]

One might speculate why Havel was attracted to this play. After all, this is his first variation on his earlier theme. So far as his political surrounding is concerned, the source of inspiration could not have been more 'legitimate.' After all, the main themes of Gay's play – exploitation, the vices of the upper classes, the power of money that can buy anything, including justice – are a perfect way around censorship because they sound like the recipe for Socialist Realist works. On the surface, therefore, Havel conforms to the demands of the political climate by taking up this early 'revolutionary' work and rewriting it for the present. After all, Bertolt Brecht, whose credentials as a Communist playwright were (at least in theory) not to be doubted, had taken up the same play and sharpened its message by revealing the hypocrisy of Christian ethics, by pointing to greed and ruthlessness as the pillars of the bourgeois value scale, by providing a miniature vision of revolutionary hope, romanticized and therefore powerfully appealing, in the song about the dishwasher-girl Jenny who administers justice and ushers in a new order.

Brecht had opposed the gallant back alley crookery of Macheath with the hypocritical business crookery of Peachum. Havel too makes this parallelism the basic premise of his play, but in a different sense. Both Peachum and Macheath are chiefs of criminal organizations which are in competition with each other and ultimately hope to ruin and absorb each other. Polly, Peachum's daughter, has been asked by her father to use her female charms in order to get Macheath to reveal to her the secrets of his organization. She is successful with the charms (which is not difficult with ladies' man Mackie) but soon finds herself saddled with a similar request from Macheath with regard to her father's organization. Faced with the dilemma of having to betray either her father or her husband, Polly gets into increasing difficulties until the author mercifully removes her from the action.

In *The Conspirators* we witnessed the tricks of the power game and recognized them as such. In *The Beggar's Opera* we no longer know when anyone is pretending and when he is not. As in a Pirandello play, the role and the player seem to fall apart and come together again as motives become transparent and mystifying in turn. And it is this tantalizing uncertainty that crystallizes the main theme of Havel's play: betrayal. It recurs in many guises and versions throughout the action, with each character in the role of deceiver and deceived. Peachum, for example, the boss of a criminal's organization, wants his daughter Polly to deceive Macheath whom she married, allegedly secretly but basically with the consent of her father who is trying to find out the dealings of Macheath's organization in order to be able 'finally to liquidate his organization, confiscate its property ... and discover at the same time sufficient evidence of his activities so that he could denounce him and achieve his deportation for life.'[48] Peachum, however, also works for the police for whom he acts as a sort of intelligence agent whose duty it is to gain and keep the trust of the underworld, so that he can act as a valuable informant. Peachum is therefore both a private businessman in crime as well as a government employee concerned with surveillance over and, we presume – incorrectly, as we find out later – the ultimate extinction of criminal activities.

As the play proceeds and new layers of Peachum's activities are discovered, the audience ends up totally confused as to the capacity in which Peachum is acting at the moment: whether he is pretending to be a police-spy in order to have a good camouflage for his criminal activities, or whether he is holding on to his position as the boss of his criminal organization only for the sake of being able to inform the police. At the end the impasse between guarding the law and breaking it is perfect. We can no longer tell which is which. We fail to distinguish the pretense of crime in order to preserve the law from the pretense of legality in order to preserve crime.

As usual, the last ten minutes of Havel's play have yet another shock in store for us. Lockit, the chief of police, having talked Macheath into collaborating with him, settles down to a pleasant dinner at home during which he casually reveals that he, too, is the leader of another, larger criminal organization which now has 'the whole underworld at its command.' Moreover, as his wife comments when she passes him the soup, 'No one knows about our organization and everyone serves it!'[49]

The deceit and betrayal theme is concentrated in the figure of Jenny, the only woman worthy of Macheath's attentions. Jenny betrays Macheath three times to the police, an archetypal pattern of betrayal. Macheath, who sees through the machinations of everyone else, falls for her false explanations every time. So does the audience.

The first time Jenny wins Macheath's trust by means of the romantic tale about the abandoned maiden: when she first meets Macheath she tells him he seduced and abandoned her five years before (Mackie's memory, overcrowded with such incidents, cannot check the accuracy of the story), and she claims to have been pining away ever since, untouched by men, faithful to his memory. As Macheath melts and they fall into each other's arms, she calls for the police and charges him with attempted rape.

The second time (Macheath, as we know, usually gets out of prison as quickly as he gets into it) she wins his trust by claiming to have been forced to betray him by the political system. 'They promised me,' she tells a sullen, suspicious Macheath, 'that if I did it, my father would be pardoned. You see, he has been sentenced to death –.'[50] Unrequited love had moved the romantic criminal; now political oppression moves the man who believes in individualism. In the brothel Macheath waits a second time for Jenny's embrace but she sends the police instead of coming herself.

Jenny's third betrayal occurs near the end of the play. She visits Macheath in prison and gradually convinces him to trust her once again, by presenting him with a brilliant argument couched in pseudo-dialectics and logical fallacies. The gist of her argument is that her love for Macheath has caused a split in her personality, so that she no longer is identical with herself, which in turn means that she has ceased to exist as an individual. In other words, she had to betray him to preserve herself – she acted in self-defense. As Macheath once again passionately declares his love for her, she wistfully remarks that he loves her only for her betrayals. Macheath decides to turn down the tempting offers made to him by the various criminal organizations and flee with Jenny to build a new and better life 'where no-one will find us,' but moments later he finds out that the chief of police has been informed about these intentions – that Jenny has betrayed him for the third time. It is now that Macheath capitulates and gives in to the ways of the world.

We see that Havel has kept John Gay's main themes – dog eats dog, life is more often a dirty game than not, deceit manipulates people under the guise of friendship. But he changes the thrust of the play in a significant way. Gay's Macheath has been granted grace as a literary character whose sins and crimes were merely meant for entertainment. The puritan solemnity with which Gay's play was condemned as glorifying vice,[51] totally missed this point.

Havel's play could also in a sense be interpreted as glorifying vice, but it is a very different form of vice from that which caused dignified eighteenth-century citizens to attack John Gay's operatic burlesque. Gay's Macheath is a character who escapes punishment for having indulged too deeply in the ways of the world. Havel's Macheath undergoes an initiation into the ways of the world. At the end he makes the decision which Alfred Stein of *The Conspirators* could not make: to play the game and stay alive. Like Wedekind's Marquis von Keith who throws away the revolver and grabs the bank note before pronouncing his credo, 'life is a roller coaster,' Havel's Macheath decides not to 'refuse the rules of the game which this world offers to a man,' shelves his ideas of honour and heroism, and joins in the game.

A word should be said concerning the première of *The Beggar's Opera* – the only one of Havel's plays written after 1968 that was actually, though only once, performed in Czechoslovakia. Like its predecessors, Gay's *Beggar's Opera*, that enfant terrible of eighteenth-century propriety, and Brecht's equally 'scandalous' *Dreigroschenoper* two hundred years later, Havel's play had an extraordinary first night performance. But it was of a different kind than Gay's tempestuous première which ushered in an unprecedented long run in January 1728, and Brecht's equally exciting first night after which a sort of 'Threepenny Opera fever'[52] swept Berlin in 1928.

The première of the third version of this mysteriously timeless play had very different repercussions. It took place in the small Bohemian village of Horní Počernice on November 1, 1975 – indeed an extraordinary first night performance for a play by an author of world reputation. The play was produced by a group of amateurs and ran for one single night. The audience was composed of local citizens but also included a large number of intellectuals from near-by Prague who were closely watched by the secret police. Most of those who had come to see the production were then interrogated and some lost their jobs as a result. For Havel himself, however, it meant that after many years he again experienced theatre in that deepest and best sense: 'that electrifying area of joy, truth, freedom and collective understanding.' For the author it became the première 'which I value more than any other I have ever had.'[53]

Although completed only in spring 1976, most of *The Mountain Resort* was written before the two short plays *Vernissage* and *Audience*. This is important because in this play the author tried to summarize his former dramatic production. *The Mountain Resort* is meant to be, he informs us, 'a peculiar scenic poem "about nothing," a play which ... becomes its own single theme, therefore being able to tell about the world only that which such a play, "a play about itself," would be able to say.'[54]

This somewhat abstract statement could be interpreted in two ways. First, it represents – whether Havel himself realizes it or not – an aspect of that general malaise now affecting the dramatic genre much more than the novel. The novel has been pronounced dead by various academic voices but (particularly among Czech writers) is alive and perhaps healthier than ever.[55] The dramatic genre, having born the brunt of various artistic Weltanschauungen for a long time, finds itself suddenly bloodless and – despite such writers as Dürrenmatt and Stoppard – short of breath. As a result it has become self-conscious and self-analytical. Havel's amazingly fine ear for the general heartbeat of the modern world seems to have caused him to share this self-analytical tendency in his own way.

Second, of course, the play is a logical outcome of the author's earlier work. Throughout his earlier plays Havel had explored the impact of mechanization on thought and behaviour. In *The Mountain Resort* he takes this approach to its 'absurd' conclusion by allowing it to take over the entire action. It is as if he had fed a number of attitudes, actions, gestures, and dialogues into a computer and let the computer rearrange them until they represent an organized, geometrical structure. The result is a seemingly well-constructed five-act play, in which, however, phrases, movements, and gestures have become autonomous, and the characters entirely interchangeable.

The action takes place on the terrace of a mountain resort; the characters are a group of holiday-makers. They include, for example, a writer, a count, a middle-class couple with a tea thermos, the director of the hotel, a beautiful young woman, another somewhat older woman who switches easily from knitting to mechanically portioned-out passion in her hotel room, and a maid serving fruit juices at equally well-spaced intervals. But apart from punctually reappearing comments, objects, or gestures, like filling the tea thermos and leaving for love-making, distribution of fruit juices and reminiscing about glorious days in Paris, there is nothing constant in the play. The characters speak each other's words, remember each other's pasts, go through each other's movements. To put it in another way, the gesture or word is there, but the character who carries it out or speaks it changes from act to act; the memory of Paris is there but in each act someone else remembers and someone else forgets. Havel tried to make these occurrences the subject matter of the play, in order to find out 'to what extent they are capable – all on their own – to create meaning.' The themes of the disintegration of human identity and existential schizophrenia which Havel has repeatedly called his main concerns, are obviously apparent again insofar as they can be expressed solely by these 'automatized occurrences.'[56]

Although the play depends on the visual impact of the repeated, as if scenario-controlled, gestures and movements, it remains to be seen whether it will ever be made into a successful stage production. However, the author claims to have written it for himself rather than for an audience. As a laboratory piece, a sort of test for summarized literary techniques, the text might have considerable possibilities if it were used as a film scenario where the camera could act as a sort of central consciousness, observing and analyzing the fragments of human identity.

The two one-act plays *Vernissage* and *Audience* (see chapter 9 for a discussion of the latter), both with strong autobiographical components, were rapidly written, and meant basically for the entertainment of friends. The author never thought that they could be of interest to anyone abroad. Paradoxically, they have become more successful abroad than any of Havel's other works written since 1968. Starting with the Vienna Burgtheater in 1976, they have had a considerable career on stage, radio, and television, from London to Israel to the Canadian Broadcasting Corporation. Havel felt a little embarrassed when foreign critics talked about his having found himself again, and called the plays examples of contemporary 'model-drama.' However, the success of the plays re-emphasized to him what he had known since he started writing: that he must 'write for someone,' for a definite spectator, and this conviction may well decide the basic direction of his work in the future.

Vernissage is a play about a couple who have invited an old friend to see their new apartment. When the curtain rises, the visitor, Bedřich, is standing at the door with a bouquet of flowers behind his back while the host and hostess, Michal and Věra, are ushering him in and offering him a drink. When the curtain goes down, an hour or so later, Bedřich, who has been trying to leave for some time, has been made to sit down again, a new record has been put on, another whisky is about to be poured and the whole thing can begin all over again. By now the circular structure has become Havel's artistic trademark. As in the companion piece to *Vernissage*,

Audience, the end of the play is at the same time a new beginning, the action is reduced to a link in a chain, and the merry-go-round character of the situation is brought relentlessly home to us.

Our yearning for some kind of crisis, some intimation of catharsis, has probably grown in intensity during the action, but we are denied any such resolution. We leave the theatre with the feeling that what we have seen happening goes on ad infinitum. We escape while Bedřich, the poor guest, must stay on. Or need we not be sorry for him? After all, he is treated royally to music, exotic dishes, and the best whisky; he is confided in, and shown that he is important; he is given good advice on how better to manage his affairs, how to help his wife come out of her depression, and so on.

They are his friends, after all, and mean so very well! They show him all their wonderful new furniture, their objet d'art (which Michal brought from abroad), they tell him about their lovely little son who teaches them to live more profoundly; they reveal to him that Michal is an ideal father and Vera is not only an imaginative gourmet cook but also – if he cared he could watch later on – an incredibly passionate and resourceful lover; they demonstrate their new almond peeler (also from Switzerland, naturally) and venture the opinion – gently and benevolently, of course – that Bedřich had simply somehow opted out: that he had passively resigned, because 'you are disgusted by having to strive, to struggle, to cope with difficulties.'[57] He should, they both feel, finally come to terms with himself, settle things at home with his wife, start a family, fix up his apartment, economize his time, start going to the sauna, live a bit more decently, healthily, rationally, and so on.

Throughout the conversation Bedřich repeatedly tries to make the point that he likes his wife's cooking and that they actually like each other, that he does not quite see the reason for having a confessional as an objet d'art in one's living-room, that he basically lacks the feeling that he is living a rotten life. But he hardly gets a word in edgewise. When, however, he tries to leave, he is called 'a disgusting, unfeeling, inhuman egoist! An ungrateful character! An ignoramus! A traitor!' When Věra throws Bedřich's flowers on the floor and bursts into hysterical tears, her husband turns to the guest with gentle reproach: 'See what you've done? Aren't you ashamed of yourself?' Bedřich hesitantly puts the bouquet back into the vase and sits down again. Immediately the two hosts are entirely normal, smile and suggest they might play a little music for dear Bedřich. As Michal eagerly puts on the record player, loud music fills the theatre from all outlets; perhaps some international 'hit' song, the author suggests, like Karel

Gott's 'Sugar Baby Love.' The music continues full volume 'until the last member of the audience has left the theatre.'[58]

Havel has revealed to us this realization: the closer his writing reflects a situation he knows personally, the better he writes and the broader his appeal will be. *Vernissage* is a parable on the hollowness of a successful life. All the clichés of 'Happiness' which have moulded the imagination of the average man from Prague to New York, from Sydney to Stockholm, are juggled throughout the play, and produce a terrible, hollow sound. It is a happiness which depends on an audience, for it is meaningless in itself; with an audience it loses its reason for being. It is remarkable that this play emerged from a 'Socialist' society and was written by an author who felt he 'had to lean on what [he] knew.' As a comment on contemporary Czechoslovakia it is certainly a fascinating document about a society, the official, constantly reiterated ideals, aims, and evaluations of which bear no relation whatsoever to the values of an individual who thrives under this regime. However, from a Western point of view *Vernissage* can plainly also be regarded as a critical comment on the materialistic values of an affluent society. Although Havel, with typical modesty, calls his two one-act plays 'miniatures, written on the side,' [59] both succeed in communicating strong meaning on an international scale.

Havel's most recent one-act play, *Protest*, draws even more openly on the author's basic experience as a 'dissident' writer. Translated into pithy German by Gabriel Laub,[60] it is to have its première in Vienna in the near future. In *Protest* Havel takes the bull by the horns and writes about the most acute problem not only of Czech writers and intellectuals but also of creative men anywhere in the world where freedom of expression has been harnessed by a stultifying ideology. *Protest* is a brilliant dialogue during an encounter between two writers. There is Staněk who has managed to swim with political currents, who is on good terms with the authorities, and whose works are still produced on television and in film studios. He knows the ropes, he writes what the regime approves of. Although he admires the dissidents, claims to be glad that there are still 'some people who are not afraid to speak the truth aloud,'[61] and avidly reads their works which circulate underground, he has steered clear of any involvement with their cause.

The other writer, Vaněk (a partly autobiographical figure who also appears in *Audience*), is a playwright whose works used to be staged successfully in Czech theatres but who, after a drastic change in the political climate, has become ostracized and persecuted by the regime, writing for underground circulation only, and spending most of his time and energy in composing petitions and letters of protest which find their way into the press abroad but which have little effect on circumstances in his own country.

The play consists of a visit Vaněk pays to Staněk, whose success with things in general is reflected in the superbly blossoming magnolia tree outside his window, his recently acquired villa, and the surrealist painting in his elegant study. In the course of the conversation between the two – Vaněk shy, clutching a briefcase, in stocking feet; Staněk effusive, pouring cognacs, offering cigars and his own slippers – we discover that after years of non-communication Staněk had asked Vaněk to visit him; we hear that Vaněk has been in prison and that Staněk's success is marred by his realization that 'everywhere is only selfishness, hypocrisy, fear ... sterility and intrigues.' We witness Staněk's admiration for Vaněk's courage, for those 'protests, petitions, letters – the fight for human rights,' but also his feelings that the dissidents have taken upon themselves 'an almost superhuman task: to rescue from this bog the remainders of ethical consciousness.' Vaněk shuffles his feet in his host's slippers and objects against so strong a praise. But Staněk continues his attentions, pours more cognac, comments knowledgeably but in a rather off-hand manner on other dissident writers, and offers knowledgeable and by no means unfair criticism of Vaněk's last play. Finally, as his motivations become increasingly puzzling, he steers the conversation to its inevitable aim: he would like to ask Vaněk to initiate 'some kind of protest or petition'[62] on behalf of composer-singer Javůrek who has recently been imprisoned.

However, as Vaněk (and the audience) are trying to cope with this extraordinary request, it becomes clear that Staněk's motivation is not indignation about the persecution of innocent people but that he has a personal axe to grind – his daughter is expecting a child by Javůrek. For once Vaněk responds with assurance and efficiency. Rummaging in his brief-case he produces a petition of the kind Staněk had had in mind. Staněk scans it with surprise and agitation, cannot abstain from making some editorial comments but finally congratulates Vaněk on his excellent style and on the fifty signatures which had already been collected.

However when Vaněk, encouraged by so much praise and concern, ventures the hesitant question whether he, Staněk, would not like to add his signature to the petition, the benevolent host embarks slowly but with increasing rhetorical power on an argument which proves, with irresistible logic, that he would do great harm to the cause of the dissidents if he did sign the document and that, due to his solidarity with those who tried to preserve the moral fibre of the nation, he would have to abstain from what he basically would like to do. Before Vaněk can assure him for the third time that he respects his decision, the news arrives that Javůrek has been freed. Generously Staněk offers Vaněk his own furnace to burn the superfluous petition in, and takes him to the garden to give him a shoot of his lovely magnolia tree.

In addition to its weighty political meaning *Protest* is an incontestable proof of Havel having grasped a basic ailment of our age. Psychology, ideology, and scientific objectivity have taught modern man to rationalize his moves. His knowledge of set patterns of behavior make him act consciously in relation to such patterns. This can be inocuous or sinister. It can spell mediocrity or evil. In his three one-act plays Václav Havel expresses what he is striving to portray, namely 'the existential dimension of the world.'[63]

In a way all Havel's writings are a critique of the reassuring first line of the Gospel according to St John: 'In the beginning was the Word.' That does not mean that he has created characters who indulge in the language of silence (like some of the characters of Beckett or Peter Handke). On the contrary, language is 'the primary moving force'[64] in Havel's plays and his characters talk a lot, too much in fact. But the more they talk, the less they say. Their conversations read like parodies of elementary phrase-books with sections like 'How to converse about world affairs with a sixty-word vocabulary'; or 'how to chat about the difference between the humanities and the sciences at a cocktail party.' It would take a volume in itself to define and order the great and resourceful variety of stock phrases in Havel's plays. All we can do here is suggest a few and point out the thing they have in common: they consist of words which no longer express reality but obscure it. Isolated from the real world, they create a solipsistic universe of abstractions which obliterates both rational thought and common sense.

In this sense Havel's language is at the end of a long line of development. It seems that the crisis in language that began at the beginning of the century has left its mark more strongly on the theatre than on other literary genres. The playwright – because he is dealing with the spoken word – seems to reflect most acutely the new awareness that man does not use language as his personal tool but rather that language, with its inherent structures and meaning, rules man. We may think of the conversation between two characters of the Austrian playwright Ödön von Horvath. In a simplistic two-pronged aphorism they summarize what they feel the twentieth century has done to human nature: 'Nobody is allowed to do what he wants,' complains one of them; the other complements: 'And nobody wants to do what he is allowed to.'[65] Or we may remind ourselves of the scene in which a Ionesco character reduces all communication to the word 'cat';[66] or perhaps of the two Pinter characters whose critical assessment of another man has shrivelled to whether he is 'funny' or 'not funny.'[67] However, we have not witnessed there a sustained display of the corruption of intellect and emotion by language. For that we have to go to Havel. Whether you choose to quote hollow statements like 'I myself – sort of personally – fancy art. I think of it as the spice of life'; soap-bubble morality like 'He has his faults, you know, but does his share'; vacuous encouragement such as 'You must not lose your hope, your love of life and your trust in other people!'[68]

One area of Havel's critique of language that provides ample comedy is his treatment of the unnatural quality of bureaucratic language mechanically tied to bureaucratic procedures. Take the conversation between the director and Hugo Pludek in which they plan well-balanced training sessions for inauguration and liquidation and arrive at the conclusion that 'Another training will have to be organized. Inaugurationally-trained liquidation officers training liquidationally-trained inaugurators and liquidationally-trained inaugurators training inaugurationally-trained liquidation officers.'[69]

But there are also some jewels of pseudo-humanist jargon: 'We are concerned with the man in the round,' says one character, 'a man whose complexity has not been simplified, whose human uniqueness has been preserved.'[70] Ironically, these words are spoken by the member of a research team computing samples of human individuality. Or listen to the sales talk of Madam Diana in Macheath's favourite brothel when she comments on the personalized service in her establishment: 'I am of the opinion that services of this kind must not be provided as on an assembly line, and I abhor those large anonymous gatherings which mechanize and dehumanize the whole thing, and debase it to the level of the consumers' attitude.'[71] This statement is mechanically repeated twice verbatim to two different customers. The fact that the remarks are totally false as such (the girls sell only what there is to be sold and consider any show of tenderness a vulgar breach of business ethics), is amusing but less interesting than its wider implication.

Our primitive ancestors believed that once a force was named, its power-spell was broken. Contemporary man, by constantly repeating the great cliché nightmares of his age, somehow believes he is dealing with them. Modern psychology has frequently used this ancient insight: formulating your fears and doubts will help you to overcome them. Havel shows us again and again that this act of the recognition of a problem can be useless if it takes place in language only. He modifies the psychology-textbook theory as well as the archaic beliefs behind them, 'if you name it you put yourself under the illusion of having mastered it,' and you can then afford to dismiss it. But under the protective shelter of your words the power of the illusion continues. The words can prevent rather than further the act of recognition.

In this instance the meaning of Havel's works for our Western society becomes particularly obvious. Although certain forms of standardization and mechanical conformism have for some time been the targets of attacks by some of those believing in 'individualism,' another form of standardization has developed among them. The 'non conformists' have formed another standardized group, whose reactions and type of language (not to mention clothes or haircuts) have become as predictable as those of the 'conformists.' Havel's comment on this kind of phenomenon has not been matched by a Western playwright.

Another target of Havel's is folksy wisdom mechanized by habitual thoughtless usage. In *The Garden Party* the hero's father, Pludek senior, reacts to most things with comments that have the ring of proverbs but are sheer nonsense. The form is empty, the content has gone: leather-bound volumes of Shakespeare and Milton contain whisky bottles, the opening line of an ancient song is used to sell shaving lotion. When old Pludek quotes proverbs, only the grammar is right: 'Well, have you ever seen a Hussar of Cologne carry hemp seed to the attic alone?'[72] We hear the proverbial rhythm, note the implied comparison to an actual situation, the built-in warning and good example – all is there, only the sense is lacking.

One of the best examples of Havel's linguistic inventiveness is of course the actual creation of an artificial language, Ptydepe, which is the thematic core of *The Memorandum*. A rich variety of comic effects is obtained from the actual use of this language on stage. There are, for example, the Ptydepe lessons – a MUST for all employees of the establishment – conducted by Ptydepe teacher Lear:[73]

LEAR And now I shall name, just for the sake of preliminary orientation, some of
the most common Ptydepe interjections. Well then, our 'ah!' becomes
'zukybaj', our 'ouch!' becomes 'bykur', our 'oh!' becomes 'hayf dy doretop',
English 'pish!' becomes 'bolypak juz', the interjection of surprise 'well!' becomes 'zyk', however our 'well, well!' is not 'zykzyk', as some students errone-
ously say, but 'zykzym' – ...

Later we get the following exchange of dialogue:

LEAR *correcting pronunciation* Listen carefully: m-a-l-u-z-
THUMB *eager student* M-a-l-u-z-
LEAR Your pronunciation isn't too good. How do you say well?
THUMB Zyk.
LEAR And well, well?
THUMB Zykzyk.
LEAR Zykzym!!
THUMB I'm sorry, I forgot.
LEAR Mr. Thumb! Mr. Thumb! Yippee!
THUMB We haven't learned yippee yet, sir.
LEAR Don't try to excuse yourself. You simply don't know it. Hurrah!
THUMB Frnygko jefr dabux altep dy savarub gop texeres.
LEAR Goz texeres!!
THUMB I mean, goz texeres.[74]

Another instance is the shouted behind-the-scenes conversation between the hero Gross (sadly ignorant of Ptydepe) and another official (well versed in Ptydepe):

GROSS Well, why didn't you answer me?
GEORGE *off stage* I wanted to test you out.
GROSS I beg your pardon! Do you realize who I am? The Managing Director!
GEORGE *off stage* Habuk bulugan, avrator.
GROSS What did you mean by that?
GEORGE *off stage* Nutuput.
GROSS *looks at his watch, then walks quickly to back door, turns at the door* I won't put up with any abuse from you! I expect you to come to me and apologize. *exit by back door*
GEORGE *off stage* Gotroch![75]

The patterns of repetition in Havel's plays seem at first arbitrary, even chaotic, but on closer inspection one discovers highly structured, almost geometric forms. Scenes are re-enacted with reversed characters; identical situations have opposite meanings because the context is different. Like a hall of mirrors Havel's work reflects itself. For example, Huml's request, made in quick succession to his wife, then to his mistress, that they straighten things out between them, is countered indignantly by both women in virtually the same words: 'For heaven's sake, what would that look like! Nonsense! You have a word with her today and that's that!'[76]

What must not go unmentioned is Havel's sustained ability to create a grotesque counterpoint between the characters' linguistic abstractions and their preoccupation with physical needs. Take the following example from *The Memorandum*. Trying to get some information regarding Ptydepe, Gross tries to approach a group of officials:

GROSS Miss Helena –

HELENA Why don't you call me Nellie, love? What is it?

GROSS Miss Nellie, do you issue the documents one needs to get a translation authorized?

STROLL Goose, vodka, and a cigar, that's what I call living.

SAVANT What a cigar!

GROSS I said, do you issue the documents one needs to get a translation authorized?

HELENA *calling towards side door* Where do you get water?

MARIA *off stage* I'll get it. *runs in by side door, iron in hand, grabs kettle, and runs out back door*

HELENA *to Gross* What?

GROSS Do you issue the documents one needs to get a translation authorized?

HELENA Yes. To anybody who hasn't recently received a memo written in Ptydepe.

GROSS Why?

SAVANT Downright heady!

STROLL I should say!

GROSS I said, why?

HELENA *calling towards side door* Where do you keep the cups?

MARIA *off stage* Coming![77]

In *The Increased Difficulty of Concentration* this theme has a subtle new implication. The central character Huml, caught in the complex mechanics of his relationships with women, uses the necessity of attending to his body's biological needs as a sort of haven from the increasing pressures of his life. Observe his conversation with his mistress, Renata, who is getting impatient with the situation and wants him to get a divorce:

RENATA If it's not worth your while to break it off on my account, you ought to do it for your own sake – just look at yourself! Can't you see the way you're slipping?

HUML I told you, didn't I, I want to do it in stages. What about some lunch?

RENATA I know your blessed stages, so far you haven't budged!

HUML What do you mean? Only this morning I began to prepare the ground.
RENATA Did you? How? Did you tell her you love me?
HUML For a start, I said I find you sexually exciting.
RENATA Well, that's at least something. What did she say?
HUML She insisted I should part with you. What about some lunch?
RENATA I hope you didn't promise her any such thing!
HUML She was so insistent, I had to agree – on the surface. But deep down I kept
    my own counsel and I didn't commit myself to anything definite.
RENATA Really? And then? Did you suggest to her you want a divorce?
HUML I said you were rather counting on it – prospectively. What about some
    lunch? There's some stew –
RENATA I'll have a look –[78]

In the same play Havel explores the most disturbing aspect of the
destruction of man by language. When Renata wants to know whether he is
still in love with his wife, we hear the voice of Huml (who is busy hanging up
her coat back-stage) 'You know very well I stopped loving her long ago! I
just like her as a friend, a housewife, a companion of my life –.'[79] In this
brief scene Havel shows us how the cliché can be used to prove or disprove
anything. A clichéd image of 'love' has taken over the form of the word like
a parasite and pushed out its real content. Here this process of forcing out
the true meaning of a word is demonstrated before our very eyes. The word
we are left with becomes an empty shell.

Toward the end of most of Havel's plays the protagonist gives a lengthy
speech in which he summarizes his outlook on man, society, and life in
general. The speeches are highly amusing conglomerations of logical fallacies, pseudo-dialectics, and false analogies. With his acute sense for the
mechanizing power of the word, Havel explores man as the victim of the
language he has created. He does so by exploring the area where the system
and the individual meet, where standardization penetrates into every fold
of life. It has been pointed out repeatedly that this is obviously the work of a
man who has grasped the enormous effect of a centralized political system
on the life of the average man.

But it would do injustice to Havel's dramatic genius if his work were to
be interpreted merely from a political point of view. The playwright himself
has told us that 'the theatre shows the truth about politics not because it has
a political aim. The theatre can depict politics precisely because it has no
political aim. For this reason it seems to me that all ideas of the so-called
"political theatre" are mistaken...'[80] By trying to give expression to the

tensions between the individual and the social system in his own society – and there is no question as to who remains the victor there – Havel has also made one of the most intelligent artistic comments on man in modern mass society in general – applicable in New York as well as Prague, Stockholm, Rome, or Warsaw.

He does this by taking to task the nature of language itself, particularly the catch-phrase or slogan whose power, well known to dictators of all kinds, is mostly misjudged by well-meaning defenders of the humanistic values of a free society. It is here that Havel's main contribution to the Theatre of the Absurd is to be found. For example, take the incident in *The Garden Party* where Hugo Pludek reproaches his father for a simplistic question: 'You think a question can be put in such a simplified way? No matter how you answer this kind of question – you can never attain the whole truth, always only a limited part of it.'[81] So far so good. Hugo's words can hardly be disputed, and his subsequent statement about human nature is still equally acceptable. Who could deny that man is 'rich, complex, changeable and multi-form'? It is only with the next words that Hugo's reasoning begins to crack up under the absurdity of his language. While we still find ourselves nodding in agreement, the argument becomes the very opposite of rational. 'There's no word, no sentence, no book, nothing that could fully describe and contain him [man]' says Hugo.[82] On the surface the statement seems true. No book can describe man in his entirety, no sentence, no word…, and here we hesitate. This is obviously a nasty cul-de-sac. How did the playwright ever get us there?

Havel has forced us into literal logic. Beginning with a sort of Kantian proposition that man cannot perceive or express truth in its entirety, he then reverses the argument by reducing the possibilities of expression to *one* word. He therefore implies that, under certain circumstances, one word *could* express a complex phenomenon. In other words, Hugo claims that one single word can wield great intellectual weight – which is, of course, a fallacy, but is also an astute observation of the power of slogans which carry a built-in, incontrovertible evaluation. This is explosive material in quite different types of modern society where slogans – whether they be 'enemies of the people' or 'women's liberation' – with their absolute evaluations are part and parcel of the daily life of the average citizen.

Also the next page of Hugh Pludek's speech bears quoting: 'And today we've passed the time of static and unchangeable categories, when A was only A and B always only B; today we know very well that A can often be simultaneously B and B simultaneously A … that under certain circumstances even F could become Q, Y, indeed even Q with a nasal! … The truth is as complex and multiform as everything else in the world – the magnet, the telephone, Branislav's verse, the magnet – and we are all a bit what we were yesterday and a bit what we are today; ... as a matter of fact we all are constantly a bit and constantly we are a bit not ... so that no-one among us completely exists and at the same time no-one exists completely ... '[83]

A political scientist in the audience might interpret this as a parody of Engels' theory of constant change; a humanist might consider it an example of a pretentious, half-baked display of scientism; while others may merely enjoy it as a brilliant show of lopsided logic. Havel's 'dialogue' with any audience occurs on many levels.

Josef Gross, the hero of *The Memorandum*, delivers his tirade on man for the benefit of the loyal secretary Marie, who, by trying to help him keep his position, lost her own. By now Havel's linguistic weapons are sharper and cut more deeply. Again Gross begins with an indisputable truism: 'Dear Maria! We're living in a strange, complex epoch. As Hamlet says, our "time is out of joint". Just think, we're reaching for the moon and yet it's increasingly hard for us to reach our selves; we're able to split the atom, but unable to prevent the splitting of our personality; we build superb communications between the continents, and yet communication between Man and Man is increasingly difficult ... Like Sisyphus, we roll the boulder of our life up the hill of its illusory meaning, only for it to roll down again into the valley of its own absurdity. Never before has Man lived projected so near to the very brink of the insoluble conflict between the subjective will of his moral self and the objective possibility of its ethical realization. Manipulated, automatized, made into a fetish, Man loses the experience of his own totality; horrified, he stares as a stranger at himself, unable not to be what he is not, nor to be what he is.'[84]

This is surely an irresistible string of arguments. Havel uses dialectics like a bouncing see-saw, and hurls images and banalities with the finality of a visionary. Marie has, understandably, no answer to all this, and her whispered comment: 'Nobody ever talked to me so nicely before,'[85] is the final stroke of deadly irony before the curtain falls. Again Havel starts safely with a comment we might hear any day on the street. Then he brings in the well-known quotation from *Hamlet* which legitimizes his whole speech by supposedly anchoring it in our cultural heritage. The three contrasts which follow might be a lesson to any public speaker. Their obviously fallacious aspects (the use of verbs in a literal sense in an image that does not bear literal interpretation) somehow strengthen the argument because the speaker seems to have used them quite frankly as rhetorical devices. This impression is, of course, dispersed as soon as the Sisyphus image is brought in. From now on the argument races uncontrollably to its disastrous conclusion – the nonsensical equation that cancels itself.

Here Havel has take up the dominant themes that have caught the critical imagination of our age: the march of science as opposed to the 'static' values of the humanist; the crisis of man's identity; the inability to communicate – all providing fertile soil for catch-words and slogans to sprout and proliferate. Finally Havel conjures up the figure of Sisyphus, the patron saint of absurdist writing, and creates an existentialist hodgepodge of images that makes our heads spin – but not enough not to realize that the parody constantly moves precariously close to reality. And here comes Havel's prime move. For a brief moment he uses Gross, the main example of manipulated and automated man, as the play's raisonneur, by letting him comment critically and lucidly on the predicament of modern man. For one flash the 'absurd' world of the play and the 'real' world of the audience have become one. The effect, if utilized by a perceptive director, is bound to be strong.

In *The Increased Difficulty of Concentration*, Dr Eduard Huml launches an impassioned attack on the automatic calculator that was to register his reactions and compute them into an orderly, predictable sample of individual behaviour. Not only does PUZUK, the hapless calculator, break down, but it also goes berserk over its task. Huml, who considers the whole project 'nothing but an unfortunate mistake,'[86] explains his attitude by taking on the whole question of scientific predictability versus philosophical speculation. And he makes no bones about being a humanist – a man who believes in feelings! For example, he remarks: 'your endeavour to isolate the element of coincidence and use it as a means of shaping human individuality bears no relationship to science whatsoever. Moreover, it is bound to miss its goal completely ... In other words, the personal, human, unique relationship which arises between two individuals is so far the only thing that can – at least to some extent – mutually unveil the secret of those two individuals. Such values as love, friendship, compassion, sympathy and the unique and irreplaceable mutual understanding – or even mutual conflict – are the only tools which this human approach has at its disposal ... Hence, the fundamental key to man does not lie in his brain, but in his heart.'[87]

Again, as in the other two speeches, the argument is circular and cancels itself: man's complexity, it turns out, can be dealt with after all; only the place that provides the key has been switched from one area to another – from head to heart. Abstraction and reality never meet. Phrases like 'the secret of man' and 'unrepeatable human understanding' have taken the place of 'the coherent pattern of received information' or a 'condensed model of human individuality.' Ptydepe has been replaced by Chorukor. We may be surprised, indeed disturbed, by the way in which this use of language reflects certain situations in the daily life of this society – be it in an insurance office, or at a 'teach-in.'

Macheath, the gallant big shot of the underworld, also likes to give speeches. In fact, he gives three of them in the course of Havel's *The Beggar's Opera*. The playwright has expanded the area of his critique of language with excellent results. In his first bout of rhetoric Macheath convinces Lucy, who is visiting him in prison, that he still loves her, despite his rampages with other women. He paints for her a glowing picture of an eighteenth-century lover's utopia from the viewpoint of an average citizen of a twentieth-century socialist state: 'You must believe me, Lucy! ... If you only knew how much I have been thinking of you! Every day I have been conjuring up in my mind a little country castle built of red brick ... surrounded by green meadows and beech groves – and I have imagined the way the two of us setting up house there, romping around in the meadows with our greyhounds, riding on horseback, hunting exotic game, bathing in the nearby brook, gathering mushrooms, cooking ancient Old-English dishes, arranging soirées for the neighbouring rural aristocracy, growing sunflowers – and I have imagined afterwards, in the evening, sitting by the big Renaissance fireplace, gazing into the flames, telling each other about our childhood, reading together old books from the castle library, sipping mead – and then – slightly intoxicated – retiring to the castle bedroom – ... drowsily taking off our clothes, and lying down together in our big canopied gothic bed and then first of all kissing each other tenderly for an awfully long time, and then loving each other and loving each other – our hot, sun-tanned bodies intertwined in spasms of frustrated love – and then finally, ecstatically happy and sweetly exhausted – we fall asleep – to be awakened the next morning by the sparkling summer sun, by birdsong, and by the butler, bringing in bacon and eggs and cocoa.'[88]

The playwright has managed to summon all the clichés of latter-day romanticism, mixing confused scraps of history and former cultures with the banal desires of a chambermaid, and concocting an irresistible pot-pourri of 'dreams come true.' Again it is language which has moulded fixed images, used in order to conjure up false pictures of happiness. The talker achieves his purpose and the stale models work on Lucy, who bursts into tears and promises to find a hacksaw and get her Mackie out of prison.

Macheath's second speech, also addressed to the female sex, is another feat of rhetoric like Marc Antony's speech to the Romans. It begins with a vocative, after which it launches into a series of protestations of love and devotion. The only unusual thing is that the speech is addressed to two women instead of one. Polly Peachum and Lucy Locket, both of whom have a claim on his love, have come to the prison cell to get things straightened out. The scene is famous in Gay's as well as Brecht's version. In both cases it is the women who carry on the battle of rhetoric and deride the 'perfidious wretch'[89] for having deceived them. In Havel's version the silken tongue of the man with the gift for language settles the matter again, reducing the girls to tears and the realization that they have 'done him wrong.' Macheath's successful speech consists simply of expounding the situation as it is and making the best of it: 'What, tell me, have I really done wrong? Was it my fault that I married you both?[90] What should I have done when I was in love with you both? Naturally what is more acceptable for society nowadays and more comfortable for a man, hence more usual, is another procedure, namely that a man takes as his wife only one of the beloved women and – making acceptable excuses to his legitimate wife – he reduces the other one to the debasing position of a so-called mistress, that is, a sort of superior courtesan, whose duties are almost identical with those of his wife, but whose rights, in comparison with the wife, are decidedly severely limited ... The situation of the wife is, however, no more advantageous: the mistress knows about the wife and often, one might conjecture, discusses her at length with her lover, the latter's husband, while the wife, on the other hand, must remain submerged in the swamp of ignorance which naturally alienates her from her husband ... Are you aware how ruthless such a solution would be to both women? And you mean that I should have proceeded in this way? No, girls, if I wanted to fulfill my duties toward you to the best of my ability I could not follow the actions of other men in this matter, and I had to strike out on my own, take a path perhaps not yet walked upon, but definitely more moral, namely the way, which gives you both the same amount of legitimacy and dignity. Such is the truth: Please judge me on its basis! ...'[91]

When Macheath finishes his speech to his two wives with a final flourish about the happy moments that the three of them will *not* be able to experience (after all, he is going to be executed in the morning), the two women fly to his chest and weep with gratitude for having been spared the ignominy of being either the deceived wife or the downtrodden mistress. Macheath has not only been forgiven but has also convinced them that he acted logically as well as morally and, above all, honourably. By basing his whole speech on rigidly clichéd concepts, Macheath develops a seemingly logical argument which no-one notices to be based on a false premise. With the help of two words he establishes two isolated areas of values which, though based exclusively on a theadbare and banal stock image, carry great weight with minds that do not respond rationally but emotionally. With a humorous insight that seems to me unmatched in contemporary theatre, Havel explores the theme of 'man at the mercy of language'[92] – a problem that has gained increasing importance in our century.

Macheath's third speech, delivered at the end of the play, is no longer a parody. It seems that here the playwright has ceased to use language as a false front. Macheath, caught in the mesh of pretense, no longer able to distinguish a lie from the truth, betrayed three times by the woman whom he had thought an exception to the general corruption, draws his conclusion: 'If everyone around me betrays me, as has become obvious, it does not mean that they expect anything else from me, but the exact opposite: by acting in this way they offer me some sort of principle of our mutual relationship.'[93] Accordingly he decides to play along on the principle, 'when in Rome, do as the Romans do,' or 'if you can't beat them, join them.'

Macheath's speech, supported by a number of significant arguments, strikes a puzzling new note in Havel's work. Is Macheath, the professional betrayer of women, the boss of a shady organization, the ruthless businessman, to be taken seriously as Havel's raisonneur? Like Gay and Brecht before him, Havel has engaged all our sympathies for the gallant crook who, by means of his wit, generosity, and ability to deal with life in a grand manner, had distinguished himself from the petty schemers around him. Does his parodistic 'existentialist decision' mean that he will join the ranks of those petty schemers? Is Havel serious about the uselessness of heroism or is he merely presenting us with another logical fallacy under the mask of a seemingly rational argument – namely that corruption can be fought by adding more corruption? Waters run deep at the end of Havel's most boisterous work.

Havel's most recent play *Protest* takes his exploration of language as a vehicle for a certain mode of thought still another significant step further. In a long speech, Staněk, faced with the request to sign a petition on human rights, explains to Vaněk (who has handed him the petition) that, if he wants to act 'truly ethically,'[94] he must abstain from signing the document. The arguments which lead to this conclusion seem to me to contain the most brilliant tour de force of logic which Havel has written to this point. In fact they are so irresistible in their lucidity that it remains to be seen whether the play will not make its impact as a plea to consider the dilemma of those who have decided to live with the regime, to think of their families, and avoid unnecessary destructive struggles against forces much too powerful to be affected.

In *The Memorandum* Gross's argument had gone up in a cloud of contradictions; Huml, in *The Increased Difficulty of Concentration* had indulged in a circular argument which cancelled itself in the end; Macheath of *The Beggar's Opera* moved precariously closer to reality by raising the question of the uselessness, in fact the pig-headed arrogance, of heroism in a world where betrayal had become the common form of behaviour. Staněk in *Protest*, assessing the consequences of certain political moves in a totalitarian country which tries to cope with a small number of people who try to show that they do not agree with the regime, does so with the foresight of a brilliant chess player. 'Let me tell you something, Ferdinand,' he explains to Vaněk, 'without noticing myself I have become used to the perverse thought that the dissidents are taking care of morality. But they themselves – without becoming conscious of it – also got used to that idea! ... What if I, too, were yearning finally to become a free human being? What if I, too, wanted to renew my integrity and throw off this burden of humiliation?' And he continues, revealing that 'after years of uninterrupted vomiting I would – if I were to sign your paper – win back my lost freedom and dignity, perhaps even the recognition of those who are close to me ... I would be able to look without shame into my daughter's eyes ... My son would not be able to go to college but he would respect me more than if I had assured his acceptance by refusing to sign the petition for Javůrek whom he worships ... This is the subjective side of the whole matter. And how does it look from an objective point of view?'[95]

It is clear that Staněk's description of the situation is realistic. Indeed his argument does not seem 'subjective' at all. If the allegedly 'subjective' point of view was so loyal to the truth, the 'objective' point of view would have to be more than perfect. In our age we gladly allow for distortion in what we have come to call 'subjectivity,' but at the promise of 'objectivity' our eyes brighten with immediate credulity. The popular credo for our times could easily be: If it is objective it must be good. Havel has prepared us well for what is to come.

'What happens,' Staněk says, launching into his 'objective' argument, 'when among the signatures of a few widely known young dissidents ... there appears ... also my signature? The closed circle of notorious signers (whose signatures are gradually losing their importance because they do not have to be paid for by anything, since those people have nothing more to lose) will be broken ... The political powers will want to demonstrate that they are not likely to panic and cannot be unbalanced by such surprises.'[96]

What is left to discuss is the question of what influence Staněk's signature would have on the vast circles of those who are trying to conform, who don't ask many questions as long as they can afford a holiday, or in some cases a car, or perhaps a weekend cottage. Here again Staněk makes his deductions with relentless logic: those conformists basically dislike the dissidents because they see in them their own bad conscience and as a consequence they would be bound to regard him, Staněk, as a victim of the dissidents' cynical appeal to his humanism. The police, of course – no need to conceal that fact – would support and try to spread this attitude. Moreover, 'the more intelligent people will perhaps observe that this sensational news – my signature – detracts from the issue itself, i.e. the matter of Javůrek, and in the final analysis makes the whole protest appear in rather sinister a light by raising the question of whether you really wanted to help Javůrek or show off me as a freshly baked dissident.'[97]

There might even be people who would claim that Javůrek had become the dissidents' victim because the latter used his misfortune for purposes which had nothing to do with his fate. Now Staněk is ready for the final moral sum-up: 'Considering all these circumstances, the question must be asked: What is more important – the liberating feeling which my signature would give me, paid for by its basically negative consequences? ... In other words: If I want to act truly ethically – and I feel sure you will not doubt now that I do – what shall I go by? By relentless objective reflection or by my own subjective inner feeling?'[98]

I could easily envisage a critic who would interpret this string of oddly indisputable arguments as an attempt on Havel's part to reveal a moral dilemma where it is rarely looked for: not in the dissidents' glowing beliefs but in those grey hangers-on of the regime who compromise and keep silent, who – as Havel's Macheath, pushed by circumstances, finally did – would play the game that everyone played. In a way the imaginary critic would be right. The moral Struggle in *Protest* surely does not take place in Vaněk's mind. But – and here we see Havel's finest display of a writer's profound grasp of the world he lives in – it does not really take place in Staněk's mind either.

Staněk's weighing of pros and cons corresponds to reality but only to a reality within the patterns of thought which permeate a society which has been forced to think in these patterns. Staněk has applied the reasoning process of a closed system of thought to a simple ethical question: Should I lend my voice to try to help an innocent man who is in trouble? The whole intricate net of reasoning which he unfurls before our eyes is the type of reasoning he has been taught by the system he lives in. It is pseudo-reasoning, and totally false in absolute terms. It is, in a nut-shell, perhaps the best portrayal of perverted 'rational' thinking that has ever been put on stage in modern theatre. As such, Staněk's arguments are also more important than might appear at first sight for a Western democratic society where moral norms are questioned and relativistic points of view have often become ethical guide-posts. A Polish cartoon sums up the issue in a humourous way: Two men are having a discussion. One has just finished his argument. The other scratches his head thoughtfully: 'Clearly you are right ... But ... from which point of view?'

There is no question that Havel's plays deal with the burning issues in his own society. However, they not only turn out to contain surprisingly apt comments on another society that wrestles with different kinds of problems, but they also reveal themselves in their timeless aspects – wisdom expressed in terms of excellent theatre. Havel himself seems to know how these things work: 'Drama's success in transcending the limits of its age and country depends entirely on how far it succeeds in finding a way to its own place and time ... If Shakespeare is played all over the world in the twentieth century it is not because in the seventeenth century he wrote plays for the twentieth century and for the whole world but because he wrote plays for seventeenth-century England as best he could.'[99] Without wanting to compare Havel with Shakespeare we can nevertheless see that the principle is the same. Havel writes for Czechoslovakia as best he can, *therefore* (as he would say) his work carries so strong a message outside its borders.

In his by now famous *Open Letter* to the General Secretary of the Communist Party of Czechoslovakia written on 4 April, 1975, Havel makes a statement which describes the arid atmosphere he is trying to reveal in his plays, by pitching his artistic imagination against the stultifying order of rigid values and suppression of truth. 'True enough,' he writes, 'order prevails: a bureaucratic order of grey monotony that stifles all individuality; of mechanical precision that suppresses everything of unique quality; of musty inertia that excludes the transcendental. What prevails is order without life.'[100] In one play after another Havel reveals the life-destroying nature of rigid forms of 'order.' The spectrum is vast and the consequences differ greatly in significance; they can affect, say, a university curriculum, the categories of behavioral psychology, or the rules governing life under totalitarianism. We cannot escape the bitter realization that Havel in his letter not only describes the fictional atmosphere in his plays but also the real situation in his country. And yet another, brighter, thought is bound to emerge: abstracted from the situation in which they were written, his words formulate a diagnosis of mass society throughout the world.

3
Pavel Kohout

INTERVIEWER What is more important for your life, politics or the theatre?
KOHOUT Politics, because I defend the theatre with politics.
INTERVIEWER What do you need more for living, love or the theatre?
KOHOUT Love, because I write for the theatre out of love.

PAVEL KOHOUT in a fictitious interview

'Pavel Kohout was given to our theatre so that there would not be any peace and quiet.'[1] With these words a well-known Czech critic begins his essay on Kohout in the course of which he commiserates with an imaginary scholar whom he casts in the role of a critic writing a book on contemporary Czechoslovak theatre. Faced with this enfant terrible of the Czech stage, who has evoked more praise and more abuse than any other contemporary Czechoslovak writer, the hapless imaginary scholar would apparently feel himself 'sliding down a curving ramp' which would permit neither foothold nor sense of direction. Appreciative of this unsolicited a priori description of the problematic nature of the task at hand, I will merely try to suggest some areas of interest and value in Kohout's colourful body of work which developed within two decades from crude ideological lyrics about the social accomplishments of the Stalinist era (the author himself read or declaimed them at political youth group meetings during the early fifties) to the complex, sardonic comedies of the seventies.

To date Pavel Kohout is the author of two volumes of poetry, some nineteen plays and adaptations for the stage, ten filmscripts, and two prose works, in addition to numerous essays and commentaries – an impressive output for a man who has just turned fifty. The body of criticism which has built up around Kohout's work covers the whole spectrum from enthusiastic praise to barbed attacks.

Generally speaking, we might distinguish three critical camps whose claims, though all justified in one way or another, are completely contradictory. First, there is a body of well-disposed critics who, delighted by such colourful theatricality coming from Eastern Europe, write about Kohout's sharp sense for topicality and his ability to express what is in the air. This view, emanating mostly from outside Czechoslovakia, where Kohout has become one of the most colourful figures of resistance against a politically repressive regime, was in fact also shared by some Czech critics when they were still free to write dispassionately about Kohout as a literary figure, and found that he had the peculiar ability to put into words a mood that 'is already there but is still missing.'[2] Second, there is a group of critics – East and West – who see Kohout as merely wanting to please at any cost, having a nose for what will sell and writing just for the box office. And third, there are those Czech literary men who have seen Kohout change colour too many times. They witnessed his career as a young performer celebrating the new British ambassador to Czechoslovakia a year or so after the war; a few years later they watched him give readings of fervent Stalinist poetry to youth groups, and at the age of barely twenty-four, rise to the heights of theatrical success with his first play, *The Good Song*, as crude ideologically as it was dramatically. It should be mentioned that as late as 1960 he wrote plays according to the Soviet recipe of Socialist Realism, the last one being *The Third Sister*, hardly surpassed in meticulous adherence to this particularly anti-creative literary genre. No wonder that his acrobatics on the see-saw of political developments have been watched with some resentment.[3]

It must be left to future scholars to explore and analyse the exceedingly complex cultural and literary climate of those years between the end of the Second World War and the events of August 1968. Such work will doubtless throw new light on the equally complex figure of the man himself. In this context, however, it must suffice to say simply that, from the vantage point of a discussion of Czech theatre in the sixties and seventies, Kohout is an exciting writer. The very ease and nonchalance with which he manages to turn out one work after another – extremely varied in nature, each seeming to bear the imprint of a different type of creative genius – makes his work a cornucopia of surprises.

During the autumn of 1967 Kohout, already known to theatre-goers in Germany from recent productions of his Švejk play and *War with the Newts*, became the object of more general interest. The German weekly

Die Zeit published a number of open letters exchanged between Kohout and Günter Grass.[4] Sparked off by a momentous occasion (the publication of an article, allegedly a 'Manifesto of Czechoslovak Writers' published on 3 September 1967 in the *Sunday Times*), the topic of the letters quickly expanded to basic politico-philosophical questions. The occupation of Czechoslovakia by Soviet troops – which followed less than a year after the first letter was published, suddenly turned the correspondence into a fascinating document of one of the great political changes of those years.

Space does not allow for consideration of all of Kohout's plays, nor of his entertaining and provocative prose writings, some of which have appeared in German in large editions.[5] By discussing the most important of his plays and adaptations, this chapter is meant only to provide some insight into his dramatic work and the way in which he blends the social and human problems of his time with showy, sparkling theatricality.

Such a Love had its première at the Realistic Theatre in Prague in October 1957. It was an immediate success. In Czechoslovakia alone it became the most frequently performed play – 770 performances within four years of its appearance. For over two years it also held the same position in East Germany where it ran for 574 performances in thirty theatres. Further afield it was widely performed in the Soviet Union, throughout Eastern Europe, but also in the rest of Europe from Finland to Greece; even in Turkey, Israel, and South America.[6] This tremendous success is all the more surprising if we remind ourselves of the almost banal theme of the play: a two men/one woman situation that ends in the suicide of the girl.

The main reason for the impact of this well-worn story is that Kohout had told it in a special form. Not that this form was particularly new. Among others Brecht had used it, and Pirandello before him. But Kohout seems to have found a particularly happy way of building the play around a court room scene and gradually illuminating the motivations of the characters involved. 'You may smoke,' are the opening words spoken by an unnamed character identified only as 'The Man in a Legal Robe' who throughout the play acts as a sort of judge-confessor, conducts cross-examinations, and makes the characters re-enact scenes of the past. After having thus established his authority the Man in the Legal Robe pronounces the accusation: 'I herewith open the proceedings concerning the case of L. Matysová and Co. The public prosecution considers you all guilty of a number of antisocial actions which have resulted in various injuries but particularly in murder.'[7]

Then the judge begins to question the four main characters – Lída

Matysová herself, her rejected fiancé Stibor, her lover Petr and his wife. At the end of each examination the accused is asked whether he feels guilty. The answers vary from a definite 'yes' to a definite 'no.' Now the actual story begins to unfold, as the characters re-enact past events the way they happened. In the end Lída Matysová, caught between her fiancé's desperate pleading not to leave him, the knowledge that her lover preferred to return to his wife, and her own inner certainty that she could not live without his love, jumps out of a moving train. As the past events of this seemingly simple story are brought to light, definite concepts of 'guilt' and 'innocence' fade and it becomes less and less possible to use these absolute terms with regard to the characters' actions.

It is here perhaps that we find the essential reason for the great success of a work which, despite its virtues, is unquestionably no more exciting as drama than, say, James Saunders' *A Scent of Flowers* (1964), which deals with a related topic. For the first time since the hiatus of the Second World War an Eastern European writer had written a play about an insoluble problem. The basic questions raised by the play – who is guilty of the tragedy? who is to judge where the borderline between guilt and innocence lies? – were new and provocative in a society where an unquestionable system has been providing unshakeable truths.

With this acute sense for the 'hot topic' – a quality that has been called his glory as well as his downfall[8] – Kohout had written a play that responded to people's increasing need to give thought to those regions of life where relationships are multi-levelled, where the smooth road of predictable development turns out to be a delusion. The raisonneur in the play, the Man in the Legal Robe, reaches no verdict over those who have driven the girl to her death, not with evil intention, but by acting according to their weaknesses, petty vanities, fears, and jealousies. 'Do you know a law according to which you could be punished?' he asks. No one does. The pronouncement of the final verdict is shifted to the audience. Before slowly and thoughtfully leaving the stage, the Man in the Legal Robe points to each of the characters and then to the whole audience, asking them to judge – if they can!

One other point should be made. By staging Kohout's play, the Realistic Theatre in Prague had broken with realism of detail and stressed inherent theatrically – an area in which Czechoslovak theatre was to excel a few years later. The production used only the most indispensable stage props. With the help of sound effects and visual projections it created that true theatricality which is the very opposite of the earlier realism.[9]

Like Bertolt Brecht, Pavel Kohout has been chided for his willingness to use and adapt other writers' material. The fictitious interview we mentioned earlier also contains a forthright section on this potentially delicate topic. 'Don't you have the feeling that you are wearing someone else's laurels?' enquires the interviewer during a discussion of Kohout's adaptation of Jules Verne's *Around the World in Eighty Days*. 'Apart from a few of your own bits of humour, it was M. Verne who filled those two hours! You have taken over his story, his intrigue, his characters, even whole passages of his text, without showing the slightest sign of embarrassment! Isn't that a kind of rearranging rather than creative work?' Kohout's answer, typically crowded with images, shows none of the embarrassment his interviewer seems to expect. 'I admit, I have more fun with adaptations for the stage than with my own plays. Writing is like a game of solitaire; the author plays against himself. An adaptation, on the other hand, is like a duel. You must force the picture to leave its frame and become alive. You must breathe life even into a collection of newspaper clippings.'[10] Without digressing into the question of the precision and fairness of this opinion we can see that Kohout thinks the main task of the playwright-adapter is to add 'a third dimension' to a two-dimensional work of art.

The possibility of adapting *Around the World in Eighty Days* occurred to Kohout suddenly on a summer evening in 1961. During a discussion with a friend[11] on the subject of favourite books, it turned out that both had recently re-read Jules Verne's classic as a result of the Russian astronaut Yury Gagarin's first flight around the earth. Immediately the playwright began to plan how to stage a work that would require about a hundred actors, a sophisticated revolving stage, and at least one elephant. The solution was provided by a collage-illustration on the dust jacket. 'I imagined on stage old M. Verne who has just decided to write the book, and next to him a contemporary of mine who knows it by heart. While the former goes through the tremendous effort of inventing the action, the latter impatiently betrays the outcome of the action ... In this way both are given the opportunity at any moment of stepping out of the action and criticizing it, moving it ahead by a stage and then, like conductors, getting on board again.'[12] This technique solved the problem of the frequent change of scene.

The problem of the numerous roles to be filled was dealt with by having the same actors play different parts. Seven male actors handled all the secondary roles (including that of the madam of a bordello), with just enough time to change their costumes. This constant time pressure backstage, the playwright argues, had an additional beneficial effect on the vitality of the play: the audience, 'witnesses of a fictitious battle of Mr. Fogg against the stage-time of his journey around the world, are at the same time witnesses of the real race of the actors against the real time of the stage performance.'[13] Even the actors' bows were integrated into the sparkling theatricality of this dramatic tour de force. Stepping singly outside the closed curtain, the seven supporting actors took their bows, then changed costume backstage and took another bow in the next role. This continued until each of them had taken ten bows in ten different costumes, so that they took the applause for seventy different roles in one uninterrupted procession. The audience, the author tells us, roared with delight.

With great skill the playwright also managed to integrate a double time shift. There is Jules Verne himself, constantly criticizing his novel, yet playing its main part as the Englishman, Mr Phileas Fogg, who in his London club makes the famous bet to travel around the world in exactly eighty days. The other time shift, introducing a much more radically anachronistic element into the play, is created by the guest from the twentieth century, who reveals his true identity – during the 'journey' he has acted the role of Passe-partout – only in the last line of the play.

The well-known adventures whirl past the audience with breathtaking speed: an Indian widow is whisked from her husband's funeral pyre; a roaring typhoon sweeps over the scene; an attack by American Indians alternates with an encounter with Mormon missionaries. The time pressure increases and it seems that Mr Fogg will lose his bet. But the international dateline as modern deux ex machina provides an unexpected extra day and a happy ending.

An age in which a journey around the world not in eighty days but in eighty minutes has become an accepted matter puts on a show of its own greenhorn past. It regards it partly with knowing superiority but also displays the wistful awareness that 'progress' is short-lived and the great achievement of today is reduced to a fumbling attempt by tomorrow. 'Don't worry, M. Verne,' says the Young Man from the twentieth century during the final moments of the play: 'You have written about your time, you have sketched pictures of strong, active people. Your books will still be read when the journey around the earth will last no more than eighty minutes.' And when the older man expresses his uncertainty about things and admits that 'this evening I often had the impression that people were laughing about me,' the Young Man answers: 'That was no derision, that was the eternal smile of youth. And those who travel around the world in eighty minutes will in turn smile at that youth. And in this smile there will always be emotion and admiration.' Asked about his name, the Young Man shrugs: 'It wouldn't mean anything to you, M. Verne. Yury Neil Gagarin-Armstrong.'[14] Then the curtain falls.

For about ten years Pavel Kohout had been toying with the idea of adapting Karel Čapek's prophetic novel *Válka s mloky* (*War with the Newts*) for the stage. This complex piece of writing, which is considered Čapek's greatest work in the utopian mode, is a collage of a wide collection of material – fictitious newspaper articles, scholarly commentaries, memoirs, and numerous other documents.

The author pretends to be a historian who reconstructs the story of the Newts from documents. Once man has discovered the species of the Newts, living in the warm and shallow lagoons of Pacific islands, he begins to use them as slaves, teaches them to speak and work, and sells them, initially as cheap labour, and later on as soldiers. In the end the Newts, having gradually become aware of the powers they have been unwittingly given, unite and begin a terrible war in order to gain more living space. Čapek's author-historian does not foretell whether man will survive the battle with this monster which he bred himself. The novel ends with a sort of inner dialogue during which the author envisages the day when a 'world war of Newts against Newts'[15] might erupt, in which they would exterminate each other and people would gradually emerge from their hiding places as after the biblical deluge, telling tales of mythical countries like England or France that had existed before the great war and the great flood.

It is obvious that the broad epic dimensions of Čapek's prose work seemed the very antipode of dramatic form. Why try to put it on the stage? When the artistic director of the Vinohrady Theatre in Prague asked Kohout to write a play for the 1962/63 season, the playwright gave him a list of ten literary works which he had thought of adapting for the theatre at one time or another. The result was the 'Musical mystery' *War with the Newts*, conceived – and here again lies Kohout's sure dramatic intuition and flexibility – as a 'live television coverage of the destruction of the world, with documentary photographs about the cause and the development of the apocalypse, relayed by the last yet unsubmerged television tower.'[16]

The whole stage was conceived as one giant television screen. A chorus-like group of reporters propelled the action. Individually they would step out of the group in order to reenact the most important incidents of Čapek's novel. Then they would merge again with the unified chorus which recited in hexameters the terrible story of the rise of the Newts, thus giving the events the timeless awe-inspiring character of Greek tragedy.

Čapek's work had been expanded into Kohout's 'third dimension,' and had become something like a lightweight Gesamtkunstwerk, combining the explosive spectacle of a contemporary war film with the stark serenity of Greek tragedy.

The play was a huge success. Open to a variety of interpretations, Čapek's masterpiece of a utopian allegory about creatures initiated in methods of destructiveness by man himself, when placed on stage, radiated a variety of meanings that was electrifying to an audience which was anxious to hear the opposite of a single-minded ideological message. But how about censorship? Kohout's play took that hurdle too for several reasons. Čapek's work could clearly be described as anti-fascist. The satirical thrusts which are scattered throughout the novel had been variously interpreted as directed against Nazism. Moreover, in Eastern Europe Čapek's novel had been read as a satirical attack on capitalism, and as such was a prime example of good socialist writing. In addition, Čapek's *War with the Newts* appeared in a Russian translation in the late thirties and became a favourite with Russian state authorities who officially assessed the value of literary works. The author had indeed been praised for exposing the evils of capitalist society, its ruthless use of technology, and its materialistic policies.[17] So much for the novel's earlier political career.

However, after 1948, when Čapek was about to fall into political disfavour again, an ironic incident,[18] which demonstrates another one of the truly absurd touches in which recent Czech cultural life is so rich, saved him for Czech literature and thus provided Kohout's play with a respectable background. In this way, most ironically, Čapek's work found itself with just the right credentials to pass the censorship despite the fact that it consistently attacks non-democratic systems in any form as the prime enemies of all human culture and intellectual freedom.[19]

The Czechoslovak audience of course understood. And Kohout knew them well; he speaks as one of them when he writes: 'I wanted neither to correct nor to draw to a conclusion Čapek's *War with the Newts*. There was no need for that with this play – this disturbing fairy tale for adults, this parable which was given a new meaning by our restless times. I did not want to do more than read it with the intellect and the feeling of a man who has lived to see those times ... I merely added twenty-five years and a third dimension.'[20] During the final moments of the play one of the characters asks the same agonized question which is found on the last page of Čapek's work: 'And what about people?' But instead of the latter's quiet withdrawal into philosophic silence – 'I don't know what will happen then,' is Čapek's last sentence – Kohout launches an appeal, the vagueness of which does not mitigate its emotional urgency. As the waters begin to rise on stage as a sign that the flood of the Newts is upon us, all of the actors come rushing to the front of the stage and call into the audience:

> People! Let us not be poor in spirit!
>   Let us not stand on the volcano five minutes
>   before it erupts!
> Only cattle go to the slaughterhouse!
>   People never do!
>   They put up a fight to the last
> People! He who hesitates will perish!
>   Let us fight, people, the war with the Newts ...![21]

Then the lights go down on stage. When they go on again after a while, the stage is empty but for a large portrait of Karel Čapek.

A year after having completed his adaptation of Čapek's novel Kohout began to work on Jaroslav Hašek's *Osudy dobrého vojáka Švejka* (The Good Soldier Švejk).[22] This was a difficult task, as the playwright well knew. About thirty dramatists had tried their hands on Hašek's great comic epic, including Bertolt Brecht whose fascination with the talkative dog-catcher in uniform went back to the late twenties when he had worked on a dramatic version with Erwin Piscator.[23] Kohout was well acquainted with Brecht's version of Švejk. He also knew why the German playwright's adaptation would not particularly please a Czech audience: not only would it be impossible for them to recognize in Brecht's figure the Josef Švejk whose favourite expressions they all knew by heart, but they would also resent Brecht's total misconception of the atmosphere of occupied Czechoslovakia, not to speak of the glaring mistake of envisaging him as a Czech soldier in the German army. Other dramatic adaptions of Hašek's novel, many of which were by local Czech authors, were, for different reasons, not much more satisfactory.

In his version Pavel Kohout 'wanted to discover a technique that would leave to Hašek what was Hašek's and give the adapter the opportunity to make his own contributions.'[24] First of all, the playwright concentrated only on the first of the novel's four books which is the most colourful one from the point of view of characterization and which also most clearly reflects the basic conflict – that of the individual against power. Hašek himself regarded it as 'a sort of condensed course in unarmed self-defense.' Second, Kohout again used the approach that had proved so successful in *Around the World in Eighty Days*. The protagonists were given their parts and the remaining twenty-four parts were distributed among a type of chorus, 'a sextet of actors.' Kohout's third aim was to quote as much as possible. His very subtitle reflects this: *Josef Švejk*, or *'They've knocked off our Ferdinand' and other quotes.* Many speeches from the first part of the novel were transferred to the stage verbatim or with only minimal deletions. Kohout, who regarded the finished dramatic product as something like a musical theme on which the pianist improvises, claimed that he adapted Švejk because he wanted to stage the play himself. He envisaged it from the start as team-work and felt that the staging was 'an example of happy collaboration that eliminated the borderlines between the text and the performance: both grew simultaneously.'[25]

The performance was conceived on three levels. The first one was that of the protagonist and several main characters directly involved in Švejk's adventures. The second level, in strong contrast to the realistic encounters of the main characters, consisted of a colourful running commentary on contemporary problems provided by the 'sextet of actors' who danced and sang their way through the performance, appearing in turn as officers, prisoners, judges, policemen, spies, and others. In this way the production succeeded in separating contemporary implications and jibes against present circumstances, which would catch the audience's imagination, from Hašek's actual text so well-known to the Czech audience. A third level developed from the combined effect of the stage set, the music, and the choreographed movements of the actors.

On a screen backstage the titles of the various scenes were projected on the portal of a movie theatre. Then the screen was lifted and the historical events were acted out by a group of dancers who moved with the cramped and jerky speed of characters in old films to the sound of typical silent-film music. Kohout himself gives us a vivid description of the most successful of these scenes: '... the wonderful scene of the soldiers' mass on the drill-ground at Motol near Prague, a mass which is being read for the regiment going to the firing line by military curate Katz who is quite drunk, with godless Švejk as altar boy. Both are given the order that the mass must be "carried out rapidly and skillfully, because in a modern war the movements of the armies must be carried out equally rapidly and skillfully." The actual reason for the hurry is that the officers wish to get to the casino as soon as possible. It is a scene of world-proportions, both *crazy* and full of *horror* [Kohout actually uses these words in English] at the same time. As background music Jan F. Fischer used the waltz from the *Blue Danube*. Played at a slow and ceremonious pace at the outset, its speed was doubled whenever it was repeated. Švejk's altarboy bell took over the function of the triangle. Jiří Němeček [the choreographer] constantly increased the speed of Katz's movements at the altar as well as those of the soldiers "on the screen" who kept kneeling down and getting up more and more quickly, so that the mass turned into a sort of monstrous sports event. All in all the scene lasted one minute and fifteen seconds; and the audience reacted according to its striking brevity.'[26]

When Kohout and his team took their *Švejk* production to Hamburg in 1967, commentators, remembering Piscator and Brecht, tended to speculate critically on the tameness of the songs that 'had no bite,' and on the non-aggressive treatment of the power theme.[27] However, the Hamburg Schauspielhaus was sold out every time *Švejk* appeared on the program.

Kohout's three dramatic adaptations discussed here have proved to be among the most highly demanded items of Czechoslovak literary export. Part of the appeal is caused by the very choice of material; in each case he has adapted a well-known work of literature for the stage. Further, the playwright-adapter has managed to preserve the paricular genius and quality of the original work and at the same time to suggest in a highly imaginative way its meaning for the contemporary world. In addition, Kohout and his team (the good work of which he mentions at every opportunity) have created in each case excellent theatrical entertainment which, after all, has been the key to the best writing for the theatre ever since the ancient Greeks.

When Kohout was asked to write a play for the Vinohrady theatre in Prague in 1962, he said he preferred to do an adaptation because it would be easier to have it accepted by the censors. Four years later, in 1966, the Vinohrady theatre was still struggling under the pressure of censorship and had just been forced to take three plays off its playbill. Since he was closely affiliated with the theatre Kohout shared its problems – a feeling which he put in his typically histrionic way: 'For quite some time I have felt like a clown who waits behind the curtain to be called into the circus-ring, gets slapped in the face by the manager, takes a bow, and disappears in order to wait some more!'[28]

The enthusiastic reaction of his colleagues to this remark resulted in the creation of another 'team' and Kohout's new play, *August August, august*, which opened on 12 May 1967. The action consists of a circus performance with trapeze artists, an elegant top-hatted Circus Manager using flowery language, a band which plays resolute marches and slow waltzes, and sounds fanfares according to the varying nature of the circus acts – and, of course, the inevitable clown who comes racing into the ring, asks awkward questions, believes anything anyone says, gets his face slapped, and delights the audience.

The figure of the clown had always fascinated Kohout as belonging 'neither to a nation nor a race; his mask purposely hides all distinguishing features, so that he is more than, say, a Czech or a Jew.'[29] The playwright was of course also aware of the theatrical possibilities inherent in the clown's relationship to his fellow men, expressed most succinctly by St Chrysostom who described the clown as 'he who gets slapped.'[30] By being the laughing-stock, the clown caters to the feelings of superiority of the audience, and the half-comic, half-painful punishment, administered on his forever grinning face, provides a type of crude amusement which has lost less of its appeal in the course of time than one might expect.

Kohout makes plentiful use of these slappings. No sooner has August spent a minute or so in the circus ring on stage than he gets slapped by the Circus Manager for lack of respect. He undergoes a test administered by the Circus Superintendent who – jovially making the audience his accomplice – promises August ten crowns if he can stand getting ten slaps in the face. August happily agrees. The Superintendent gives him nine slaps and then walks off.

There is another, subtler quality about the ancient figure of the clown, however, and it is this quality which primarily seems to have stirred Kohout's artistic imagination. No matter how often he gets beaten up, the clown is none the worse for it. He is never allowed to become a victim for more than a moment. His naïve joy of life is not tempered by the blows he receives, his dream is never crushed. An instant after having been slapped, August can leap with delight at the thought of beautiful white horses. Like a cork he bounces back on the crest of the wave, regardless of how often he has been submerged. Kohout's August is never shaken in his belief that his own great dream – to train eight white Lippizaner horses for an exquisite dressage performance – is shared by the entire audience:

AUGUST ... *running excitedly along the outside of the ring calls into the audience*
    That's beeeeeeeautiful! That's ... that's ... that's ... beeeeeeeautiful!
SUPERINTENDENT What is beautiful, August?
AUGUST To polish eight white Lippizan horsies!
SUPERINTENDENT And you would like to train them too, August?
AUGUST That would be super!
SUPERINTENDENT So why don't you try it.
AUGUST That'll be super! *Racing delightedly to the curtain backstage* Horsies –
    horsies – chickee – chickee – chickee![31]

As the Prince in a fairy tale is prepared to face horrible monsters and dangers to rescue the beautiful Princess from the clutches of whatever monster may hold her in his power, August is ready to accept any 'condition' put to him to achieve his dream object, the horses. Perhaps we remember Samuel Beckett's clowns who also have to deal with a condition – that of waiting. We may feel Kohout is overstating the case when he claims that 'those conditions which my August is given by the Manager, become the basic condition of human life.' However, we cannot fail to realize that the rising and ebbing waters of joy and disappointment, of hope and despair in the play are conceived on a much deeper level than a clown's bouts of laughter and tears. Kohout, as always writing not *for* the stage but *with* the stage, knew that heavy-handed symbolism was the enemy of the theatre. He had to avoid 'letting the circus roof be crushed by the weight of the allegory, and turning the circus ring into a mere symbol.' What was needed were all the trimmings of a real circus performance with its roars of laughter, its breathless tension, its gaudy colours and screeching sounds.

August August, august is a work that has to be approached like a Russian doll which contains another doll, which contains another doll. The play contains an idea within an idea within an idea. The first idea is that August, the circus-clown, will never learn to handle life's situations and will always be beaten up. Holding on tenaciously to his wish-dream – those eight magnificent Lippizaner horses at his gentle command – August will never learn about the impossibility of realizing his dream: his personal inadequacy (he is totally ignorant of horses and calls them as one would call chickens); his inadequate position in society (the Manager would never entrust his clown with a dressage act); and the overall impossibility of such a situation ever occurring (the modest circus has no chance of ever owning such priceless animals).

There is nothing new about the literary figure of the dreamer. He has a long line of ancestry from Don Quixote onward. But there is a ring to Kohout's play which had a definite meaning for the Czechoslovak audience. The top brass of the circus never deny the possibility of August's dream coming true, in fact they keep referring to it in a friendly manner. However, the dream material is carefully measured out and when August overdoes his dreaming he gets a lesson that causes a rude awakening. At a certain point a man's dream becomes punishable: one should be careful not to overstep the limit. The analogy needs no further elucidation.

There is another way of looking at the dream-theme in the play which is more fruitful for literary analysis. Like a true clown August is completely naïve. None of his actions are 'sicklied o'er by the pale cast of thought.' He takes everything literally because, in Santayana's words, 'he sees the surface only, with the lucid innocence of a child … He is not at all amused intellectually; he is not rendered wiser or more tender by knowing the predicaments into which people inwardly fall; he is merely excited, flushed and challenged by an absurd spectacle.'[32] August's logic is completely literal. Among the many instances of humorous effects produced by the clown's literal-mindedness we might mention the conversation with the Superintendent who reads a letter alledgedly addressed to August in which an unknown lady expresses her infatuation for the clown.

SUPERINTENDENT *reading* 'Dear Sir' … *to August* What are you looking for?
AUGUST I am looking for that Sir.
SUPERINTENDENT But that's *you*, don't you see?
AUGUST Me? That's super!
SUPERINTENDENT 'Dear Sir. From the moment you appeared in our town I have been lost!' Where are you racing off to?
AUGUST To look for her.
SUPERINTENDENT Stop! That was only a turn of phrase.
AUGUST Where did it turn?
SUPERINTENDENT Nowhere. She's gone overboard about you.
AUGUST Did she drown?
SUPERINTENDENT No. She wasn't even near the water.
AUGUST So where does she write me from?
SUPERINTENDENT Silly fool. She is simply all beside herself.
AUGUST So why doesn't she get back into herself?
SUPERINTENDENT Oh, forget it. What I meant to say was that she isn't herself.
AUGUST So who is she then?

And a little later, as August answers a question put in the letter:

SUPERINTENDENT She is asking you that question.
AUGUST I know. That's why I'm answering her.
SUPERINTENDENT She can't hear you.
AUGUST *sobbing* Huhuhuhu!
SUPERINTENDENT What's the matter?
AUGUST So she's deaf![33]

The deadlock in communication, illustrated by a number of contemporary playwrights, has here become something entirely different. The Superintendent's inability to communicate with August is based on the mechanical use of habitual images and the effect is a refreshing revival of the sense of language rather than the sense of stultification we get, say, from Ionesco's *The Bald Soprano*.

However, despite brilliantly entertaining moments, one cannot escape the feeling that in this play Kohout has given us rather too much of a good thing. The first act is much the better of the two and the repetition does not yet jar on us. August and his identical clown-wife Lulu – a large doll come to life – produce a child despite the fact that they have not been able to find a stork. Stuck between the generations – his own clown-son, August junior, who wants to imitate him, and Bumbul, his clown-father-in-law, who wants to prevent him from realizing his dream – August tries but fails to kill Bumbul with a sledge-hammer because a fly was sitting on Bumbul's skull and August, as we all know, cannot harm a fly.

After the intermission however, when the audience have been sold sausages, sandwiches, and beer by attendants walking through the aisles as in a circus, events on stage begin to multiply and we get the feeling that the playwright's teeming inventive imagination got the better of his dramatic sense. Although he finally comes back to the central issue of the play – the dream – the dramatic tension has been lessened too much to be recovered. When August, with Lulu and his child as spectators, is given tails, a top hat, and a whip, and is asked to perform his great dream-number, the horse dressage, we sense something sinister brewing. During the preparations a huge cage is set up, beastly roars are heard from outside, and Lulu, who is asked to take a seat in the cage, expresses increasing anxiety.

The Manager's last warning is ominous: 'A dream should remain a dream, August. Otherwise you kill it. Do you understand that?'[34] August's affirmative answer is, of course, meaningless. The only thing he understands about a dream is that 'a dream is a dream if it is dreamt,'[35] and the only thing he wants is to perform his dressage with eight white Lippizaner horses. August is incapable of understanding that his great wish is only a dream and that it will be destroyed once it becomes reality. Instead of the white dream-horses the audience catches a fleeting glimpse of the first ravenous tiger rushing toward August as the lights go out and a deafening drum-whirl fills the air. When, a few seconds later, the lights go on again, the performers take their bows from an empty circus ring. With flowery solemnity the Manager speaks the final words to the audience, wishing them 'the very best for your way homeward and for our further common way into the future –.'[36]

The playwright tells us that these final moments of the play were a great problem for the director and himself. This, however, was not for the reason we might think. The fact that the clown-figure had to disappear caused a technical problem due to the curtain calls. To our hypothetical question: why not simply leave the clowns backstage and so stress the whole point of the play?, Kohout replies: 'The bow is an indispensable part of the production. It can be its crowning glory or ... it can erase the impression of the performance. In *August* it was particularly important. For over two hours we were balancing on the narrow path between circus and allegory. If the clowns did not reappear at the end, the play would become distinctly allegorical. If, on the other hand, they took a normal bow, their deaths would appear as a cheap circus trick.'

Playwright, director, and main actor solved the problem as follows: 'When the performance was ended, all other performers took their bows to the tune of hearty march music. During the ninety seconds that elapsed since their last scene in the cage the four clowns had taken off their make-up and put on civilian clothes. When they came into the ring, the applause stopped for a moment. It was as if they had taken the audience's breath away. Then the applause redoubled. Four pale, tired actors' faces formed just as striking a contrast to the motley circus than had the four clown masks previously. There was indeed not a trace of the clowns left but at the same time they had risen. The circus and the allegory were united again.'[37]

On 15 February 1974 a double bill with two one-act plays on it by Pavel Kohout opened at the City Theatre in Ingolstadt, Bavaria. The program contained a letter by the author to the director which comments on the nature of both plays, *Bad Luck under the Roof* ('un petit grandguignol' – 1972) and *Fire in the Basement* ('a fiery farce' – 1973). Together with the slightly older *War on the Third Floor* ('a military play' – 1970) which had been performed earlier, they form 'a trilogy of one-act plays under the overall title *Life in a Quiet House* ...'[38]

The three plays are variations on a theme that could be defined as a humorous version of a Kafka nightmare. State authorities of undefinable but obviously vast powers penetrate into the peaceful habitat of average couples and destroy their lives within the dramatic time at their disposal. In each case the powers' interference occurs in the same, seemingly inexplicable way. Servants of the state suddenly appear in the guise of postmen who have passkeys, firefighters sliding down a pole, masked guards emerging out of closets. Within a matter of seconds they have changed the quiet rooms – bedrooms in each case – into a hectic scene of an uncannily military nature. They shout orders, telephone secret higher authorities, conduct cross-examinations of the stunned tenants and thwart their questions with incomprehensible 'official' language.

In each case the victims are a couple – similarly surprised, harrassed, and driven to unforeseen extremes. Each time they are in bed – either in reality or in wishful thought. In *War on the Third Floor*, a peaceful middle-aged couple is awakened from their post-midnight sleep; in *Fire in the Basement* a young couple, married three days before, are caught frolicking happily in their new marital bed; in *Bad Luck under the Roof* a shy young woman visits for the first time a shy young man in his apartment, and, although the official intruder finds them still sitting up, the idea of a bed and what goes with it is not far from their minds. In all three plays the privacy of a bed, with all its connotations of the joys of intimacy, peace, and safety from the world outside, is put in glaring contrast to the uniformed officiousness, punctilious legality, and omnipotence of superior powers which, by the end of the play, have taken full possession of the scene.

Of the three plays, the first one, *War on the Third Floor*, is, in its parabolic simplicity, the best and strongest of the pieces. An obscure citizen, Emil Bláha, is fetched out of his marital bed and told that he has been chosen to engage in a fight with a representative from another nation because, as one of the officials readily explains, society has finally 'succeeded in eliminating wars which formerly used to extinguish whole nations. However, responsible politicians have expressed the fear – a fully justified fear – that warring is part of those atavistic tendencies which cannot be eliminated by a mere signature ... Therefore on the top level the secret decision was made that in future wars should take place in a quasi-private way.' History, the official continues, has once again inspired this new political idea; we know from the ancients that 'when the armies were exhausted, for example at the gates of Troy, each side simply chose a man who fought representing them all.'[39] And so Emil Bláha has been chosen with complete scientific objectivity by a computer. His opponent, a wine merchant from Saarbrücken, chosen by similar means, is just arriving fully armed on the train and is expected within a few minutes.

Bláha's protestations, his attempts to call the police or his lawyer become progressively weaker. Finally even his wife, giving in to the mounting pressure, begins to egg him on, at first inspired by fear: 'Emil, for God's sake, start shooting, or else he'll kill us!' Later on, as grenades explode and shots riddle the windows and furniture, his wife begins to repeat hysterically the battle-cries of the observing officers: 'Emil! Move forward into the hall! Throw the grenades ... Pump him full of lead! Make mincemeat of him!'[40] In the end both 'representative warriors' have been killed and the generals, standing over the corpses and discussing the unfortunate deadlock, play with the tentative idea that it might be better after all to return to the old, tried methods of waging wars.

Two years after this bitterly funny and theatrically powerful play was performed in German in Oberhausen in 1971, the director and manager of the City Theatre in Ingolstadt asked Kohout to write another play expressly for this theatre. The result is the two short plays, *Bad Luck under the Roof*, and *Fire in the Basement*, which the playwright considers as sequels to the older play, forming the trilogy *Life in a Quiet House*. The theme and dramatic structure of these two later plays closely follow their forerunner. In *Bad Luck under the Roof* a timid painter, who has been working on a portrait of his beloved for four years (alone with her for the first time he may find the courage to confess his passion), is suddenly confronted by a man stepping out of his own clothes closet and accusing him of being a murderer. Shedding a false belly and beard, the man explains jovially that he is only a link in a chain of command, that he only fulfills the order of his bosses 'who know exactly what they are doing,'[41] and if the painter wanted to use the time before the Examination Officer arrived and jump into bed with the lady – after all, it was only natural – he, the Man, would gladly retreat to the kitchen for a while. As the girl becomes increasingly suspicious and finally believes the painter to be really a murderer, the latter, driven into a frenzy, shoots the intruder as well as a number of policemen who break down the door at the end of the play.

The author tells us that the play explores the way in which 'a constantly repeated lie or absurd claim, supported by all the means a modern power has at its disposal, becomes a reality.'[42] We are reminded not only of Goebbels' notorious dictum but also of well-known plays as different as Bertolt Brecht's *Mann ist Mann* (*A Man is a Man*, 1926) and Max Frisch's *Andorra* (1961), both of which explore the way a system can change an individual. In Brecht's play, the hero takes on his new identity because he is threatened and brainwashed. In Frisch's parabolic model the pressure of a constantly repeated idea – the image society has of the hero – results in his being imperceptibly moulded to fit this image. Kohout's farcical version falls somewhere between the two, steering equally clear of Brecht's activist lesson and Frisch's depth psychology. Kohout has telescoped the hero's development and lightened the burden of the central idea by letting farce and high-spirited theatricality take over the action.

The third part of the trilogy, *Fire in the Basement*, is theatrically superior to *Bad Luck under the Roof*. The horseplay of the two naked newly-weds, made stageworthy by a shaking bed, tangled legs hanging over the bedside, and heads popping up and down, reflects Kohout's reputed sense for theatricality. Equally appealing is the idea of having the fire-fighters constantly sliding down and creeping up their pole, in full fighter's uniform, weighed down with all kinds of complicated equipment, the essential or non-essential nature of which they constantly discuss with clipped professionalism. The difference between these heavily clad, officious, self-possessed intruders and the naked, dazed young couple provides an irresistible effect.

The fire-fighter's claim that the kitchen is on fire turns out to have been a lie, and the smoke issuing from the kitchen door whenever a fire-fighter heroically enters it, turns out to come from a smoke bomb. But by the time the young couple discover this, they have signed an expensive insurance policy and are left with no way in which to prove that they have been deceived. Their wedding clothes, the only property to have been salvaged – their small savings disappeared with the efficient fire-brigade – look sadly wilted on their sagging figures. Moreover the pleasure of taking them off again at the end of the play and returning to love-making is marred by an intense question in their minds. Have they been manipulated by ordinary thieves, or by a power the workings of which they do not comprehend? As the young man again begins to undress his wife, he suddenly freezes: 'And what if they weren't any thieves after all?' She (anxiously): 'What if it's only sort of by the way that they ...'[43] Both (in unison): '... steal?'

Kohout tells us that *Fire in the Basement* deals with the features of a power that is beyond public control. 'The more totalitarian it becomes, the more extensive areas of an individual's life become the private hunting grounds for all those who are permitted or dare to act in the name of this power. Such mini-powers are more dangerous than the maxi-power because they act violently in the private sphere of the individual, without ideological explanations and with undisguised cynicism.'[44] As usual, Kohout's theoretical comment is catchingly formulated but contains a mixture of ideas, some of which are fuzzy. However, this does little harm to the theatricality of his play.

There is another play, *Poor Murderer*[45] – a bold experiment, it seems – that ought to receive some attention here, not only because it was actually staged on Broadway in the autumn of 1976, but also because it reflects Kohout's theatrical genius in all its aspects. It is another adaptation, but this time the playwright has gone far beyond the original work which he has used merely as a touchstone rather than a model.

The theatrical possibilities of creating a character who acts 'abnormally' are vast. Uncertainty as to whether the character is acting abnormally because he is a madman or because he is merely pretending to be insane increases the tension on stage. The audience are left with an open question which creates the intrinsic tension that is the basic ingredient of good theatre: is the character's behaviour a game played in order to achieve a certain purpose, or is it total lack of reason that prompts his actions? Playwrights have known the magic of this tension all along. *Hamlet*, of course, comes readily to mind but there are also Büchner's *Woyzzeck*, Pirandello's *Henry* IV and, more recently, Peter Weiss's *Marat/Sade* which explores the borderline between sanity and madness from a vast and constantly shifting variety of angles. It is not surprising that Kohout's sense of theatre led him to attempt an experiment of this sort, creating a stage where, in Pirandello's words, 'everything is in the making.'

Kohout found the material in the Russian writer Leonid Andreyev's story, *Mysl* (1902) – the title could be rendered as 'Thought' as well as 'Mind' – which analyses a man's psychic condition. The story consists of the hero's confession addressed to a board of psychiatrists trying to determine whether he is sane or insane. The hero, Kerzhentsev, a physician by profession, is to be tried for murder, and he records his state of mind down to the most minute detail, as he reconstructs the history of the murder from the moment when he first conceived the idea of killing to the moment of his arrest. Andreyev's story analyses the murderer's mental state with such precision and insight that it stirred discussions not only among the general public, but also among contemporary psychiatrists.[46] In order to evade legal punishment, Kerzhentsev pretends to be insane for some time before he commits the deed which, he reasons, will then be ascribed to his abnormal psyche rather than to criminal intentions. His downfall comes after the murder when his assurance that he had been deceiving others suddenly turns into the shattering realization that he may have been deceiving himself.

Kohout's dramatized version, *Ubohý vrah*, was written between June 1970 and July 1971, and is built around these two basic tensions: sheer intellect pitched against intuition and emotion; madness against sanity. However – and here lies Kohout's originality which he would call the 'third dimension' – the borderlines between the two opposites constantly merge and switch sides, so that the problem remains fluid. The playwright achieves this effect by making the main character not a physician, as in Andreyev's story, but a famous actor. The official examination which is to determine his sanity or insanity, is conducted as an experiment, a sort of shock treatment through 'reconstruction of his imagined crime [which] would bring order to his shattered mind.'[47]

Kerzhentsev is to act a part in a play performed on an improvised stage in an asylum where he is an inmate. The chief psychiatrist, the 'Professor,' has devised the experiment and plays the part of the audience during the 'play.' Actors – former colleages of Kerzhentsev – play the other parts; Kerzhentsev plays himself. Interrupted by discussions about props, the Professor's occasional interventions, actor's asides, and the protagonist's marginal explanations, the 'performance' rambles along, operating on several levels at the same time. We witness scenes from Kerzhentsev's childhood and adolescence; his revenge on his hated father; his fanatical belief in the supremacy of reason; his declaration of love to beautiful Tatyana and her refusal because she thinks he is just playing another role; the moment of decision to murder the hated rival. Under medical supervision the murder itself is re-enacted, as a sort of therapy for the actor. Kerzhentsev does indeed commit the murder but he 'kills' in his 'role' as an actor. In the role of Hamlet killing Polonius – snatches of *Hamlet* are recited throughout the restaged 'performance' in the asylum – he commits his planned murder while in full view of the audience during the bedroom scene with his mother, the Queen.

At the very end of the 'performance' comes the final twist of the intermingling of reality and fiction, truth and pretense. After Kerzhentsev has completed his part and, as Hamlet, 'killed' his victim as Polonius, the Professor asks another actor to play the same scene again, the way it really happened in Kerzhentsev's earlier performance. The new Hamlet, instead of thrusting the weapon through the curtain behind the Queen's bed, suddenly falls to his knees and begins to howl like a wounded dog. This, the Professor explains, was what Kerzhentsev really did during that fateful performance. Now Kerzhentsev has been shown the real truth. The murder had been the fiction of his imagination; in reality he had failed at the crucial moment.

His mind had tricked him and he is left with the terrible question 'Have you pretended to be insane, to be able to kill – or have you killed because you are insane?' And it answers itself: 'You believed you were pretending but you are really mad. You are just the stupid, decadent little actor Kerzhentsev ... the mad actor Kerzhentsev.'[48] It is now that the professor declares that his experiment has failed. The great actor's mind was to remain permanently clouded.

But just as his friend and intended 'victim,' Tatyana's husband, expresses his regret about the failure, Tatyana herself, who has been watching the whole 'performance,' declares that she is now sure she had wronged

Kerzhentsev whose declaration of love she had dismissed as being merely another 'role' he was playing. She calmly expresses her decision to leave her husband and attempt to nurse Kerzhentsev back to sanity. As she leaves the stage, her husband opens once more the curtain on the improvised stage with the words: 'Kerzhentsev ... You really did kill me!'[49] Kerzhentsev is still sitting there as before, flanked by two attendants of the asylum. There is a smile on his face.

There is no question that the play is a brilliant piece of sheer theatre. Like Pirandello's *Henry* IV, it manages to erase the borderline of reality and imagination by opposing the ordering, formalizing quality of the human mind with the deceptive and incalculable quality of life itself. Like Peter Weiss, Kohout is able to stack levels of reality and imagination within each other like boxes with interchangeable lids: Weiss's own comment on *Marat/Sade* could apply to Kohout's play: 'it is theatre, we act out a reality for you, and in this reality we act out a play within a play.'[50] The play within the play here lacks the philosophical depth of Weiss' drama, and it also lacks the formal perfection of Pirandello's experiments. Nevertheless, by sustaining with great dramatic skill the tension between the destruction of fiction by reality and of reality by fiction, Kohout has given a form to a problem that has preoccupied man ever since he became conscious of the powers of his imagination.

August 1975 saw another premiere of a Kohout play, this time in Lucerne, Switzerland. *Roulette*[51] was written in 1974/75 and, is also based on a short story by Leonid Andreyev. In *Mind*, Andreyev explored the psychological recesses of the tension between sanity and madness, whereas the story *Darkness* is more philosophical in that it deals with the complex, multilevelled, and perennial theme of human idealism versus materialism.

Andreyev's tale has a semi-political history which throws light on the dynamic nature of its theme. Among the many stories told to him by Maxim Gorky (who supported Andreyev greatly in the early stages of his literary career), there was one relating to the socialist revolutionary terrorist Rutenberg whom Andreyev actually met in Capri in 1907 while the former was in hiding. Andreyev recalled the story later as follows: 'The episode was very simple. The girl in the brothel, sensing in her guest a revolutionary hunted by sleuths and forced to come to her, conducted herself towards him with the tender solicitude of a mother and the tact of a woman who was fully capable of feeling respect for a hero. But the hero, a tactless, bookish man, answered the impulses of the woman's heart with a sermon on morality, reminding her of that which she wished to forget at that time. Insulted she struck him on the cheek – a thoroughly deserved slap in my opinion. Then, understanding the whole coarseness of his error, he apologized to her and kissed her hand ... That is all.'[52]

When *Darkness*, obviously based on this incident, appeared late in 1907, Gorky felt that it was a distortion of the truth, and that what he had hoped to be an inspiring tale had been perverted. He was never able to forgive Andreyev for having changed the ending. Almost seventy years later, when the Revolution had gone through many stages, Kohout in turn provided a new change to the ending. We will never know how Andreyev would have reacted to this different outlook, but it seems fair to say that the displeasure Gorky showed is not likely to have repeated itself.

Andreyev's hero is also a revolutionary during the Tsarist regime who seeks refuge in a brothel in order to escape the police. His encounter with the prostitute Ljuba reveals his detachment from life, his isolation in some moral zone outside real experience. When Ljuba asks him what right he has to be good and virtuous when she, forced by circumstances, is unable to be either, he begins to realize that he has hitherto led a false life. Ljuba demands that he give up his past completely – his ideas, his comrades, his books, and paradoxically he feels strengthened by this loss. With the transformation of his hero, Andreyev presents a profound paradox: the vulgar, greed-ridden existence of the brothel purifies the idealist's life, frees him from his arid egoism and makes him genuinely capable of a truly human deed. Ljuba in her turn is ennobled by the immensity of his moral sacrifice.

Kohout's revolutionary Alexej, the hero of *Roulette*, who is about to commit a political murder the next morning, pretends to be an English officer when he enters the brothel to get a few hours of sleep before carrying out his dangerous mission. The scene during which he is invited by an eager madam to survey and choose, is a typical Kohout scene in its sparkling theatricality. Western critics who worry that his work is suffering from his enforced isolation from the theatre should feel reassured that he has lost none of his histrionic sense.

In Alexej's scenes with Ljuba, Kohout follows Andreyev's basic idea. Her unpretentious reactions to his idealistic political pretensions begin to confuse the puritan activist. When he tells her about 'the real enemies of Russia ... its rulers,' and about himself, whose 'fate it is to awaken the people,' she is none too pleased because she has enough trouble as it is and doesn't want to ask for more. When, puzzled by his behaviour, she enquires whether he perhaps prefers boys, he silences her angrily. 'I have no time for such things ... I have dedicated my life to an idea.' When he preaches to her that 'Happiness comes from sacrificing yourself for others,' she makes a face: 'Is that so?! Then I'd practically be swimming in happiness!' When he asks her why she does not look for 'a decent job' because, after all, she is '*still* (my italics) a good human being,' she laughs bitterly: 'I'm an ordinary whore, darling.'[53]

The quiet dialogues in Ljuba's room are interrupted twice by lively group scenes in the reception-room downstairs. At first Alexej, trying to leave the brothel because the restful hours he has looked for have not worked out, is stopped by a group of Tsarist officers who question him about the attributes of English women while constantly refilling his glass with champagne (he is totally unused to alcohol). As the laughter becomes louder and tempers hotter, Alexej gives a performance of Russian roulette. He presses the trigger of a loaded revolver three times as he holds the weapon to his temple. Luck is on his side. Had the Tsarist officer, to whom Alexej hands the gun, then had the courage to match Alexej's bravado, he would have blown out his brains, but when he pulls the trigger he points at the mirror and only Madam cries with grief at her shattered property.

The second time Alexej comes down from Ljuba's room he has begun to change. Wanting to experience what he had denied himself and despised all his life, he orders champagne and music, and calls for the girls, who have to be wakened at his command. As Ljuba, who is also undergoing a process of change, watches with mounting anxiety, he indulges in fun with the girls until Ljuba breaks up the party and takes Alexej upstairs again. However, the old servant, whom Madam fired in a moment of anger, had seen Alexej move in a way that raised his suspicions and made him feel he might get himself some money. As the two finally fall into each others' arms in the room upstairs, he scuttles out of the house and returns with the officers who break open the door to Ljuba's room before she has managed to get Alexej out by the window. In a final scene of dramatic tension, Ljuba shoots Alexej in order to prevent his being tortured by his captors. The commissar's astonished 'Why?,' spoken to the rhythm of a well-known popular song, is the final word of the play.

In the course of the action the two main characters, the whore and the soldier, the unconscious victim of circumstances and the conscious activist who intended to change them, moved, as it were, toward each other. He tasted the life of the senses, she reached awareness of a region beyond the one she had known. But the two miss each other on the way; the world in which they live does not permit a rapprochement beyond a moment's embrace. In the end they have lost each other forever. The saviour has not carried out what he thought to be his act of salvation; the victim has not been saved.

In fact the roles have been strangely reversed. It is here that Kohout brings in the twist of his new ending. The lesson of real life has taught the idealist the senselessness of individual action: Alexej stands there apathetically as the officers arrest them. He has failed to affect reality by means of a violent action, but he has affected it in a way he never expected to: he opened a victim's mind to a new awareness. In the end it is Ljuba who commits the active deed, although with the intention of saving only a single man from suffering. The deed of salvation which hovers above the whole action has been reduced to an embrace on the one hand and a fraternal gesture on the other.

The German critic discussing the play's Lucerne première may have been right in criticizing Kohout for not having worked out fully the credibility of the psychological change the main characters undergo;[54] nevertheless, apart from being an extremely lively and fast-moving piece of theatre, the play is political in the basic sense of the word. On the one hand we might say that it is merely another version of an old literary war-horse, the spiritual struggle of the revolutionary intellectual who must act in a way that transcends the average individual's conscience, who cannot afford to live by the laws of average mortality.

From Dostoevsky's Raskolnikoff to Sartre's Hoebiger of *Dirty Hands*, to Peter Weiss's Robespierre of *Marat/Sade*, to Camus's Kaliayev of *Les Justes*, the problem of the moral dilemma of the man who undertakes violent action for – at least in his own eyes – valid political grounds, has haunted many modern writers. Kohout's play does not offer anything new in that respect. But this does not seem to have been his intention. He wanted to take Andreyev's story, anchored so closely in actual, and moreover recent, political reality, an important step further. The Russian writer's 'pre-Revolutionary' view of common people as the salt of the earth, no matter how politically unaware they were, is taken up by the Czech writer, three 'Revolutionary' generations later.

Kohout still presents them as incapable of political understanding but he shows them as capable of acting, once their personal sympathies have been engaged. These personal sympathies arise from a disinterested sense of loyalty, an instinct to prevent suffering, a sudden burst of inexplicable courage in the face of brutality. Even if Ljuba's desperate shot solves nothing, it is fired from an awareness of a certain value, the birth of which is the second main point of the play, the first being the death of abstract idealism. Of the shots fired in the roulette-game of life, most go off triggered by the wrong idea; the shot Alexej had in his revolver that was to be used the next morning was such a shot. It would have been morally unacceptable. Ljuba's shot was different. Unhampered by a structure of moral justification, it was an instinctive act of salvation.

But we must not overburden Kohout's writings with interpretive ballast. Despite the fact that his work has moved markedly closer to psychological and philosophical areas in the years when he has been isolated from the actual stage (contrary to his talent, his former habits, and his needs), he remains a writer whose imagination is largely histrionic. To fill the last half-hour of a play with events during which a callous prostitute is spiritually ennobled and a purpose-ridden revolutionary not only gets swept away in a passionate embrace but also gives up the idea of firing *his* 'political' shot –; makes an irresistible ending for a dramatist whose world is the stage. If, as in this case, a thinker's insight goes together with a flash of histrionics, so much the better.

Throughout Kohout's work we have witnessed his particular characteristic – which is also a characteristic of Czech theatre – the fierce awareness that the actual text is only part of the whole structure of the play; that the word is only one of the many ways of reaching an audience. Moreover, these other ways have a distinct advantage over the spoken word, for they belong solely to the stage and have therefore a more immediate impact. Brecht was equally aware of this and discussed on numerous occasions the importance on stage of 'Gestus' (a Latin word conveying the idea of the whole range of acting motions and techniques). It is here that we may find the hidden root of the strong bond between the social topicality and the circus-like quality of Kohout's work. We are reminded of the *Volkstheater* of nineteenth-century Vienna, which nightly played a variety of farces, musicals, and fairy-tale shows to sold-out houses.

In the tradition of this *Volkstheater* and indeed even in the tradition of Punch and Judy shows and travelling players of country fairs (though on a more sophisticated level), Kohout's theatre seems to have developed apart from general theatre repertory, as a response to the general public's need to be offered topical entertainment drawing its subject matter from their familiar contemporary scene. In 1974 Kohout entered into a surprising cooperative literary venture when, with Klíma, he adapted Kafka's *America* for the stage.[55] This seems to open yet another vista on his writings and offers yet further proof of his seemingly limitless versatility.

Kohout's prolific and uneven literary output has laid him open to all kinds of more or less justified criticism;[56] his stature as a Czech playwright may for a time be overshadowed by the realization that his path of development as a writer was for a long time full of twists and bends. Yet his moral consistency of the last decade has been remarkable. In an interview given to the *Frankfurter Allgemeine Zeitung* in the winter of 1976, Kohout comments on the way his work has moved from critical topicality to a more philosophical preoccupation with the general theme of the human being as such. Surely it was this development that accounted for his involvement with the work of Franz Kafka, a writer who might, at first sight, seem completely alien to Kohout's artistic intellect.

Kohout himself explains this new philosophical component in his work by referring to the deep shock over the political events of 1968, a shock which each Czech or Slovak writer had to cope with in his own way. 'It is, after all, no negligible thing to analyze the reasons for a catastrophe at a time of almost completely interrupted communication ... It seemed to me as if I were writing my plays on water and I am grateful to all those who have put them on land somewhere with all the risks involved in performing actions of saving.'[57] The attitude expressed here is surprisingly close to that of Václav Havel, a writer of such a different nature. Whatever we may feel about Pavel Kohout's work as a whole, one thing is certain: he uses every aspect of the stage with unfailing intuition and to the delight of any theatre audience. He has delighted people in Hamburg, Graz, Athens, and New York, as much as those in Prague. He is, one might say – entirely without irony – truly a playwright of the people.

4

Ivan Klíma

OFFICIAL But ... doesn't this story bore you?

K. No, it entertains me.

OFFICIAL I am not telling it to entertain you.

K. It entertains me by giving me an insight into the ridiculous confusion which under certain circumstances decides the existence of man.

FRANZ KAFKA *The Castle*

If we want to talk about Ivan Klíma, we must first take another look at Kafka and director Jan Grossman, the man who brought Kafka into the Czech theatre. Before Grossman decided to put Kafka on the stage, he asked himself a searching question. Was it fair to mould Kafka's highly personal prose into dramatic form? Was it not doing violence to Kafka's genius to adapt his work for the stage, to make him a dramatist? But Grossman immediately dispersed these doubts by explaining what he regards as the true nature of drama: 'We must not think about theatre as a genre that "exists" but as a genre that is forever reborn and changing. The theatre as a structure is electric: it constantly borrows from the areas of those genres which at a given moment contain the most experience and harmonize most sensitively with the intelligence and sensibility of their time.'[1]

Kafka's prose, so cryptic and so full of inexplicable tensions, that it constantly provokes totally opposed interpretations, has an activating dynamism that makes it highly dramatic. Only the reader's reaction gives Kafka's prose its full concreteness, its full sense as a work of art. The reader becomes a partner whose mind is provoked into a dialogue. This dialogue is the chief prerequisite for modern theatre. And if this dialogue induces the reader to realize that the illogical has a logic of its own and that the borderlines of common sense suddenly disappear in a strange vacuum – as happens again and again in Kafka's work – he goes through an experience identical to that of an audience during the performance of an 'absurd' play.

And so Jan Grossman put the great ancestor of absurd theatre where he thought he belonged – on the stage. He staged his own dramatic version of Kafka's *The Trial* with great success in Prague. K.'s whole life span between his arrest and his execution takes place on the same sparse stage set. In addition to a staircase backstage, there is only one chair, K.'s bed which later becomes a bench, and his writing desk which later becomes the judge's seat. In this way the three areas of K.'s existence – his private life, his professional work in the bank, and his situation as an accused are visually interrelated on stage. This is also the way Grossman has constructed the play. The three spheres of K.'s existence are all present and alternate in the first third of the play. In the second part K.'s private life has been suppressed; the scenes alternate only between accusation and bank: the trial has penetrated his professional life. In the third part the bank, too, has disappeared and the action is reduced to the trial authorities and K.'s hopeless struggle to discover the nature of his guilt. Thus we see K. as a private person in the beginning, an official in his job halfway through the play, and as nothing but an accused man at the end.

Under Grossman's direction the last scene, when K. is taken by two guards to his execution, was performed in such a way that the guards remain outside but close to the revolving part of the stage; several times K., trying to escape them, begins running along the revolving part, stumbles and falls over parts of the furniture, and in the end finds himself every time face to face with his guard-executioners who have remained motionless. Gradually he resigns himself and apathetically awaits his end. At the same time as the audience, K. realizes that the world in which he has been moving is a cage. The visual impression of the stage makes this cage much smaller and increasingly more claustrophobic than the epic dimensions of Kafka's novel which covers a whole year on almost as many pages as there are days in it.

But the world around K. is conceived as abnormal, incomprehensible, absurd. It consists of deformed, exaggerated characters, one of whom, for example, is played in the Prague production[2] as a sort of human insect, slimily wriggling around the lawyer in disgusting subservience; another is Titorelli, the painter, who combines clownish acrobatics with the smooth politeness of a head waiter and the half-hidden insolence of an arriviste. The visual impact of the stage forces the viewer more radically to identify with the hero than the longest description of the same circumstances could on a printed page. While reading we can raise our eyes, reread K.'s reactions, disagree with them, quarrel with him as we undergo the nightmare of his experiences.

In the theatre, however, we are prisoners of the events unravelling on stage at a concentrated speed with relentless force. The audience sees and hears the world the way K. sees and hears it. When K. uses the telephone, the audience hears over a loudspeaker the voice that K. hears in the receiver. They know no more nor less. In the scenes with the functionaries of justice K. is literally pushed aside to a place sidestage and becomes, as it were, a member of the audience. By using stylization and deformation of characters, by combining the actors' voices with reproduced sounds and voices, counterpointed by completely silent figures, the director gains this particular kind of uncertainty, manysidedness, and strangeness that has come to be called 'kafkaesque' even by people who have never read a line of Kafka.

Grossman does not aim, he tells us, at an interpretation of Kafka, but at a factual reproduction of his prose on stage. This is why he is critical of the version dramatized by André Gide and Jean-Louis Barrault who approached the novel psychologically, interpreted some of the events as tortured dreams, and totally missed Kafka's most basic quality, that tension between everyday reality and inexplicable occurrences.[3]

In October 1964 another 'Kafka-play' appeared on a Prague stage – Klíma's *The Castle* – again directed by Grossman. Despite its openly sailing under Kafka's flag – this is reflected not only in the title but also in the hero's name, Kan – the play's relation to Kafka's novel is curiously inverted. It seems important to try to see this relation with some measure of clarity because it reflects on essential questions of Czechoslovak theatre, and accordingly I have given more space to *The Castle* than the play deserves as a theatrical work.

The plot of *The Castle* concerns Josef Kan's arrival at the Castle in order to work together with the renowned scientists, artists, and 'deserving' politicians who inhabit it. The play begins with a shock effect. The stage instructions are as follows: 'In the darkness a long choking scream is heard. The scream is heard again; the terrible scream of a man who is being choked and frees himself for an instant from the choking grip. It dies away, stifled. A moment of silence. Quick steps of a person; the partition is moved to the side. The light illuminates a hand that is extended toward the string of the chandelier. The chandelier is lit. Centre scene is a bed with dead Ilja, at the bed stands Cyril, putting something into his pocket. Bernard as always at the window, which he opens. Emil is sitting motionless on a chair that faces the cupboard with a mirror. In the room there are several more chairs and an old fashioned writing desk. At the side wall a large decorated partition. When the light goes on Filipa comes running in, her hair loose obviously as if she were just going to comb it.'[4]

As the characters on stage begin to discuss this event, the hero, Josef Kan, arrives, apologizing for the clearly inconvenient time of his visit. During the following scenes we find out more about the inhabitants of the castle. Their alleged work, to which Kan refers initially with deep reverence, consists of doing precisely nothing. They stuff themselves at meals and tell dirty jokes. They show off with stories about their past great deeds in the world outside but have obviously lost all contact with it. They look alike, whistle alike, think alike. They squabble and obviously suspect each other of the young scientist Ilja's death, but it gradually becomes clear that they murdered him in unison. It also appears that Kan has taken the victim's place in every sense of the word. The very night of his arrival he is forced to sleep in the bed where his predecessor has just died.

As Kan begins to realize that the circumstances surrounding the death are highly suspect, justice seems to be on the way. An official arrives who has been delegated to find out the truth about the murder. He stages interrogations and finally reconstructs the circumstances of the deed by asking each of the group to play the role he played during the murder. Kan tries to add his own observations but is silenced. The final irony comes as a shock: the face of justice was a mask. The official, satisfied with what he has found, delivers an ambiguous speech and withdraws with polite wishes for successful further work, leaving the scene free for the inevitable final scene: the murder is re-enacted with Kan as the victim. The play ends with the lamp being turned off by the same hand that had lit it in the first scene and another terrible scream rises from the darkened stage as the curtain falls.

The play evoked from Western critics two types of reactions that were contrary to the playwright's intentions. First, it was considered a successor to or an extension of Kafka's novel. When staged in Düsseldorf in 1966, critics' comments had headings like 'On Kafka's Tracks,' 'Kafka-Variations,' 'A Breath of Kafka on the Düsseldorf Stage.'[5] Such a reaction could not surprise anyone, not even the playwright who had built his play around the central symbol of Kafka's novel. Yet Klíma tells us that his inspiration came from other sources. First there was his visual and histrionic sense. He imagined 'the terrible cry of a strangled person even before the curtain rises, only then the light goes on, the murdered one is lying on the stage and all the characters talk about his death – it is clear that one of them had to be the murderer.'[6] This is an old trick à la Agatha Christie (whom Klíma read at the time), but one that always works. The second source of inspiration was his personal experience in the Castle Dobříš which the Czech Government had assigned to the nation's writers as a pleasant and quiet place for them to compose works about life 'outside' the castle walls. Klíma, who spent only a brief time in Dobříš, soon realized that the atmosphere of exclusiveness, peace, and freedom from want amidst a restless, suffering world had a disastrous influence on creative minds.

The second reaction of Western critics was conditioned by a newly discovered, conveniently topical master-key to Eastern European absurd plays: the realistic impact of absurd situations on stage and the topical political meaning they had for the audience. For example, the Düsseldorf performance of Klíma's *The Castle* was called 'a thinly disguised critique of a society moulded by Stalinism.'[7] To be sure, in a society where the individual's life is so closely surveyed by the system, the audience's highly trained political awareness will tend to relate what happens on stage to what is happening in real life. It is probably impossible for a play in a totalitarian society to have an entirely non-political effect. Moreover the Czech audience was likely to catch the sardonic allusion to Dobříš Castle. But to strip these eloquent comments on today's world of anything but a localized political meaning, is not only to do them an injustice but also to miss their deeper and more lasting levels.

The critical essay that appeared together with the Czech edition of Klíma's play *The Castle* contains an interesting section: 'Klíma followed the steps of the land-surveyor K. to our own days. He did not think them up in unpleasant dreams, he really found them here. He, too, came face to face with the Castle. Today it is deprived of terror, because we are able to realize that it was created by men and that which is created by men can be changed by men.'[8] Kafka has been turned inside out. The inhabitants of the Castle – mysterious figures with secret powers which are transmitted by mysterious messengers – have become hollow, sterile creatures whose cliché-bound thinking and primitive sensuality present a danger only in so far as they are in power. What Klíma actually does in his allegedly kafka-esque play is quite unkafkaesque: he explores a state of rigidity and petrifi-cation in a similar manner to Albee in *The American Dream*. For example, the writer in Klíma's play still calls himself 'a writer,' although he has not written a line for ages; Albee's impotent 'father' and his sterile mate call each other 'Mommy' and 'Daddy' only to keep up the appearance of the role. These characters stultify and ultimately destroy the young generation.

This similarity of 'message' between the Czech and the American writer is interesting for the simple reason that it occurs quite rarely. It occurs rarely because Czech 'absurd' theatre is hardly ever didactic, while American 'absurd' theatre often is. The Czechs and Slovaks have clearly noticed this emphasis.[9] (I will discuss these tendencies more fully in chapter 9.) For the moment what concerns us is that Klíma's The Castle brought the great outsider of Czechoslovak literature, Franz Kafka, to the centre of attention. To use Kafka as a spring-board was a good idea because the famous borrowed name of the play helped it to be staged in Germany and sparked immediate attention among Western commentators who never fail to mention it in even the briefest assessments of Czech theatre. But the real merit of the play lies elsewhere, in its being the first work openly to integrate the work of Kafka into Czech literature.

Yet some Czechs saw more deeply. Jan Grossman, who directed the play, saw it as a forecast of Klíma's later works. In his essay on Kafka, Grossman discusses the nature of K.'s guilt. Although K. – and this is true also of Klíma's character – at first refuses to accept the senseless and therefore alien reality, he refuses in principle only. In principle he considers it nonsensical or absurd but in practice he goes along with it. We are reminded of a contemporary satirical sketch by another Czech author that shows a huge YES which, on closer inspection, turns out to consist of innumerable little 'nos' and a huge NO that is made up of little 'yesses.'[10] By accepting in practice what is happening to him, K. 'legalizes, conventionizes and normalizes'[11] the absurd situation. It is obvious that we are knee-deep in the problematic nature of society – be it the systematized, rigid value-structure of totalitarianism or the fluidity of democracy where any value has become a matter of 'opinion.'

In Prague, of course, people saw the play their way, despite the fact that the director studiously avoided any explicit reference to a topical situation. He even created a sense of alienation on the stage-set itself by featuring a circular horizon, a huge baroque painting of a monster, and organ music. With a mind raised on Kafka he managed to let the uncanny, terrifying element arise imperceptibly – as it does in Kafka's work – from concrete details, the slight shifting of which suddenly produces a sense of horror.[12] But an audience constantly subjected to the pressures of a non-democratic society outside the theatre are bound to grasp the play in a highly realistic way. The very idea of guilt becoming arbitrary is pregnant with political meaning. In the West we have had several versions of Kafka on the stage, yet we have not been particularly struck by the political explosiveness of these problems. This merely shows that political theatre in the West must be explicit in order to be recognized as such. In Eastern European countries reading between the lines has become a game, almost to the point of obsession. In most Western countries, where there is less need for political criticism to wear a mask, the game fails to create tension and generate excitement.

Kafka's great novel is about a young man who is trying to get into the Castle to do some work there but who never succeeds and who becomes old in the process of trying to find his way into the complex alien hierarchy. Klíma's play is about a young man who arrives at the Castle in order to work there but is murdered by its inhabitants. Kafka's hero is prevented from what he considers to be his duty – carrying out his calling – by having to cope with endless difficulties so that all his emotions and mental energies are used up in constantly intensified efforts directed toward a constantly diminishing goal. Kafka's hero cannot get *into* the Castle; Klíma's hero cannot get *out* of it. The struggle to find out about the reality of the Castle has turned, for Klíma's hero, into an awareness of that reality. The unknown enemy has become known. This, of course, is no longer Kafka. But then, Klíma did not want to become Kafka's follower and we must free him from this image for which he himself was responsible.

Yet here too we must pause and reflect. At the end of one of Klíma's later plays, *The Double Room*, the main characters are exhausted from their struggle to achieve what they believed in achieving, and in their numb resignation there is a recognition that reminds us of K.'s attitude. They know there are still things to be done and lives to be lived but not for these people. In the first chapter of Kafka's novel the hero gazes through the clear air of the winter morning in the direction of the castle towering in the distance. At this moment he is aware of its promise of 'fulfilment';[13] only later does he realize his 'ignorance of the circumstances.'[14] Klíma's earlier play wore only Kafka's mask, whereas his later plays have grasped the core of Kafka's meaning.

As we saw earlier, Klíma returned to Kafka once again in 1974 when he collaborated with Pavel Kohout on a dramatic version of *Amerika*.[15] Was his spiritual affinity with Kafka so strong that he felt he had to steep himself in the work which had received less dramatic attention than the other two? Was he encouraged by Kohout, whose clown character August (discussed in chapter 3) shares certain psychological aspects with Karl Rossmann, the victimized yet strangely indomitable hero of *Amerika*? These are questions that may be answered by future commentators. The fact is that in a unique bout of cooperation, the two writers shaped a play from Kafka's novel in which they kept meticulously to Kafka's original text. This was possible by means of a narrator who bridges the various scenes and provides a commentary on the events.

Kafka's powerful, densely packed first two sentences, which describe and allude to images, situations and concepts which dominate the rest of the book, are read as Prologue at the outset of the dramatized version, thus setting the scene for the whole play: 'As Karl Rossmann, a boy of sixteen, who had been packed off to America by his poor parents after a servant girl had seduced him and got herself pregnant, stood on the liner which was already slowing down as it entered the harbor of New York, he saw the statue of the Goddess of Liberty, sighted long before, as if it had been illuminated by a suddenly increased burst of sunshine. The arm with the sword rose up as if recently stretched aloft, and round the figure blew the free winds.'[16] From there on one adventure or mishap of the hero follows the next in quick succession. Kafka's text is only shortened; no other changes are made.

The two adapters' loyalty to the original is so consistent that it raised sceptical comments among German critics after the première at the Krefeld Theatre in March 1978. One of them, for example, felt that the Czech authors had radically reduced the complex novel to the 'external shape of the various events.'[17] This judgment was partly justified because of the unfortunate nature of the production which ignored the carefully worked out psychological dynamics of the play as well as the finer philosophical points which the adapters had taken care not to obstruct.

The production at the Vienna Volkstheater[18] which opened in the autumn of 1978 came closer to the secret chiaroscuro pattern of the novel which reveals how the land of unlimited dreams gradually becomes a land of unsuspected horrors. An initially mercurial and chaplinesque but later more and more tormented Karl Rossmann tries to cope with a surrounding which was undergoing an increasingly grotesque and uncanny metamorphosis (a ship, a hotel, a brothel, and the big theatre in Oklahoma were suggested with minimal but powerful props on the revolving stage set).

A close analysis of the Czech dramatization and a comparison with the original work should yield most interesting results, but in this context we must limit ourselves to one aspect only – the treatment of law and guilt. Karl Rossmann, during his employment as an elevator operator in the Hotel Occidental in New York, abandons for a short while the elevator of which he was in charge. He is found to have neglected his duty and thus broken the regulations governing the hotel staff. To be sure, he had begged one of his colleagues, whose work he had taken on that night, to oblige him in return and take charge of the elevator for a little while (while he, Karl, quickly took care of a drunken friend who would have caused disturbances of all sorts in the elegant hotel). The neglect of his duty, therefore, weighed against the possible embarrassment to the hotel management if the drunk had been noticed by the guests, was indeed much the lesser of two evils (after all, nothing at all went wrong with the elevator during Karl's brief absence).

However, the powers that be in the hotel took a different view. During a cross-examination, conducted by the Head Waiter and the Chief Desk Clerk, Karl's guilt towards the letter of the law as well as towards persons of authority in the hotel hierarchy is amply proved. He is cross-examined, humiliated, and fired.

During the cross-examination, the following exchange takes place:

HEAD WAITER *craftily* Perhaps you were suddenly taken sick?
KARL *giving him a scrutinizing look (actually wondering whether the Head Waiter had noticed the unfortunate mess the drunken friend had made by being sick into the elevator shaft – an occurrence that gave Karl the incentive to leave the elevator and get the drunk out of the way)* No.
HEAD WAITER *shouting loudly* So you weren't even sick? ... Then you must have thought up some grand lie. What excuses are you going to offer? Come on, talk!
KARL I didn't know that I had to telephone to ask for permission.
HEAD WAITER That's really priceless! *seizing Karl by the collar and almost slinging him across to a list of elevator service regulations which was pinned to the wall – the Desk Clerk follows them* There! Read! ... Aloud![19]

Karl subsequently explains that he has carefully read the service regulations but that he forgot the exact wording because the particular paragraph is rarely needed – besides, he had been working at the hotel for the past two months and had never left his post for a minute. This reasoning is flatly rejected of course, and Karl Rossmann's downfall takes its course. The accused had tried to apologize for his transgression by referring first to the insignificant aspect of the rule he had broken, and secondly to its rare applicability. He put forth this reasoning in the hope that it would make sense to his superiors. By so doing, however, he imposed relativistic values on legal points and thus came in conflict with the absolute concept of the letter of the law.

His 'guiltlessness' – not having consciously done anything wrong –

therefore turns to 'guilt' in the absolute eyes of the law – not having observed the law precisely, and having depended on a private promise rather than on a legal agreement. The personal aspect had taken the upper hand in his actions; complex human loyalties had led him to ignore the letter of the law. But such considerations have no room in Kafka's universe. The human being is deformed into performing mechanized functions according to abstract and absolute instructions. On Kafka's heroes these gradual and painful deformation experiments are performed, and with meticulous care Kafka observes the various stages of deformation.

When, in about 1963 or 1964, Ivan Klíma read Dürrenmatt's *The Accident*[20] in Polish translation, he felt as if he were having 'a revelation.'[21] The Swiss writer's story (which is also known in a radio play version) is about an average man – not evil, but no angel either – with the usual mixture of human weaknesses and ambitions, a little bit of ruthlessness when needed, and an occasional touch of self-indulgence.

This Everyman is stranded one evening in a small town and is invited to spend the night in the house of a retired judge who also invites his old colleagues, a prosecuting attorney and a defending lawyer, for dinner. During the sumptuous meal, when the greatest delicacies are served, the three old men entertain themselves and their visitor by staging a mock court case in which each of them carries out his judicial function and the visitor is cast in the role of the accused. In brilliant legal arguments developed between coq au vin and crêpes suzette the three representatives of justice manage to convince their defendant of being 'guilty' in all walks of life. Next morning, when they come to his room to tell him how they enjoyed the evening, they find him dead: he has carried out their playful verdict and has hanged himself from the window frame.

This was what sparked Klíma's imagination. In Dürrenmatt's story a verdict was spoken and a man carried out what he took to be justice. Perhaps he hung himself merely in order to avoid the question of how he could go on living after his eyes had been opened to the fact that guilt had crept into his life, not with a dramatic breaking of the written law, but as an imperceptible process, edging its way through the loopholes of seemingly inconsequential weaknesses and allegedly necessary aggressions. Was he unable to bear the awareness of being guilty without having the glory of being a great man? Dürrenmatt does not tell us. But what he implies – and what fascinated Klíma – is that justice as a system knows only extreme positions, and refuses to acknowledge the vast spectrum, for it is in the ambiguity and variety of life that the artist finds his material.

Ivan Klíma's main concern as a playwright is basically as much akin to

Kafka as it is to Dürrenmatt. The best example of his kinship to both writers appeared a whole decade after his version of *The Castle* and his discovery of Dürrenmatt: *Games* (1974), a full length play, brilliant both theatrically and philosophically, reassesses the complex issue of man's rights and the forms of his guilt. Klíma's particular closeness to Kafka and Dürrenmatt lies in his exploration of the secret, highly charged connection between 'right' and guilt and the way they can create or cancel each other. The right to have an opinion, for example, is directly connected to the guilt of not making the correct choice. The right to assert yourself is related to the guilt of overcoming others. And so on. Such thematics sound forbidding for the stage, but Klíma clothes his speculations in so colourful and imaginative a form that his plays are not weighed down by ideas but remain stage-worthy.

Although Klíma has written more prose works than plays, his feeling for the stage is obvious. Less analytical than Havel and less poetic than Topol, he tells us his plays are usually sparked off by a particular event and, he says, rapidly written. He knows how to use cliché, slapstick situations (two lovers alone, interrupted by funny incidents), or well-worn stage-tricks (cakes, some of which are poisoned – the audience can't keep track which – being passed around and eaten) with complete assurance as to how they will work on stage. All this, of course, seems far from the bleak rigidity of *The Castle*. But the basic unity is there. Klíma's earnest search for justice has merely decided to put on fancy dress in order to perform its task anonymously.

On the face of it, Klíma's *The Master* (1967) looks like a conventional detective story. A carpenter delivers a coffin to a family home, and claims that it has been ordered. None of the inhabitants of the house knows anything about it. Yet later it appears that the delivery of the coffin was not based on a mistake, for one member of the family is found to have died in his room upstairs. Moreover it appears that he died under suspicious circumstances, after having drunk poisoned milk. This is, of course, a perfect situation for a detective story: the four inhabitants of the house are all under suspicion; even the master-carpenter who brought the coffin is a possible suspect. He becomes a sort of confessor for every single member of the household, and discovers each of them to be a potential murderer. Again, in the tradition of the detective story, the circle of suspects decreases, and the members of the household die, one after another, until only the dead man's daughter is left. The revelation of the truth seems imminent.

Unlike a detective story, however, this play has no revelation. Obviously none of the suspects committed the murder, and the fact that the master-carpenter might conceivably be the guilty one seems not only unsatisfactory but also irrelevant. This feeling of the irrelevance of the whole 'case' has been wedging its way into the mind of the reader since he first has the inkling that he is being led up the garden path by a false detective story. However, the playwright's deception of the reader as to the actual nature of his play is counteracted by the fact that he provides clues that would reveal this deception: he does this by suggesting that the conventional detective secret – who is the murderer? – conceals within itself a further, much more complex secret.

It is the secret of the hidden forms of guilt every man – unless he be a saint – incurs by not fighting constantly for what he believes to be true and good. In the play the paralysis of moral indifference is represented as a kind of death. Klíma has embodied it in the strangely aloof figure of the master-carpenter who stalks death with his ever-ready coffin but who also dispenses a consolation that results in euphoric numbness and submerges the will to act.

The master-carpenter constantly refers to an ideal place which he describes as a desert where the stars are near and anguish is burned away in the clean sand. All the inhabitants of the house fall prey to the reassuring beauty of this vision; only the young woman Františka withstands it. No longer able to distinguish between guilt and innocence (all her relatives have fallen dead and the murderer remains unknown), she still refuses to be lulled into irresponsible oblivion of the here and now. When the master-carpenter wants to take her to his 'desert,' she says she would rather go to the police station. 'You know how to speak beautifully,' she tells him, 'but what are these words in a world where words have been completely separated from deeds? Your desert? What is that desert of yours? ... Do you believe in it? And what if you long ago stopped believing in anything except those words which flow from your lips of their own accord, still beautiful and still alluring? ... You care for nothing but your vision. You would be capable for its sake ... to use everything ... even our pain ... And the fear you awakened in us.' (Softly) 'It is so close: consolation and death-hope and despair ...'[22]

The implication of such a passage is obvious to anyone aware of the Communist vision of an ideal future in the name of which deeds of violence are justified. But Klíma has written more than a topical play. Descending to a deeper and more universal level of meaning we find that self-justification by means of a selfless aim is a widespread disease – and as soon as we have said so, we are bound to question the use in this context of the word 'disease,' wanting, perhaps, to substitute it with a non-committal term like 'phenomenon,' and having thereby provided a perfect illustration of the general confusion about the meaning of 'guilt.'

The Master was never performed in Czechoslovakia. Apparently no director could be found who could understand it. When it appeared in print the heady intellectual excitement of the times was not favourable to a speculative study of this sort. People were not in the mood for detective stories that ended in metaphysical question marks. Although the problem of an individual's guilt was highly topical material, there was a need for more clarity. Even if the nature of justice was revealed as remaining beyond human grasp, there was some need to define the villain more clearly than by means of a passive death-wish in man. Although Czechoslovaks of the sixties were ready for Beckett and Pinter, they seem to have been able to accept a local work of metaphysical complexity only if it was a work of poetry. It was Josef Topol who provided this type of writing for the stage. Klíma never pretended to be a poet. This is why this remarkable work never reached the Czechoslovak stage. Klíma seems to have learned his lesson: the 'murder case' of his next play does not require the audience to brush up their metaphysics.

The second and last of Klíma's plays to be performed in Czechoslovakia was *The Jury*, a remarkable tour de force that takes up the question of a man's guilt with a combination of philosophical ambiguity, grotesque legalism, and dramatic momentum. The very title makes us alert. We are prepared for something like this: a group of people having to decide the fate of another man; an assessment of guilt or innocence based on the objective opinion of disinterested fellow men; a man to be judged on the basis of legal evidence and common sense. The absurd twist of Klíma's play – as the audience and the jury find out about half-way through the play – is that the accused man is dead already and the jury's verdict will be merely a theoretical judgment of a case that has in effect been closed.

The motley group confronted with this unusual situation consists of a former army captain, a barber, a milkmaid, an engineer, and an archivist. It does not take long to gather the reasons for this choice of characters. The 'case' will be assessed by the soldier bent on carrying out commands, unused to asking questions and quick to dispense labels like 'traitor'; the manager of a small business whose success depends as much on how he can entertain and occupy people's thoughts as it does on the way he trims their hair; a simple-minded country woman frightened by the task, frantically taking notes about everyone's speeches because she is afraid she will forget what she is supposed to remember; a young engineer, pragmatic and impatient to 'have the thing clear'[23] and get the job finished; and a conscientious scholar for whom 'justice' is a big word and who worries about the ethical implications of his decisions.

The man on whom the group is to pronounce judgment has been accused of murdering a young woman but the event remains so vague and is referred to in such contradictory ways that the audience is unable to form its own judgment. Gradually, however, they realize that the accused is of minor importance; it is the jury who is on trial here – a group of ordinary people faced with the choice between making a decision to the best of their conscience and putting a stamp of approval on a case that has already been decided. Clearly, the authorities want the verdict to be 'guilty.' They make sure that the jury realizes this. Not long after the beginning of the play the question in the minds of the audience is no longer 'is the accused guilty or not guilty?' but rather 'will the jury perform its task as puppets of an authority that has made up its mind?'

The verdict has become merely a matter of principle, no longer related to the actual fate of the defendant. The playwright subtly suggests the characteristics of the members of the jury and reveals how their minds give in under steadily mounting pressure. Even after learning that the accused is already dead – beheaded, as the Engineer finds out, and not shot while escaping, as the authorities claim – the jury is not allowed to close deliberations; they have been locked into the building and soldiers are marching up and down outside, urging them on to pass a 'just' verdict. And so they begin to realize what the audience has known for some time, that they must pass a verdict not on the alleged murderer but on themselves.

Gradually they become aware of a predominant feeling that is directly connected with the moral decision they are facing. It is the fear of contradicting the authorities. The army captain, accustomed to act rather than to think, is the first to pronounce the verdict 'guilty.' Gradually he is joined by the Barber and the Milkmaid and finally even the Engineer who, realizing that the whole thing is a show prepared for public consumption, no longer cares.

Only the Archivist, conscientiously repeating the contradictory aspects of the accusation, remains unswayed and makes his ethical gesture by pronouncing the accused 'not guilty.' However, even this act of moral courage becomes part of the system it is trying to oppose. In the words of the Judge the Archivist's verdict 'contributed to the certainty of the complete independence of the tribunal;'[24] in other words, it helped to provide the image of justice before the public eye. Alone on the stage during the last few minutes of the play, the Archivist bitterly assesses the role he has played in furthering manipulation and injustice.

The Czech reviewer who compares the gradual change of the jury's attitude to that of the citizens in Ionesco's *Rhinoceros* seems to have overlooked the basically different motivation. Klíma's jury changes on the premises that 'it's all the same anyway,'[25] whereas Ionesco's people change because 'one has to keep an open mind ... and we must move with the times.'[26] The former decision is based on the awareness that heroism is not only dangerous but also useless; the latter is prompted by thoughtless gregariousness and the refusal to be different. On the whole Klíma's people *know* that their decision has nothing to do with what they think is right; Ionesco's people think their decision is based on what is right. The characters in the Czech play watch themselves changing into rhinos, never losing sight of the human image they are abandoning; the characters in the French play invert the values: the rhinos become people and the people become monsters.

It is surprising that *The Jury* was staged in Prague as late as April 1969 when, naturally, it caused agitated applause and obvious excitement among the audience. The reason that it was censored only at a later date may be found in the fact that the play could be and indeed was interpreted[27] as a comment on the false claims of democracies that pretend to let the people have their share in decisions. That the play can be taken as a comment on the problem of justice in entirely different social systems shows that Klíma's play plumbs greater depths than the manipulations of justice in a country that is being 'normalized' back into a system.

On closer inspection it appears that the manipulators themselves are passive parts of the system and play their roles as a result of circumstances rather than by free choice. 'We all know it,' confides the Judge to the Archivist (whom he significantly now calls a 'colleague'), 'Murderers are among us. Certainly we ask ourselves the question whether one can live like that, not to speak of passing judgements. But every question has its time. And each of us has his role.'[28] Klíma implies that the Judge, who in this play seems to be at the head of the manipulation, is only another wheel in the big machinery. He knows it and accepts it.

The anonymity of modern mass society permits people to dispense with a personal conscience. In fact there seems to be no place for it. Consider the Archivist who had a personal conscience. What good did it do? Like Friedrich Dürrenmatt, Klíma seems to claim that it is impossible to represent justice on today's stage because all forms of power are 'submerged in faceless abstraction ... Today's state has become anonymous, bureaucratic ... and can be represented only statistically.'[29] But, also like Dürrenmatt, Klíma creates individual figures who oppose this machinery in their own, perhaps ridiculous and imperfect way. And although their efforts come to naught, although they too inevitably contribute their drops to an ocean of guilt around them, still they show – as Dürrenmatt thinks – that there is still some courage left in man, and – as Klíma thinks – that 'in a deaf and blinded world a kindred soul can be found.'[30]

Is this too modest an aim for a contemporary playwright? Perhaps. But as soon as we ask such a question we are involved in the complex argument whether, as Shaw and Brecht thought, the playwright ought to try to change the world, or, as Ionesco and probably Pinter think, he should merely attempt to express an incommunicable reality. Klíma himself worries about these questions and is both cautious and humble in formulating his response.[31] He feels that the very process of asking questions leads a writer to recognize the attempts of other related writers to answer them. This inspires him to ask more questions and makes him aware of the magical power of human language.

Four highly theatrical one-act comedies followed *The Jury*, and at first sight one would hardly recognize the author of *The Castle* and *The Jury*. The author's vivid stage sense seems to have come with his decision to provide amusement because 'what sense is there in torturing minds that are already filled with anxieties.'[32] Despite this rather gloomy incentive Klíma has written very funny plays, though the laughter they evoke is none too comforting. But then – as we have been shown from Aristophanes to Molière and Shaw – laughter somehow rarely is.

The four plays have catchy and, of course, rather misleading titles: *Klara and Two Men*, *Café Myriam*, *A Bridegroom for Marcela*, and *The Double Room*. In each of them the central character strives to attain something. That something is very simple; in fact, in three of the four cases it could be called dire necessity: To be alone from time to time; to choose your mate yourself; to have a place to raise your family. The fourth one is a little more demanding: it is the wish to be happy. But that does not mean that the other wishes are more easily attainable. All are thwarted. In each instance Klíma has built his play around one of his 'kindred spirits' who summons the courage to refuse to join the doings of the world around him, whether it means refusing to trust anyone, or getting things at the cost of others, or letting the system consume your private life.

None of the four plays has been performed in the author's home country.

No member of a Czech or Slovak local audience had the opportunity to let the author know whether he had achieved what he considers to be any playwright's basic task: to make the audience feel that 'whatever is happening on stage is about themselves, that each of their problems, emotions or words – no matter how insignificant – is familiar to the characters on stage.'[33]

Klara and Two Men had its first production in German at the Atelier-Theater in Vienna in 1971. It is an amusing yet deeply serious one-act play about how and whether to enjoy life. 'I like to be happy,'[34] says the naïve heroine of the play who is surprised that there seem to be people who do not seem to share this preference. Her world is one where pleasures are considered the only legitimate goal in life and the harassments which stem from problems perennial or topical are simply pushed aside gently with the reminder 'don't think about that now.'[35] We are reminded of the lesson the tensely conscientious English writer learned from Zorba the Greek who believed that a man should dance as often and as long as possible.[36] However, Klíma does not grant his Klara the full victory of the passionate Greek. The play, written rapidly during a short spring holiday, starts out looking like a bedroom farce and ends with an existential outcry into silent darkness. The scene is Klara's room, cluttered up with potted plants, radios and transistors because, although she likes many things, one thing she does not like is silence.

When the curtains open, Klara enters with a bunch of flowers and a man. The first line explains the situation: 'Man: (looking around ...) So this is where you live.'[37] The audience has been alerted for what is likely to follow: a first attempt at love-making interrupted by all kinds of difficulties. This is indeed what does happen, but the difficulties are different from what we expect. It turns out that in the next room Klara's former lover is dying of cancer and his faint voice carries through the wall, begging for forms of help that seem as absurd to Klara's visitor as they do to the audience: the voice asks for wire and dogs. Klara, who has been providing both for the last weeks, calmly explains to her puzzled visitor that there is nothing strange about these requests.

KLARA Wire. He always wants wire ... He'd been in prison probably and knows when there is wire all around, he can't get away. And now he doesn't want to go away. He wants to stay here. Here. With me. And altogether – here. Later he'll want me to bring the dog.

MAN The dog?

KLARA They were probably watched by dogs there.

The faint but insistent voice on the other side of the wall keeps interrupting the Man's increasingly half-hearted attempts to make love to Klara (who obviously is perfectly prepared to do so):

VOICE Klara!
MAN Klara!
KLARA *her head had been resting in the Man's lap* Pardon?
MAN He is calling you!
KLARA Don't think about it.
MAN *desperately* He wants the dog.
KLARA I have no dog.
VOICE Klara!
MAN *desperately* But he will keep calling again and again!
KLARA Don't listen to him.
VOICE Klara!
MAN I can't stand it!
KLARA Well, then you have to go and bark.
MAN I should go and bark? ... Klara, I came to you and now I should bark?
KLARA Oh, don't think about it.
MAN On all fours or upright?
KLARA He doesn't see you anyway. It is dark. He only wants to hear the dogs.
MAN Alright, Klara, I am going.[38]

The Man does not have to bark long. Soon the fall of a body is heard. Under Klara's orders he has to help her bring the dead man into her room and put him on the couch where he remains until the end of the play, by which time the Man predictably leaves without having done what he intended.

So much for a realistic obstacle regarding the Man's endeavours – a death (though not his own) thwarted the embrace. But there is another dimension to the play which opens up a quite different reality. Throughout the action all sorts of inexplicable things keep happening. Several times the phone rings and voices ask for the Man although he protests 'no one knows that I am here. Half an hour ago not even *I myself* knew that I'd be here.' Another tenant rings the bell at midnight with suspicious requests. All these incidents visibly unnerve the Man, whereas to Klara they seem perfectly normal occurrences. Everything is natural for Klara. At one point, when the Man has gone into the room next door, she actually picks up the phone and talks to God, to her 'friendly, fat God who wears sandals,' to whom she has always prayed whenever she has broken off with a lover. But now her God does not answer, she cannot even see him as she is used to; her desperate assertion 'But I want to – I want to be happy!' and her plea 'This one time, a last time, one more last time ... Don't leave me!'[39] remain unanswered and the only sound that is heard as the light goes out is water running from the tap she has turned on in her desperate attempts to break the unbearable silence.

And so the bedroom farce has turned out to be a play about human fear: the whole spectrum of fear beginning with the concrete fear of being caught in an illicit love affair, moving on to a more general anxiety generated by mistrust of other people (the Man is uneasy about the woman tenant at the door), and ending with a constant sense of some kind of persecution (he examines the phone, worries about who might have seen him come).

At the end of the play the fear expands and deepens; it becomes a kind of existential terror, a 'Weltangst,' that engulfs the whole world of the stage, including Klara herself. No longer able to find the answer to life in seeking pleasure, no longer able to conduct amicable conversations with a friendly paternal God, she cries out into the silence in a final scene that reminds us of Camus' *The Misunderstanding*, in which an equally desperate plea for the meaning of an absurd event meets with stony silence.

Thus the ghost of fear forces its way relentlessly into the comfort of a well-lit room resounding with modern rock music. The words of the man next door, for whom the loss of freedom in the past has become the spiritual haven of safety in the delirium of death, acts as a grotesque subplot to the theme of fear. The visitor, who knows no cure for his own fear, is made to dispel the fears of another by absurdly summoning the fears of the past.

With Klara's character the playwright asks an open question about human happiness in today's world. The apparent banality of the question should not deceive us about its urgency. 'By trying frantically to see only that which we wish to see,' Klíma asks, 'can we hope to wriggle through the barbed wire, suffering, horror, pain, humiliation and hopeless dying which surround us on all sides? Are there sounds that will drown out the anxiety that slumbers on the bottom of our souls?'[40] The most resourceful critic would find it difficult to interpret *Klara and Two Men* as a comment on a certain social structure. It is simply about contemporary man's loss of value, loss of sense of direction, loss of self. In speaking about Klíma we sound as if we were speaking about Pinter, Frisch, Arrabel, Beckett.

Café Myriam, written in 1968, is an entertaining black comedy which ostensibly deals with the shortage of places to live. It is perhaps ironic that this most localized of Klíma's plays was performed in the United States[41] where shortage of apartments is certainly not one of the main problems society faces. The author, although he refuted the idea that the play was meant as social criticism – 'I had a lot of fun trying out that black humour for the first time'[42] – tells us that it was inspired by the desperate shortage of apartments in Czechoslovakia. In a situation where young couples have to wait for six or seven years for an apartment, live in the meantime in cramped conditions with in-laws, and have to pay a horrendous deposit in order to be put on the waiting list, an apartment gradually becomes the focus of dreams and desires. The disastrous psychological consequences for the characters of otherwise harmless and kind people provide the background for *Café Myriam*.

The café sells a 'speciality of the house': delicious cakes in the shape of a mushroom, covered with marzipan and soaked in brandy. Anyone who has visited a mid-European pâtisserie is familiar with this kind of pastry which is often prepared in bright colours that actually make it look like a beautiful but highly poisonous mushroom, well known to Europeans for its combination of attractiveness and danger. The chief pastrycook of 'Myriam' – a burly muscleman who looks more like a butcher – bakes two kinds of sweet mushrooms: both are equally delicious but one kind is poisonous, causing certain death to the consumer.

A young couple appears in the café, lured by an advertisement that 'Myriam' can provide apartments within a few days for a relatively low price. As the couple try to find out how this splendid proposition works, they are gradually enlightened as to its real nature. Apartment-seekers find an elderly person who has an apartment, establish friendly relations, take him or her for a treat to the pastry shop, attend the funeral a day or two later, and are promptly presented with the papers for the apartment by the efficient manager of Café Myriam.

Not only have the police and the representatives of justice availed themselves of this successful housing service, but a government minister is actually the founder of the establishment. In impassioned speeches he explains to the young couple that it is all being done 'for you, my children, so that you have a roof over your heads. So that you can procreate in peace.' The young man is appalled: 'Can you live where murderers live unpunished? Where the authorities protect the murderers?'[43] Admirable ethics, to be sure. But, like the honest Archivist in *The Jury*, Klíma's young man is denied a role of honour. He is carried off on the shoulders of the butcher-cook, cheered by the others as keeping alive the image of purity and idealism so badly needed in this guilt-ridden world to which we all belong. Stunned with what is happening to him, he is integrated into the poisonous production as a holy picture of innocence that punctually revives the theory of guiltlessness while everyone around shares in guilt.

The black comedy here has given another sardonic twist to the theme of *The Jury*. Although we are likely to laugh throughout this vivacious and fast-moving play, the question that forces itself on our minds is no less serious than the one posed by *The Jury*. A system that is able to arrange things in such a way that the most elementary needs of man are presented as privileges has the power to control people to a frightening degree. Moreover, there is an equally frightening power in the pull of togetherness; if everyone does it, it surely can't be all that wrong? Collective guilt, although we have done much talking about it in the last few decades, does not weigh as heavily as individual guilt. In fact, it strangely loses the face of guilt for those who do not want to see it. There is, it turns out, only a short step from the absurd Café Myriam to the great social questions that rock our age.

A Bridegroom for Marcela concentrates openly on the themes of arbitrary guilt, free will, and violence. Again the fable that illustrates these questions is amusing, at least at the start: the quiet clerk Kliment is asked to present himself at a higher office because, he is told, he apparently wants to marry a young woman, Marcela Lukášová, who lives in the same apartment block. This is a complete surprise to Kliment whose connection with the girl is limited to having once helped her with the groceries. Far from having amorous designs on Marcela, he says he has his own girl whom he intends to marry. When he is finally ushered into the office after having had to wait for eight hours in the unheated waiting-room, he is tired, hungry, and cold, but he is certainly not guilty of what he is accused of – namely, having seduced Marcela Lukášová who is now expecting his child.

In the course of the play three officials work on Kliment with methods varying from moralizing rhetoric about conscience and love, to blows and a loaded pistol. At one point they actually bring in the 'bride' who shows obvious signs of a similar official interrogation and considers Kliment no less a stranger than he considers her one. The play ends with Kliment, reduced to a babbling, croaking bundle of wretchedness, collapsing of a heart attack.

The author, who had written the play in feverish haste while on a visit to London during the fateful month of August 1968, felt disappointed on later hearing about the Viennese audience's reaction to the play. Protesting against what they regarded as cynicism and violence, they completely misunderstand its intention. The beatings on stage which had offended their sensibilities were actually quite unimportant. This was proved in the later radio-play version where the author eliminated any reference to physical violence which he considers only a minor aspect of spiritual violence, for 'what could human brutality achieve without the murderous deafness, deadly dissembling and lies which are the forces that activate brutality?'[44]

It would, of course, be easy to interpret the play – particularly if we consider when it was written – as an allegory on the political events of August 1968. But while these events may have provided the momentary impulse, the play is conceived on a deeper level and deals with questions related to the great fables of mental violence of our age, like Ionesco's *The Lesson*, Dürrenmatt's *The Visit*, or Max Frisch's *Andorra*. The core of the play is actually a critique of language used as an instrument of power. Klíma had long been aware of a general and potentially dangerous development, 'the increasing distance of words from their original meaning.'[45] We can all think of instances in this cliché-ridden world of ours when the confusion between concepts such as 'conviction' and 'prejudice,' 'conformist' and 'individualist,' 'right' and 'privilege' is such that we throw up our hands at a loss for any word to define the situation. Hamlet still thought himself sure of the difference between cruelty and kindness but he suggested that there is room for switches of meaning and confusion of concepts.

This deep-seated confusion of concepts is Klíma's concern. He regards it not only as 'an instrument of propaganda, as many people superficially believe, but also as an important means to undermine normal human communication – an indispensable postulate for every false image of the world.' The ordinary man in Klíma's play suddenly faces a power that does not accept what is doubtless the truth about his trivial little life. Everything he says is either ignored or turned against him. The truths he wants to communicate are blocked. But they are blocked on purpose. And here we have the basic principle of Klíma's play: 'the purposefully caused impossibility of communication.'[46]

The usual laws of language and logic have lost their value in the office where Kliment has to account for his life. When he assures the officials that he does not love the woman they want him to marry, he gets a lecture on emotions 'that beautify human relationships and are a prerequisite for a happy future of all citizens;' when he tells them that he loves his own girl, he is reminded that the office is not interested in old memories but rather 'in what you are doing today;' when he tries logic and argues that, after all, he cannot love the girl they have for him because he does not even know her, he is told that he is 'emotionally confused;' when, in the end, exhausted and delirious, he crouches on the floor and calls for 'one human being ... At least one human being ...' the officials interpret triumphantly: 'He is calling for her.'[47] They mean Marcela, of course.

It is here rather than in *The Castle* that Klíma brings Kafka 'up to date.' The conversations in Kafka's work often give the impression that the other characters speak on a different level from the hero and attach a different meaning to words. This secret change of meaning – a source of irritation and anguish to Kafka's character – Kafka sees as something mysterious and incomprehensible because the reader shares the hero's frame of mind with all its suspicions, hopes, and perception of limitations.

Klíma formulates this change in a concrete way: words are used in full awareness of their changed meaning. Take the phrase 'service to our youth'[48] repeated by the clientele of *Café Myriam* in several variations. The word 'service' here actually means 'murder.' Or consider the way the officials who try to find a bridegroom for Marcela use terms designating humanity: 'We too are human,' says one official when it is getting late and he wants to go home. 'Are you even human?'[49] another asks of Kliment. The words are used in full awareness of their changed meaning. We are reminded of Ionesco's Professor who uses language literally as a tool to commit murder. 'After all we are civilized,' writes Klíma, 'and know how to humiliate, violate, torture and kill without a single blow, without any noticeable use of force.'[50]

The Double Room, written in 1970, is a farce about a young couple, Roman and Juliet, who have rented a hotel room for a horrendous price in order to be alone together – a luxury which they have never enjoyed during their previous love-making on sofas and floors with relatives sleeping, or not sleeping in the next room. As in *Klara and Two Men* the initial situation – 'finally alone together' – quickly changes. But instead of the phone calls and a dying man next door, *The Double Room* is invaded by a motley group of people who intend to settle down for the night. The stage becomes a scene of increasing confusion, as characters pour into the room, invade the bathroom, pull out fold-away beds, beat a big drum (some of them belong to a travelling band), bicker and make passes at Juliet, as her lover looks on helplessly.

Communication between the couple and the intruders is impossible. In this respect the play reminds us of *A Bridegroom for Marcela*. However, unlike the wretched 'bridegroom,' the young couple here learn how to use the weapons that are being used by the intruders. By accepting aggressiveness, egotism, lies, and total disrespect for others as the basic rules of conduct between people, they manage to get rid of the whole crowd. Finally they are again alone in their room but their attitude has changed. The night of love can no longer take place. Sitting next to each other on the bed, their faces buried in their hands, they know that they will never be the same again. The author, surprised that one of his friends thought the work his first 'optimistic' play,[51] tells us that, on the contrary, he feels this to be 'the strongest expression of his scepticism,' because it shows people who overcome their problems by accepting and perpetuating the workings of inhuman surroundings.

With Klíma's *The Double Room* we have come a fair way from the Kafka with whom we began. Josef K. of *The Trial* had incurred guilt by rejecting in theory but accepting in practice the accusation against him, thus becoming the victim of absurdity, but also its co-creator. The absurdity in that case can crudely be defined as feeling guilt where there is none. Similarly the characters of *The Double Room* are as much the victims as they are the perpetrators of absurdity. However, the absurdity in their case could be crudely defined as refusing to see guilt where there is some.

Thunder and Lightning (1972)[52] is a hilarious one-act farce about life in one of the many regimented recreational establishments at which totalitarian regimes excel. A number of citizens arrive for what is to be a relaxing holiday at a mountain resort and soon find themselves in situations diametrically opposed to what one imagines by the free and easy holiday spirit. They are forced to take part in classes learning how to make beds according to a certain method; failure to cooperate results in not being given any breakfast, or lunch, for that matter. They are handed out keys with confusing instructions as to which doors they unlock, and soon they find out that the rooms have neither furniture nor water-tight ceilings.

As the audience laugh their way through an hour of fast-moving slapstick they get to know the individual characters: the couple who kotow to any regime; the he-man who volunteers for jobs to impress the ladies rather than for idealistic reasons; the sceptic who resents being pushed around but who backs down when he is reprimanded 'officially' through a loudspeaker; the paranoid with the persecution complex who enjoys other people's fights; the adolescent who translates manuals on sexual behaviour to any female who will lend an ear; the military vacation-group leader who mouths completely arbitrary and absurd rules and regulations with a gospel teacher's intensity and a robot's mechanistic phraseology.

From the first moment the audience know that the vacationers are bound for disaster. As the speed of the action increases, a thunderstorm begins to roar outside and the group leader assigns the vacationers to a variety of incredible jobs, such as holding up the lightning rod on the roof or the grounding cable near the oil-storage and handing out rubber-soled boots and notebooks for metereological notations for greater efficiency. When, after a terrible clap of thunder and a flash of lightning, one of the characters comes staggering onto the stage with singed clothes to call for help because lightning has struck, the leader of the group cannot be found. He has departed with the most attractive of the lady-vacationers to provide her with refuge and holiday pleasure in his sheltered villa in the valley, which has not only a swimming pool but also a canopy-bed and a lightning-rod.

The message is clear: the rules are arbitrary and exist for their own sake; truth, as the cynical saying goes, has been buried so deep that no one can find it; people who have come to escape routine and seek freedom and play find another form of regimentation; people's sense of guilt is used as a lever for any action; crass rule of power masquerades as objectivity; the slogan 'equal opportunity' provides a smoke screen for arbitrariness, favouritism, and force alike.

An East European audience – which, of course, has not seen the play – would obviously savour the basic situation portrayed in *Thunder and Lightning* in an active way because the play derives its humour from vast exaggerations – but not necessarily distortions – of the reality they know. A Western audience could enjoy the high-spirited theatrics and, on a more thoughtful level, they would be bound to recognize certain aspects of their own lives. The implication, for example, that a place of pleasure can quickly engulf those who are taking care of it in unpleasant, harrassing, and even dangerous tasks might strike a bell for many people, from the weekend cottager to the owner of a sailboat or a coin collection.

Here again a startling thought wedges its way through the argument. The audience of Eastern Europe has someone to blame for the characters' predicament. Their reactions – lucid recognition of parallels to reality, informed amusement, pleasure in seeing on stage the revelation of unmentionable topics – will be anything but ambiguous. The Western audience, if indeed they recognize the threads that lead to their own lives, will be puzzled and perhaps none too comfortable. Kafka, even in fancy dress, is never comfortable.

But then again, as Topol's Vena puts it: 'That's not inclination. That's life.' Kafka's Joseph K. would have liked this quotation. So, surprisingly, would many twentieth century dramatic characters who are put by their authors into situations where accepting and perpetuating – or stopping to question but then carrying on – has become their chief concern. Herr Everyman of Max Frisch's *The Fire Raisers* has as much claim to this as Beckett's Winnie from *Happy Days*.

Games[53] was written in 1973 and translated into German from the typescript (the playwright made some changes to the Czech original while the translation was taking place). Here Klíma takes up the theme of guilt and innocence in yet a new way. As was apparent in the four black comedies, the initial atmosphere of the play seems miles away from Kafka's world. However, while the characters play the 'games' announced in the title, a dark, threatening reality begins to emerge from the cheerful surface like a terrifying monster from the bubbling waves of a peaceful lake.

Again the play revolves around the concepts of right and wrong, freedom and justice, but the lattice-work of guilt and innocence is much more complex than in Klíma's earlier plays. For example, while the 'victim' in *The Jury* or *A Bridegroom for Marcela* was clearly innocent, Kamil Sova, the man who is about to be hanged innocently at the end of *Games*, is partly a volunteer with complex motivations, partly a relativist, and partly an uneasy cross between idealism and resignation whose active imagination makes him sympathize as much with the average citizen who pulls the wool over his own eyes as with the revolutionary who believes 'We must buy weapons, print books, influence world opinion.'[54]

However, despite this seemingly undramatic complexity, *Games* shows Klíma's dramatic genius at its best. The action consists of a group of people meeting at a friend's house for an evening of games. The friendly hostess, Irena, had thought it would be nice to invite a few people and 'just play games rather than talk about politics and such awful things.' – 'You know,' she explains to the guest who arrives first, 'simply forget that we are grown-ups and that the whole ugly world pushes itself on us.'[55] Gradually the other guests arrive and several games are played – though with resistance for various reasons by the people taking part.

There are six games: three in the first act and three in the second. The scenes are named after the particular games: Meddling, Charades, Taking Hostages, Court Procedures, Spiritual Affinities, and Execution. The games become increasingly sinister and dangerous. Imperceptibly, while all kinds of fun are choreographed on the stage and the audience are brilliantly entertained, they are made to witness how a game turns into reality, how guilt and innocence are judged arbitrarily, how the past of each participant comes into play and changes the nature of the game, how the elusive phenomenon of implicit guilt becomes more frightening than a real, explicit crime, how a henchman and a victim are found and accepted, and how each character plays his or her part in the general destruction of justice.

Again the characters are a cross-section of modern society. There is the perfect hostess and excellent cook, Irena, the naive inventor of the disastrous games idea, a sentimental, motherly woman who would not harm a fly but who, if something terrible is happening close by, bends over her salad bowl, slicing and measuring, paying meticulous attention to the delicate balance of the ingredients. Obviously she is too busy to notice anything else. Besides, although she knows that 'fate is evil,' she is also convinced that 'we people are not.'

Her husband Filip, a former judge, is haunted by the accusing ghosts of his past verdicts. He cannot stand games in which people are blind-folded and the thought of loaded guns makes him shiver. When, during the charades, he is made to represent the Statue of Liberty (incidentally a dramatically brilliant and hilarious scene), no one is able to recognize his representation of freedom. In a later game, he prefers to act the Court Attendant who simply ushers people in and out and watches the proceedings as an outsider who is not responsible for anything.

During the last game, the Execution, however, he is once again cast in the role of the legal authority who reads out the verdict. This time he takes on the part with gusto because it gives him the opportunity to deliver an impassioned speech in which he claims that the position of a judge 'is nothing but a codified form of injustice because it serves power and not justice'; he confesses, 'I tell you, I have known for a long time that whenever I put on legal robes I become an actor who can do nothing but improvise.' And he continues, telling his listeners about the throngs of persecuted people of all times who died on galleys, in exile, in gas chambers, on the gallows, in ditches; as he sees this mass of people moving toward him, huge and relentless, he knows that there is no way out but to repeat his initial verdict, to judge them, 'to judge again, once again, to condemn those innocent ones, because they are the ones who call most passionately for a justice that does not exist.'[56]

Among the guests is the fat and prosperous Deml, who can afford a beautiful young actress for a mistress. It is Deml whose past, as the games reveal more and more clearly, is the truly criminal one. He has murdered a young woman whose body he disposed of in a garbage truck. But this crime seems melodramatic, crass, and unreal amidst the complex games of right and wrong. As the surface of the game cracks and Deml's murderous past comes to light, his crime seems like a decoy, realistic yet unreal, somehow out of step with the vast dimensions of the rest of the play.

Eva, his mistress, is the most enthusiastic game-playing guest. Apart from sexual games, which she plays to perfection, she likes any game at all. She eagerly acts any part, from charade guesser, to hijacked passenger, to prosecuting attorney, to henchman's assistant. She does it all with panache, finds everything fascinating, and does not mind much which of the other eligible males she will seduce the next evening – the muscleman or the bookworm.

The former, Jacob, is an avid sportsman who flies around the world wherever his team is sent, who communicates in the clipped sentences of the sports 'pro,' who acts the witness for the prosecution with the same slow-witted pedantry with which he does muscle-building exercises 'according to the Kaiserschad-Kowalski method.'[57]

His opposite, Peter, a thoughtful scientist, cool and collected behind the book he insists on reading most of the evening, is the ironic observer of the cruel ways and games of man. His occasional aphorisms reveal him as the author's spiritual kin: he remarks that 'not only he who carries out violence serves its purpose but also he who submits to it;' or else he refers to 'judgments which will be made only years later. Or centuries later, or never.' It is Peter who plays the Judge during the trial of the real crime, who knows whenever anyone plays the part best suited to him, who, after having asked in vain whether anyone wants to hear the verdict before they hang an innocent man, draws the conclusion which makes up the last words of the play: 'They don't hear me. How very busy they are.'[58]

Then there is Bauer, a nondescript bully of fifty, who becomes sociable only when he talks about guns or tells stories from his own – if we are to believe him – colourful past. Chagall, he claims, once gave him one of his priceless paintings just as a small tit-for-tat gesture; or Duke Schwarzenberg shared his bunk during their internment in the fifties. It appears that Bauer 'made always good,' as he would put it himself in his crude lingo. Fascinated by the loaded gun which he has detected on the wall, he begins to handle it playfully and soon wields it with much pleasure and know-how, whether acting the part of a Revolutionary or a member of the State Militia. The last game, Execution, is Bauer's own idea, and he organizes and casts it with great efficiency. At the end it is Bauer who gives the command for the hanging which is interrupted, not by anyone shouting 'Stop it!' as the guests had hopefully imagined, but by the falling curtian. The audience will never know the end of the game.

Last but not least there is Kamil Sova, a gentle homespun philosopher who is the first guest to arrive. He is intrigued by Madame Irena's salads from the culinary as much as from the philosophical point of view (because he realizes that the relationship of certain ingredients and how they affect each other could be transferred to an abstract argument of values with most revealing results). Sova – incidentally the only character who has both a first and a last name – is rather a poor actor but he has a lot of imagination. Too much, in fact. He has imagined what it is like to be a prisoner, what a man feels before he is executed, how one would talk to a man before he goes to his death; he used to dream of being a revolutionary but somehow he has lost the belief that the world can be changed. The ingredients are such that the salad – or the world – is bound to turn out to be of a certain kind.

But it is Sova who recognizes the symbol of freedom even in its most awkwardly represented form: Filip impersonating the Statue of Liberty. Sova's roles, we realize, probably run parallel to the roles he played in his real life. They progress from an idealistic hijacker (who has written books like 'On Truth, Justice, and its Enemies') to witness for the defence of a real criminal, to innocent victim at the Execution. However, as his hands are tied, he lifts them into the air and calls out his own credo of freedom: 'These are not the worst fetters. Power and false beliefs put us into much tighter chains.' To be chained and rendered helpless is for Sova 'an extraordinary experience ... only now do I become aware of its [the world's] real dimension ... all of a sudden, by means of this (lifts his tied hands) I feel unified with all those who perhaps have not even a notion that their hands are tied too.' As he climbs the improvised scaffold, appealing to his friends not to abandon an innocent man to the henchman's hands, Peter, the commentator, raises his eyes from his book: 'He acts brilliantly! Finally he has found the part that's right for him.'[59]

If in *The Double Room* Kafka was turned inside out, in *Games* he is conjured up. As Kafka's seemingly innocuous corridors, offices, pubs, or studies become threatening places where dark forms of guilt are relentlessly revealed, so the cosy living room where a hostess welcomes her guests for an evening of fun gradually turns into a solemn court of justice – a grim place of execution. Kafka's haunting metamorphosis of an average young man into a giant beetle is at work in Klíma's play: a sex bomb becomes the henchman's helper; a kindhearted matron, who would unlock the chains of any prisoner if she got the chance, becomes an indifferent witness of brutality; a judge becomes a robot; an academic becomes a policeman. Kafka's salesman had changed into the beetle in his sleep before the story started. In Klíma's case the metamorphosis takes place before our very eyes; when we realize what has happened, it is too late. The deformation has taken place. The one man who has not joined the general behaviour is isolated and stares in horror at his fellow men.

Klíma's Kamil Sova[60] expresses three emotions when he mounts the scaffold at the end of the play and the end of the 'Game': horror of his fellow men, conviction that he is innocent, and regret about the loss of human dignity. 'It is all so undignified!'[61] are his last words. It was Kafka who spent his life drawing for us a meticulously graphic picture of modern man's loss of dignity, of his deformation into performing mechanized functions, of his loss of human consciousness. Jan Grossman, calling Kafka 'the first poet of automization of the modern world,' put it in these words: 'Dostoevsky's characters are people subdued by deformation who strive against it. In Kafka's case the main character is deformation itself which still keeps its human likeness and strives against humanity.'[62]

In 1974 Klíma and Kohout decided to dramatize Kafka's novel *Amerika*, six years after the Prague Spring and after all creative voices except those who completely adhered to the Communist party line had been silenced. Theirs was a poignant attempt once more to illuminate – literally, put into the limelight – Kafka's prophetic and, in the most basic sense of the word, *political* vision of the horrendous danger of man's automization. The danger can manifest itself in the organized murder of people or in – a spiritual kind of murder – the organized destruction of human individuality and dignity. From *The Castle* to *The Jury*, from *Amerika* to *Games*, this realization is the deep bond between Kafka and Klíma's work.

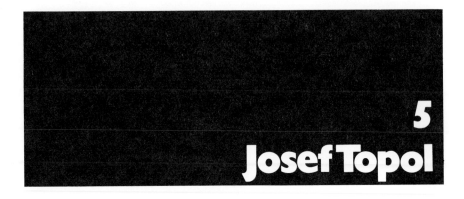

5

Josef Topol

VÉNA What are you afraid of?
EVI Nothing. Especially of nothing.   Josef Topol *Cat on the Rails*

Josef Topol has been called the greatest poetic talent in the Czech theatre
since the Second World War. His genius was recognized when he was still
very young and he had the invaluable attention and co-operation of outstanding men like Otomar Krejča and Karel Kraus. It is impossible to
predict his further development but it can be said that his work, as it stands
now, occupies a place in Czech literature similar to that of Samuel Beckett
in English and French literature: the poet-philosopher struggling with life's
timeless questions and the craftsman re-creating the language of people
around him with inimitable precision.

   In 1964, when Topol's *The End of the Carnival* was produced at the
National Theatre in Prague, the path seemed clear for a Czech version of
Beckett to make its entrance. However, Topol's spiritual kinship to the
great Western poet of futility is by no means immediately apparent. It
emerges gradually. In fact everything about Topol seems to happen gradually. His particular way of disclosing the basic problem of each play slowly,
even hesitatingly, as if he were avoiding facing it openly, can also be
applied to his whole development as a dramatist. The plays which overtly
explore the absurd aspects of human life were written only after he had
completed three full-length plays which cover the spectrum from historical
romanticism to contemporary realism.

   Wind at Midnight – his first play, produced when he was in his early
twenties – is a poetic drama on a theme from Czech history modelled on
Shakespeare's history plays. It was immediately hailed as the work of an

outstanding poet. Much was expected from this writer's future. It was felt that if Topol would fully recognize the nature of his own talent, *Wind at Midnight* would turn out to be 'only a modest prologue to the rest of his dramas.'[1] Indeed, Topol worked out his responsibility to his particular type of genius step by step until the moment when he, too, had to fall silent.

His second play, *Their Day* (1959), was about life in a small Czech town. Although there are definite signs of Topol's later 'absurd' style, *Their Day* is still contained within realistically conceived family life. In this play the urgent questions about life's meaning are still embedded in a conflict between youth and age which masks their existential nature. The play could be said to be about 'the generation gap' but in reality it is much more complex. The intricate pattern of relationships involves a whole network of tensions between those grasping for security, believing in making the effort to gain 'firm ground under your feet,' and those who 'are always looking for something and never finish looking.' The climactic scene, a discussion between father and son, crystallizes these tensions into an opposition between imaginative man who believes that a human being is more than a bundle of bone tissue and biochemical reflexes and realistic man who believes in science with its 'logic, law and order' and who considers symbolist painting and literature 'charlatanism and irresponsible game-playing.'[2] It is a problem that is as old as it is new: Hamlet's questioning spirit will always clash with closed mentalities whose rigid beliefs are based not on knowledge but on ignorance slumbering behind a wall of clichéd thoughts and half-truths for popular consumption.

In Topol's third play, *The End of the Carnival* (1963), this type of conflict has become the central concern; but it has also become increasingly difficult to define. The complexity arises from the intricate use of a dramatic device Topol had already touched upon in *Their Day* – the play within the play, the mask pretending to express reality and the face under the mask.

A Czech critic reviewing the première of one of Topol's plays introduced his remarks with a quotation from a poem by Vladimír Holan:

Because she had glued on freckles and a wig
she testified how much more real a tree is in artificial light
Because we are not nature.
That is where our fear comes from,
fear of death ...[3]

If Holan had intended to write a poem about the 'stuff' Topol's plays 'are made on,' he could not have done any better. From *The End of the Carnival* on the playwright's work pivots on questions involving the nature of illusion, the nature of death, and the reality of ideas as opposed to the reality of matter. All this, however, does not mean that Topol's work is weighed down by philosophical abstractions. In fact, it is most important that his plays be seen on stage and not only read. Otomar Krejča, aware of how the author had prepared the theatrical possibilities of his plays and how he had counted on the dynamic tension between his written dialogue and the bodies and voices of the actors, used his talent to magnify this tension. He did it by 'obstructing the words with theatre;'[4] by counterpointing the characters' groping search for meaning with a gracefully assured choreography of their bodies.

Once Topol had arrived at the theatrical economy of his three one-act plays, *Cat on the Rails, Nightingale for Dinner*, and *An Hour of Love* (written between 1964 and 1968) he had moved into the radius of Beckett's and Pinter's absurd worlds. *The End of the Carnival* (1963) seemed a far cry from Beckett's tramps. *Cat on the Rails* (1965) and *Waiting for Godot*, however, have much in common. *Nightingale for Dinner* (1965), with its ritualistic inevitability, again reminds us of Pinter. As in the latter's *The Birthday Party*, for example, we have the feeling that we witness a kind of timeless ritual – but a ritual without belief. This is not to be taken in the sense that these playwrights regurgitate Nietzsche's badly maltreated aphorism of God being dead, but rather in the sense that, as they unfold one question after another, the possibility of finding any kind of truth gradually seems to fade.

When Topol's producer Karel Kraus, himself an outstanding literary critic, distinguished the playwright's work from the dramatists of the Absurd, he made one particularly important observation: The Theatre of the Absurd, Kraus argued, does not really demonstrate the fundamental situation of man – the incoherent, senseless nature of the world – but rather establishes it as a given entity. It is therefore 'the author himself who fixes the rules of the game.'[5] This attitude of inequality in relation to the audience remains alien to Topol who, like Beckett, entices – or inspires – the spectator to follow the author to increasingly deeper, more rarefield, yet at the same time more universal levels of meaning.

At the end of the mysterious *Two Nights with a Girl* (1969), for example, the characters suddenly stop in their high-spirited chase around the table, and each stands frozen in another place staring in a different direction. Then one of them slowly asks: 'What are we laughing at, we fools?'[6] The audience, having joined the characters in their uncalled-for merriment for some time, are likely to stop laughing with a start. What indeed have they been laughing at? A kaleidoscoped performance of a man's confusions, disappointments, hopes and fears?

Because of Topol's highly developed sense of the theatre, his plays will vary greatly with the intellect and perceptions of a particular director. For our purpose they are best regarded as magnificent works of dramatic poetry – a parallel to W.B. Yeats comes to mind – which refuse to yield their full meaning no matter how often they are read or seen.

Like Harold Pinter, Josef Topol has an acute sensitivity for spoken language with all its repetitions, unfinished thoughts, non sequiturs, pauses, and awkward formulations. Like Václav Havel and Peter Handke he is, on the one hand, aware of the increasing alienation of words from their original meaning, and on the other, of the concealed power of language to mould and change man's intellect and his perceptions. Havel attacks clichés – bureaucratic, emotional, and conceptual. His target is clear and we can take an intellectual delight in the precision of his attack. Topol is more complex then Havel, and like Handke – but nonprogramatically and without the latter's intellectual aggressiveness – he takes on the whole area of language and communication as such. The interesting thing is that this is at first hardly noticeable.

Topol's concern with language is part of his general quest for the meaning of life or the nature of truth. It seems to be just one of the natural results of his explorations of the human psyche. If we think of Handke as arriving at his definition of man through studying his language, we might say that Topol, more like Pinter, arrives at his definition of language through studying man. His characters communicate in a defective, rambling, interrupted way which demonstrates how fine an ear the author has for the average person's language.

Yet, despite its deceptively realistic cadence, the language of Topol's characters is not a mere copy of the language spoken in, say, a Bohemian village or the streets of Prague. Without losing its colloquial immediacy it constantly reaches down into the subconscious of the character and reveals his struggle to understand himself and others. In *Cat on the Rails*, for example, we get the following exchange:

EVI *Reproaching her lover for not wanting to marry and let her raise a family* You are afraid of your duty, that's it. You just don't want to face up to it.
VÉNA I'm not good enough for it.

EVI If everybody thought like that! What about actors?

VÉNA Oh, they just play it.

EVI Don't you see the way things are organized? Some things you do for yourself. Others are – well – written out for you.

VÉNA Who wrote them out?

EVI God. City Hall. How do I know?

VÉNA Nobody knows. They just pretend they know. Everybody pretends to everyone else. And nobody knows a damn thing.[7]

We may notice that in the course of the conversation there suddenly comes a point when the words seem to become transparent and we realize that the author is talking about something quite different from what he seemed to be talking about. It is as if another dimension has appeared behind the situation at hand and allowed us to look through the texture of the language, beyond the place and hour at which the action takes place. Past and future open up and the next thing we know, in the middle of a conversation on a rather banal issue, we are made to think about life's unanswerable questions, about the nature of time and the certainty of death, about the ambiguity of love and the imperfection of man's understanding of his fate. It is as if Topol put to our eyes a pair of strong binoculars: every detail becomes magnified, almost touchable in its clarity and closeness; then all of a sudden the playwright imperceptibly reverses the binoculars and we see the same situation removed, merging with its context so that its details become blurred and only the basic, abstracted outline remains. This change of focus, this mingling of realistic detail with a mystical search for the nature of life, is the main key to Topol's work.

To achieve this is, of course, not an easy task for a dramatist. Topol knew it: 'Modern science and technology have given power into man's hands,' he remarked. 'Man can change the world into heaven or hell. There are only these two possibilities. Everyone bears his responsibility. In such a precarious situation man truly becomes the key: also ignorance and passive indifference can commit great evil. And what should the poet do?'[8] When Topol said this he was still very young.

It was during the painstaking rehearsals of *Their Day* at the National Theatre[9] during the 1959–60 season that the young playwright had the invaluable opportunity of working with two outstanding men of the theatre, Otomar Krejča, who directed, and Karel Kraus, who produced the play. As a closely working team the three men kept polishing the play's language and perfecting it to the smallest detail, continuing their work even after the play had begun to run. It takes a great deal of mental discipline and artistic assurance for a young author to stand such a test. But Topol stood it. We are told that he changed some of the dialogue even after the eighty-fifth performance of the play.[10] It was during those months of intense work, supported by his own experience as an actor, that the playwright developed the unique dramatic style we find in his later plays from *The End of the Carnival* (1963) through *Two Nights with a Girl* (1969).

On the face of it *The End of the Carnival* (1963) is a realistic play about a village which is celebrating the end of winter with a traditional masquerade. During the festivities an old problem is revived – the tension between those villagers who have adopted commune farming and the old farmer Král who has persistently refused to join the commune. In their high-spirited mood of celebration and fun the masked villagers play a trick on Král by talking his feeble-minded son Jindřich into playing the 'corpse of winter'[11] in their procession and letting them carry him around in an open coffin. His father, appalled when he finds this out, punishes his son in the presence of the assembled villagers. This humiliation awakens feelings of revenge in the child-like youth and ultimately leads to his death. It is Raphael – a young man from town courting Král's daughter Marie – who accidentally kills Jindřich. At the end Raphael faces justice (something he has been avoiding all his life) but also wins Marie who publicly confesses her love for him.

Taken like this, the play sounds like a work straight out of nineteenth-century German Poetic Realism; or else, if we stress the subtle individualization of the characters, it might pass as a Naturalistic dramatic reproduction of a locality; or else, if we read the entry on Topol in Crowell's *Handbook of Contemporary Drama* and find that the play is described as dealing with 'the life of the younger generation in the new conditions of cooperative-farm villages,'[12] we are bound to think that the play is a latecomer to Socialist Realism and we may doubt that Topol could find a place on the roster of international playwrights. What kind of a play is it then? Why then has it been produced most successfully in Germany as well as in France? Why – and this is even more surprising – did its Prague producer Karel Kraus write a lengthy essay[13] in which he spent several pages distinguishing Topol's work from the Theatre of the Absurd? Surely he would not need to do this if Topol had merely written a study of Czech village life.

As we will see, in Topol's work following *The End of the Carnival*, knowledge of the story tells very little indeed about the work itself. Consisting of a complex field of relationships and tensions, his plays contain a symbolic pattern that counteracts the realistic elements of the plot. In this way we get highly dramatic and realistic incidents combined with an overall effect that is symbolic and lyrical. It is as if throughout *The End of the Carnival* the audience were made to witness how the raw stuff of life is transformed into a poet's work of art under their very eyes. Both the realistic and the poetic levels of the play have their focal point in Jindřich, Král's child-like son, who provides the tangible reason for the clash and at the end becomes its victim.

At one point Jindřich, surrounded by the masked villagers whose leader is dressed up in a Hussar's colourful coat, playfully borrows the Hussar's sword and begins to draw an image of himself in the sand. Studying his drawing, he comments thoughtfully: 'It is as if I was alive but something was missing':

MASK dressed as a Hussar *seizing the sword and pushing it with a thrust into the drawn figure* This!
JINDŘICH *catching his hand* What are you doing!
HUSSAR You are dead.
JINDŘICH Oh no, I have a wrinkle on my forehead.
two masks are bringing in the coffin without a lid
HUSSAR It's time, your majesty.
JINDŘICH Ah yes. *steps into the coffin*[14]

The relationship between the named, indentified villagers and the anonymous, unpredictable throng of masks indicates another aspect of the tensions between the realistic and the poetic level of the play. The three young people, for example, whose fate is at the centre of the action – Marie, her brother Jindřich, and he lover Raphael – become for a brief spell members of the masked crowd and merge with it beyond recognition. Indeed, the fact that one of them cannot be recognized for who he really is turns out to be the cause of a tragic death. It is in the mask of the Hussar that Raphael accidentally kills Jindřich. Earlier Jindřich's image in the sand had been 'killed' by the Hussar; later the living Jindřich is killed by the image of the Hussar with Raphael hidden beneath.

Each of the three young people joins the masks for the wrong reason: Marie in order to escape the man to whom she will vow loyalty at the end of the play; Raphael in order to hide the identity which he must fully confess in the final scene; Jindřich because he has the literal mind of a child and does not grasp the difference between symbol and reality (he also takes the coffin balanced on four shoulders for a horse) – a tragic confusion that brings about his early death.

To regard the play therefore as a Hegelian drama of social tensions where the old order (Král's belief in individual property) finally succumbs to the values of a changing world (the new cooperative order) is about the same as interpreting *Hamlet* (as Brecht once did – playfully though) as a work about the replacement of a rotten monarchy by a new progressive government. Czech critics themselves are quite aware of the relatively small importance of the play's sociological aspect. Even in the program notes to the production at the National Theatre Karel Kraus stresses the broad meaning of the play. 'Where the social tensions between the members of the organization and its structure as a whole have been solved, the existential tension between the complex and never completely organizable world of the individual and the world as a whole emerges with increasing urgency.'[15] This, on the one hand, leads back to classical tragedy but on the other is directly related to Ionesco's plea that 'if anything ought to be demystified, it is ideologies that offer ready-made solutions ... Everything ought to be constantly re-examined in the light of our anguishes and our dreams ...'[16]

This is precisely what Topol does in his next play, *Cat on the Rails*. He examines life through the consciousness of two people's anguishes and dreams and does not tell us whether a solution can be found.

The first of Topol's short plays, *Cat on the Rails*, was written in 1964 and produced in November 1965 at the Theatre Behind the Gate under Otomar Krejča's direction. The play is essentially a dialogue between two people who, though young, are not as young as they used to be (both are nearing thirty). Nor is their relationship – limited to week-ends, when they go into the country with rucksacks – as exciting as it was seven years ago when it began. Things have gone a little stale all around. The action takes place late one Sunday evening when, after one of their habitual weekends, the couple wait at a railway-stop for the train that is to take them back to their lives in the city – her to her work as a waitress, him to his work as furniture mover and his life at home under the daily influence of his nagging mother.

Their conversation as they wait *is* the play. Surrounded by the darkness of night they talk and fall silent, play and attack, caress and tear at each other, reach out and push back, tell lies and speak the truth – gradually unmasking themselves and each other until they sit exhausted on the rails that lead back where they do not want to go. At the end of the play the roar of the approaching train deafens the audience's ears as the stage falls into darkness. The question of whether the couple die on the rails or take the train back to town should not have worried critics as much as it did. A prominent Czech critic, for example, feels that the end is absurd and not worthy of the play because it contradicts not only its general meaning but also the character of Evi, the girl.[17] A German critic, on the other hand, regrets that this brilliant piece of writing ends with facile tragedy like a cheap novel.[18] Others, again, believe that the author intended an open ending.[19]

Whatever the intention of the author, the ending is simply not that important. Whether the two die there and then or go back to their deadly lives in town where 'nothing is of any consequence anyway,'[20] does not change the fact that the whole play has been a show-down with what life and death really mean. During their inimitable discussion – held (according to stage instructions) while they sit, run, creep on the roof of the shack, balance on the railway track, try to light cigarettes without matches, lie in each other's lap or play games – they cover the spectrum of human life. Take their exchange on the sources of joy:

EVI You could play tennis.
VÉNA Tennis!
EVI White trousers, racquet under your arm –
VÉNA Knock myself silly chasing that ball? And run after that white phantom until you go nuts –
EVI Oh well, if that's all you see in it ... what is one to do with you? Your rob yourself of so much beauty – and you don't even know how.
VÉNA I got you – just enough for me.
EVI I'm cold.[21]

A little later Véna admits his ambiguous attitude to emotional commitment and the nature of responsibility: 'I would tell you that I love you, cross my heart, if I could be sure I wouldn't live till tomorrow.' Or take the couple's two-line aphorisms on loneliness:

VÉNA *complaining that Evi is talking too much* One should be alone.
EVI One is alone, anyway.

And then there is the act of waiting itself, that long wait for everything in life which does not necessarily come:

VÉNA The train isn't coming – I've got to do something.
  EVI Does something have to happen all the time? Can't we just be ... just like that?

VÉNA You can't even wait just like that ... mouth keeps going.

EVI The way we used to go off to the country ... just take off – It was marvellous. It was quite enough for us. It was beautiful.

VÉNA You know, you can lead a horse to water but one day the river's dry.

EVI Oh, forget it.

VÉNA Well, stop needling me.

EVI As if *I* could needle you. Me!

VÉNA You sure can.

EVI I know, time seems too long when you're with me now.

VÉNA God, how I love it – that long time growing longer ...

EVI Ah, pipe down![22]

Composed like a work of music, with the same themes coming up in different keys in the three parts (the author calls them 'situations'), the dialogue gains in depth and urgency as both partners become increasingly honest and bring to the surface the innermost traits of their characters, their mutual relationship, and their lives as a whole. Three times the outside world intrudes and distracts their attention from each other, only to bring them back with a redoubled intensity. At the beginning of each 'situation' we get a snatch of the story of Ivan, a boy from a neighbouring village who had been dancing at a barn dance with someone else's girl, and was now being pursued by the jilted lover together with the girl's brother. At the beginning of the play Ivan and later his two pursuers come rushing on stage, and the audience is informed about the incident at the same time as Evi and Véna. Again, as in the case of *The End of the Carnival*, there is an additional audience on stage. The difference, however, is that Ivan's story turns out to be on the periphery of the play and of no great interest to either audience.

As things proceed, the fortunes of those other lovers from the village dance become increasingly incidental, even disturbing in relation to the main concern of the play. The author is well aware of this: step by step he reduces the importance of these intrusions – both in dramatic intensity and in the time period they occupy. When Ivan first comes rushing in in order to hide in the station shack, he literally steps on the couple in the dark and the play actually begins with a shriek of physical pain from Véna, quite unrelated to the pain of living he will reveal in the time to come. The pursuers, irate avengers in the first part, return in the second part with their tempers considerably cooler. Showing unmistakable signs of the wear and tear of their unsuccessful pursuit, they are anxious to get home irrespective of whether their mission is completed.

In the third part only the boy returns once again, very quietly this time –

the stage instruction calls for a whisper – and very briefly. The respresentatives of the world outside have rapidly diminished. Furthermore, while in the first part Evi and Véna discussed the village event for some time after the pursuers had gone, the last appearance of the boy only triggers a bitter exchange about their own relationship. The more acute the tension between the lovers, the less interested the audience (and they themselves) become in the peripheral plot of the other lovers. However – and here Topol is at his theatrical best – as our indifference to the village lovers grows, we begin to regard the interruptions more and more as a kind of relief from the emotionally draining exchange of the main characters. And as the dialogue becomes increasingly a question of life and death, we need these moments of relief as much as the main characters need them.

One of the strangely magic qualities of this little play is that everything in it at the same time is and is not. What seemed to be a plot turned out to be an inconsequential murmur from the world outside; what seemed to be an indifferent wait for a weekend train revealed itself as a time of reckoning with life. This same ambiguity applies also to the main characters: they are a couple and yet not a couple; they live together but only on weekends; they sleep together but never in a bed; they cannot face the thought of the future with each other because, as Véna puts it, 'We are each other's past. We remind each other of each other.'[23]

Nightingale for Dinner was written in 1965. The English title does not convey the ambiguity inherent in the original Czech title, *Slavík k večeři*. In English we might think of an exotic dinner party where song birds are served stuffed with delicacies; the Czech connotation is quite different. Besides meaning nightingale, 'Slavík' is a fairly common Czech name, and to have Mr Slavík to dinner is as likely an occurrence as entertaining a Mr Brown or Mr Smith in an English-speaking country. The fact that Slavík, the song bird, can be had as a dinner guest or a dinner bird gives the Czech title a semi-sinister ring.

This one-act play has again a very simple plot: Mr Slavík has come to have dinner with a family consisting of Father, Mother, Son and Daughter. In the course of the evening he gradually realizes that his hosts intend to kill him and bury him in their garden among the graves of their many previous dinner guests. At the end of the play, Father and son perform the killing job upstairs while Mother and Daughter, regretfully but calmly, wait below.

The theme of the unsuspecting stranger who is murdered has been used before. We may remember George Lillo's *The Fatal Curiosity* (1736), in which a long absent son is taken by his parents for a rich traveller and killed;

or Zacharias Werner's German melodramatic tragedy *The Twenty-Fourth of February* (1810), a variation on the same theme. With *The Misunderstanding* (1944), Albert Camus attempted – not very successfully perhaps – a twentieth-century 'existentialist' version of the same theme. Another variation is the German writer Tankred Dorst's play *The Curve* (1966) where two mechanics make a living from repairing cars wrecked on a dangerous curve on a mountain highway; the drivers are buried with pomp and circumstance in their rock-garden cemetery.

In all these versions, however, the author provides some way of explaining the motivation for the murders. Usually it is economic: in the case of Dorst's work an additional psychological element of destructiveness is present. Not so in Topol's play. Like Pinter's *The Birthday Party*, it does not provide motivations and reasons for behaviour. An audience which looks for a rationally explicable story will fail to be satisfied by either Topol's or Pinter's play.

Beginning with what seems to be a concrete picture of average life – a family dinner with a welcome guest – *Nightingale for Dinner* (1965) is neither about a dinner nor about a murder. In fact the dinner and the murder merely frame the action: one ushers it in, the other concludes it. The play provides a poetic model of man's awareness of being and dying; his uncertainty about what is real and what is a dream; his experiences in getting used to the fact that he will never know why he was born and why he must die; his surprise at being able to experience the joy of life in the very moment of realizing the inevitability of his death – his slavery to but also his victory over time. This sounds, of course, very much like Beckett. But it also harkens back to the works of great writers of the past giving expression to the timeless tension between man's dreams of freedom and the fetters of reality: we may remember Calderon's *La vida es sueño*, Cervantes' *Don Quixote*, Shakespeare's sonnets and *The Tempest*, or Kleist's *Der Prinz von Homburg*.

When the curtain opens, dinner is almost over (though the dishes and glasses remain on the table throughout the play) and the play begins with one of the miniature 'audience on stage' scenes in which Topol excels. The family is watching while Mother is dancing with the dinner guest to the music of a shaky record player. A moment later the needle gets stuck and the same notes are repeated over and over again, forcing the couple to go through the same steps. Nightingale offers to stop the record but his partner won't let him because, after all, he is 'the guest.' There is a shouted conversation but no one makes a move to stop the unbearable repetition until the dancers, accidentally knocking into the table while passing, cause the needle to take a jump and the tune continues. The period of relief, when things again move on in their old order after the suspension of time is over, is punctuated by three remarks made by the 'audience' – the non-dancing members of the family. Father says: 'Well, there was such a lot of screaming and now, you see, it's all done.' The Son who had been beating out the repeated bars on his thigh, begins to yawn and asks: 'What now?' The Daughter gets up with the words: 'The comedy is finished.'[24] These same words, although later they are spoken in Italian, are part of her very last verbal comment in the play. After that she only hums a quiet tune.

In this way the play is introduced by a miniature grotesque – or, if you like, absurd – version of its own theme: the eternally moving pattern of growth and decay has been arrested; time has come to a stop. How has this happened? The dinner guest who bears the name of the exquisite song-bird – perhaps, though we are never explicitly told, he is a poet – has come to bring the gift of never-fading beauty. His hosts, however, fail to make an important distinction: that between the real timelessness of a dream of beauty and the deceptive timelessness of repetition. The moment of timelessness created by the repetitive sound of a mass-produced gadget is referred to at the end of the play with the same words as the actual killing of the song-bird.

The members of the family that 'kill the dream of beauty' have no names. They are rigidified in their roles as Father, Mother, Son, and Daughter, and go through the gestures sanctioned by habit with the predictability of automatons. The Daughter sits on the Mother's lap, the Father tousles his Son's hair, the Son gulps down the rest of the food from other plates. As they tell their visitor about their lives, their complaints and petty aggressions toward each other take on growing proportions. Nightingale can hardly get a word in edgeways and is limited to monosyllabic reactions. They use their guest, as they admit themselves with increasing honesty, as 'a live piece of stage property,' as 'a mirror into which we can look.'[25]

As the evening proceeds the dinner guest begins to feel increasingly uneasy. The merry atmosphere at the beginning has given way to a feeling of anxiety and guilt. The visitor begins to try to justify his existence by complying with anything that seems to be asked of him. This process is surprisingly close to Kafka's work. From an everyday, ordinary situation we are led by forces which we cannot fully grasp to face questions of crushing magnitude. Objects attain an oppressive quality, and we move with increasing uncertainty through a forest of strange signs.

One of these signs is a bouquet of flowers which Nightingale brought for the hostess. As she looks in vain for water to put them in, a discussion ensues about whether the flowers need water at all because they are probably not real. The visitor claims twice in the course of the play that 'they were real when I brought them,' but the Daughter is sure they are artificial. The Mother discovers them to be real about half way through the play, basing her conclusion on the fact that a fly has settled down on a blossom, and surely 'it wouldn't sit on an artificial one.' At the end, when Nightingale is killed upstairs, the Mother, plucking petals from the flowers, hides her face in the bouquet. The Father's final words to the Daughter are 'Think about the flowers. – You are singing to yourself? Why?'[26] These are also the very last words of the play. The remark can be taken as a reference to the care needed for a new grave in the garden – a task usually entrusted to the Daughter; but it also refers to Nightingale's bouquet – the one tangible (and perhaps living) proof that he had been there. The Father's reminder of the flowers is immediately followed by the Daughter's song. Why does she sing?

What are we to make of this play which Czech critics came to regard as Topol's 'unsuccessful journey into the Absurd?'[27] If we tried to cap it with a definitive symbolic interpretation, we would be behaving as the Mother with Nightingale's flowers: we would look for a proof of its artistic 'reality' outside its own nature. There is, however, one scene that seems to contain the central core of the play. As the death of Nightingale becomes more and more an accepted fact, there ensues a discussion between the Father and the visitor about the reason for living. It is the only time in the play that Nightingale talks at any length. In essence the two points of view are reflected in the following comments:

FATHER You are a nightingale, the king of singers, but you too depend on who is listening to you ... For one it may mean heavenly delight! And for another? A delicious little tidbit, something to sink his teeth into, nothing else ... though we walk on the ground the ground walks on us the same way, that's why we are worn out in the evening and have worn boots! – We breathe the air and the air breathes us, we spend life and life spends us ... You play a game and the game plays with you. Or doesn't it? ...

NIGHTINGALE And if you love a human being? *silence; they look at each other* If you love one, with your whole soul – *silence* If you love – ... With a human being it's different. *Nightingale approaches the Daughter* Why is it different, why? Why is it different?[28]

This question rings in our ears when we leave the theatre. If, as a Czech critic suggests, we take the figure of Nightingale as representing 'man's eternal dream of beauty and happiness; a dream that must always die when touched by everyday life,'[29] we will have found an interpretation that 'works' on all levels. But we are also closing doors which the playwright is desperately trying to open. A play that equates literal-mindedness with death in life does not deserve to be systematized by interpretation. Besides, Topol's hero goes to his death with the words, 'And whatever might happen, it will be a dream from which I will awaken.'[30] This semi-grotesque self-assertion reminds us as much of Kafka's Hunger Artist as it does of Beckett's clowns, constantly busy in asserting and proving their existence. Besides, Topol warns us of tugging too resolutely at the play's veil of mystery: he subtitles it 'a Play in a Dream.' His next work, *An Hour of Love*, takes this process a step further. Once again simple, even trivial events, acquire a metaphysical dimension and become mysterious, awesome signs. It is here that Topol's kinship with Beckett is most in evidence.

An Hour of Love (1966–7), Topol's third one-act play, recasts the theme of *Cat on the Rails*, but reduces it to essentials. Again there is a couple at the centre of the action but they are no longer anchored in a specific setting as were Evi, the waitress, and Véna, the furniture mover. Called El and Ela – man and woman – they can no longer be related to any specific social context. Rather they live, like Beckett's characters, in a vacuum of space and time. It is as if their relationship were abstracted from any incidentals; the murmur of the world outside that had interrupted Véna's and Evi's wait for the train has fallen silent.

The plot is so simple that it can hardly be called a plot at all. The setting is a room where Ela lives with her ailing aunt. At the beginning of the play her lover El arrives with the news that by order of some authority – the nature of which we never find out – he will have to leave for good. The lovers have only one more hour in each other's company. Just before the end a message arrives that cancels El's departure. When leaving he assures Ela that nothing has changed. He will be back as usual. Their last hour of love has turned out to be repeatable; a link in a monotonous chain.

The play is all about the way the two people spend what they take to be their last hour together. As in Topol's two other one-act plays the stage action and the duration of the play are equal. The audience is made to experience with painful accuracy how the moments pass – one after another, as the lovers harass each other, each trying to experience the other fully for the last time.

ELA My God, how much time we have! How much time we still have! All those seconds!

EL Only people that are desperate count in seconds.

ELA And criminals. When I say three I'll shoot. One, two, three –

EL *rocking his head from side to side* four, five, six –

ELA Seven, eight, nine, ten –

EL One, two, three –

ELA Four, five, six –

EL Seven, eight, nine –

ELA Ten. – Twenty seconds with you. *motions him to be silent* No, it's a pity!

EL A pity, a pity, a pity –

ELA Stop it! *Rises and walks about the room*

EL If we keep silent it doesn't go so fast?

ELA I'm sure it goes more slowly.

EL But the clock's ticking.

ELA *stops the clock* No more.

EL It's getting dark.

ELA (lights the lamp on the table) No more. *sits on his lap*

EL Your heart is beating.

ELA That I can't stop. – That keeps measuring my time! That keeps measuring our time!

EL We get older by seconds, by minutes, and by days.

ELA Now we are still young. One more hour!

EL No more. Not a whole hour. Now only –

ELA *interrupting him* You aren't supposed to count! ...[31]

Two elements in the play interrupt the couple's painful awareness: the call of duty and their dreams. The former takes the shape of Ela's elderly Aunt who, lying behind a partition in the same room, can hear everything, and joins into the conversation at the most inopportune moments. She complains about her doctors (but has already outlived two of them), incites Ela to play tricks on El (whom she dislikes), comments on life (for which she seems to have all the answers), and above all, interrupts the 'hour' by constant demands for her medicine, a cup of tea, or a drink from the bottle El has brought as a present. Although Ela feels 'tied down' and responds to these duties with obvious weariness, she knows that 'if I am alone, I cease to exist,'[32] and anchors her life in these daily duties which make her measure time in terms of meals and doses of medicine rather than in minutes that carry away youth.

The other element that permits the couple to escape the prison of time consists of those moments when their imagination takes over and they roam freely through past and future, telling of dreams and fears, dreams within dreams and hopes. The action is broken up into little plays within plays as the characters recount their dreams or re-enact scenes from the past – the day they met, their first experience of love, moments of particular crisis. We are never quite sure whether these things actually happened, or how much they have changed in the characters' minds by being retold and reshaped during their relationship. We hear about El's nightmare of trying to hide from irate pursuers on a tiny island with only a single tree on it (a dream which the aunt immediately interprets with 'Women's Column' platitudes); we hear about Ela's horrifying waking dream of being stuck in the earth head down after falling from the lofty heights of a tree. At other moments the lovers re-enact their first meeting: Ela, having swum across a river to dare another man who used only safe bridges, meets El on the other shore and entrusts herself to his care. Or else we witness their first night of love which was spent rather uncomfortably because Auntie was, as always, close by. But then she went to work next morning and the lovers had the whole day to themselves.

In the course of the intricate blending of past and present, imagination and reality, we see Ela gradually get physically weaker, as the certainty of being loved, which gives her the self-confidence of being able 'to walk along the edge of an abyss and not get hurt,'begins to wane. On the other hand the Aunt – in whom we gradually begin to recognize the inevitability of dying, of the flesh relentlessly taking precedence over dreams – becomes stronger and more youthful. Toward the end of the play, in the course of which she actually appears only twice, she has become a young woman sitting before the mirror with loosened hair. It is now that El tells the Aunt of his realization that the freedom without which he had thought he could not live does not exist. After some time 'A man finds out that he carries his cell with him ... drags it around everywhere, does not take a step without it, sleeps and eats and loves in it, and can't escape it ...' This is not news to the rejuvenated Aunt. With a knowing smile she retreats behind her partition.

When at the very end of the play El receives the news that he does not have to leave and 'everything can stay the way it was,' the lovers are unable to rejoice over this change which cancels all the agony of their last hour together. It had been the last hour of their love after all, as the Aunt's voice sings softly from behind. The beautiful dream of timeless love is cut short:

EL Time is not merciful. It breaks off in mid sentence. As it did to Hamlet: I can't tell you any more – And he dies.[33]

A dark play indeed. Surely the darkest Topol has written. And yet so charged with human energy that it affirms life in spite of stressing acutely its transitory qualities.

Topol's next play *Two Nights with a Girl*, completed in 1969, was not published in Czechoslovakia. On the surface it appears to be a play about a family (two daughters and two sons) who have just buried their father. In the course of their deliberations about the past and the future two visitors (or rather opportunistic intruders) arrive, falsely claim to be the late father's friends, and after causing all kinds of havoc, leave at the end of the play, having tried (unsuccessfully – a better thief beat them to it) to steal the family jewellery. The family is left alone with their father's cryptic testament, with their momentary relief at having survived the onslaught of the thieves, and with their recurring moments of confusion about the meaning of life.

This threadbare summary of the plot is, however, completely misleading. *Two Nights with a Girl* is Topol's most ambitious and complex play. It is a rare combination of slapstick and symbolism, language play and philosphical insights. The movements of the actors are described with great precision, so that the reader becomes aware that the playwright has conceived the play as a pattern of movements as much as a pattern of words. The action takes place in a house and adjoining garden. The room is crowded with a jumble of odd pieces of furniture and all kinds of musical instruments; the garden causes the characters all sorts of physical difficulties, ranging from stumbling over protruding roots to getting stuck in bogs and caught on low-hanging branches. Furthermore the stage instructions establish a rhythmic pattern of night suddenly changing into day, and vice versa. This pattern has no obvious relation to the actual passing of time but presents a dream sequence of moods such as we find in Strindberg's *A Dream Play*.

Despite the highly realistic surface action of Topol's play we soon begin to realize that the inhabitants of the house, the four children of the deceased musician-father, must not be interpreted according to a handbook of psychology. On one level they seem to represent basic human traits. There is Rosa, the rational daughter, who is trying to keep the family together but tends to be deceived by appearances; Dolf, the self-indulgent but loyal son; Emmi – the only one who could manage their late father when he was in one of his 'moods' – the down-to-earth girl whose common sense saves most situations and who always has food and drink stored in some hidden cupboard when everything seems empty and everyone is almost starved. Last but not least, there is Rudolf, the family's 'golden boy,' who has inherited his father's traits, his love of music, his wisdom, and his ability to talk to his own dreams.

On one level the play could be regarded as an allegro or capriccio variation on the *Waiting for Godot* theme: the family is trying to survive, until two strangers appear and shake their beliefs in various ways. The strangers' behaviour is alien and destructive: they not only steal jewellery and food; they also try to make off with the big prize of life, 'the fairy princess,' the ideal woman – but this venture is unsuccessful. The princess drives off in their car and they are left to pedal on to other tasks on a borrowed bicycle. When they have left, the family is no further ahead than Didi and Gogo at the end of Beckett's play.

One significant aspect of the play is the author's ability to give visual presence to even the most subtle thought process or philosophical speculation. The best example of this is the concept of the 'girl' in the title of the play. It refers partly to a figurine which dominates the stage visually from the very first moment. Later we hear that the figurine was brought for Rudolf's benefit from his brother's tailor shop. We hear Rudolf converse with it, and his sister refer to it as 'his Girl.' After the figurine has been burned in the garden, it is replaced by a living girl who moves from one male character to another, bestowing her favours and representing for each what he wants her to be. At the end no one gets her, and she makes off with the family's jewellery in a stolen car. Rudolf is the only one who grasped her essence – her changeable nature, her play-acting, the impossibility of possessing her except for an instant. Was she life? – truth? – happiness?

All through the play we feel that we are walking through a forest of symbols and that the reality we perceive is only a reflection of another reality. Realistic details – and there are many of them – somehow disintegrate in the dream atmosphere of this double reality. The apricot tree in the garden is suddenly referred to as a cherry tree, the spaghetti prepared on the stove never gets cooked, the calendar seems to work backwards (Sunday comes before Saturday), a fist fight reduces one of the characters to a twitching marionette; secondary characters appear in stylized fairy-tale numbers – for example, the cast includes Seven Musicians with Wind Instruments, Seven Hunters with Rifles, Three Men with Flashlights.

There is another aspect of the play which is very important: the linguistic. The playwright may suddenly have two characters embark on a dialogue in which they play on words and concepts, reveal the confusing power of language, and shift the meaning of the scene to an entirely different level. Take the following example:

GIRL You stay here and can calmly go on playing –

RUDOLF Who? What?

GIRL For example love.

Rudolf laughs, makes her sit on his chair, and stands behind her

RUDOLF There are many cases in human life. It's the third one that is important: With whom?

GIRL I am still staggering hopelessly around the first one.

RUDOLF Who of them, who of us.

GIRL I dread the fourth one when I get old.

RUDOLF Over whom, over what.

GIRL And you?

RUDOLF Without whom, without what, when you don't stand before me any longer.

GIRL I know another preposition.

RUDOLF You mean behind?

GIRL I mean under.

Rudolf bends down to her, they kiss ... [34]

Although in English some of the sharpness of this grammatical analysis of life is lost, we nevertheless see that the author is trying to explore and reconsider our relationship to language. He makes us rediscover, like children, the mysteries of structures which have become so familiar to us that we no longer notice them. As Ela says in another context to her lover: 'She [the Aunt] has become so used to you, that you no longer exist for her.' [35] It is habit, smothering life and gobbling up man's existence like a ravenous monster, that Topol exposes in each area of his mysterious poetic work.

In the eight plays Topol has written to date, the setting has changed considerably to accommodate the variations on his themes. The early plays are historically defined and realistically localized. *Wind at Midnight* takes place at a certain period during the Middle Ages and *Their Day* is located in a typical small town in central Bohemia with its neon signs above the pubs doors, its stodgy living rooms, its smudgy railway station with red benches and dust-covered flowers planted in wooden barrels. Although Josef Svoboda, who designed the set, used a multi-screen projection process in order to intensify the dramatic conflicts, the overall impact was a realistic one, 'as if a camera had shifted the view of a panoramic whole into the inside of several people on a certain Sunday in a certain small town.' [36]

Topol's third play, *The End of the Carnival*, which established him as a playwright of international stature, still has a concrete setting – a village with its farm houses and fields, and its barber shop. The stage here is reminiscent of a Breughel painting of a small community, half at work, half at play, teeming with life and activity. In comparing this setting with Topol's fourth (and first one-act) play, *Cat on the Rails*, one finds a surprising difference. The action takes place at night at a railway-stop – not a station but merely a stop somewhere in the country where the train passes a wooden shack by a big tree, where someone may or may not be waiting. The stop is a strange, half-real place, its existence defined only for a few moments at a time, namely when the train stops and unloads or takes on an occasional passenger. Afterwards the place sinks again into anonymity until the next fleeting moment of identification when another train stops by.

No longer a Czech town with middle-class homes, no longer a village with farms and a dance hall, but a place 'in the middle of nowhere' that has its reason for being only in having people arrive from somewhere and leave for somewhere, in directions indicated only by two seemingly endless rails. Moreover the number of characters is drastically reduced. *Their Day* has twenty-six, *The End of the Carnival* twenty-five characters. The cast of *Cat on the Rails* consists of only five characters, three of whom are on the stage only briefly and are of no central importance. Basically the play consists of a conversation between two people.

Topol's second one-act play, *Nightingale for Dinner*, moves the action into a home again. However, it is not a home conceived as part of a village or town but rather a room sealed off from the outside, where remnants of food remain permanently on the table, the only sound of the world comes from a worn-out record player, and the view is limited to a piece of garden where visitors who cannot leave – and none of them can – will be buried in a shady spot. The wide sky above the village of *The End of the Carnival* where trees were swaying in the wind has given way to a closed-off garden where nature is fostered as the guardian of death – shading and beautifying the graves of men. The only other way out of the room is the staircase leading upstairs – an area that becomes more and more sinister, as the certainty grows that this is where the visitor Nightingale will be killed. The open railway station where one stops only in order to leave again has become a locked prison with no way out.

The room in Topol's third one-act play, *An Hour of Love*, does have a door, but whoever goes out inevitably comes back. The only window is a mirror into which the girl makes a grimace at the end; a symbol of the starry sky is flattened against the prison wall, a zodiac sign – stage instructions say – is painted on the partition from behind which the authoritative voice of the Aunt crushes any notion of freedom. In Topol's second full-length play, *Two Nights with a Girl*, the room with its arbitrary assortment of furniture, its array of musical instruments which no one plays, its adjoining garden illuminated by the straying flicker of a flashlight, its stripped chandelier where only one bulb works, is, for all its seeming concreteness, a no man's land of human habitation, a place that neither is what it seems to be nor seems to be what it is. Like a house in a parable it could be found almost anywhere at any time; its reality is the higher reality of a symbol.

Topol's relation to his stage has some similarity to Ibsen, who narrowed down his dramatic world from the universal dimensions of *Peer Gynt* to the stifling rooms of *The Wild Duck* and *Rosmersholm* and then expanded it again to the airy mountains of *When We Dead Awaken*. In his staging of Topol's plays Otomar Krejča revealed his understanding of the playwright's changed expression; he realized that the increased spareness of 'realistic' and localized detail required a more fully structured inner rhythm. In his famous staging of *Cat on the Rails*, for example, Krejča achieved this rhythm by using 'the dynamics of the actors' bodies as well as their language.'[37] Especially where the lovers fight and tussle, the director managed to work out a pattern of animal leaps, a fascinating visual mixture of strength and brutal elegance.[38]

The mask, as Pirandello has told us, is a frozen form in which we constantly try to capture life because we can only perceive life when it does not move. Kierkegaard, using an opposite image to express the same thing, called life a white horse galloping past us on the other side of a high fence so that we are at any one time only able to see a fraction of it. If we were to give a label to Topol's work, we might call him the dramatist of the mask. He uses masks in each of his plays, sometimes explicitly, at other times symbolically. The 'demasking' process is a central theme in this work. We are well aware of the ambiguous quality of the mask: it hides and reveals at the same time. By concealing the identity of its wearer it releases him from personal responsibility and ushers him into the amoral sphere of anonymity.

But just because of this release from law and order it reveals and frees certain suppressed qualities; by sweeping away the borders of convention and habit it becomes a provocation to intimacy and a new form of freedom. He who dons a mask no longer plays his habitual role; having lost his set form of behavior he is free to let his innermost qualities come to the surface. In other words, the mask may identify him as the man he really is. This is precisely what has happened to one of the main characters of *The End of the Carnival*: Raphael, who, as a result of an action performed while he was masked, must now for the first time in his life face up to individual responsibility. In his case the mask meant a true identification.

The End of the Carnival is partly about a play within a play. However, not the players but the on-stage audience wear the sign of the theatre, the mask. The events taking place in the village are witnessed by the villagers who have masked themselves to celebrate traditionally the feast of Shrove Tuesday, the end of the Carnival season. The audience in the theatre thus see not only the events themselves but also observe the other audience – the masked villagers – who are instrumental in bringing about the catastrophe without being aware of their active part in it.

Faced with a sort of mirror image of themselves on the stage, the theatre audience are made to observe an attitude common to most people in everyday life: that of a partly informed onlooker who makes judgments on very scanty information, the scantiness of which he fails to realize himself. What is shown on stage therefore is an event and at the same its interpretation by society. Unlike Brecht, however, who instructs his audience carefully about the reasons for the events taking place, Topol does everything possible to avoid evoking definite judgment. On the contrary, the image of justice in his plays remains unclear. Because the playwright refuses to freeze it into a certain form, to give it a mask of timeliness, it remains unreachable, even inconceivable in its entirety, like Kierkegaard's white horse on the other side of the fence.

At first glance Topol's next play, *Cat on the Rails*, is a play entirely without masks. But its staging at the Theatre Behind the Gate in Prague during the 1965/66 season proved otherwise. The double bill announced an unlikely companion piece for the evening: Ghelderode's farce *Masquerade from Ostend*. As it turned out, however, the two plays were not strangers at all. Even before the lights went down, fragments of taped conversations of *Cat on the Rails* were heard in the audience, and as people were leaving, the main musical motif from *Masquerade from Ostend* accompanied them out of the theatre. When Ghelderode's play had finished, the masks taken off by the characters were left lying front-stage in full view. During the second part of the evening two people were taking off their masks metaphorically while sitting by a railway track in the place where the masks had been lying before. At the end of the play, as the train for which the lovers had been waiting approached, the rising roar of the engine mingled with the musical motif of Ghelderode's play, increased for a brief moment to an almost unbearable fortissimo, and then abruptly ceased, and the stage fell into darkness.[39]

Topol's third one-act play, *An Hour of Love*, was also staged in a play-within-a-play context. It ran at the Theatre Behind the Gate together with Arthur Schnitzler's *The Green Cockatoo*, a short play about the French Revolution.[40] Again this unlikely choice turns out to have been the result of Krejča's deep insight into the nature of the plays he worked with. *The Green Cockatoo* deals again with theatre within theatre: an improvised play about revolution is interrupted by the revolution itself. The fictitious action is ironically pierced by reality which spills into the artifact and, by destroying it, proves its theme to be a fact.

Topol's subtitle for the second play of the evening, *An Hour of Love*, is 'a Dream in a Play.' It is as if the subdued trio of actors, taking up the theme from the symphonic treatment of Schnitzler's play, now gave an intimate variation on the subject of man's imagination versus reality. The important thing, however, is that the form of the imagination in Topol's case varies with the reality against which it wrestles. Schnitzler explores how man's imagination wanted to oppose reality by conjuring it, getting ahead of it, as it were. In *An Hour of Love* the characters try to oppose reality by contradicting it, and the flights of their imagination take on various shapes in the course of their struggle. Again and again Ela acts out her fancies to ward off the approaching extinction of her greatest dream – the dream with which 'everything stands and falls for her.' In the end this dream is crushed not by reality proving it to be no dream at all, as in Schnitzler's case, but – a more contemporary and grimmer image – by reality making it 'change under [her] hands,' wearing it away 'drop by drop, pebble after pebble.'[41] Ela gives up her dream once she has found that it no longer has a relation to reality and has become senseless for her.

In *An Hour of Love* the playwright is pushing the theme of the role of man's imagination to its very limits. Whether the play is as stark and hopeless as some Czech critics have found it, has to remain an open question. Seen in the context of the three one-act plays, which I regard as variations on a theme, it does not seem to reveal quite as dark a vision as they would have us believe. Repeatedly the playwright imitates what Evi and Ela did by thinking up new ways of letting the mind play its magic game and turning the tables on the finality of death. 'Only death is real, time is an illusion,' says the Father in *Nightingale for Dinner*, to which his visitor, at the door of death, responds with the impassioned question: 'And if there is someone who turns it upside down? Who realizes himself within the limits of time so completely that he makes death an illusion?'[42]

Topol once gave us his definition of a happy man as 'a man who lives in harmony with himself, who realizes himself to the greatest extent, who really *is*.' The playwright was very young then and his formulation sounds obvious, if not commonplace. His definition of the opposite of this kind of life is much better: He refers to 'those who have simply got used to our world, who have settled down in their own way, and not only do not know but never even ask themselves the question "why and for which reason all this is."'[43] Here particularly we see the spiritual kinship between Topol and Beckett. Remember Estragon and Vladimir with their carrots?

ESTRAGON ... Funny, the more you eat the worse it gets.
VLADIMIR With me it's just the opposite.
ESTRAGON In other words?
VLADIMIR I get used to the muck as I go along.[44]

At the heart of each of Topol's works there is a tension between two ways of looking at life. Generalizing, and therefore necessarily oversimplifying, we might call it the tension between the man who collects answers and the man who collects questions. These two basic poles of the human spirit have been called many names. The Greeks personified them by two gods; Nietzsche considered these gods in turn the key symbols of modern western thought; Santayana told us that one cannot exist without the other, because 'unless irrational impulses and fancies are kept alive, the life of reason collapses for sheer emptiness.'[45]

The problem of the tension between these poles of man's inner life was central to Topol's work from the very start and grew with him, gaining in depth as he matured, paralleling his own development as a man and an artist. When the playwright was twenty-three, he presented the problem with the assured clarity of a young talent. For the 'scientifically minded' middle-aged Mr Dohnal of *Their Day* all the answers to life have been provided because 'nature has pulled it off from the biological cell to *homo sapiens*,'[46] and he can settle back into his self-satisfied life without aims and dreams, and the responsibilities that come with them. The playwright obviously encourages us to write Mr Dohnal off as a negative figure and suggests that the sooner the young generation struggles free from his influence, the better.

By the time we meet the next of Topol's negative figures, the efficient village barber in *The End of the Carnival*, the playwright is much less explicit. Smrt'ak (a nickname playing on the word 'death' – something like 'Deadfella' perhaps) is no longer an obviously destructive figure; rather he is nondescript, average, and can be called 'a villain' with little more justification than any of the other villagers. Everyone is in some way responsible for Jindřich's death; Smrt'ak only a little more tangibly so, since he provided the make-up and the coffin for the procession.

Still, Smrt'ak is the destructive figure of the play. The fact that the evil he spreads has become less obvious is only due to the playwright's matured vision. Having rapidly outgrown a tendency to be too literal, Topol now moulds the figure with subtlety. Smrt'ak is a tidy man. He likes order and takes every opportunity to urge others to do 'one thing after another;'[47] he deplores waste and can get indignant when someone does not finish his drink; he himself hardly drinks (his excuses vary from gall-bladder trouble to kidney stones); and anxiously sticks to all rules and regulations. Even when he was a little boy (he has never left his native village) he was so well behaved that he was chosen as altar boy for the church service.

Smrt'ak has few pleasures – the chief one is seeing others get into trouble. Of course he never gets into trouble himself and quickly leaves whenever anything 'stops being funny.' In passing we learn that he directs the local amateur acting group and does the casting according to his knowledge of the villagers' weaknesses and secrets. During the mask festivities, too, he plays the role of the organizer. 'It all depends on me,' are his first words in the play. Even this feast of spontaneous joy he wants to organize according to the rules of his own limitations – for he is incapable of the sheer joy of living. For him the only enjoyable aspect of the masquerade will come when he sees the tragicomic figure of Král's son in the coffin: 'and with that funeral procession you wait until half past five when I close shop,' he orders the masks, 'that I wouldn't like to miss!'[48]

In *Cat on the Rails*, Topol recasts the same figure even more subtly. Determined to work out the character to the last detail, the playwright has moved him into the centre of action. Véna is a man who knows that 'whatever I can't get my hands on gives me trouble.' He is literal-minded and unable to see beyond factual evidence. Evi puts it in her own perceptive way: 'When you laugh you cry! – What do you do when you cry?' Of course Véna never cries, perhaps because he thinks that there must always be a reason for everything. When Evi tells him a story about an actual event, he frets: 'So why do you tell me that? Where's the moral lesson of the story, where?' He cannot grasp the girl's impulsive joy, he cannot join her in her dreams because he has no inner harmony. There is a dark animal in him which he calls 'the mole,' and he is 'never sure who of the two is really me, the one who enjoys or the one who destroys.'[49]

El of *An Hour of Love* is Véna's kindred spirit. He too abhors heights of any kind and when Ela, re-enacting a scene from the past, pretends to be standing precariously on a high rail, he shouts at her just as Véna had shouted at Evi when she had climbed on the roof of the railway shack. None of the men can understand the desire to seek heights even if it involves danger. 'I love heights! I love heights!'[50] calls Evi perched against the sky. 'My God, what sense does it make?'[51] grumbles El when Ela is balancing on the back of the sofa.

In *An Hour of Love* Topol has penetrated even further into the recesses of human nature. After having given 'the mole' in man the upper hand in *Nightingale for Dinner* and letting it destroy the messenger of joy, he now faces it in *An Hour of Love* with redoubled intensity. At one point Ela drapes herself in a table cloth with a flower pattern. At first El prefers these flowers to real ones 'because they don't grow. And what doesn't grow, doesn't change.' But when the penetrating voice of the Aunt informs him from behind the partition: 'What has got life, has got death,' El draws a 'logical' conclusion: 'So only that which is not alive remains forever? That which is not, is eternal?' Whereupon he shouts at Ela to 'take off that table cloth. Take off that eternity.'[52] El misses Topol's significant distinction between merely living, and really *being*. Drawing his literal conclusion, he arrives at the closed door of an absolute statement. He fails to grasp Nightingale's dream about making death an illusion. Neither would he be able to follow Santayana's thought that 'literalness is impossible in any utterance of the spirit, and if it were possible it would be deadly.'[53]

When Topol wrote *Two Nights with a Girl* he no longer tried to represent 'the enemy of life' in one character. The destructive and life-denying quality becomes less tangible and much more widely suffused. At various moments each character seems to share in this quality. It could be summarized as materialism and greed, an inability to perceive beauty, a refusal to try – with all the imperfections of trying – to arrive at some form of truth. In other words, it is lack of spirituality. The quality appears most obviously in the two intruders, the Doctor and David, who prey on the family's material and spiritual resources.

However, unlike Smrt'ak, the quietly vicious barber of *The End of the Carnival*, these two characters do not project a definite form of 'evil.' When Rudolf, assuming that David has taken off with the Girl, calls him 'a hired murderer,' the Doctor quickly deflates this moral judgment: 'You Romantic. He is a common thief.' Furthermore, as we find out a minute later, David is an unsuccessful thief. At the end the two 'thieves' dejectedly depart, two sorry figures pushing an old bicycle, hiding their faces in their upturned coat collars. The Doctor's last words, 'Night, the black cave of our minds,' pronounced as he leaves the threshold, sound strangely absurd. But not as absurd as Figaro's buoyant aria which resounds immediately afterwards from the record player. The dark forces in man's soul are crowded out by the irresponsible rhythms of a popular virtuoso theatrical performance. Perhaps it is 'all only play. And why not play for a while?' as Rudolf tells the Girl earlier. In play our dreams are released and perhaps only in play can we fill the empty silence which follows our questions about the meaning of life.

In his note to *A Dream Play* Strindberg tells us that 'Time and place do not exist. On a flimsy foundation of actual happenings, imagination spins and weaves new patterns: intermingling remembrances, experiences, whims, fancies, ideas, fantastic absurdities and improvisations, and original inventions of the mind. The personalities split, take on duality, multiply, vanish, intensify, diffuse and disperse, and are brought into focus. There is, however, one single consciousness that exercises a dominance over the characters ...'[54]

These words could well serve as an introduction to Topol's most profound and, in its exquisite combination of histrionics and philosophy, his until now most challenging play, *Two Nights with a Girl*.[55] From *The End of the Carnival* on Topol has established himself as a playwright-poet who keeps asking the eternal question: 'What is life and what does it mean? Who is man and what does he mean?' And although he knows that this question can never be answered, he bravely sets out to ponder again the nature of good and evil, happiness and sorrow, hope and despair. 'They don't understand you,' Rudolf says to his figurine-ideal once she has come to life and wins all the games everyone tries to play with her. 'They all approach you with sheer reason, they cut off your most beautiful branches, the yellowish green ones, on which not even a bird perches because they break when touched ever so lightly.'[56]

In this paradoxical image lies much of the secret of Topol's play. By reason alone we find no way to the 'meaning' of the play. Its logic is the logic of a dream; its reality combines the invented and sensed reality of a dream merged with physical experience; its time and space become questionable as abstract entities and exist only in the imagination of the characters. Strindberg's *A Dream Play*, in which he placed the whole of humanity on trial, ushered in the drama of the twentieth century. Almost three-quarters of a century later a young Czech writer takes up the heritage of the great prophet of tortured humanity and reshapes it for the generation that knows Samuel Beckett.

6

Ladislav Smoček

MAN Listen, is it really a real maze?
GATEKEEPER What do you mean by really real?   Smoček *The Maze*

Of the four small theatres that achieved international fame during the
sixties the Theatre On the Balustrade under Jan Grossman and the Theatre
Behind the Gate under Otomar Krejča have received some attention in the
preceding pages. There remain the Drama Club and Semafor,[1] the last a
particularly interesting feature of the theatre life of Prague. Semafor
emerged in the late fifties from informal musical entertainment in a wine
cellar, and was launched formally by Jiří Suchý[2] whose talents ranged from
acting to writing plays, from singing to composing. Together with Jiří Šlitr
he led an ensemble in the centre of Prague, filling the theatre evening after
evening by putting on witty and intelligent cabaret shows, sometimes
whole plays, usually written by himself.

Semafor became a household word in Prague, and the performances
provided the city and indeed the entire country with not only hit songs and
topical jokes but also with fictional characters who reappeared in different
contexts on the Semafor stage and became so well known to everyone that
they became part of the daily reality of life. Peter Brook attended some
Semafor performances in the early sixties, and praised their artistic qualities and their important contribution to what he considered the necessary
and urgent deflation of the 'snobbish attitude to art which was characteristic of the last century.'[3] The tremendous popularity of the Semafor performances was, however, due to another reason of which Peter Brook did not
seem to be aware.

Semafor responded to the urgent intellectual needs of the audience. As a
member of the founding group put it: the members of Semafor felt that 'the

theatre should respond to its period. That means it should answer its questions or else formulate questions for it. The question of each period in time are very real and urgent ones and basically they are always the same questions about being or not being ... The level on which the answer is given is not important. It can be given by Shakespeare but also by a cabaret.'⁴ And so it appears that the least 'literary' of the important small theatres of Prague fulfilled an existential need among the population to an extent that has not yet been measured.

Today Semafor still exists and plays to full houses. Watched by the authorities, it is tolerated as a sort of vent for laughter, provided that it does not overstep its limits. The 'existential' aspect and the critical voice of reason are still there but they are hushed and expressed with the veiled caution of someone who believes that survival with compromise is better than having one's gesture toward intellectual freedom cut short by being silenced.

The last of the four small theatres to be examined is the Činoherní klub (the Drama Club) which, of the four, has staged the largest number of Czech plays.⁵ The ensemble worked particularly closely with the stage, resulting in a type of play writing which has become characteristic of the Drama Club. It was with this lively and creative group that Ladislav Smoček was affiliated while exploring various highways and byways of the theatre before he began to write plays. Initially he intended to become an actor; later, having completed his studies in directing at the Faculty of Theatre in Prague, he worked for several years in theatres outside Prague and gained some reputation as a promising young director. After a brief period at Prague's Laterna Magica, which apparently did not further his best qualities, Smoček returned to the limelight of the Czech theatrical world as the director of his own plays.

In 1965, together with Ivan Vyskočil, he founded the ensemble of the Drama Club, perhaps the most tightly knit artistic group among Czech theatre companies. One reason for its extraordinary collaboration and artistic self-sufficiency was that the Drama Club ensemble included several resident playwrights: in addition to Smoček, there were Alena Vostrá (wife of the co-founder of the Drama Club) and Pavel Landovský (himself a leading actor of the ensemble). Their plays are also discussed in this book. Led by excellent directors with multiple talents – Smoček, Vostrý (also a drama critic), and Jan Kačer (also an actor) – the Drama Club, despite its restricted quarters, quickly became one of the most noteworthy theatres in Prague.

Ladislav Smoček did not become a playwright overnight. But he used his pen as director from the first. Throughout the rehearsals of a new play he never hesitated to make changes in the text so that the work would yield its best dramatic quality. Vyskočil goes as far as to claim that Smoček began to write plays because as director he was dissatisfied with the available dramatic texts.[6] There always remained something to be said that could not be expressed with another writer's work. And so, after several years of work with other dramatists' writings, Smoček began to write his own plays.

It is difficult to point out a chief characteristic of Smoček's plays. We might say that they are primarily built around a dramatic situation. One has the distinct impression that he conceives a situation from the stage and then expands it with ideas. (This is, incidentally, the very opposite of Havel's approach to play writing.) In Smoček's world we have, for example, five soldiers bivouacing in the jungle; a person half-heartedly trying to gain entrance to a mysterious establishment; an elderly man losing his place to live; a number of people meeting in a country house. Around this situation Smoček builds his imaginative theatre. His medium is the word on the stage; what he wants to express he could express neither with his own words and someone else's stage work, nor with his own stage work and someone else's text. In other words, he works with neither the text nor the performance alone, but with both.

In his farce *Dr. Bell Burke's Strange Afternoon*, for example, Smoček directed the actors to stalk about with jerky movements, reminiscent of old films, creating the impression of some mechanical inadequacy, perfectly balanced with the simplified nature of the characters. Or take the way he directed the final scene of the same play, when three characters sit down to a meal of soup, bread, and yeast cakes. In print the text is only one page long but in the performance the scene was drawn into great length and seemed to take forever. The conversation during the meal – reduced to plodding slow motion, as the characters chew and munch – is about plucking chickens, straining soup, fetching beer; about the 'golden, blessed hands'[7] of the motherly cook; about the potential thief who might steal some of this earthly delight; about the happiness of eating and eating more. Smoček here manages to give the impression that each greasy word spoken has been soaked in thick gravy. The impact on the audience is devastatingly funny.

Another instance of Smoček's use of the stage is a scene in *Cosmic Spring* when a young man and a young woman in their first moments of sexual attraction begin to touch each other. This happens while they are picking up pieces of broken glass (the girl has just broken a window by accident). Since they are flushed with excitement and careless, they cut themselves and each other; blood begins to flow and as they stain each other the 'love scene' becomes something of a bloodbath. The playwright's imagination obviously works strongly on the visual level.

On the whole it might be said that Smoček lacks the unmistakable dramatic signature of the other playwrights discussed in individual chapters. Nevertheless, he is an important figure precisely because he has managed to realize his double talent. Perhaps we should think of him less as a dramatist as such but rather as we tend to think of some film-makers of our era. In their case we no longer separate the word from the image and we accept their work as a unit of sound and sight.

Smoček's first play, *Picnic* (1965), although it is about Americans, would most probably be less interesting for a Western audience than his other plays. It is built around a situation that has worn a little thin in the English-speaking world. Popular art forms have used it, numerous good and bad American films have moulded it almost into a cliché. Although in the best cases it still works, as a theme it has become threadbare: a group of people are put into a difficult situation under various pressures (usually connected with survival) which bring certain hidden qualities and suppressed characteristics to the surface.

In Smoček's play the 'group under pressure' consists of a patrol unit of four American soldiers camping for one night in the jungle of a Pacific island during the Second World War. They have no duties other than to wait for their officer Crackmiller who has gone on a dangerous reconnaissance patrol to find out the Japanese enemy's position. While the four men are waiting – constantly and increasingly aware of the fact that Crackmiller might never return – their innermost qualities come gradually to the fore. All this sounds familiar.

Smoček's play steers clear, however, of the usual man-against-officer clash on the one hand, and the strong-boy-with-weak-character and vice versa on the other. Unburdened by the American 'image' of the American soldier, Smoček is purely interested in what happens when a man-to-man relationship is put under unusual stress. He is conducting an experiment with highly explosive material which he puts under increasing pressure until the point of explosion is reached. In that clearing in the jungle – which, as one of the group ironically feels, would make a nice picnic site – the four men are isolated from their habitual surroundings; not only from their safe households back home but also from their orderly military division (they now form a small independent patrol unit) and from their trusted source of command (Crackmiller has gone away).

The dramatically interesting aspect of the play is its shift of the focus of tension. About half-way through, the audience is bound to realize what they took to be the dramatic aspect of the play was in fact unimportant; what they took to be the expected crisis was a side issue; what seemed to be the plot is never brought to a conclusion. In the end the officer has not returned, and the enemy's moves have remained undiscovered. Instead the real tensions of the play emerge with increasing urgency, and the men's fear, anger, uncertainty, touchiness, suspicion, envy, and intolerance begin their irrational play of forces. In the course of petty conflicts, during which the tension mounts, the weaker of the four – dreamy, kindly Rozden who believes in raising a family and having a clear conscience, and hot-headed but basically sensible Burda – gradually drop out and the power struggle is concentrated between the two strongest characters, sarcastic, aggressive Smile, and taciturn, stubborn Tall.

Throughout the play, the characters in turn disappear into the thick jungle that surrounds the clearing. While everyone listens with baited breath, sounds of rustling leaves, cracking branches, and bodies breaking through the undergrowth are heard. The frightening mystery of the surrounding jungle increases as the four soldiers begin to imagine the murdered body of their commander in the thicket, the watchful eyes of the enemy, and some other dreadful danger they are unable to formulate. As Rozden, the dreamer, invents fantastic stories about growing wings, as if in a fairy-tale, and flying off to safety and light, there seems to be an increasingly strong sense of violence in the air. Finally the inevitable bloody encounter takes place. Both Tall and Smile disappear in the jungle; after ominous sounds a scream is heard and when the opponents reappear, one of them, the tough joker Smile, crawls back lacerated and bleeding.

The play ends with the soldiers leaving the clearing in the jungle while dawn is breaking. In a few monosyllables Tall announces that he will go to find out what happened to their commander. The other two bustle about, taking care of Smile's wounds and broken teeth; then they leave, with him on a stretcher between them, and Rozden repeats the absurdly human comment: 'Oh God! Such a nice place! Just made for a picnic ...'[8] As it grows lighter the stage is empty; all we hear are jungle noises and the sound of men fighting their way through the undergrowth – both sounds have attained a certain terrible familiarity in the course of the play. Suddenly – the stage instructions are precise – the breaking of foliage stops and shots are heard in quick succession, and after a short silence a grenade explodes. Silence. The lights go down, there is the sound of ocean waves crashing against the shore. A sign appears: 'ON THE PATH THE AMERICAN PATROL MET WITH A JAPANESE ONE ... DEW APPEARS, THE PLANTS

BEGIN TO STEAM.'[9] As the sound of the ocean waves increases and then abruptly stops, the author's instructions call for equally abrupt light in the audience.

The question has been asked why Smoček chose to write a play on this topic. To write in problem-ridden central Europe a play about the Japanese-American war seems far-fetched indeed. The playwright's choice may be partly due to his first encounter with US soldiers at the impressionable age of thirteen, when the American army marched into his native Plzeň in 1945. The basic reason, however, as suggested by Jaroslav Vostrý,[10] was that Smoček wanted to avoid any trace of what might be called 'national psychology.' The varied genealogy of the Americans, he felt, would make any explanation of motivation by means of national characteristics impossible. Indeed, to make doubly sure of eliminating all national traits, Smoček resorts to alcohol – in the course of their wait the men consume a fair amount of liquor.

The author felt he had thereby reduced the men to essential human qualities, basic emotions, primitive instincts and impulses. Some of us might want to question the theory that alcohol erases differences in nationality but this is of little importance here. What is important in this play is the author's attempt to find ways to reduce human nature to what he considered its basic qualities. He was more successful at this only in his later plays when he had discovered his own particular idiom and no longer needed external help.

Although it has its strong moments, *Picnic* remains an exercise of sorts. It has a certain claim to fame, however, since it was during the work on *Picnic* that the core of the Drama Club was formed. For that reason it is perhaps appropriate that the play was never performed at any other theatre in Prague but remained exclusively attached to the actors of the Drama Club. Later Smoček directed a film version of *Picnic* but despite – or perhaps because of – the much greater possibilities of creating the jungle atmosphere on the screen, the film was not as successful as might be expected. The claustrophobic tightness of the stage was needed to put across the meaning of the play. The jungle turned out to have been quite unimportant.

Smoček's next play, although it followed *Picnic* within two years, seems of an entirely different nature. However, on closer inspection we find that it is based on the same two basic artistic principles as the earlier play: the exploration of a certain situation, and the reduction of human nature to its essential features. Smoček had now become much more adept at both.

The plot of *Dr. Bell Burke's Strange Afternoon*, this 'feigned comedy,'[11] as the author subtitles it, says next to nothing about the play itself: Dr Burke, an old bachelor, a lover of literature and nature, returns to his flat with his pupil-assistant after several months' absence. He learns that the landlady's daughter has finally found a husband and intends to set up her new household in his quarters. Dr Burke reacts violently, even attempts murder, but to no avail. He has to leave what had been his home and the young couple settles in. Curtain.

When told in this way, the play sounds more like a modern tragedy or at least a serious social-problem-play. In actual fact it is a farce. The action contains all the slapstick elements expected of a farce: three characters are knocked out and subsequently stuffed into a cupboard from which they promptly emerge at inopportune moments; dozens of cakes are pulled out of drawers or hurled at the door; one character swallows a key; another ends up lamenting over the liquid evidence of his disgraceful failure to get to the bathroom. While all this happens, snatches of inappropriate music and the well-timed chirping of sparrows provide a shrill counterpoint from back stage.

What Smoček has done is to write a script – one might almost call it a libretto – for the most essential feature of farce: deflation. The stronger the deflation, the funnier the farce. When a young man in a smudgy sweater and with paint on his jeans slips on a banana peel we laugh; but but we do not laugh half as much as if the man who has slipped is an immaculately dressed executive emerging from a chauffeured car. Although we may argue that in our age and society bent on equalization and the elimination of social differences (at least in looks) this type of farce has a harder time in eliciting amusement than it used to have, the above example still carries some meaning. The harder the fall, the funnier it is; the more obvious the deflation, the better the farce. Farce, the most extreme form of comedy, exploits in the most simplified way possible the contrast between what people pretend to be and what they are not, and between what they are and what they do not want to be.

Dr Burke pretends to be a humanist-philosopher, a sensitive intellectual who claims to live according to the laudable motto, 'seek goodness within yourself.'[12] In actual fact he is selfish, revengeful, and stupid. Svatava, the glowing young bride, is neither young nor glowing, and her appropriately starry eyes are fixed on her future husband's bank-book. Václav, her fortunate (bottom-of-the-barrel) choice, a crude lout from the village who promises to buy Svatava a honeycake heart, bagpipes, a television set, a car, and a whole mountain of eggs (in that order), is so ridiculous from the start that the principle of deflation could hardly work with him. Yet it does. At one point he beats his head against the wall, screaming: 'I'm not a primitive! I'm not a primitive!'[13] Although he does not pretend to be anyone he is not, he does not want to be what he is.

Even Tichý, Dr Burke's modest and shy pupil-companion, whose outlook on life seems to be that of a wise man: 'We are blind and imagine that we can see! ... we are cowardly and too vicious!'[14] is kicking the furniture as he is pronouncing these philosophic statements and soon the audience realizes that he is using them only to detract his mind from his need to get to the toilet. And so we have false culture and false naturalness and a false happy end in this anatomy of deflation. As events multiply, the farcical element comes more and more to the fore – characters who merely hid knives behind their backs earlier on, now sit on bunches of roses, throw soup into each other's faces, stick pots on each other's heads, and lose their false teeth by biting other people in the backside.

The climactic scene was played under the playwright's own direction. The way this was done bears repeating here. Václav, the suitor, believing that he has been jilted (in fact his bride – believed dead by the audience – is ten feet away from him in Dr Burke's cupboard) alternates between threatening Burke with a knife and bashing his own head desperately against the door, whereupon, out of breath and dazed, he flings himself on the floor and remains sitting there with his tongue hanging out. In the meantime Burke writhes with pain caused by the swallowed key, Tichý dances about tortured by the growing urgency of his need, trying to encourage himself with slogans like 'Tycho de Brahe stick it out ... just imagine that it is for your fatherland,' while Svatava watches the whole scene with a silly smile and her mother tries to make peace by admonishing everyone to 'love each other. The neighbours will hear it!'[15] Smoček directed this farcical furioso in such a way that he slowed down the action and let the situation linger so that the audience could watch and savour the behaviour of each character as well as the complex choreography of the whole scene.[16]

The playwright used and balanced the features of traditional farce with the assurance of someone who knew exactly how things will work on stage. However, he does not let the farce affect the audience as mere visual articulation of funny situations. By opposing the potentially tragic emotional aspect of the story with the funny physical and even physiological aspect of the individual scenes, Smoček achieves a particular tension which Eric Bentley would call the 'farcical dialectic ... the interplay between the direct and wild fantasies and the everyday drab realities.'[17]

But Smoček takes this dialectic a step further. Not only does he illustrate it with the wild antics of the characters' farcical actions but, on another level, he intensifies the awareness of this tension in the audience. They hear a character on stage talk glowingly about the beauties of the surrounding countryside while other characters wash the floor and obviously see nothing beyond that floor; they are plied with comments about the future happiness of 'the children,' the young lovers, yet they witness that the bride is ugly and in her forties, and the groom is fifty and squints; they hear Dr Burke holding forth on culture and Goethe, and simultaneously learn that he keeps his books stored away in a dusty, dark attic where no one (including himself) can find them. At the end of the play the audience's feeling of sympathy for the now homeless old man and his pupil is undermined by a mixture of embarassment and physical discomfort as they watch them retreat – one with a key in his belly and the other one with wet trousers.

Bludiště (*The Maze*), written in 1965 and staged at the Drama Club in 1966, seems at first sight a far cry from *Picnic*. And in many ways it certainly is. The play reflects a situation which combines elements of Kafka and Beckett. It is about anxiety, about waiting, about trying to understand something in the wrong way; but it is also funny and farcical.

A man – average in every way, it seems – finds himself in front of the entrance to a maze situated in a park and designed for the pleasure and enertainment of people. This at least is the description given by the gatekeeper who, after all, should know the establishment to which he also sells entrance tickets. From the moment the curtain opens, the stage is dominated by the presence of the Maze of which the audience see only the entrance gate. The stage is described as follows: 'The Maze forms narrow streets lined by high thick hedges. It expands under the open sky into the distance. It pulsates like a distant swimming pool. On the outside it is surrounded by a fence made of wrought iron. There are three signs, one says "The Maze," one "Entrance," and a smaller one "Information." There is a chair, an old case of beer, a small stove and a Gatekeeper with an official cap who is selling tickets. Next to the entrance stand a broom and an old bicycle. Birds are heard in the park. Sidestage stands a Man with a hat and a briefcase to which a small parcel is tied. He wants to begin a conversation. A Soldier and a Girl hold hands. The Soldier carries the Girl's handbag. The Gatekeeper finishes his beer from the bottle.'[18]

Nearly the entire action of the play consists in a discussion between the Man and the Gatekeeper in the course of which the former makes all sorts of enquiries about the nature of the Maze: whether it has an exit; whether it would be possible to enter by the exit and exit by the entrance; whether people could 'spend years, trying to find a way out.'[19] As in Kafka's world, the answers to these increasingly urgent questions are not only totally unsatisfactory but reveal the general uncertainty of the situation to such an extent that they reduce the question itself to ridiculously small proportions and reveal its irrelevance.

The Man's initial question whether this is 'really a real maze,' is countered by the Gatekeeper with another question: 'What do you mean by really real?' When the Man expresses concern about those who have gone in: 'How will they get out? Could it be that they won't find the exit? Would you help them in any way?' the Gatekeeper ponders for a good while until he says: 'I haven't ever thought about that, Sir. They wanted to get in there, so let them be there. Let them lose their way! After all, that's what this is for!' When the Man, increasingly disturbed, wants to find out about the fate of those who perhaps failed to find the exit, the Gatekeeper shrugs: 'Well, Sir, I can't know everything, can I, that's not my worry, as I say. If you are that curious, buy yourself a ticket and you'll find out for yourself, won't you?'[20]

These conversations are occasionally punctuated by two types of interruptions. One type comes from within the Maze, the other from outside. The latter includes for example, two talkative elderly ladies knowledgeable about crime stories, a peasant wanting to gather mushrooms, and a naturalist hunting butterflies. They all arrive at the Entrance, buy their tickets, and unceremoniously disappear inside the Maze.

The other kind of interruption, much more mysterious and unsettling, is caused by the Maze itself. From time to time strange figures emerge at the Entrance, showing obvious signs of a prolonged stay inside. A bearded man appears with moss sprouting on his hat; a shadowy figure trying to find 'some hole through to the outside' hits the Gatekeeper over the head with a block of wood – an attack that goes completely unnoticed by the intended victim; a rattling skeleton wearing a hat and carrying a shoe is chased back by the Gatekeeper like a stray dog. Moreover there are confusing sounds emanating from the Maze, which vary from the twitter of birds to lively marches (played by a band of whom the audience sees only the marching feet parading past). Here and there heterogeneous objects come flying over the hedge – a piece of cake, for example, or a human hand in a sleeve which is promptly flung back by the Gatekeeper who mutters about people's messiness with the garbage while the Man wonders with horror whether 'someone didn't perhaps get murdered inside.'[21]

As the Man repeats his questions with growing anxiety but also, we realize, with growing fascination, a gradual change comes over the Gatekeeper. Not only does he become arrogant and abrupt but he also grows more and more aggressive. Finally he tears off the Man's jacket, accuses him of maltreating children, threatens to beat him up and, when the Man tries to leave, sends his watchdog after him to chase him back. When the Man crouches there, terrified and exhausted, signs of a strange understanding between the Gatekeeper and the Maze begin to fill the air. As the former begins to play a tune on his mouth organ, voices from inside the Maze join in; when he cracks a joke, responsive laughter from inside is heard. Finally the Man, pursued by the Gatekeeper with a hatchet, seeks refuge by rushing into the Entrance of the Maze.

With this instant the terror has gone. The situation is momentarily changed to a normal working day. With habitual care the Gatekeeper begins to 'close shop': locking the gate, putting away the utensils, picking up things that were left lying around. In the course of cleaning up he finds the Man's jacket, fingers its pockets for some change which he promptly pockets himself, and then throws the jacket over the hedge to the man: 'So that you wouldn't say that I'm a thief! What's yours is yours!' He is just about to leave when a young woman comes rushing in and asks for an entrance ticket although she knows it is getting late. The Gatekeeper gets out his ticket book and opens the gate for her. When she thanks him for being so kind, he sighs: 'If they were all that appreciative, young lady, things in the world would look different, believe you me!' As he closes the gate for the second time, puts a chain lock on the broom, gathers his things and begins to push his old bicycle off the stage, he stops for a moment and looks back at the Maze, muttering something about 'perhaps some exit somewhere.'[22] The Maze pulsates and the stage darkens.

The playwright works with two thematic inspirations, one ancient and one modern. Implied by the title and substantiated in the text itself is a reference to the well-known Greek myth of Theseus out to slay the monster of the labyrinth, the Minotaur. Theseus is protected by the shrewdness of Ariadne who supplies him with a clue of yarn to help him find his way back to the light of day. On another level the play reminds us of one of the great haunting scenes of modern literature, already mentioned in the Introduction – Franz Kafka's parable *Before the Law* (which also forms part of his novel *The Trial*). It describes, as we remember, the arrival of a man before the Gate of Law requesting permission to enter, and the perennial ambiguous rebuttals of the gatekeeper who, after a lifetime has passed, informs the dying old Man that 'this entry was meant for you only. Now I am going to close it.'[23]

Among the numerous and varied interpretations of Kafka's cryptic parable there are those that claim that the Man from the Country did not gain entry because he was waiting for the Gatekeeper's permission rather than braving official reasons and striking out on his own while he still had the strength to do so. Smoček's character suffers from a similar lack of spiritual strength: he neither decides to buy the ticket nor makes up his mind to leave. When he does decide, it is too late. The Gatekeeper's power has grown to such an extent that he has him chased back. Kafka's Man is shut out, Smoček's Man is shut in. Here we notice a parallel to Klíma's *The Castle*. Both Klíma and Smoček imply that their characters have suffered a defeat. In both cases, however, the defeat seems to be in the nature of things.

Smoček's play thus works with these two themes: the idea of getting lost under the shadow of some lurking danger and not being able to find the way out; and the idea of not being able to pass through an entrance for complex reasons of indecision and paralyzing anxiety on the one hand, and the presence of a seemingly all-knowing power on the other – the Gatekeeper. At one point in *The Maze* the Greek myth of coping with the powers of confusion by not losing sight of where one started is taken up clearly. The Man suddenly has an idea: 'An intelligent person would never get lost in it! He would just take along a spool of yarn and if he couldn't find the exit, he would simply follow the thread and get back here.' However, this classical solution makes no headway with the Gatekeeper: 'Then you would really make a mess of it;' he mutters; 'we send those back right away, Sir. It is prohibited to exit here. Right there it says perfectly clearly "Entrance." That means that it is the Entrance to the Maze and not the Exit, get that? ... It is all clearly described on the ticket. And that counts for everybody, Sir, and I am here to see to it that it does.'[24]

The essence of Smoček's two-pronged play might be formulated like this: a human being, faced with the possibility of entering an unknown area which promises to hold both pleasures and dangers, seeks assurance that he will be able to leave as he came. He learns that this is impossible. There is no way back. There is no certainty to be found by waiting, except the certainty of never finding a certainty.

This dilemma, of course, is Kafka's point. Smoček, less of a mystic and more of a visual artist, conveys the ambiguity of the situation by letting the Gatekeeper have the last word. Unlike Kafka's story, where the Gatekeeper finally reveals his terrible knowledge – that the entrance was only for the Man from the Country, and was to be closed, unused, at the end of his life – Smoček's Gatekeeper admits his own ignorance about the nature of things, about whether or not there possibly is an exit from the Maze.

As to the meaning a maze surrounded by high hedges would carry for a Czech audience, they would have associated it at once with the maze at Hampton Court near London which they knew from the then immensely popular film version of J.K. Jerome's *Three Men in a Boat*.[25] That it also carried a topical implication, as did, for example, Miloš Forman's film version of Ken Kesey's novel *One Flew over the Cuckoo's Nest*, is more than likely.

Needless to say, Smoček was attracted by this potentially philosophical topic because he saw it as a situation that would make good theatre. The constant visual presence of the Maze, the mystery of which is increased both by confusing sounds and strange figures, and by the Gatekeeper's laconic yet oddly ambiguous comments, form a focal centre of tensions which hardly lessen throughout the play. In addition, the audience experience a visual tension while witnessing the reduction of the Man from a sceptical citizen with hat and briefcase to a coatless and dishevelled creature, panting on the Gatekeeper's chair in vivid contrast with the Gatekeeper's growing stature, as well as the increasingly inquisitorial nature of his questions. All these cross-developments, visually enacted before our eyes, provide, of course, exciting theatre.

The sceptic's question whether in Smoček's plays 'good theatre has crowded out ideas' is not really relevant. The play does raise all kinds of speculative questions which are far from being shallow. Take, for example, the polite invitation to enter which becomes a brutal chase from which there is no escape. What was masked as free will becomes action under threat. The political alertness of the Czechoslovaks could hardly miss this implication. But a Western audience are equally able to relate the play to their own lives and to feel its insight into the human dilemma. We may, say, remember the lines reiterated by Beckett's clowns who by now have become an integral part of the contemporary imagination when they witness Lucky's dilemma under Pozzo's whip: they respond with a two-voiced refrain – 'It's inevitable,' and 'It's not certain'[26] – repeated five times. It is the inevitability of uncertainty that Smoček's Man at the Entrance of the Maze experiences just as Kafka's Man experienced it almost half a century earlier.

Cosmic Spring, one of the very few post-invasion plays under discussion here to be performed in Czechoslovakia (in March 1970), is Smoček's most ambitious venture – as playwright as well as director. Here he takes on the problem of modern man in general. It seems as if playwright Smoček had decided to write a philosophical parable and director Smoček seized the opportunity to stage a director's dream – a complex interplay of figures and voices, a carefully planned emergence of characters presenting views and problems in flashes and submerging again, as snatches of conversations are heard, fragments of dilemmas are revealed, expressions of man's joys and sorrows flash across the stage.

As the audience begins to grope its way through the intricate pattern of voices and characters (unnamed at first) it gradually becomes aware of the following situation: a country house is about to be demolished or confiscated in the interest of some kind of scientific progress which, however, is revealed as being of dubious value. We never find out the precise nature of the problem but the characters' frequent references to heaps of slag moving closer to the house and poisonous smoke filling the once-clear air never let us forget the impending change.

The house is filled with relatives and guests of all kinds, floating in and out of the house, discussing any subject under the sun, eating, drinking, quarrelling, making love, generating hate, being petty, curious, agonized, frantic, joyous, elated – crowding the air with the motley stuff of human life. The Master of the House, who dies of a terminal disease in the course of the play, is trying, during the few hours that are left to him, to formulate an answer to the confusing questions of life.

In a quiet central scene, which is interrupted here and there by his concerned relatives and friends who come tiptoeing in to see whether he is still sleeping, the Master of the House holds a philosophical monologue in which he ruminates about the blessings of the average unthinking man, the perennial curse of aggressive mediocrity assuming leadership, the animalistic aspect of the average life, man's grotesque yearning for a happy end, his bloodthirstiness, sensationalism, and ignorance, his presumption in calling himself the master of the universe, and his infinite resourcefulness in masking his self-love, his fears, and his uncertainties. While the talkative, self-assured physician gives him his daily injection and false pep talk, the Master of the House wonders about this small planet earth revolving somewhere in the universe with all its teeming life of plants and animals and people reduced to microscopic dimensions.

In the brief Epilogue to the play we hear his spiritual testament. While a home-made movie shows the old man sitting in his arm chair, silently talking to himself, his niece Jana reads his last thoughts in which he encourages those who come after him to continue to think and search, so that he himself and the whole past of man would not be an illusion. It is here that the parabolic aspect of the play emerges: 'go on researching what kind of a being I was. Perhaps we strive for other worlds and eternity, who knows? Above me there is a roof, it protects me from the heat of the sun, the coldness of the winds. Behind it, beyond the clouds ... there is space in all directions. Light comes here all the way from there. And within me there is a light as in a spider crawling over rough plaster and casting a shadow. It is imprisoned in us and does not come out ... you can see far into space.'[27]

As the girl reads, the old man on the screen raises his face and looks upward, the film gets progressively lighter until it fades into white. The screen is empty. It was the end of the film in the camera. The lights go down. This is obviously a strong ending after the passengers on this ship of fools have filled our ears for the past two hours with frantic chatter about nothing.

However, the playwright/director's real strength emerges in the crowd scenes rather than in the meditational moments of the play. The audience is put through the steps of having to acquaint themselves with the characters. In the first part of the play we meet them as unnamed numbers only. It takes quite some time before we realize that one is the doctor, one is the Master's hard working, homespun sister-in-law, another is his niece torn between her sexual drive and a desperate sense of futility. Then there are a lecher and a fraud, a nervous lady, a common-sense realist, a guilt-ridden puritan, and so forth. Only when we have grasped what types of characters they are does the playwright reveal names and their social labels. Thus – a quaintly realistic and modern aspect of the play – we perceive their human quality before we know their names. The name itself seems incidental and unimportant; a name does little to relieve modern man's anonymity.

There is no question that the play is a lively piece of theatre. Whether it stands on its own feet as a philosophical comment is the wrong question to ask. By trying to span the chasm between the trivialities of daily life and man's deepest agonies and hopes, the author may have stretched too far beyond his potential. Yet there is intellectual power in the old man's rejection of all the cherished concepts of today's Western civilization – be it in Eastern Europe or in the West – notions of progress, equality of men, systems of perfect societies.

Again it is not so important that this intellectual insight fails to be matched by the vague emotional sense of hope which emerges from the Master's last words and which provides the audience with a vague visionary satisfaction comparable to the final bars of dissolution in an opera.

However, in its refusal to believe, in its determination to see clearly, in its rejection not only of despair but also of bitterness, the play is a very interesting artistic comment to emerge from Czechoslovakia at a time when the decision to dispense with illusion and to give in neither to bitterness nor to despair must have struck a chord in every member of the Czechoslovak audience. Moreover, the play would be sure to fascinate a western audience that enjoyed, say, T.S. Eliot's *The Cocktail Party* or Tom Stoppard's *Jumpers*.

7

Life in a group

... Oh God,
why did you burden my soul with this terrible longing? Perhaps it is easier to say:
There is neither good nor bad. There is only what the weak ones decide among
themselves. Or what the strong ones with their power force on them. Do I belong to
the strong ones? Am I strong enough to do what I feel is right? ...

Antigone in MILAN UHDE *The Whore of the City of Thebes*

Eric Bentley has drawn our attention to the difference between the playwright's concern with individualism and his concern with the individual.[1]
He illustrates this initially puzzling statement with the cases of Ibsen and
Chekhov who were hostile to the individualism of a freely competing
economy precisely *because* they were friends of individuality. Their concern with the individual human being who has a particular, unrepeatable
life-story behind him was, Bentley argues, the most original feature in the
new drama at the beginning of this century. I am not certain that this
interesting speculation adds much to our understanding of Ibsen and
Chekhov, but it may help us in approaching a group of Czech plays and a
Slovak play, the wide variety of which makes it difficult to bring them
together into one chapter.

These plays display the reverse of the above situations; they seem more
concerned with individualism than with the individual. Their characters
have no particular life story behind them, but rather represent variations of
the same story. Their lives have been affected by a certain way the world
has been going, and to be concerned with their individuality would be to
start crossing bridges before one comes to them. Perhaps Bentley should
have added that Ibsen and Chekhov's interest in the individual was possible

because these writers had a type of individualism to rebel against. The Czech playwrights, trying to reassess the precarious position of the individual in a totalitarian society, had to begin with the idea of individualism before they could get at the deeper level of the individual himself.

The Czech prototype for this kind of play is František Hrubín's *A Sunday in August* which was first performed in Prague in the spring of 1958, and became a great theatrical event. It is a hushed, Chekhovian play, about a group of people who spend a steamy summer day in the country near a lake in southern Bohemia. As the heat of the day gradually changes into the coolness of the night, the surface of the lake is rippled by the evening breeze and, simultaneously, the characters' passions, misunderstandings, hatreds, and confusions rise to the surface.

The play has no distinct plot. As in Chekhov's plays, the basic structure is in the unfolding and concealing of emotions rather than in the actual happenings. The language used is an intricate poetic orchestration of dialogues during which each character speaks his own idiom and follows his own trend of thought, incapable of concentrating on others. As with Chekhov we experience the moment at which the conversations about everyday topics – the weather, the evening's party, the weight of a suitcase – become transparent and reveal the speaker's emotional patterns, which have nothing to do with the topic discussed.

Apart from its artistic value, Hrubín's *A Sunday in August* is interesting as a landmark in the revival of drama after the artistically fruitless period of Stalinism. By dealing with states of mind and spiritual crises, with people's sense of uselessness on the one hand, and their urgent need for a little joy and love on the other, the author has written a philosophical play without a tangible social reality. His explorations of man's nature and his subdued questions about what life was all about resounded loudly through a country where such topics had not been touched for years.

Czech critics quickly launched an eager discussion about the play's values which, interestingly enough, ended up precisely with the very question with which we started out: the difference between individualism and the individual. Though aware of the subtle character sketches, they detected a certain difference in comparison with characters from Ibsen's or Chekhov's pen. As one critic put it: 'Hrubín ... sees his characters as social beings, types of society, and individualizes them only within that – restricted – framework.'[2]

Whether this observation is correct need not concern us here. What interests us is that Czech writers first of all had to usher in the very idea of individualism as an abstract principle in order to break the ground in bringing the concept back into people's minds. It was an extraordinary event when, after the total disregard of individual man under Stalinism, a play appeared that seemed to claim that each person ought to have a story, even within a system where the number of stories was decidedly limited. Once an outstanding writer had made such a statement – no matter how veiled and implicit – successive writers could be released into new areas of spiritual and intellectual adventure.

The year 1958 also saw the première of another very different play which implied that there was being attempted an artistic reassessment of what it meant to live in a collective, ideologically anti-individualistic society. If Hrubín's *A Sunday in August* is a low-key, poetic exploration of emotional patterns, Vratislav Blažek's *The Third Wish* is a rambunctious, partly simplistic, partly ironic story about an average Prague family who are taught a lesson about human happiness. Whether they actually learn the lesson is left an open question. The play is a sort of modern fairy-tale in which a jovial magic Grandfather promises the hero to grant him three wishes. According to fairy-tale pattern, the first two wishes are easily and uselessly squandered, and the third and only remaining wish presents a major problem.

The young couple, Petr and Věra, have many urgent wishes: an apartment of their own (daily life with the in-laws, though they are kindly people, is not exactly a bowl of cherries), a better job for Petr, some nice clothes for Věra, a car, a holiday at the sea ... the list could easily be expanded. Eventually they hit upon a great idea: a package-deal wish. After all, if they had all the things named above and perhaps a little more, they would be truly satisfied. Petr calls on the magic Grandfather and expresses his third wish: the wish 'to be satisfied!' The Grandfather, though realizing the problem, grants the wish and things take their inevitable course. The couple get their own apartment, Petr is promoted, they enjoy their television set, Věra can give up her job at the post office, serve lobster sandwiches, and drink French wine.

Despite all this, of course, things don't work. Satisfaction remains a receding spectre on the horizon. A true fairy-tale ending would have called for a voluntary change back to their former lives with a 'moral' realization that material goods are unrelated to life's real values. The author, however, leaves the ending open. As Petr is challenged to give up his present position and life-style in order to help a friend who is in trouble, the curtain falls without his having rung the magic bell that will bring back the Grandfather and demonstrate his 'moral' decision.

Told like this, the play sounds very naïve. And in a way it is. Why then did it run in theatres all over the country for 348 performances within a year, and another 418 performances within another year, with sold-out houses evening after evening? It was the first time since the establishment of the Communist regime in 1948 that a new Czech social comedy reached the stage – a play which discussed actual circumstances from the average person's point of view, in lively everyday language and with a combination of good-natured humour, intellectual irony, and biting satire.

In other words, the play was a *first* of sorts and as such it was immensely successful not only in Czechoslovakia, but in Hungary, Bulgaria, East Germany, and even the Soviet Union. When the play was published in the popular *Divadlo* series nine years later, when contemporary social satire was no longer (or once again!) a stranger to the Czechoslovak stage, the edition included a number of commentaries and essays in which critics celebrated the play as 'a real satire,' 'a hot chestnut which the author took from the fire and put into the audience's hand,' the presentation of 'a serious and highly topical problem,' 'an unpleasant fairy-tale ... which we need like salt.'[3]

From our point of view it is most interesting that this very well-written but rather obvious play, which tells the audience that money isn't everything, could take the country by storm. Moreover this success is certainly remarkable in a society which is based on the premise that the unequal distribution of material possessions is the root of all of man's problems. The more we think about Blažek's play, the more clearly we realize the revealing political implications of its strong impact. Why did people need to be told that possessions don't matter when they were living in an allegedly egalitarian society? To return to the main thread of our argument, was Blažek's play an attempt to tell people that one's 'own story' was not to be obtained by means of the simplified image of social equality which had been formed in the average person's mind under the pressure of the public media?

And so, with two well-timed original writers at its threshold – Hrubín, the poet, and Blažek, the humourist – the complex question of man's right to his own story in a homogenized society became – during the following years and particularly during the political thaw of the sixties – the topic for a number of outstanding playwrights with varied intellectual leanings and artistic talents.

The plays which I will discuss now are all about people with much the same story behind them; or better, the same lack of a story. In other words, they have no individual stories that have become the watermarks of their lives, and the characters themselves may be only dimly aware of their loss.

We might say then that the plays are about the possibility or impossibility of individualism in today's world. Most of Chekhov's characters live lives that are different from the ones they dream about living. Ibsen's characters, less prone to dream, picture the alternatives offered by the future more concretely; they imagine how life would look after some definite change had taken place.

The Czech characters we are about to discuss never get so far. Their energies are spent in trying to cope with the model of the world to which the playwright has fettered them, and their vague if urgent notion that somehow they have the right to be more than a cog in a system, never gets beyond its initial stage. Thus the plays are about individualism rather than individuals.

Perhaps in today's world – East or West – it is impossible to write plays about individuals. Today's man, though well stocked with scientific answers about how his heart, his brain, his feelings work, can no longer recognize his 'own' story. Playwrights from Schnitzler to Beckett have told us that man is not even sure whether he is happy, what his life is all about, or who he really is. The belief in individualism has taken on a different face than it had in the late nineteenth century. It has taken on a passive form and the question is no longer how the individual can act but rather how he can be left alone to live out his own story.

As said before, the plays discussed in this chapter are quite different in nature from the western European tradition. They share, however, a common starting point. All seem to agree that the world they are depicting shows little direction, that the social structures it contains are arbitrary and confusing, and that the individual is at best unfulfilled, at worst destroyed by having to cope with his relationships with the world around him – with authorities, colleagues, neighbours, elders, lovers. The playwrights – and here we have the difference between 1900 and 1960 – are more interested in these relationships than in the individuals themselves.

The member of the audience who looks for a 'rounded human being with a unique story' will not be satisfied by these evocative and highly theatrical explorations of situations and ideas. But then, the time of interest in unique psychology on the stage is over; the life-stories behind Gerhart Hauptmann's or even Tennessee Williams' characters do not interest us as much as they used to. We have become aware of the contemporary playwright's struggle to find a way to represent our complex world and the kind of character that would capture and reflect it in all its aspects.

It has been said in various ways, most eloquently perhaps by George Steiner, most memorably probably by Friedrich Dürrenmatt,[4] that our world has lost its claim on tragedy. The plays we are about to discuss seem like pointed illustrations of this theory. With the possible exception of Milan Uhde's version of the Antigone story they are all, despite their obviously serious concern, irresistibly funny. There is slapstick and word-play; there is humour of character and ironic communication with the audience. The entire complex scale of comic responses is evoked and, on the whole, the plays seem perfect examples of Pirandello's definition of the comic attitude[5] as the flexible and powerful instrument with which the audience can be controlled while the image of the play is being formed in their minds.

I

No age has had as much trouble with what is called man's 'self' as the twentieth century. There seems to be a general anxiety that it is getting lost. Humanists have fastened on Samuel Beckett as the great poetic preserver of the self. Martin Esslin, for example, calls his chapter on Beckett 'The Search for the Self'; Frederick J. Hoffman chooses the subtitle *The Language of Self* for his study on the same author.[6]

There is a whole group of contemporary plays that could be called 'plays on the loss of the self.' These plays appear in the West as well as in Eastern Europe. Ushered in by Expressionism in the first twenty years of our century and subsequently expanded and deepened by the playwrights of the Absurd, these explorations of man's loss of himself tend to take on the form of deadpan presentations of an insanely power-mad, obsessive, materialistic world in which the single man has little chance of surviving as an individual being, as a 'self.' The spirit in which writers conduct these explorations varies from acid bitterness to speculative hope, from macabre gloom to knowing laughter.

These problems of man lost in society like a drop in an ocean are shared by Western countries and Eastern Europe in greater measure than might appear likely. In both areas the writers' imagination has been fired by the theme of the automatization of man, the condition of the human being who has lost his reasoning power through pressures of society, tradition, ideology or habit, and whose reactions are merely conditioned, automatic responses. It is no over-statement to say that literally thousands of pages have been dedicated to critical discussions of this topic. Open any book or journal dealing with contemporary drama and you will find an essay or chapter dealing with it. The idea of man's irrational responses fascinates the contemporary mind, which spends more time and energy on observing the behaviour of apes than on studying the writings of its great philosophers.

The theme of automatization is, of course, by no means new. It has appeared in many guises for almost a century. When, for example, Peter Stockman in Ibsen's *The Enemy of the People* (1882) informs his wayward brother that 'as an official you have no right to any private opinion,'[7] or when, in 1920, Karel Čapek writes a play about man-made robots which fulfill their assigned tasks without understanding the nature of the tasks, these authors are obviously concerned with related problems. However, what had for a good many years been on the periphery of the writer's vision of man and his world has now moved into the centre of his attention.

Few plays do not in some way or other touch upon these problems which have become part and parcel of the life of everyone who has not withdrawn into a mountain cottage or a shack on an isolated beach. The writers of a systematized society such as Czechoslovakia feel, more acutely than the writers in an – albeit imperfect – democracy, the reduction of the human being to a particle in the system. It is much less apparent, even surprising, that the former have found a more amusing and playful way of expressing their misgivings, even agonies, about it than Western writers.

In this chapter I will consider a group of highly entertaining plays dealing with the rather grim subject of man's irrational, strangely automatic grab for power, and the terrible, ludicrous forms this power-struggle can take, the absurd situations it produces, and the way it reduces man to grotesquely small proportions, all the time deafening him with the message of how important his welfare is. The parallel of this kind of a situation to daily life in a totalitarian system need not be pointed out. Yet it also makes sense as a comment on certain aspects of Western societies.

We have watched the theme in Havel's grotesques about language taking over not only man's thoughts but also his soul. We have seen it presented in Klíma's juristic fables as well as in his grim comedies, we have recognized its implicit dangers in Topol's poetic visions and in Kohout's wry fables. The group of plays we are now about to discuss consist of variations on the theme. 'Man and the system,' 'the individual and society' have become clichés in Western literary criticism. Having been applied cheerfully to playwrights from Sophocles to Stoppard, these phrases now carry that amorphous pseudo-meaning which is dangerous not in its own right but because it prevents clear thought on the matter while seeming to encourage it.

The following three plays take up this theme with fresh verve and imaginative insight. They explore the worst aspects of the power structures man continues to build, and reveal their arbitrariness, their mechanistic nature, their fanaticism, their alarming powers of furthering the worst qualities of human nature. But none of the plays stops at the power machinery. Each of them explores the substance of the living oil that drives those machines. Here is where the individual comes in, the 'unique man' with his 'unique self.' Without exception the plays present the people, those groups of individuals, as confused, glad to have answers (almost *any* answers will do), cherishing their own little comforts, indifferent to the point of being brutal, afraid of nearly everything under the sun (but rarely the real dangers), wanting to make the best of the little they have.

It is interesting that these plays do not tend to reflect the playwright's bitter indignation about mediocrity – a trait that we find in many Western plays. The faceless crowd of the Czechoslovak theatre are not blamed so harshly. Rather we are constantly and humourously reminded that the world does not consist of magnanimous heroes, and the little Hamlets it contains have no Claudius, no 'kindless villain,' to blame for the world being out of joint. Their situation is much more like that of Peer Gynt facing the invisible monster, the Boyg, who is all around him but can neither be seen nor attacked.

Three plays illustrating the ways of the fertile monster of power approach the problem from three different angles. *King Vávra* by Milan Uhde (1964) is akin to Havel in the sense that it focuses on the power of language; *The Great Wig* (1964), by the Slovak playwright Peter Karvaš, explores the staggering power of a single idea; and Milan Uhde's version of the Antigone myth, *The Whore of the City of Thebes*, brings the ancient clash of the powers of social laws and individual conscience to a new and drastic conclusion.

King Vávra, subtitled 'nonstop-nonsense,' written for the satirical theatre *Večerní Brno*, is a sparkling satire of an authoritarian state.[8] Conceived in a highly theatrical way, with songs interrupting the loose structure of the play, *King Vávra* has an impact of striking immediacy. Growing out of the lively awareness of cabaret and 'little theatre' activities, the play transcends the limits of the cabaret satire while keeping the personal atmosphere of the small stage.

King Vávra, a sort of mechanized King Ubu, rules over half the world (envisaged by the playwright – with unintended irony – as centered in Ireland which constantly fights England) filled with ventilators, refrigerators, water-closets, ancient record players, and similar objects of man's technological inventiveness. The physical presence of these objects as the curtain opens, gives the audience immediate visual proof of a utopia based in every sense on mechanisms. This chief feature of King Vávra's empire is conjugated throughout the play. Mechanism is the chief symbol, the ultimate authority, the final aim and reason for being in Vávra's world. It appears in the gadgets in his study as well as in his conferences with his councillors and his communication with his people. The population, grotesquely dehumanized by being constantly referred to as 'inhabitants of both sexes,'[9] is part and parcel of the mechanism. Its passivity, its dependably mechanistic response, its indifference and willingness to carry on according to the laws of mechanized habit is the fuel needed for the smooth running of the mechanized empire. And it does run smoothly.

The representative of the people, the 'Nation's Uncle' as he is called, is another perfect example of mechanization. He moves around on the wheels of his invalid chair and his mind moves on the wheels of habitual thinking. He represents a kind of mechanized national memory: press a button and you get the story of a certain great battle, press another one and you get a folksy proverb. A certain word in the general conversation sets in motion the mechanism of the Uncle's brain, and he promptly delivers his speech with unfailing accuracy. When someone, for example, speaks about 'real life,' Uncle immediately rattles off his story about the battle at Woodford when, while delivering food to the frontline, he had to outwit a traitorous driver.[10] This, of course, keeps the audience continuously amused, particularly if it has been constantly exposed to certain canned versions of heroic tales from past revolutionary history.

With an additional twist of satire the playwright makes the cybernetic machine break down at one point. The Uncle has dozed off and misses the weatherman's information about an approaching storm. According to the way things should go, he is now expected to launch into his story about the English having been forced into hasty retreat during the battle at Killberry. But the Uncle does not respond. It is the Secretary of State who saves the situation. He pokes the Nation's Uncle in the ribs, repeats the signal word 'wind' into his ears, and – in order to assure proper results – he turns the ventilator so that it blows straight into the Uncle's face. This makes the mechanism function again and we promptly get the story about the battle at Killberry.[11] The credibility of the mechanistic world is complete. Even automatic gadgets are not foolproof and can break down. A seemingly broken alarm-clock, when gently shaken, can render additional years of dependable service.

Throughout the play there are various instances of resourceful play with language. We have sardonic literary allusions: 'Man was born and is here in order to become what the world needs, said Jiří Wolker;'[12] amusing logical fallacies: 'It is not important what facts we see but from where we see them ... that is why the position where we stand is so important because it decides what we will see;' refreshing examples of political dialectics: 'Act according to the principle of preferring the better to the worse! But you have to show people right away concretely what is better and what is worse, so that nobody gets the idea that he could decide it himself.'[13]

The crowning idea of the play is that this smoothly operating utopian society has mechanically accepted a false premise on which the entire system is built. King Vávra, the ruler, has a highly individualistic physical feature about him which he is anxious to conceal. Knowing what it is, we fully understand his desire. King Vávra has ass's ears. Everyone in the country is legally forced to wear long hair; to be a barber is to be a traitor. But actually the inhabitants have known for a long time about Vávra's closely guarded secret; only they don't think it worth their attention because they feel that 'we ordinary people just want to go on living ... never mind King Vávra's having ass's ears.' The play ends with an initially charming, wistful song about a merry-go-round, on which swans, fish, and painted horses move in a never-ending circle. As the refrain is repeated, however, it builds up with an increasing anxiety which is intensified into an desperate, urgent plea for release:

Please Mister Merry-go-round man, could you return my fare?
I've really had enough of it, it gives me such a scare.[14]

The Great Wig, by the Slovak writer Peter Karvaš, has an idealistic General who wants things in order and sets out to clean up the overall mess of society – a worthy endeavour, to be sure. Himself an orderly man, who dislikes fuzziness and ambiguities of any kind, he goes about his task with the methodical assurance of a man who knows how to achieve what he wants to achieve. He decides it is necessary to indicate clearly the causes for the problems which trouble society. In other words – and here we feel the playwright using the sting of his sharp satire – people must be told who are their enemies: who are good and who are bad.

The experienced sovereign shrewdly reasons that since an enemy of the people is not all that easy to define, he must be invented. After having rejected some of the possibilities that offer themselves, the General's choice for the invented foe falls on bald-headed citizens. When someone ventures the obvious question: 'But why bald-headed ones?' he is reprimanded that his question is 'politically wrongly formulated' because 'politics cannot be made from a position of negation and doubt.' When a worried high official enquires how such a decision can be explained to the Parliament, he is given a brief political lesson: 'For heaven's sake never explain anything! Does anyone explain why it rains or why it is quarter after nine? As soon as you begin to explain anything, you are sowing doubts.'[15]

Thus begins the simplistic separation of people into Good Ones and Bad Ones: into those who are in power and those who are persecuted. The terrible magic of such a separation soon begins to work. The new point of view provides a new system; the new system starts to function, begets its own mechanism, and soon the idea, which seemed to be utterly senseless, derives sense by becoming a reality. It is the people themselves who put it into practice and make it a reality. The people, unsure of values, confused about ethics, are only too glad to be handed a system that liberates them from making difficult and soul-searching moral decisions. Once they have accepted the idea that people must be divided into two groups – and man's religious, political, and cultural history contains enough evidence that such a division is close to his heart – the rest is easy. As a successful citizen in King Vávra's state has told us: 'It does not matter what facts we see, but from what point of view we see them.'[16]

With this all-too-human material Karvaš shapes his hard-hitting, yet highly amusing play. The theatrical possibilities of an enmity between bald-headed and hairy people are obvious. Once the ideology has caught on that all social and economic difficulties are to be blamed on the bald-headed citizens, the natural result is that hairless people do their best to 'go along with the attitudes of the day,' to 'be with it.' This naturally means that the wig business not only flourishes but becomes a highly political activity. A hair tonic, which allegedly causes hair to grow, becomes the chief product of chemical manufacturers and is purchased in wholesale quantities by all citizens.

It later appears that, through some unfortunate misunderstanding, the tonic furthers growth only for a short time and then causes complete loss of hair. The whole nation begins to wear wigs and once again confusion reigns as to who are the Good Ones and who are the Bad Ones. The possibility of wearing a 'bald' wig and revealing one's real hair only at a given moment, provides a new and original angle of testing one's neighbour's feelings about political matters. Toward the end of the play the audience, seeing all sorts of 'covered' and 'uncovered' heads milling around on the stage, share the characters' total inability to tell where the scalp ends and the wig begins.

The playwright's finest touch is that he sets off the whole plot against fragments of Hamlet's tragedy. The central character – the anti-hero, if you wish – is Hanjo Hraschko, a wig maker and hair-stylist for the 'Grand Theatre' of the nation. When the audience first sees him, he is just in the process of preparing for the stage a bearded king's councillor and a particularly terrifying version of the ghost of Hamlet's father. Rosencrantz and Guildenstern, characters who notoriously spend more time waiting in the wings than acting on stage, are playing cards in stage costume and discuss rumours about the new hair tonic. As actors they are proverbially easily confused; as ordinary people they create no confusion whatsoever since, ironically, one of them is bald.

But Hanjo, the talented hair-dresser, has no interest in the political aspect of his profession. He simply wants to do a good job and takes pleasure in sending onto the stage, say, an irresistibly coiffeured Ophelia. Nevertheless, he still gets into political trouble: the new hair tonic with its apparently redeeming but actually disastrous effect happened to be his – at the time totally unpolitical – invention. As he is struggling in vain to keep out of political involvement, there resounds from backstage (which is frontstage in the ongoing *Hamlet* production) Hamlet's soliloquy about the weary, stale, flat, and unprofitable uses of this world. The actor playing Hamlet, we are informed in passing, has been provided with a particularly attractive wig underneath which he is – quite bald.

Hanjo, the hair-stylist, who was rejected by the army, who likes poppy-seed cake, and whose big wish is to live without fear, because ever since he could remember he has always been afraid of something – jaundice or competition or marriage or the revenue office – is imprisoned and sentenced to death by both the Hairy Ones and the Bald-Headed Ones (who overthrow the Hairy government at the end of the play). Hanjo, whose only decisive action was that he shaved his head in order not to belong to the oppressors, is considered the enemy of both regimes because he refuses to see why people should lie about what is underneath their wigs.

The political necessity of an ideology simply does not make sense to him the way it makes sense to everybody else. Or does it only seem to make sense to them? Do they only act as if it made sense? Have they made absurdity real by acting in accordance with it? In a sparse but brilliant scene, reminiscent as much of the gravedigger scene in *Hamlet* as of Arrabal's *Pique-nique en campagne*, two gravediggers in army uniforms exchange remarks about the advantages of wearing a helmet: 'It's enough to put helmets on people's heads and right away everything is brought to order. Isn't it?' The gravedigger's colleague agrees: 'You wouldn't believe it, such a helmet is even better than a wig.'[17] At the end of the scene – which frames Hanjo's execution – the two gravediggers' work has made them feel hot. They wipe their foreheads and take off their helmets. One has long locks, the other is completely bald. As the lights go down on stage, the two stand there, staring at each other in silence.

Milan Uhde has written an *Antigone* for our times. Friedrich Dürrenmatt, in his 'Problems of the Theatre,' cites the tragedy of Antigone as an example of the fact that in our formless, violently changing world the tragedy of an outstanding individual can no longer be written: it is 'Creon's secretaries who deal with the case of Antigone.'[18] The famous clash between the statesman who guards the law and the pure spirit who guards the ideal is reduced to a bureaucratic procedure: Antigone has become a 'case' to be dealt with by regulations and paragraphs. However, though she is reduced in importance, Dürrenmatt still sees Antigone as clashing with the man-made law, and dying, even if deprived of heroic dimensions, for her beliefs.

The Antigone about whom Milan Uhde wrote in 1967 has lost not only the sense of the importance of her death but also the sense of the importance of her whole fight with Creon. She goes on living. All Antigones of the past went to their deaths as absolute postulates of their truth as opposed to the political compromise of Creon. Even Anouilh's Antigone (1942) dies, though no longer in order to oppose Creon but rather because she does not *want* to understand that the real world demands the surrender of absolute stands and ideals.

Milan Uhde's Antigone is paralysed by two discoveries: both are tragic in terms of her action but comic in essence. She realizes Creon is not the source of evil but only a small, in fact an exchangeable part of it; and she loses sight of the borderline between good and evil, and she can no longer define it – not even within herself: 'Perhaps it is easier to say: There is no good and no evil. There is only what the weak ones decide among themselves. Or else what the strong ones force upon them with their power.' Uhde's Antigone has fallen victim to the relativism of the modern world. To her horror she finds that her truth changes once she begins to analyse it: 'Shall I harbour a thousand souls inside me? Judge and forgive – and lose myself in that mess just as you do?' she asks Creon. She does indeed lose herself and her desperate attempts to hold on to her former moral convictions are futile. 'Are you ice or a flame? Good? Evil? Tell me that you are one as well as the other! I wanted only one of the two.'[19]

A terrible new awareness dawns on her as she realizes she can no longer think in clear moral distinctions: she feels part of Creon within herself.

What she had believed to be her own truth, defined by 'the command in her blood,' pales before that new insight. When she approaches Creon with a dagger in order to kill him, he tells her about his own agonies which closely resemble hers. With the very same words she had used before, he now describes his 'terrible yearning' for perfection; his contempt for the Thebans 'who make themselves at home in any dirt;' his last hope that rests with Antigone's own purity that would 'wash away' his guilt, and give the Thebans a new life. As Antigone recognizes her own struggles in Creon's words she begins to grasp that 'we both come from the same blood. What Polyneices was for you, Creon, you now want to be for me.' Her ultimate refusal to play her part in this handing on of roles is based on her realization that, by carrying out the demands of her ideal, she would merely again act out Creon's stale role. Instead she becomes a whore and plays the part of becoming a whore – of selling out to the world – over and over again. The play that began as Antigone's timeless tragedy becomes a hackneyed comedy about 'a beauty becoming a whore instead of you, and daily presenting her image, instead of yours, to be spat at.'[20]

With this version Uhde has written a modern 'tragic' Antigone. To go on living because there is no cause to die for is potentially more tragic than to die for a belief. And yet it seems that the very term 'tragic' is no longer applicable to Uhde's vision. 'Laugh about it, it is a comedy, only for tears,' counsels Antigone herself. 'Cry. A tragedy in which no one dies is usually funny. Laugh, the two go well together. It is one single miracle on this earth, so common that no one notices it. I feel that with a mere intake of breath man gives in to power. As sex it penetrates into our bodies and souls, dominating, it spreads lust in me, pain, laughter and tears, so that I want to give thanks. But to whom? And what for?'[21]

This is no longer the recasting of a classical theme, this is a contemporary writer's outcry against the impossibility of rendering today's world with the old forms; not because the forms are outlived but because modern man has lost the sense for moral action, because he is no longer sure what morality is. Reduced to patterns of behavior, exchangeable like roles, he plays his game, enjoying it or suffering, and not knowing why. And unlike Antigone – and this is why she is still an outstanding figure – he does not ask why.

II

Chekhov once said: 'It is necessary that on the stage everything should be as complex and as simple as in life.'[22] In his best plays he puts on the stage a group of people and makes us watch them in their complex simplicity. It has often been said that very little happens in Chekhov's plays and what does happen is almost commonplace and makes no claim to be tragic. When Aïda is buried alive in the subterranean vault, a whole orchestra conjures up the tragedy of her death; when the old servant Firs shuffles up in the last act of *The Cherry Orchard* and finds that he has been locked in the abandoned house, no sense of tragedy is allowed to develop. Old Firs does not mind. The clock time of the outside world no longer has meaning for him. As he sits still on the sofa behind the bolted door, we hear 'a distant sound ... coming as if out of the sky, like the sound of a string snapping, slowly and sadly dying away.'[23] A snapping string is scarcely tragic. At best it is a tragic moment, presented in comic terms. It seems that after this mild snapping sound on Chekhov's stage, tragedy has become impossible.

Czechoslovaks have a very close relationship with Chekhov. Anyone who has seen a Chekhov production in Prague, Bratislava, or Brno is bound to realize how fully local directors and actors respond to the great Russian's genius. The Drama Club of Prague is particularly successful in producing Chekhov. Several plays have been written by the actors and artists of that club. Chekhovian in spirit, they are of surprising literary value in addition to their theatrical immediacy. Centred around the average lives of average people, they reflect an artistic reality indeed 'as complex and as simple as in life.'

Alena Vostrá's *On the Knife's Edge* produced at the Drama Club in Prague in 1968 is a perfect example of Chekhov's dictum about simplicity and complexity. The play describes life in an apartment house close to a railway track. Passing trains regularly drown out conversation, make the windows shake, and cause dust to gather on dishes and beds, thus providing a nerve-shattering but generally accepted punctuation of daily life. The cross-section of a house with its inhabitants seems at first sight blatantly naturalistic. There is a henpecked caretaker who sublets a room to two medical students; a doctor who lives with his old-maid sister who has never changed her hair-style; an overworked lady schoolteacher who shows interest in the utopian blueprints of her engineer neighbour for reasons not altogether connected with architecture; and a foreign musician who plays the piano and has an eye on the caretaker's teenage daughter. The cross-section of the house is shown on stage, in its entirety, with all rooms simultaneously visible, and each illuminated in turn. The tenants run up and down the stairs with shopping bags, study for university examinations, borrow six cubes of sugar, play a masquerade with hats. So far so realistic – perhaps even so banal.

Beneath these everyday activities, however, there is another layer of existence. The characters of that other layer become ambiguous and can no longer be explained in terms of their lives. Dream and reality become inextricable and take on threatening shapes, while the audience continue to laugh at the funny incidents. The main current of the play is comic, but the undercurrent is tragic. Each of the characters has settled down, more or less comfortably, in the everyday, comic shape of his existence. The custodian, Mr Hrdina (which means 'hero' in Czech), whose intellectual curiosity makes him wonder why a fly can hold on to the ceiling without falling down, goes on, throughout the play, getting bread and carrying buckets of coal; the schoolteacher immerses herself in her exercise corrections although she makes the psychologically interesting admission that she is attracted by what she is afraid of; the doctor's sister, who knows how to skin rabbits like a butcher, harbours the philosophical conviction that people know nothing about themselves.

One evening everyone in the house gets drunk in the caretaker's kitchen and the usual routine is broken. The reason for this sudden abnormality is allegedly the fact that one of the medical students has passed his examinations, but the real reason is much more mysterious than that. At an earlier point in the play Hrdina admitted that 'I always used to think about how many things I am going to learn ... how many different and interesting things there are in the world ... and somehow I didn't make it.' After that remark, made to a tenant over the usual coal bucket on the stairs, Hrdina enters his kitchen and, going through the motions of his daily chore, he begins to wash the perennial pile of dirty dishes; then, as if lost in thought, he takes the big kitchen knife, lifts it over his head, and drives it with all his might into his skull. There follows a mad dream scene in which Hrdina gives a nonsense lecture to his applauding tenants, and leads them in a jubilant song about

That thing I've got in my head, you know,
it sure feels quite unreal;
those heady thoughts, they come and go,
can't tell you how I feel ...[24]

The euphoric wish-fulfilling dream recedes and Hrdina, back to his old anxious and orderly self, wants to get rid of that thing in his head which disturbs his mental balance. As he is trying to use an old top hat as a fig leaf to cover his shame, his tenants stage a 'fancy hat' drinking party in imitation of his grotesquely inappropriate attire (carrying coals with a top hat on one's head is not exactly what one would habitually do). During the general confusion everyone in the house (with the exception of the strait-laced, humourless Mrs Hrdina) has his or her brief flight of freedom, when awkward habits and thoughts are shed and unheard-of things are done with ease, charm, and courage. Hrdina manages to have one of the medical students remove the knife and bandage his head so that he returns to the party with another fancy head-dress – white gauze instead of a black top hat.

The play ends on an ambiguous note. Hrdina still has his thirst for knowledge but the implication is that it is the wrong sort of knowledge. The playwright does not tell us whether his existential act of courage and the subsequent moments of mental freedom will affect his further life. Just before the curtain falls Hrdina asks for a pill to relieve an ache in the part of his body that has always given him the most trouble – his head.

The interplay of simplicity and complexity, of the tragic and the comic, becomes more cerebral in Milan Kundera's *The Blunder*. Vostrá's *On the Knife's Edge* had almost entirely dispensed with a plot and the event with the knife, although unexpected, became the secret centre of the play and the focal point for the other events. Kundera's play, too, deals with an 'absurd,' secret action, performed by the hero, but here the whole plot develops out of this action, and the hero's ultimately insoluble tragi-comic situation is a result of his own doing as well as of the surrounding circumstances.

The central character of Milan Kundera's *The Blunder* is a high-school Principal whose reputation of manly charms is based on the fact that he is supposed to have had 400 women – a much-discussed secret that causes admiration and awe among the members (both sexes) of the teaching staff. Concerning the rest of the Principal's life, there is nothing much to be said; it is quite ordinary until a certain day.

On that day – and this is where the play starts – the Principal does something extraordinary – at least, for a Principal. Doodling on the blackboard in an empty classroom, he makes a drawing which at first seems to be of a geometric nature but, as he keeps adding more lines, turns out to be an obscene sign. To top off this highly inappropriate activity, he prints his own title 'The Principal' in front of the drawing and connects the word to the drawing with an equation sign. The meaning is unmistakable. When it is found on the blackboard the school goes into an uproar. As the Principal surveys the excited confusion, his initial amusement turns into horror as he watches the teachers produce a student culprit who promptly confesses to being the author of the drawing. Observing with growing dismay the perversions of moral indignation on the one hand and the perversions of justice on the other, the Principal gets more and more involved in the network of the complex, indeed 'absurd' relationship between crime and punishment until he himself is caught in the power web and pays for it for the rest of his life.

On the surface he will continue living a dutiful, contented existence, taking care of his school during the daytime and spending his evenings pleasantly with his charming new wife (who takes pride rather than displeasure in her alleged 400 predecessors). Beneath this varnished exterior, however, the Principal is at the mercy of a lecherous woman who nauseates him and forces him to satisfy her desires once a week – on Wednesday afternoons – when her husband, his superior, the School Inspector, regularly visits his mother. What had started as a schoolboy's joke, a high-spirited attempt to invert the cards and harrass the authority of which he himself was the representative, ends with a lifelong slavery which is the more distressing to him because it is imposed with the mechanical puntuality of a clock.

If we approach the play from another aspect – the power-structure of the school – we get another picture. The Principal, although he holds absolute power over the teachers in his school, is in his turn a stooge of the Inspector who is a mamma's boy, morally so vulnerable that he asks the 'experienced' Principal to try to seduce his fiancée and then report to him on her moral fortitude or lack of it. The Principal undertakes the delicate task with little glee – not only does he despise the Inspector but he also abhors the fiancée. One thing leads to another, the tensions of the power-structure multiply, and the situation becomes increasingly complex as success in someone else's bedroom becomes a way to humiliate one's hated superiors. The Principal takes his revenge, has his Pyrrhic victory and is promptly ensnared by blackmail. In a highly amusing bedroom scene he becomes another type of stooge *cum* unwilling gigolo to the Inspector's new wife. As the lights go down on stage and he performs the enforced rites of love in silent fury, the rhythmic creaking of the bed bears witness to his new slavery.

Havel's Gross brought about his downfall as a human being because he submitted unquestioningly to an absurd system; Klíma's family fell victim to the perverse lure of the Master because they failed to distinguish between true and false hope; Topol's simple-minded Jindřich became the villagers' dupe because in his childlike mind he was unable to tell a symbol from the real thing.

Where has Kundera's Principal failed? Has he also brought about his own downfall? He has indeed. But the reason is different. The Principal has given up his role as the leader in the school. He has suddenly stepped out of his own situation and seen himself as the somewhat perverse autocrat that he was. He expresses this inner discovery in a manner that one of his pupils might have used. Had he been willing to go all the way and openly admit how he regarded himself, he might have lost his job but not ended up in sexual slavery. Rather than embracing it fully, the Principal only played with honesty, letting it drop as soon as it touched his position of power. When he asks the schoolboy why on earth he has taken the blame upon himself, he gets a coldly reasoned answer:

PRINCIPAL You didn't do it! And you aren't interested in who really did it?

PUPIL I did it.

PRINCIPAL You're an idiot.

PUPIL I am not, Sir. After all, you must take into consideration that the investigating commission weighed things logically. It is much more likely that I did it than that I didn't do it.

PRINCIPAL Are we trying to find out likelihood or truth?

PUPIL What is truth, Sir? All human certainties are, if you permit me to say so, only forms of likelihood ...

PRINCIPAL You aren't only an idiot, you are a scholar.

PUPIL But Sir, please do try to understand. If I maintained that I didn't do it, nobody would believe me, they would say that I am lying and would punish me much more. In this way, although I am guilty of having made the drawing, everyone is bound to realize that I speak the truth and that is a great moral advantage for me ... Please understand that it doesn't matter one bit whether I really wrote it or not. The decisive thing is that the guilt happened to fall on me. Don't think I didn't try to deny it at the beginning. But then I realized that it really doesn't matter. And that the best thing for me to do is just to forget altogether that I got into it innocently.[25]

Critics have tended to regard the play as a parable on power through sex and have called the Principal's revenge – his bedding with the Inspector's wife – 'his fight with power [which is] the expression of his will to subdue life itself.[26] It may be that the time (January 1969) when the play appeared was a time when Czechoslovaks were particularly sensitive to the problem of power and its usage. At any rate, although the power theme is obvious –

especially when the play is considered within the context of Milan Kundera's prose writings[27] – the interwoven themes of a drastic breaking with your 'public image,' as in the case of the Principal, or the creation of such an image, as in the case of the pupil, yields less obvious but more interesting food for thought.

Through their drastic actions – in shrill contrast with the habitual pattern of their lives – both the Principal in Kundera's and the House Manager in Vostrá's play discovered their other, private selves which had not been moulded by the power structure or the mechanizing pressures of their jobs. Hrdina, expected to unlock doors and carry coal, has a secret self, intellectually curious and avid to find out about anything, from geography to chemical processes and man's anatomy. The Principal, expected to be rigorous and objective, responds readily when a young woman teacher discovers his 'other face, different from the one we know.'[28] He eagerly explains the difficulties and dangers of having to manage two faces and of not knowing at times which of the two is the real one.

Both characters perform the action that alienates them from their previous lives by doing something completely opposed to their 'roles.' When Kafka's Gregor Samsa wakes up and realizes that he has been changed into a monstrous insect, or when Havel's Josef Gross finds an incomprehensible memorandum on his writing desk, the impetus for alienation from their surroundings as well as their former selves comes from an outside source, inexplicable in Kafka, theoretically explicable in Havel.

The two characters of Vostrá's and Kundera's plays, however, are the active agents of their own alienation. Although both perform the action as if in a state of mental numbness and almost despite their own will – both playwrights make sure this is specified in the stage instructions – there exists no tangible reason for them to act the way they do. Following the authors' implicit hints we might say that both try to crack the nut of their existence, one by splashing dirt over his public face, in order to find his private one, the other by performing on himself, as it were, a living autopsy in order to find out what his brain contains. And so it becomes clear that these two so very different plays have a common core; it also shows again that the stories behind the characters are at heart the same stories. They are stories about the possibility of individualism, rather than about individuals.

Among this group of plays that try to reach out to the audience with particular urgency (Alena Vostrá even stated that she wrote *in* the theatre and not *for* the theatre) we might also consider Pavel Landovský's *Rooms by the Hour*. The play, written in 1968, is his first one. It is a lively piece of dramatic writing, full of verve, humour, and playfulness; it combines awareness of the stage with psychological insight and literary subtlety.

The theme is an almost farcical one. Two garrulous, sloppy old men rent their sleazy room by the hour or by the night to young couples who have no place to be alone with each other. The prices are moderate but clients prefer to bring their own bedding since the old men's linen is not exactly fragrant. Once we get beyond the potential slapstick of the situation, the play reveals itself as an original exploration of a sort of inverted generation gap. It is the old ones who have their flights of fancy while the young ones are ruled by their watches and their habits. It is, indeed, the old fellows who reveal themselves as the heroes of the play.

The young couples who use the room are rather predictable and variations of their harrassed conversations about love, time, the future, her boredom and ambitions, his anxieties and his wife at home have often been heard on stage from Strindberg to Albee. Tonight's couple is no exception. She, confusing her own carefree attitude with moral value, criticizes him for his utilitarian leanings. 'Can you ever talk about something that has not happened? Or can you talk about something that does not directly affect you? Have you ever done anything that made, let's say, no sense at all?' He is in turn aggressive, meek, helpless, on the defensive, and mostly ineffectual. But he has his moving moment of truth when admiringly confessing to one of the old men: 'You know what just passed through my mind? That I somehow envy you that you've managed to survive all this, that you've got it behind you, and still are around.'[29]

The two old men, Hanzl and Fana, the hidden heroes of the play, are reminiscent of Beckett's Vladimir and Estragon with their mutual quarrels and needs, their urge to discuss life in depth, their clownlike behaviour. Hanzl, who holds a job as a night-watchman, is a humorous version of the philosopher in rags. For example, he ruminates about man's intellectual endeavours by pointing out that cheese is the result of man's thinking, because he has forced cows to give milk beyond their natural time, when they have calves. 'The calf for which the milk started running may already be in a better world, but the milk keeps flowing. Do you get that, Fana?' Fana gets it, but he gets it as he always does, in his literal Švejkian way that completely loses the original point, 'You mean to tell me, you ... you ... that I don't know how cheese is made?' Fana doesn't like philosophizing. In fact he claims he does not really need a brain at all, he can do perfectly well with 'a nose, a mouth and a couple of eyes.'[30] He keeps all kinds of animals in the back room and holds forth about how much less stupid than people they are because they don't use their brains.

These two old men are exposed to the nervous, tense encounter of the two young lovers. At one point the girl asks old Fana to stay in the room because she does not want to go through the usual love scene tonight. This is a very pleasant event for Fana who usually spends these nights shivering on the balcony in order not to disturb the paying guests. There is indeed no lovemaking that night, and as the disappointed lover leaves, the pouting girl shrugs her shoulders: 'It makes no sense, anyway.' Hanzl, who has arrived from his watchman's job in the meantime, takes this comment with all its logical implications: 'If you know what makes no sense, then you probably also know what makes sense ... do you know it?'[31] The girl promptly rattles of a clichéd schoolbook answer, and, in order to prevent further searching questions, she pretends to be falling asleep.

Lying there on the sleazy bed on which for fifteen crowns a night she had often made love to a man whom she did not really like, she hears old Hanzl's definition of happiness which she is likely to grasp only when she is a few decades older, or perhaps never. The playwright makes it perfectly clear that he wants to leave the question open. According to his stage instructions the girl rises in a matter-of-fact way after everyone has left, fixes her hair, brushes her clothes, and spits on her handkerchief to wash her neck, giggling from time to time. Then she walks out into the streets, displaying her feminine beauty, unconcerned about the fact that she, too, was obviously incapable of doing something that 'made no sense' – a shortcoming for which she had bitterly blamed her lover.

The opening ending of the play shows her stalking arrogantly out of the room commanding Fana to open the door for her. The night of revelation is over. For the young people it has meant only the end of a love affair; for Fana it has meant pleasant entertainment but also a loss of income. For Hanzl, however, it represents the realization that a man's fulfilment does not lie where, throughout his life, he had thought it lay – in youth, freedom, and motion – but in the realization that there was such a thing as beauty, youth, and freedom even if one reaches it only for an instant. But the young woman to whom he reveals this secret realization has fallen asleep and does not hear nor heed.

Each of the three plays I have discussed here is about a group of people, and the tensions within that group. Like Chekhov and Hrubín's figures, the characters of these plays 'act' only in response to events. Things happen to them. If they do act (as in the case of Hrdina and the Principal), it is a half-hearted pretence at acting, somehow as if performed only in order to see what would happen, and constantly prepared to withdraw.

Broadly speaking, the characters are usually separated into two groups that hold entirely different opinions, without necessarily being aware of the difference themselves. However, that difference is basic: one group believe, or seem to believe, that the world is going somewhere, that life on the whole is improving. The others – and they are the interesting group, containing Vostrá's Hrdina, Kundera's Principal, and Landovský's Hanzl – are rather convinced that the world is going nowhere, that it has no sense of direction, and that the reason for living is not only obscure but probably non-existent. This latter group believe that man neither knows what he wants nor wants what he knows.

This anything but cheerful awareness, however, does not make them grim like some of Beckett's figures. They never seem to lose their Chekhovian wide-eyed wonder at life. Perhaps that is why they are neither successful nor practical. They are house managers reduced to carrying coal, night-watchmen who like to see whether they can spit on the ceiling, engineers who design houses that float and cannot be lived in. They are fascinated by the march of science and puzzled by the fact that it has not managed to solve the simplest philosophical problem. They are true citizens of the twentieth century. Despite their outwardly seemingly simple lives, they balance the largest questions of man's life in their 'average' little heads; they worry about the nature of freedom, crave more knowledge than is available to them, and are disturbed that the widely praised 'progress of man' seems to take place with regard to wheels and wires rather than intelligence and ethics.

All three plays reflect Chekhov's spirit in that they are complex and simple at the same time, and also both tragic and comic. Madame de Staël said long ago that tragedy is simple and comedy is complex because it touches life at infinitely more points than does tragedy. Surely Chekhov's modern complexity and his sense of comedy are related. Perhaps it is impossible to write a complex tragedy because as soon as there is complexity, there is irony, shifted focus, relativism and hence no tragedy.

And here we are back at the thought that our age can no longer be approached with the values of tragedy in mind. It is tragi-comic, grotesque, absurd, anti-tragic – take your choice of expressions with which modern critics have tried to describe the literary reflection of the chaotic world of today. The contemporary playwright has been striving to express his sense of the infirmity of our world, the incapacity of our speech to describe it, the awkward way in which we are grasping for each other's understanding amidst shifting values and confusion.

Chekhov was the first to give artistic form to this awareness; Beckett represents the ultimate possibilities of this form. Perhaps the unpretentious, painfully honest, yet gravely funny Czech plays, written almost exactly a century after Chekhov's birth, indicate the beginnings of a new cycle. They too are about the failure of people to master or even grasp the true meaning of their lives, let alone to tell each other about the failure in a language that may be understood.

But – unlike their contemporaries Ionesco on the one hand and Pinter on the other – these Czech playwrights seem to point to the confusion caused by social pretences and political lies and the resulting spiritual void and emotional aridity. That confusion and that aridity are not easily defined. Perhaps the whole image of 'pointing to' something is wrong. Their form of hope is not beckoning from the horizon as a reminder of 'timeless human values' or whatever cliché modern man's frantic attempt at self-protection has coined. The Czech writers' form of hope is not so much in what they say but in how they say it. With their resourceful imagination and their sense of humour they display an inner freedom that is the affirmation of man's creativeness and hence his self-renewal and hope.

III

The idea that man plays roles is much older than popular psychology would have us believe. The art of imitating others, of taking their part and 'acting' from their point of view – natural to the little girl who plays 'mother' to her dolls or the little boy who plays 'wolf' for his playmates – is perhaps the most important quality an audience brings along into the theatre. The spectator's ability to suspend his own identity for a while and share the condition of the characters on the stage is – and this is contradicting Brecht less than might be thought – as important to the playwright as is the ability of the actors to play their parts in his play.

If the playwright chooses to play with, interrupt, and tease this ability of the audience, he can achieve a complex pattern of response that will swing back and forth between the extremes of identification and alienation (the latter meaning here refusal to identify; a desire to judge rather than to understand). The ability to impose this shift between 'becoming someone' and 'judging someone' is a powerful tool in the hands of the playwright, as Hamlet knew when he made his players act out a scene that would make it impossible for Claudius either to identify or to judge, because both attitudes would cast the action back into his own lap. He could bear neither being actor nor audience.

Three playwrights who are particularly concerned with this complex area are Zdeněk Mahler in *The Mill* and in his collage of Nestroy's works, *The Rope with Only One End*, written with Karel Kraus; Alena Vostrá in *Eeny, Meeny, Miney, Mo*; and Pavel Landovský in *Closed for Disinfection*. These plays are quite different in content and form. *The Mill* is ambitious and complex, set against a historico-political background which lends the play weight and seriousness; *The Rope* is a superb distillation of the writings of a brilliant and perceptive humourist. Vostrá's play is a light, at times slapstick, exploration of an everyday situation; Landovský's is a sardonic utopia of a totalitarian state in the 1980s. Yet, in their essential consideration of the interplay between truth and illusion, between 'being' and 'acting as if' they are closely related.

Zdeněk Mahler's *The Mill* – 'a buffoonery in ten scenes'[32] – was first produced in 1965 by the Slovak National Theatre in Bratislava with Otomar Krejča as director.[33] The work is a complex, demanding script for a production that includes showing films in which part of the action is seen from a different point of view. Basically the play is about a Jewish work-camp in the Nazi period and the events that take place during the shooting of an allegedly documentary film about the German 'liberation' of the Ukraine on the one hand and the defeated Red Army soldiers on the other. The theatre audience is made to witness on stage the real filming of a false reality: false actors playing false roles in a documentary (parts of which are later actually shown on stage); an untalented double of the 'Führer' being trained for his part in the film.

Essentially the play deals with the process by which one level of reality is used to produce another, illusory level of reality. The result is extremely entertaining. We are clearly reminded of Peter Weiss's *Marat/Sade*, first produced, significantly enough, only one year before *The Mill* was staged in Bratislava.[34] Not only do both plays deal with different levels of reality, but they are also structured as plays within plays, creating new plots which are repeatedly broken off and started again. Thus the plays form reflected patterns of reality and illusion which give a strangely confusing yet, ironically, a highly realistic effect, because they do not permit the audience to be sure what is 'real' and what is just 'acted.'

Into this pattern Mahler projects another pattern of false reality. A prison inmate who, out of despair, becomes a collaborator with the Germans, is being sent on an intelligence mission into the camp: he is to pretend that he is a British parachutist smuggling in weapons with the goal of starting a revolution. This revolution (which actually, due to all kinds of tragi-comic circumstances, never takes place the way it was planned) is thus instigated by a fake revolutionary and its aim is not liberation but the 'justified' extermination of the Jewish inmates of the camp. The levels of illusion multiply. The false Ukrainian peasants are on another level false revolutionaries or rather real revolutionaries but for the wrong reason, a pretended reason which is as false as the documentary reality of the film.

The theatrical possibilities of such a text are clear but so are the dangers of over-complexity. Otomar Krejča's production used the former to the full and avoided the latter. A Czech critic calls the staging of *The Mill* Krejča's most difficult and, in spite of this, his 'most balanced production.'[35] Krejča's stage reflected constant chaos, with actors moving pieces of furniture and acting as stage-hands during the intervals. This meant that another level of confusion was added, namely the uncertainty whether the actors were performing these tasks as part of their roles in the film, as inmates of a labour camp, or in their real capacity as actors in Mahler's play.

The director's intention was to respond with all the means at his disposal to the playwright's basic idea: the world is a mad-house in which truth and illusion mingle beyond recognition. Peter Weiss's intention is similar. His Marquis de Sade would have made an excellent director for Mahler's fraudulent film about victory and defeat.

The crowning absurdity of *The Mill* is that at the end the false parachutist, the agent provocateur, is executed as the British parachutist whose role he was playing.[36] When he is given the choice in which 'role' he wants to die, whether as a foreign agent or prisoner number 82 – i.e. in the role of an activist or a victim – he shrugs his shoulders and signs both papers because 'every word is false, only the murders are real.'[37] His execution is filmed as an uplifting finale for the documentary film, in which evil is universally defeated by good, and the Director of the whole 'show' delivers a passionate speech about truth victorious in which, piling one lie on top of another, he recapitulates the 'facts.'

Like an ominous version of a Beaumarchais play in which everyone pretends to be someone he is not, *The Mill* is an attempt to reveal the structure of what can readily be called an 'absurd' world. Every character is caught in the confusion, helpless and ridiculous, playing his part badly for the right reasons or well for the wrong reasons. A particularly grim undertone is heard with increasing urgency as the comic events take their course: there is no exit from this maze of false identities because – and the shock of this realization is prepared with great care by the playwright – real identities matter much less than seemed to be the case at the beginning of the play; the nature of the truth is irrelevant to the tragi-comic pattern of the mill of life.

Two years after *The Mill*, Mahler, in cooperation with Karel Kraus, produced a singularly interesting adaptation of works by the prolific Austrian humourist Johann Nestroy: *The Rope with Only One End*.[38] What Mahler and Kraus did was not to adapt one particular play but, with what is obviously deep insight into the puckish Austrian's mind, they chose individual scenes from different works, and merged them into what became an original, unified play with musical interludes. It was as if the adapters had distilled the very essence of Nestroy's vast and uneven dramatic work (for example, the twenty-four quotes from *The Rope* reprinted in the program were drawn from no less than eleven Nestroy plays) and moulded it into one unique miniature replica of the dramatist's world which contained all his essential elements.

Comparing it to Karl Kraus's[39] famous essay on Nestroy, the well-known critic Jindřich Černý[40] calls the Mahler/Kraus play an equally valuable comment on Nestroy's stature as a commentator on human nature and society. Thus the Czech play crystallized the largely neglected philosophical aspect of Nestroy's work, and the playwright's popular image as a writer of localized Viennese Volksstücke changes before our eyes into that of a fine humourous intellect à la Oscar Wilde, Shaw, or even Molière. Moreover, the biting social criticism of Nestroy could be related by the Czech audience to circumstances at home, while 'officially' they referred to a top-heavy, decadent, nineteenth-century Austrian monarchy.

Despite the complex mosaic of the adaptation, Mahler and Kraus somehow managed to retain a very simple main plot as well as straightforward characterization. Miraculously, none of Nestroy's own dramatic thrust was lost. Together with Josef Svoboda's stage-set and Hapek's music it was an enormous theatrical hit. An additional stroke of luck was having as director Otomar Krejča, who stressed the farcical elements of Nestroy. The result was a surprisingly new Nestroy which, however, also reaffirmed his image as it exists in the literary consciousness of our age. The success of the Nestroy pot-pourri is proven by the comments of a number of Viennese critics who took the Vienna-Prague *Vindobona* Express in order to be present at the première. They expressed high praise and indeed claimed this to be the best Nestroy play ever staged.

If Mahler had certain messages in mind when he explored the playing of roles in *The Mill* and merged different roles in *The Rope with Only One End*, Alena Vostrá tells us that although her play *Eeny, Meeny, Miney, Mo* was written with the idea of 'a play within a play' in mind, it did not pursue a 'utilitarian interest' of any kind. In other words, the author, unlike Weiss or Mahler, did not intend to catch the 'conscience' of the audience.

The interest created by the originators of the play within a play, she argues, 'does not lie outside but within the play. In a game played by people with people there are usually victims. The very originators of such a play can become its victims ... We are dealing, if you like, with the play-model of every human action ... The integration of "non-play" actions into the play on the one hand, and the play into "non-play" actions on the other is the principle of this comedy: the border lines of both are flexible ... Thus in this comedy unconscious acting and conscious acting interpenetrate each other ... the play within a play is the subject as well as the motivation, the theme as well as the organizing principle.'[41]

At the beginning of *Eeny, Meeny, Miney, Mo*, which takes place alternately in a garden restaurant, a park, and an apartment, one of the characters, a young man called Pierot, while having some drinks in the company of his friends, suddenly fixes his eyes on a certain point in the audience and exclaims:

PIEROT Mary, dear – how did you get here? *to his friend Ofsayd* Look, Mary's there.
OFSAYD *looking up, surprised* Gosh, Mary.
PIEROT How did you get home that night? Did you find that shoe? – On New Year's Eve! – Well, did you?
OFSAYD When you were sick all over Pinder's cocker spaniel!
PIEROT You honestly don't remember? *to Ofsayd* She doesn't remember.
OFSAYD She forgot.
PIEROT *as if making a sudden decision* But that's impossible. She doesn't react. *shouts* Are you dumb?
OFSAYD She's embarrassed about it. So she's acting as if she didn't know what it's all about ... Forget about her, Pierot, What if it isn't her?
PIEROT *irritated* What? You think I can get Mary mixed up with anyone? Ma-ry?
MEDIK People get mixed up. Especially if there are many of them in one place.
PIEROT *suddenly unsure* Well, guys, maybe it isn't her after all.
OFSAYD Maybe not.
PIEROT Yeah, that's it. It isn't her. It isn't Mary, it just isn't ...[42]

The implications of the scene are clear. First, the actors have identified themselves as actors on a stage before a room full of spectators, thus indicating an awareness shared by actors and audience that what is going to be represented on stage is only pretended, fictional reality. The obvious reminder of Brecht's theatre is misleading because Brecht approached the audience rhetorically, treated them en masse, while in Vostrá's case an individual in the audience is singled out and his or her past is related directly to the actor's past. Going a step beyond Peter Weiss and Mahler, the author claims not to be serious about suggesting that there exists any level of non-fictional reality on the stage.

This brings us to the second implication: By denying a differentiation between audience and actors, between onlookers and players, Vostrá's play is stating its basic premise of the inextricable interrelationship of 'play' and 'non-play.' As soon as the actor, peering into the audience, has accepted the basic principle that it is possible to confuse one person with another on the basis of behaviour, he firmly denies his initial act of recognition. If a person acts in a different way that cannot readily be related to one's previous knowledge of him or her, he or she can be considered a different person. The personality disintegrates into ways of acting.

The whole play is an exploration of games to be acted out. The young men decide on the rules of the games to be played by one of them, Ofsayd, with the restaurant's chanteuse. He succeeds – she comes to a rendezvous in the park, he kisses her at half past three on the dot, while his friends, watching from behind a tree, check their watches for accuracy. However, the game, initiated as a whim, causes infinite complications as Ofsayd gets caught not only by the girl's husband but also literally in a piece of furniture. As the slapstick scenes, in which we can no longer tell 'pretence' from 'reality,' roll on before our eyes, the play races – not to its conclusion, but rather to its dissolution.

HUSBAND What's all this supposed to mean? This whole comedy? ... What are you
    rattling on about all the time?
OFSAYD About human life.
HUSBAND What? What life? What are you dragging life into it for?[43]

These are the last words spoken in the play. Then Ofsayd launches into a song about a girl who assured him that he need not be afraid of her because she is not real, she is only a figment of his imagination – a fiction.

The role-playing theme in Genet's *The Blacks* makes use of an antagonism existing in real life, outside the theatre, and derives its particular force from experimenting with the levels of this antagonism.[44] Genet's attempt to reveal the destructive power of 'false' images is related to the message of Max Frisch's *Andorra* rather than to Zdeněk Mahler's or Alena Vostrá's approach. Genet and Frisch seem to claim that the truth is blocked by false images; Mahler and Vostrá imply that the nature of the truth cannot be known and we might as well accept the fact that, although we may be able to peek under the mask worn for a certain role, we are not likely to find out whether the face underneath is not another mask.

It would take a detailed study to discover whether the idea of 'role-playing' appears in the modern theatre of the West with the same intensity and resourcefulness as it does in the theatre of Eastern Europe. In a totalitarian society in Eastern Europe today values are fixed, one form of belief is irreversible and absolute, and behaviour is standardized – not as a result of perniciously reductive advertising as in the West, but rather because personal behaviour is closely surveyed and constantly judged in moralistic terms (we must not forget that having a view of the world that would differ from the official line would be considered not only wrong but also immoral). Such a society must impose upon its citizens the unavoidable need to play roles. Hence they project not only a public persona (which is true of the West too), but also a political persona of a certain standardized type, deviation from which would be equivalent to moral betrayal. Of the plays chosen here to illustrate this complex topic, Ivan Klíma's more philosophical *Games* (discussed in chapter 4) and Pavel Landovský's *Closed for Disinfection* are, despite their farcical aspects, the most poignant statements about a non-democratic social order.

Pavel Landovský's *Closed for Disinfection* (1976)[45] is a high-spirited, extremely funny play in which the author uses every aspect of histrionics with the unfailing instinct developed by years of varied and intense experience with the stage. The topic could be put simply as a day – or rather a night – in the lives of a group of average people in a sort of 'brave new world' of a totalitarian society in the 1980s.

It is a society which encourages its citizens to dry their garbage on ropes stretched between the windows of their homes, and thus save electricity for the state's garbage mills; a society where guests ask in restaurants whether they would be allowed to use for a minute 'the untapped phone'; where complicated loudspeaker systems are devised in order to trick the bugging systems of the authorities; where the citizens are forced to read 'Duty-Brochures' on behaviour; where professors of science secretly build conveniently noisy ventilators to exchange for four bottles of Heinz ketchup apiece; where daily 'personnel-gratitude-sessions' are staged with texts that are passed out like hymn-books before the service and mechanically repeated in order to pacify the official wire-tapper (though he is usually asleep). It is a state in which the finding of loopholes in the system has become a full-time activity.

A mere look at the list of characters will suffice to make the audience realize the nature of the people who populate (as employees or guests) the restaurant which is the scene of the action. The waiter is a former lawyer, in fact a prosecuting attorney; the guard used to be the mayor; when a physician has to be called they get him in the garbage disposal plant where he is working as a stoker. A former actor and a couple of policemen play childish jokes on clandestine gatherings and their complicated uniforms and 'protective-action-gear' do not prevent them from being more interested in chasing girls than in raiding in the name of the law. There is a Minister of Culture (*not* a former one) who his caught in bed with his mistress because a mild heart attack has prevented him from leaving the house unseen as he had been doing successfully for the past fifteen years; there is a black English-speaking foreigner who turns out to be neither black nor a foreigner but a local Czech intelligence man; there is a writer whose chief interest lies in passing around petitions to help free another writer (actually, the idea is to get him not out of but *into* prison which would be much preferable to the lunatic asylum where he was put as a result of an earlier successful petition).

These characters, if they were presented on a Czech stage, would clearly have not only a highly realistic impact but would actually play to persons in very similar situations among the audience. The rest of the characters – assorted kitchen personnel, guests, bakers, and so on, create constant movement on the stage, carefully choreographed by the author in the stage-instructions. They run into the kitchen, to the upstairs apartment, out into the street; they creep under tables, climb on ladders, unhinge doors, lower chandeliers, and pull up curtains. There is a constant hustle and bustle of comings and goings, so that we get a sort of mosaic of aborted scenes, untold bits of information, interrupted love-making, scraps of conversations from the kitchen or from upstairs, repetitions of comments and so on. As a result the whole cast seems like a group of little busybodies, lifting and rearranging equipment, carrying objects, connecting wires, pressing down keys, pulling switches – a grotesque group of dwarfs chasing about to serve technological accomplishments. The play shows man reduced to playing slave to the machine on the one hand, and to the huge power apparatus (however inefficiently or absurdly it might work) behind it.

Take the author's description of the stage set: 'A large room reminiscent of the restaurant of the seventies of our twentieth century. Everything is spick and span. On the walls hang the diplomas earned by the personnel. In the left corner the table, on it knife and fork, napkins, salt and pepper, tooth picks, perhaps cigarettes. Next to it a table with a chair for a single steady customer; the other chairs have been placed in such a way that no-one can sit down. This corner seems as if it belonged to another, more logical era. At all the other tables the chairs are placed in such a way that no guest can sit with his back to the platform on which there is a large television set of plastic (the screen can't be seen from the audience); furthermore a bust of an important statesman with an average face; a speaker's desk, a radio transmitter, a tape-recorder, a record player, a projection-screen and numerous newspapers ... [as are often seen in Europe]. That corner gives the impression of a strange altar.'[46]

Later on, when the sign 'Closed for Disinfection' is put at the locked door, these chairs and tables undergo a drastic change: the waiter pulls a switch, and from the ceiling ropes are lowered which the latter attaches to chairs and tables with routine efficiency, whereupon they are pulled up so that for the rest of the play they remain suspended about two and a half metres above the floor, which produces a hilarious effect on stage and makes the characters flit about like mice under the furniture.

On the whole the play has no plot, but there is one thread of action which, though initially peripheral, later moves into the centre. In the apartment above the restaurant (visible on the stage)[47] a love scene takes place between the current Minister of Culture and Mrs Kádová, his mistress, unbeknown not only to his wife but also – which is much more important – to the state authorities. As the characters in the restaurant below go about their nightly activities (which vary from taping political slogans cheerfully recited for the benefit of the hidden microphones, to trading in black market goods or discussing social circumstances in a way that would amuse any audience) the act of love proceeds in the apartment above, from wine and roses at the table to amorous activites on the bed, until the unexpected crisis: the Minister has a mild heart attack, which means that he cannot leave the house unnoticed as he has been used to doing in the past. In the course of the play he is moved (on an unhinged door) into the restaurant downstairs, and at the end of the play he is on his way to the hospital, carried (à la Hamlet) in a huge basket, buried under fresh buns, with a scooped-out loaf of bread for a camouflaging head cover – a plaintive Falstaff asking his 'bearers' not to forget his hat, his briefcase, and his trousers.

Nearly all the characters in this farcical parody of a utopian 'workers' state' are playing false parts. They have accepted a life which consists of pretending on every level of existence: the police pretend as much as the black market dealers. Only the various couples who manage to spend a while in Mrs Kádová's bed upstairs experience a moment of non-pretence and truth.

Mahler's *The Mill*, by dealing with a situation from the Nazi occupation, permitted the audience to adopt a distancing attitude inevitable with a quasi-historical topic; Vostrá intellectualized the proposition and experimented with the same theme, trying to show how "unconscious" acting merges with "conscious" acting.'[48] Landovský's play, though the funniest of the three, presents potentially the darkest vision, in which a drastic life-lie has become so necessary for survival that it is no longer recognized as a lie. The playwright punctuates the mechanistic, plastic, mindless order – an Orwellian universe, a gloomy utopia for West and East alike – with outbursts of the unmanageable, unregimentable aspects of man (passions, playfulness, resourcefulness, amusement); he pitches spontaneity against training, personal perceptions against the 'byzantine vigilance hierarchy'[49] of a closed system.

According to another Czech writer, Ota Filip, the state and the Party have given up trying to 'convince' or to 'educate' the citizen – they are now satisfied merely to drive him into resignation. In an essay which appeared in the program to the first production of *Closed for Disinfection*, which took place in Bonn in the autumn of 1978, Filip comments how the Czechoslovak people, made completely unsure of themselves in public life, have withdrawn into small groups and 'their real life takes place in tightly closed ghettos where they seek safety from the agressive impact of propaganda and other threats.'[50] The irony and the cynicism which they voice there keep them sane, for there are circumstances under which cynicism can be healing rather than destructive as it usually is. To survive in such a world is not easy: the spark of an independent thought, a healthy scepticism in the face of the all-pervading *Gleichschaltung*, are fragile plants prone to wither in a sterile atmosphere such as this.

Kundera's Principal still talked about his 'two faces'. Landovský shows us the difference between those who have forgotten their real face and those who still remember it. Yet, one may add, how long will they remember? This frightening realization appears again and again in the writings of the Czech dramatists. But the very fact that they write about it so insistently (let us not forget that there is a decade between *The Mill* and

Closed for Disinfection), is revealing. There seems no danger that they, the spokesmen for their people, will ever get confused about what is real and what is a lie. Furthermore, their exploration of this aspect of social behaviour, or the 'ecology of language' as it is called, places them at the very centre of modern man's consciousness, in a field being examined by literature and the social sciences alike.

8

Aspects of history

Everyone has his model of history, the approximate outward forms of which are represented by facts and dates, but the inner actions, passing through our consciousness ... are always contemporary.

FRANTIŠEK HRUBÍN program to *Oldřich and Božena*

The fact that Czech playwrights seem to be reticent in their attitude to historical themes is due to a particular combination of circumstances. Treatment of history in Czech literature had, during the last century or so, acquired, very broadly speaking, three different faces.

First came the earnest and passionate attempt to revive national consciousness in the nineteenth century, inspired by historians such as František Palacký (1798–1876) and writers such as the prolific Romantic Josef Kajetán Tyl (1808–1856). Palacký wrote the monumental *Dějiny národu českého* (History of the Czech Nation), the first volume of which was published in 1836 and the last some forty years later. He is often called the father of modern Czech history. Tyl's large and uneven literary output had a formative influence on Czech literature. Passionately engaged in the movement of National Revival, he advocated social and moral reforms, wrote impassioned historical dramas and fiction, but also excelled in a pithy and natural style.

During the nineteen twenties, various kinds of historical fiction began to appear. Ironically, this initially romantic and patriotic phenomenon, interrupted by the Second World War, reached its culmination during the Stalinist period of the early fifties, when there appeared works prompted by both the Marxist stress on the importance of history and the dictates of Socialist Realism. In these works we encounter ideological clichés about the selfless zeal of the proletarian youth, about the evils of capitalist exploitation, and the strength of the collective. Within this group we also have, after the Second World War, the so-called 'occupation and concentration camp literature' which describes the horrors of Nazi Germany as the antipode of the values of Socialism.

A third and entirely different stream goes back to Hašek's *Švejk*, that historical enfant terrible which has provoked reactions varying from sharp attack to high praise ever since it appeared. As was said before, *Švejk* represents an anti-heroic attitude which uses irony to reduce the great historical moments of the past to the mouse-perspective of a little individual. Josef Škvorecký's novel *The Cowards*,[1] which appeared in 1959, is an electrifying revival of this tradition. The action of the novel takes place under the occupation, but the atmosphere is entirely different from the traditional literature about Czechoslovakia during the German occupation. *The Cowards* makes the point that the much-stressed 'responsibility to society' can be an empty phrase and reveals the hypocrisy of cowardice posing as heroism.

With these contradictory approaches to a literary treatment of history in their files, Czechoslovak writers of the sixties found themselves in a complex situation. The black and white world of Socialist Realism was rejected; the old concern with the nationalistic aspects of Czech and Slovak history seemed strangely irrelevant, and contradicted the fresh breeze of internationalism that was beginning to blow after the turn of the decade. The hunt for false sacred cows of history that had made works such as Škvorecký's *The Cowards* or Hrabal's *Closely Watched Trains*[2] so exciting, had been replaced by explorations of the complex issues of the present, as in the plays of Havel, Klíma, and others.

This perhaps accounts for the fact that among the numerous plays written in the sixties, surprisingly few deal with historical events. Moreover, those highly individualistic attempts to deal with history are outside any of the three main literary streams indicated, and were prompted not so much by the desire to shed light on events of the past, but rather by the urge to explore that deep crisis in modern man's experience – the division between personal experience and social conflicts. Perhaps the awareness of this crisis is doubly strong in a country like Czechoslovakia which, situated at the cross-roads of Europe, has been the scene of power struggles for centuries. It almost seems that the Czechs had to learn earlier than the rest of Europe to separate experience into social and personal categories.

A contemporary footnote to this attitude is provided by a comment

František Hrubín made on the reception of his play *Oldřich and Božena*. Hrubín tells us that, while writing the play, he had 'expected the public to react more strongly to those scenes in which the struggle for power becomes apparent in all its brutality; luckily, however, even today an audience reacts not only to those discussions which are related to their feelings as citizens ... but also to those that deal with nothing greater or smaller than the relationship between a man and a woman.'[3] Hrubín realized that the audience had instinctively separated social from private experience and that his play engaged them less as a basic model of power struggle than as a moving story about a man and two women. Hrubín's expression 'luckily' in this context seems to reflect his awareness of this attitude, and he defends it as an artist.

Milan Kundera is here more didactic. In connection with his play *The Owners of the Keys* he wrote that only 'stern self-recognition makes a national literature mature. And only in the process of such a cruel self-recognition is a nation capable of developing and overcoming its own mentality.'[4] Whatever the difference between the attempts of these two authors to shed light on certain moments in history, their works have surprisingly much in common.

Milan Kundera's *The Owners of the Keys* (1963) was performed in fifteen Czechoslovak theatres, in two Russian translations in a number of Russian theatres, in Estonia and Hungary, Bulgaria and Poland, East Germany and France. It was translated into Serbian, Greek, Japanese, and English. It was (if we discount the impact that Havel and Kohout's plays had in some Western countries) probably the most successful of all Czechoslovak plays written during the 'renaissance' of the sixties. This success is quite simple to explain. *The Owners of the Keys* is an excellent piece of writing for the theatre. It is difficult to believe that it was Kundera's first dramatic effort and that at the time he knew preciously little about dramatic literature.[5] Furthermore – the thaw had only just begun – the play deals with a politically 'safe' topic: the German occupation. However – and this perhaps explains its lasting appeal – *The Owners of the Keys* carries a much more complex and many-sided meaning than the average occupation play which normally merely filled a momentary need and had little artistic value.[6]

The play contains two stories. The first is as follows: Jiří, a former student and member of a resistance group, has opted out of social commitment and withdrawn to a small town where he now lives a quiet and unobserved married life, sharing his in-laws' two-room apartment. One

Sunday morning he gets a phone call from Věra, a former fellow student who is being hunted by the Gestapo. He lets her take refuge in the apartment and – in the course of her brief stay – while his wife Alena and her parents are in another room – kills the spying caretaker with a paperweight in order to save Věra. This means certain execution for him and his family. Věra knows some way of escape. She wants to save at least the young couple. With a threadbare excuse Jiří tries desperately to lure Alena (to whom he cannot at this point tell the truth) from the house. However, supported by her parents who have always been critical of Jiří's behaviour, Alena pouts and refuses to join him. Jiří has no other way but to go alone and leave the family to their terrible fate.

The second story in the play is as follows: In a small town there live the Krůta family – father, mother, and Alena, their daughter. They have always had three lots of keys for their apartment and everyone was happy. But when Alena gets married, her husband Jiří moves in with the family and quickly manages to lose one set of keys. Since he has to be given another one, the old Krůtas are left with one single set of keys. One Sunday morning, after having received a mysterous telephone call, Jiří disappears with both sets of keys and leaves the family locked in the house. When he returns he claims to have taken the keys by mistake but the family ascribe his action to his mad jealousy of Alena whom he does not want to go to her ballet lessons. This alleged jealousy angers old Krůta to such an extent that he insists Jiří must return both sets of keys. Jiří refuses. Complications occur when a former fellow-student of Jiří's – a girl – suddenly appears out of the blue and asks him to go with her to the country to try to get some eggs, food rations being very short. Jiří asks his wife Alena to come along, and when she refuses, he tries to drag her from the apartment by force. Her mother intervenes, and Jiří, obviously defeated in every respect, leaves alone and, as a sign of his capitulation, hands over both sets of keys to father Krůta who feels the family has finally won a victory.

Obviously the two stories are of an entirely different nature. The former is a typical occupation drama with its moral decisions and its innocent victims; the latter sounds like an example of the Theatre of the Absurd, something like Ionesco's *Jack or the Submission*, in which an insignificant issue – in Kundera's case a set of keys, in Ionesco's a certain dish – takes on grotesquely magnified proportions. The interesting thing about the two versions is that the first one represents what theatre and literary critics had accepted and analysed as the 'content' of the play, and the second version was told by the author himself in the Afterword to the published edition. It was told in order to make us aware that both dramas – so opposed to each other in their basic natures – take place simultaneously, 'like the two voices of a fugue, two voices of which each has its own melodic independence but at the same time creates together with the other voice a single harmonic unity; the themes ... are taken up and worked through consecutively by both voices, i.e. by both stories. This means that all the themes in the play (the theme of judgment, etc.) are constantly revealed ... both in their reality and in their absurdity.'[7]

Kundera knew full well that he had not written merely a historical play, that he had put on the stage characters 'whom we frequently meet in our contemporary life, those owners of the truth, owners of principles, owners of morality, owners of rights to judge others – those owners who at the same time never know what things are really all about.' The playwright could not, he argues, have permitted the Krůtas to recognize the actual situation because then his play would not be what he wanted it to be: 'a myth of human pettiness on the march ... in its terrible battle for nothing – and at the same time a myth about the destruction of those soldiers of pettiness who live in self-delusion ... and die in critical situations, not realizing why, crushed by a boot of which they do not know to whose leg it belongs.'[8]

As we see, we have left the historical scene of the German occupation far behind. And here is also the answer to the play's lasting interest. At the outset the hero's moral dilemma occupies a central position in our minds: should he remain with his wife and share her fate or should he flee, in order to continue to fight the enemy, coping with the terrible knowledge of having had to sacrifice her but perhaps gaining freedom for others? Critics, too, have seized the issue of this moral dilemma and discussed the pros and cons of Jiří's action with heated concern to the point of attacking the play for being 'antihumanistic.' However – and Kundera knew this – once critics and audience had made up their minds about what they considered right or wrong in Jiří's actions, once they had solved the obvious moral problem, they could settle back and discover the real issue of the play: the playwright's passionate search to discover and grasp the nature of an average man's life in his 'battle for nothing' which, even if lost, is lost unconsciously and does not bring the light of self-recognition. This is why the play, when staged again in Paris in April 1974,[9] was recognized as presenting a situation much more ambiguous and much less timebound than the occupation drama it seems to suggest at first sight.

When František Hrubín's *Oldřich and Božena or a Bloody Conspiracy in Bohemia* was produced at the Vinohrady Theatre in Prague in September 1968, Czech critical sources responded with particular interest. The play was a work by one of the greatest living Czech poets while the rest of the new plays were primarily by young playwrights; and it looked at a well-known event from Czech history. This latter fact does not perhaps seem particularly important unless we remind ourselves that the play was rehearsed during the exciting period of the Prague Spring of 1968 and that its première took place just over one month after the country was once again occupied by an alien force, thus providing another concrete illustration of the vicissitudes of Czech history. With this in mind we will fully understand the spirit of animation with which the play was received.

František Hrubín, whose most recent dramatic work had been written in the late fifties, tells us that he was inspired to write an historical drama when leafing through the plays of an older Czech playwright.[10] *Oldřich and Božena* is based on an event from the dawn of Czech history which is as well known in Czechoslovakia as the story of Libuša and Přemysl: the Bohemian Prince Oldřich falls in love with a beautiful peasant girl Božena and takes her to his castle as his mate. The theme of a ruler tying himself to a woman whom state authorities consider harmful to the ruler as well as to the state was, particularly in the last century, a subject of considerable interest to dramatists, who were trying to illustrate the ethical problem of the clash between a man's emotions and his sense of duty.[11]

Hrubín's highly poetic play, however, is of a different nature. The central issue here is not the ruler's ethical dilemma but rather the future of the whole country: 'I have come to Bohemia to prevent the birth of a child.'[12] These opening words, spoken by Guntr, the Emperor's ambassador, set the scene for the conflict. The child which Božena will bear Oldřich – his marriage to the Emperor's niece Juta has remained childless for seven years – will prevent the extinction of the powerful family of the Přemyslids. Later on the child becomes Břetislav I, a ruler who was said to have rejuvenated Czech power and fame. Thus the image of the great national figure is present in the minds of the audience and, by merging with their school knowledge of Czech history, lends weight to the central dramatic issue of the child's survival. In the play the child represents at the same time the hope of the Přemyslids that their dynasty will survive and a threat to the opposing forces of the Emperor who is planning to assume power over Bohemia.

The play's very title focuses on those two contradictory areas in the history of man that make it impossible fully to unlock the past with the master key of historical documentation. There is man as an individual with a name – Oldřich, or Božena – and a unique relation to his immediate surrounding; there is also man as the nameless member of a group given to violence and destruction of those who prevent it from gaining power – man as part of the 'bloody conspiracy.' This double focus is kept in variations throughout the action, at the beginning and end of which there hovers the image of the child – threatened in the first words and hoped for in the last words of the play. It is as if the dim hope represented by that child, to be born of the beautiful woman whom we never see on stage, casts a bright light through the dark pattern of brutality and violence with which the rest of the play is woven. Factual reality is grim but another reality behind it yields hope. The poet is aware of and expresses both.

It is significant for an assessment of the mood of Czechoslovakia during that time that another, very different play, František Pavlíček's *The Heavenly Ascension of Saška Krist*,[13] reflects a similar balance between the world's ruthlessness and a transcending spiritual value. The play had its first performance at the Vinohrady Theatre in Prague in February 1967, and is a freely conceived variation of Isaac Babel's volume of stories, *The Red Cavalry*,[14] which deals with the Russian author's experiences during the war of 1920 when Bolshevik groups were clashing with Polish troops along an undefined battle line.

In a quick succession of turbulent encounters Pavlíček's play seizes the atmosphere of a constantly shifting front, the flucation of historical events, and the fates of people who live in perennial proximity to death. The setting is the inside of a Catholic church recently occupied by Bolshevik troups. By placing the action during Easter week, the playwright makes use of the audience's awareness of the ancient pattern of betrayal, sacrificial death, and ultimate salvation. While the brutality and turbulence of war rage outside, from time to time spilling over into the church (and onto the stage), aspects of the lives of individuals – agressors or victims – are fleetingly revealed. The audience is left suspended between wonderment about man's ability to be kind and charitable even in the midst of raging brutality and a sense of waste that these drops of individual goodness have little chance of changing the surrounding ocean of violence.

It is one of the particularly appealing qualities of the play that it manages simultaneously to contain two focal centres: one down on earth and another above the general turmoil – literally so. The mural painter Apolek, perched during most of the play on a scaffold near the roof of the church – visually high above the rest of the characters – continues working on a series of murals depicting Christ's journey to the Cross and His ascension. The painter's remarks form a philosophical commentary not only on the irrational events of the strife down on the stone floor of the church but also on the nature of revolution in general.

The audience watches the bizarre painting grow as the events of life, 'teeming below him as if on the palm of his hand,'[15] provide the artist with inspiration for the features of his biblical characters and finally also for the face of Jesus Christ which dominates the play's last moments. Towards the end of each act the action slows down and in the fleeting stillness the painter's comments on man's struggle, his madness, and his hope ring through the theatre as if they came from another world of harmony and wisdom. But they too, if considered more closely, reveal a line of development. At the beginning the painter questions the direction of all struggle: 'Does he know, the volunteer down there, where they are all marching? Progressing by what? By villages? ... By painful shocks? ... By that one single big step between fear and obsession?' At the end, in the Epilogue of the play, when the painter has died next to his completed painting of the ascending Christ, a young soldier in the turmoil below the scaffold continues the dead artist's philosophizing: 'And things continue. Continue – by one grave ... by one truth gained through a thousand bitter doubts ... By that eternal footprint between despair and hope.'[16]

The play ends on a poetic note of reconciliation between the artist's view of the fermenting world *sub specie aeternitatis* and that world itself in all its agony and hope. The life of contemplation and the life of action have been merged in two ways: the fruits of contemplation have reached the mind of a common man below; the features of a common man have reached the image of Christ above. During the final moments the playwright allows his audience to perceive a possibility – a 'footprint' – of peace and harmony, and leaves them with the image of a Saviour in the likeness of the common soldier Saška who used to be a shepherd in his native village before the Revolution taught him how to kill.

Saška, struggling along amidst the turmoil, reflects the unpretentious humanity of the simple human being who has remained untouched by brutality and violence. Before he gets killed, carrying out quietly what he takes to be his duty, he helps an orphaned girl bury her father and protects her from the cold with his own coat. Saška has strong certainties but also large questions: he is sure that a cow has a soul but he is not sure whether man is 'the grain or the millstone' of history. But, although the play's title makes Saška the hero, Apolek's religious painting and his philosophic commentary provide its structure. To lend such prominence to a figure that harbours doubts about the value of revolutionary strife, thoughts about the concealed connection 'between fear and obsession,' and about whether human fulfillment could possibly reside in 'one futile dream,'[17] is not exactly in the spirit of the Socialist Revolution.

The author has made Revolution itself – man's perennial struggle to realize his ideals – the subject of his play. This is not only an intellectually demanding task for a playwright but also requires handling of complex dramatic material and complete control of the medium of the stage. The violent contrast created by the events that take place below forms a concrete – visual and auditory – counterpoint to the philosophizing above. In addition to the impact of constantly seeing the contrast between the stylized familiarity of the biblical images above and the feverish actions of the characters below, we hear Hebrew mourning chants as well as aggressive army marches, and we hear churchbells, the detonations of grenades, scraps of a popular song from an old record-player, machine-gun fire – all in quick and dazzling succession. But we also hear terrible silences which reach our ears whenever death has claimed another victim.

The story of the crucifixion imprints its rhythm on the play to the point that the acts are named after stages in the painter's work. Yet the author prevents his play from becoming an obvious parallel between the contemplative wisdom of the artistic spirit and the madness of blind action. Apolek, the painter, is conceived as a Chagall-like dreamer whose work shows signs of visionary grotesqueness. Saška himself, whose face is later immortalized in the image of the Shepherd-Christ, admits that, though he would like to own one of Apolek's paintings – a 'small, ordinary one only' – he would like it to be more real, more the way it is 'when it is true,' because Apolek's paintings all seem to him 'somehow strange, everything a bit crooked, the way children draw,' and make you feel 'as if you were drunk.'[18] By implying that the most worthy of the active men below cannot make his peace with the artist's abstract thoughts, the playwright steers clear of ideological commitment and his own final poetic vision shares in the touch of light irony which hovers over the artist figure Apolek.

When Oldřich Daněk's *Forty Scoundrels and One Innocent Babe*[19] had its première in January 1966, the reviews were critical. He had written a dozen plays and half as many film-scripts, and it was an ambitious play by a writer whose works had always tended to be a little heavy-handed and had carried their 'message' about man's moral obligations in society with an obviousness in a way untypical of Czech artistic genius. In this new play, directed by the author himself, Daněk again tackled a particularly difficult moral issue. At first sight the complex problem implied in his topic seems forbidding for a dramatist of Daněk's kind. However, the result – although for several reasons it falls short of being a good play – deserves to be discussed here.

Forty Scoundrels and One Innocent Babe, subtitled *A Tale about the Third Seventh of the Second Cohort of the Royal Guard in the Year Zero*, is based on the well-known biblical story of King Herod who, in great wrath, 'sent forth, and slew all the children that were in Bethlehem ... from two years old and under ...,' when he heard that a new King of the Jews had been born. Herod, himself, however, does not appear in Daněk's play. He merely figures in the imagination and thoughts of a group of rough and ready soldiers who like women and drink, and who are suddenly faced with a moral dilemma: they have been ordered to go into the town and kill new-born children. Their unanimous but only temporary refusal to carry out the order, the dilemma of their sergeant, of a higher officer, of a priest and finally of the new queen who ushers in a totally different regime – this is the material from which Daněk weaves his play.

The author is not interested in obvious guilt, but in those twilight moral areas of the little man's restricted freedom to make this choice or that. He is not concerned with such modernistic set answers as 'helpless man caught up in a large mechanism with no ability to stop inevitable developments'; nor does he seek to point out clearly defined areas of guilt and responsibility. Rather he keeps suggesting that reality is much more complex than that.

A little song with which two prostitutes (who have been smuggled into the camp in crates) entertain the carousing soldiers gives a key to the seemingly merely lusty but basically morally horrendous interpretation of how a good soldier is supposed to think and act:

> Come on, you boys there, don't sit still,
> Keep livin' strong and steady.
> If you don't do it, others will,
> A whole platoon is ready.[20]

As the soldiers join in the catchy refrain, they are unaware that they are foreshadowing a later scene in which this very reasoning is used to break down their moral resistance and send them on their murderous task.

The officer puts forth the argument that 'those children are actually already dead, if you don't carry out the order, another group will; and if the guardsmen refuse, the soldiers will be very happy to be promoted to guardsmen because guardsmen get peas for their grub from time to time and not only beans. So we've got those newly-born ones strictly speaking completely dead by now.'[21] The guardsmen gradually give up and walk over to the officer (a scene of great dramatic tension on the stage) as a sign that they agree to carry out the order. Each apparently makes his decision for different personal reasons, varying from blind belief in the king's wisdom to a wish to see the ocean once again, and from a persecution complex to an inverted sense of solidarity; but each is finally swayed by the irresistible argument of the psychologically astute officer.

Had Daněk made this theme the main point of his play, he would have turned out a dramatically more unified work. But he introduces two other threads which cause unnecessary complexity and unwieldiness. First, he attempts to crystallize two further levels of moral responsibility. One level is illustrated by the sergeant who refuses to lead his men on the killer mission, though not for moral reasons but because he, a childless man, imagines having a little daughter, golden- or raven-haired, and relates the fate of the innocent victims to his dream-child.

The other level is illustrated by the ideological clash between the officer and the priest. The former is a sort of *Realpolitiker* who, although he feels perfectly cynical about the king's desire to do away with possible royal competition, nevertheless sees to it that the order is carried out because guardsmen are meant to 'execute orders without discussing the nature of the order.' The latter is a zealot who considers royal justice absolute and claims that a loyal servant 'does not ask why but simply believes.'[22]

It is decidedly a weakness of the play that the author gets involved in this polemical, almost academic argument between two positions, both of dubious morality – fanaticism and sceptical relativism – which tends to disrupt the dramatic structure of the play. Perhaps he lacks the histrionic and intellectual imagination of Peter Weiss, whose memorable polemical discussions between Robespierre and Danton in *Marat/Sade* had appeared in Ludvík Kundera's Czech translation a year earlier.[23]

Daněk sets himself an ambitious aim. He seeks to explore differences in degrees of moral responsibility – between unethical actions carried out in ignorance or in blind faith and those executed in full knowledge of their immorality. Obviously such dramatic philosophizing had strong contemporary implications. The interpretive essay included in the printed edition of the play stresses repeatedly that the play is a comment 'on the ethical questions of our times and the contemporary world,'[24] and draws parallels between Daněk and writers like Arthur Miller and Friedrich Dürrenmatt of whom, as well as of Sartre, there are distinct echoes in the play.

When one reads these commentaries one realizes once again the important formative role Czech criticism played in the reception of current writings. I have referred repeatedly to the influential and perceptive commentaries of Zdeněk Hořínek. Although critical of some aspects of the play, Hořínek speaks of it in strong terms: the guardsmen 'go and carry out an order without having any doubt about its injustice, but similarly they have no doubt that nothing else can be done. Daněk's ethical paradox is rooted in the fact that *despite this* it is necessary to do something, to refuse, to resist injustice. In such an abnormal situation (if indeed we consider good as something normal, which we definitely should!) all that is left for a normal man is to become a hero. So-called necessity does not cancel out responsibility.'[25] A public force-fed the Marxist concept of 'historical necessity' in schools, in the press, and wherever 'official' political language is used, found in such a statement not only an exciting assessment of a contemporary writer's thought but also a fresh moral challenge for themselves.

It is significant that a work with a similar theme appeared in 1964 when the Polish philosopher Leszek Kołakowski published *Keys to Heaven* in which he explored well-known biblical stories from the point of view of moral philosophy. One of his stories deals with King Herod who consults the philosophers at his court about his worries connected with the prophecy of the three wise men. The advice he gets varies according to the adviser's philosophical persuasion – there is a stoic, an epicurean, a religious moralist, and a politician – but Herod interprets all of them according to his own wishes. The children are killed, but the mission was, as we know, unsuccessful.

The devil, joining an ex post facto discussion between Herod and the advisers in the furthest recesses of hell, where they have all landed, pronounces the final philosophical verdict: 'You can judge your deeds and intentions only when they have become irrevocable. The moral aspect of every act, in contradiction to the technical aspect, is absolutely unforeseeable and can be understood and evaluated only as hindsight.'[26] In other words, ethical motivations and the means whereby one seeks one's ends can only be assessed when these ends have or have not been accomplished. A brilliant philosophical twist pulls the carpet from underneath our fragile moral codes.

Whether Daněk had read Kołakowski's *Keys to Heaven* (which appeared in Warsaw two years prior to his own play) is a moot question. It is interesting to note, however, that during the sixties various Eastern European writers felt an urgent need to reassess the moral responsibility of the individual in relation to the law, in the light of the teachings of moral philosophy and the demands of the individual moral conscience. We find this urgency in each of the four plays discussed in this chapter, although the plays are very different in nature. The first deals with an incident from the German occupation during the Second World War, the second is a poetic revival of an event from the legendary past; the third centres around a situation from the Bolshevik Revolution; the fourth is based on a biblical story. All the plays were written within a period of five years, and all share a concealed common core.

Each play contains a central character who is gentle and peace-loving and does not share the fanatical fighting spirit motivating those around him. Kundera's Jiří has withdrawn from the struggle against the occupying forces and prefers long Sunday mornings alone with his wife. Pavlíček's Saška, though a good and loyal soldier, has his doubts about the more violent aspects of the Revolution and at one point gives an aggressive comrade a piece of his mind: 'You've joined the Revolution anyway only because you wanted to get your revenge. And to kill. When you've smashed up the other side, you'll start beating up your own comrades.'[27] The ruthlessness of Hrubín's Prince Oldřich is balanced by his gentle brother Jaromír whose kindly figure provides throughout the play a lingering reminder of man's yearning for peace. Daněk's Sergeant Zupak refuses to lead his cohort on a mission to kill children.

Each play expresses in a quiet but insistent way the values of sympathy, helpfulness, and non-aggression. Yet somewhere in the course of the action each play unobtrusively seems to change course and begins to project a different sense of values. We find ourselves worrying, for example, lest Kundera's Jiří fail to give the show of strength we expect from him. Subtly the playwright suggests with gradually increasing urgency that a wife's nice waistline does not make up for her feather-brained behaviour. Although the thought of the actual execution of so harmless and innocent a girl chills us to the bone, we cannot really blame Jiří for going off to fight rather than staying and submitting to a futile death with her.

During the last moments of Pavlíček's play, Saška Krist, who started out as the good Samaritan – and never really changes – acts decisively, picks up the grenade another soldier did not dare to throw, and hurls it through the church window to extinguish the irresponsible painter's lamp. His last words are spoken just before this final act of courage which results in his death: 'we are soldiers, Mita. And we joined voluntarily.'[28]

In the case of Hrubín's play the change of direction is even more concealed. At first our sympathies are likely to be engaged by Prince Jaromír whose kindness to his royal brother Oldřich's abandoned wife Juta is illustrated in one of the loveliest and most poetic scenes of the play.

However, as political intrigues are spun and Jaromír proves repeatedly that, though good at heart, he lacks any kind of moral strength and stamina, we are alienated by what now appears as a crass weakness of his character. When, toward the end of the play, Jaromír's eyes are gouged out on Oldřich's order, we are likely to witness the scene as a further example of Oldřich's desperately brutal way in dealing with anyone who might provide an obstacle to his aims, rather than as a scene representing a tragic loss.

When Sergeant Zupak refuses his military duty, the author makes doubly sure that we are aware his decision was prompted by his pipe-dream about unborn daughters and not by a sense of the evil of murder. In fact his monotonously repeated explanation 'I didn't want to lead them ... I only didn't want to lead them,'[29] makes him appear as a childish simpleton who is totally incapable of moral decisions of any kind.

This concealed shifting of the basic undertone of the plays is also reflected in their dramatic form. In *The Owners of the Keys* the realistic scenes in the Krůtas' apartment are interspersed with four dream scenes during which the hero reconsiders the situation and, by coming face to face with the actual consequences of his decision (he sees his wife at the execution wall), realizes the enormous burden of freedom of choice. In the case of *Oldřich and Božena* the action is similarly broken by Oldřich's poetic soliloquy in which, on a stage illuminated only by a flickering flame in the fireplace, he ruminates about the sense of his life and the meaning of human freedom. In the Saška Krist play the audience has the reminder of that other dimension before their eyes, whenever they raise them to the paintings in the upper part of the stage. Here this other 'reality' grows visually until it finally dominates the whole stage.

What are we then to make of all these similarities? Is it merely a coincidence that the four best Czech 'historical' plays of the time should contain such surprisingly similar elements? If we strip each play of incidentals and concentrate on its essence, we find the chief character plagued by Hamlet's question whether to struggle actively against 'a sea of troubles' or passively to 'suffer fortune's arrows.' Ought he to follow Voltaire's advice and quietly cultivate his own garden? This, one might argue, is a dilemma so basic to any form of human endeavour that almost every play ever written touches on a variation of this theme. However, these four plays show an almost identical line of development from passive acceptance to active resistance which gives them the strangely cryptic quality that we know from Chekhov or Ibsen's late plays. The peace-loving heroes are either replaced by activists or drawn into the struggle for whatever is the current means of saving the world: the brutal order of a pagan ruler, the machinations of a Bohemian dynasty, the excesses of the Bolshevik Revolution, or the resistance movement against a foreign occupation.

However, the timeless quality of these 'historical' plays appears most strongly when the question of the actual validity of that cause, though not explicitly denied, is deliberately rendered inconsequential. In the course of each play another reality is created which counteracts the surface reality of the play. From *The Owners of the Keys*, 'the myth of human pettiness on the march,'[30] there emerges the proof of man's ability to struggle against evil even at the cost of what he cherishes most. In *Oldřich and Božena* there rises from the fanatical struggle to preserve the power of a royal dynasty the perennial hope promised by an unborn child. *Forty Scoundrels* is by no means only about the murder of small children, but also about the immorality of passivity in the face of evil. The Officer knows how this passivity works: 'Some have to be shouted at, some perhaps need to be only avoided ... Sometimes it is even enough to keep quiet.'[31]

These playwrights make us see the hidden brutality and inhumanity of those who remain passive and listless in the face of evil. They explore the concealed perniciousness of those whom Dante assigned to the deepest of hells, those 'nearly soulless whose lives concluded neither blame nor praise.'[32] They reveal the sly abominations perpetrated by those who follow the corrupt motto of the subhuman trolls in Ibsen's *Peer Gynt*, 'To thyself be enough.' Their distinct message emerges quietly but with increasing urgency from the very core of their plays about man's history.

9
East meets West

I would be happiest, if the audience – no matter in which country – were to find in my play above all a comment on the world in which they live. Should it, however, be taken as a document ... about circumstances which are alien and of no concern to the audience, I would consider it a failure.　　　　　VÁCLAV HAVEL in a letter

Since this chapter is the first attempt to consider the recent renaissance of dramatic literature in Czechoslovakia in the general context of contemporary Western drama, it necessarily involves a certain amount of speculation. However, I hope the preceding chapters have shown that these plays could enrich and significantly expand contemporary international theatre if they became an integral part of that wider context. (This means of course that more of the plays would have to become available in English which they doubtless will before long.)

I will try to suggest briefly how the Czech playwrights, despite political difficulties and persecution, give artistic shape to problems which loom just as large in the minds of English, American, German, French, and Canadian playwrights, how inventively they use the ancient medium of the stage, and how resourcefully their works explore and reflect the complexities of today's world.

For the sake of clarity I have divided my remarks into several topics: The modern hero will be considered as a figure whose trademark appears to be mediocrity and who is not good enough for heaven and not bad enough for hell; as a figure under constant pressure to show solidarity with his fellow men which results in the common, and yet exceedingly complex dilemma 'if everyone does it, can it be bad?'; and as a figure who needs to play roles which inevitably results in a version of the notorious modern 'crisis of identity.' I will examine the power of language or man as the victim of his words. There follows a brief section on what I have called 'existential aspects;' it will argue that even in a 'classless society' where every stage of human development is regulated, man urgently seeks his own personal definition. Finally I will raise some more general questions by way of comparison between Western and Czech drama, and illustrate my argument with reference to Havel's *The Audience* and *Protest* and Milan Uhde's *A Play About the Dove*.

I

When Oedipus – both guilty and innocent – finds out the nature of his crime, he accepts his fate, carries out his own punishment, and thus saves the city. Order is re-established. When Orpheus, disobedient to the gods, turns back to look at Eurydice, he is duly punished by losing her forever. What the gods decided, happened. Macbeth, murderer from ambition and weakness of spirit, receives the verdict of justice; Othello, murderer from possessiveness and rigidity of mind, metes out his own punishment. We know the magnificent and terrible order in which the relationship between crime and punishment, between the trespassing of limitations and the workings of fate, has been recast for centuries by dramatists of all nations.

But when we come to the late nineteenth century, an alarming change takes place: a new monster appears on the moral scale of man's activities. At the end of the preceding chapter we saw that period's growing awareness of that monster, of what Dante deemed the most despicable form of man's evil, namely to be 'neither for God nor Satan' but only for oneself. More than half a millenium after Dante, Ibsen's Button Moulder, who appears toward the end of Peer Gynt's life, sadly tells us that 'nowadays one hardly ever meets a sinner on a really grand scale.' Unlike the Stone Statue, who carries off the seducer Don Juan to hell without the slightest hesitation, the Button Moulder is worried about a very modern problem – about mediocrity. 'A man,' he explains to Peer Gynt (who does not meet the requirements for being doomed), 'needs strength and purpose to be a sinner.'[1] Almost a century later the Swiss playwright Max Frisch[2] has the devil send an average middle class couple straight back to earth with the explanation that, though not really good enough for heaven, they are certainly too mediocre to be accepted in hell.

Most twentieth-century literary protagonists – whether we call them anti-heroes, weak heros, non-heroes or whatever – would pass the scrutinizing eye neither of Ibsen's Button Moulder nor of Frisch's devil.

Remoulded and sent back to the earth, they would be left to repeat their petty mistakes and live their petty lives all over again, as merely the raw material of human life. Think of a remoulded Willie Loman, Jimmy Porter, Berenger, Alfred Ill, and expand the list according to your choice. What these characters share is the feeling that things have gone wrong but they don't know exactly why. The story of the dramatic hero of contemporary Western literature is the story of failure – if indeed it is a story at all. Fragmented and ambiguous, the tale of modern life becomes at best a series of flashes of awareness. Uncomplimentary images, suggesting hollowness, mechanisitic responses, faltering intellect, and dried-up emotions, have been showered on the modern dramatic hero by Western playwrights and critics alike.

Scanning the gallery of dramatic characters from the Czech plays we have been discussing, we are equally hard put to find anyone who might resemble a heroic figure. We have encountered frightened little men, who would not harm a fly, getting involved in issues far beyond their grasp; we have encountered hen-pecked husbands and shy young couples, hectic bureaucrats and romantic pensioners, prisoners who want to keep their lives, employees who want to keep their jobs – above all, people who want to be left alone!

This is an interesting discovery. Does it mean that societies as different as the systematized, ideologically regulated societies of Eastern Europe and the open, pluralistic societies of Western Europe and North America have produced the same image of contemporary man? And if so, how could this happen?

Does not the dramatist deal most clearly with the clashes between individual man's private conscience and the standardized collective? Let us listen to the characters themselves:

> I can resist these forces no longer. I will go back, murder, and say it's for a better world, for this must be said to prevent insanity. And when I'm standing, addressing the crowds of Argos, telling them what great things are to come because of my act, I will know it is nothing but weakness that brought me there in front of them ... I will do so knowing I was not great enough to create something better. [Jack Richardson *The Prodigal*]

> I'm not good-looking, I'm not good-looking. They're the good-looking ones. I was wrong! Oh, how I wish I was like them! ... I need one or two horns to give my

sagging face a lift. Perhaps one will grow and I needn't be ashamed any more – then I could go and join them ... I've only myself to blame; I should have gone with them while there was still time. Now it's too late. Now I'm a monster, just a monster. I'm past changing. I want to, I really do, but I can't, I just can't ... I'm so ugly! People who try to hang on to their individuality always come to a bad end! [Eugène Ionesco *Rhinoceros*]

And everyone would ask: where did that man get the right to distinguish himself so ostentatiously from the others, to step out of line, scorn the opinion of the majority ... I would be regarded as an arrogant exhibitionist who wanted to act as the conscience of the world; I would sacrifice myself for something that no one except me believes in; my death would therefore remain misunderstood, it would not strengthen the authority of any values, it would not help anybody, it would only create pain for some of those who are close to me. And, after all, it is understandable: although it is more comfortable to reject completely the rules of the game which this world offers to man, it doesn't usually lead anywhere; it is much more difficult but at the same time disproportionately more meaningful to accept these rules, by doing so secure the possibility to communicate with one's surrounding, and then to take advantage of this communication in order gradually to improve the existing rules of the game. [Havel *The Beggar's Opera*][3]

Consider the first and the third: both protagonists decide to go back to the world and play the game that is expected of them. Richardson's Orestes reverses his original decision to withdraw from social and political obligations, live in the country, and help his gentle wife raise their children. Only after having realized that circumstances are closing in on him and pushing him toward Argos and filial duty, does Orestes draw the conclusion that there is 'nothing else for Prince Orestes to wear but the ragged dress of yet another hero.' Richardson's Orestes is fully aware that he did not adopt the role of the hero voluntarily. It was forced on him because 'the world demands that we inherit the pretensions of our fathers, that we go on killing in the name of ancient illusions about ourselves, that we assume the right to punish, order, and invent philosophies to make our worst moments seem inspired. Who am I to contradict this any longer?'[4]

Ten years later and a few thousand miles further east, Havel's MacHeath similarly questions his right 'to distinguish himself so ostentatiously from the others ... and scorn the opinion of the majority.'[5] A strange parallel indeed. In one case the world expects a hero, in the other it resents a hero. Moreover, as we consider these arguments in favour of opposite values, both lines of reasoning seem increasingly suspect. Orestes' line disturbs us because of his defeatist attitude: the people perennially want a hero (for perennially wrong reasons) – all right, he proposes, I will impersonate one of them, but I will just go through the motions without believing in what I am doing. Havel's MacHeath makes us feel uncomfortable not so much because of his blatant diagnosis of the stupidity of the world but rather because of the underlying and somehow suspect connection he makes between utilitarianism and idealism.

The second speaker, Ionesco's Berenger, seems less aware of what is expected of him. When his friend Dudard tries to convince him that to become a rhinoceros was not so bad after all, that 'one has to keep an open mind ... to understand is to justify,' and besides, 'who can say where the normal stops and the abnormal begins?' Berenger simply does not 'want to accept the situation.' Exasperated, he shouts at the persistent Dudard 'We must attack the evil at the roots!' He has not really defined this evil because, as he later admits, he is mixing up everything in his head and all he knows is that he feels 'instinctively' that the rest of the people who have become rhinoceros – or, play the game, as Orestes and MacHeath would call it – are 'in the wrong.' Later, however, even his instinct fails Berenger, and he is no longer sure who is the monster – himself or the others. This, of course, is equal to joining forces with Dudard's relativism: 'Who knows what is evil and what is good?' When in the last three lines of the play Berenger decides not to capitulate, we distinctly feel that Ionesco's grand gesture is a catchy stage gimmick but can hardly be taken seriously philosophically.[6]

The grounds for comparison are obviously treacherous. Let us begin with something of which we can be reasonably sure: all three characters are concerned with the question of conformity. In other words, they are trying to define their values according to the values of the majority – whatever those values happen to be: pretense as justice, admiration of brute force, or the anything-you-can-do-I-can-do-better game. On the basis of the above and numerous other examples that are easily found, it might seem fair to argue that solidarity with his more or less wretched fellow men is the distinguishing mark of the modern hero. Or is this quality not so modern after all?

Is it not the ancient hero's proud allegiance to his mortal condition that makes him a true hero? Ulysses returned from the realm of the supernatural to his mortal wife and son: it can be argued that he affirmed his tie with the world in which death reigns and in which the passing of time causes ravages unknown in the world of gods. This proof of allegiance, this show of solidarity, is very much part of the consciousness of the contemporary playwright. The Polish philosopher Leszek Kołakowski has recast the story of Noah into a form which allows him to pose the question whether Noah is not a traitor to human values, an apple-polisher and yes-man, a servile character who does a job because he is told to do it and forgets that he owes some loyalty to his fellow beings. Kołakowski's fable remains cryptic and avoids the logical consequence: by refusing to build the ark and by thus drowning along with the rest of humanity, would Noah not have extinguished the human race?

The modern hero seems to have arrived at the basic realization that those forces which he had assumed to be alien and inimical to his nature – rigidity, corruption, and ruthlessness – turn out to be essential parts of himself. He discovers that he is the bearer of the world's dubious inheritance. His realization of solidarity is a two-faced coin: one side shows sympathy and affirms the bondage wrought by common suffering and shared ignorance and fears; the other side shows complicity in greed and corruption, cowardice and will to power. Is this solidarity therefore dangerous? Does it sanction streaks of viciousness in man by showing him that other people are vicious too? Does it deny him wholeness by moulding him imperceptibly into a general mould?

In his introduction to *The New Theatre of Europe*, R.W. Corrigan argues that Iago might be regarded as the prototype of modern man because he is no longer a character in the traditional sense.[7] The 'motiveless malignancy' of Iago, to use Coleridge's words, has baffled successive generations of actors, and has made Iago one of the most difficult Shakespearean roles. It is impossible to find Iago's centre, his human persona, or, as we prefer to say today, his identity. The particular reality of the character lies in the role that he is playing.

When the impassioned German Expressionists of the first two decades of our century wrote angry plays about how industrialization had reduced a man to a foot (the foot that is needed to keep a machine in motion) or a hand (that is needed to push a handle) they spoke from a social consciousness that rebelled against the reduction of a human being to a function. Few of them are likely to have anticipated that this mechanization of humanity would later take on astonishing dimensions. The hated factories that they regarded as the root of all evil turned out to be only a minor part of modern general collectivization.

In today's mass society man's identity tends to be defined exclusively by his function. This means that a man's true identity is, more often than not, never discovered. Society will not discover it because it is only interested in functional values. Man himself, if constantly assured that it is only his social function which makes him who he is – a teacher or a hockey player, a sheet metal worker or a corporation lawyer – will define himself as such and play his role accordingly. Once modern man has accepted the role thrust on him by circumstances largely beyond his control his path is clear, and his life's role, with slight variations in script, is before him.

> I am Signora Frola's daughter ... and I am Signor Ponza's second wife ... And to myself I am no one ... I am the one that each of you thinks I am.

> Look, Mack, a person can't live split into someone who fulfills the wishes of others, and someone who watches this process with disgust; all of us need – at least to a certain extent – to belong to ourselves, because not to belong to yourself means not being identical with yourself and therefore actually not being at all.[8]

The first quotation is from Luigi Pirandello's *Right you are (If You Think So)*. The date is 1917. The second quote is from Václav Havel's *The Beggar's Opera*, dated 1972. The two playwrights are obviously talking about the same thing: the problem of man's split personality or his loss of identity, his depersonalized conformism – or whatever names we wish to give to the great crisis in modern man's consciousness. But they approach it from different philosophical angles. Pirandello says that we must give up the search for objective truth and settle for personal impressions which may be right or wrong. Havel suggests something like the existentialists' differentiation between being and existing.

Bertolt Brecht told us in *The Good Woman of Setzuan* (1943) that a kind person must wear a cruel mask in order to survive in this brutal world. The greed and selfishness of one's fellow men warrant a double morality; besides, the day-dreaming gods above find this quite acceptable. But of course, Brecht implies, if we had a better social system we would not need to combat the evil of the world, we would not need to have two faces and on our real face the smile need never disappear. Leaving aside the complex problem of Brecht's political beliefs, what is interesting here is the idea of the two faces, and the occasions when they are needed as equipment for living.

When the gods withdraw and leave the worried mother, Shen Te, below, they give her one last piece of advice: not to wear her evil mask too often, 'once a month should be enough.'[9] In other words, she should ration her 'other' face and use it only when necessary. This means that a human being is expected to decide when there is time for brutality and ruthlessness, and as long as it is rationed out according to some kind of economic principle – i.e. production meeting demand – all will be well and the moral aspect of things will take care of itself.

Shen Te had decided to don her evil mask not in order to hoard riches or live in luxury but in order to be able to feed her little son. Her moral dilemma is therefore the decision between two forms of evil: either be selfish and ruthless or let your child starve. Shen Te's motherly love and her natural sense of values – 'my child comes first' – prompt her to adopt two faces. By using her freedom to be ruthless, Shen Te herself can enjoy freedom from want.

In Dürrenmatt's much discussed play *The Visit* (1956), the population of a run-down town buy the means for new economic growth, education, and well-being for each citizen. The price they pay for it is high – it is the life of one of their fellow-citizens. And yet, on closer inspection, one life is perhaps not a very high price to pay for such a vast improvement for so many. Besides, the life in question is only that of an elderly, nondescript shopkeeper, named Ill. And to top it all, he has committed a nasty deed during his youth, so he is not even a 'good' man.

By the time the citizens of the town have finished reasoning in this way, they have already concluded that their decision to sacrifice the man for the town's sake is prompted not by their desire for prosperity but by their desire for justice. Persecuted by the whole town, Ill finally accepts his execution as a form of justice. Unanimous common consent has made the victim a criminal; the citizens' act of violence has become an act of justice. The idealistic principles pronounced at the end of the play are the outcome of practical considerations, and the ideology that emerges has been prompted by crass utilitarianism.

When Ivan Klíma's hapless character Kliment faces the officials who want to force him to marry the stranger Marcela Lukášová, they ply him with variations of the argument: 'Of course we cannot force you, Mr. Kliment, and indeed we don't want to force you. But if you have decided to destroy yourself as well as the girl, then it is our duty to prevent you from doing so.'[10] Without knowing what is happening to him, Kliment, the victim, has been pronounced a criminal. Exhausted, terrified, Kliment begs for a little time to 'think it over' and consider the nature of the demand made on him.

In the Epilogue to *The Trial*, Kafka's Josef K. has been convinced that he is guilty and must be tried. Milan Kundera's high school student puts it in a nutshell: 'it doesn't matter one bit whether I really wrote it or not. The decisive thing is that the guilt happened to fall on me. Don't think I didn't try to deny it at the beginning. But then I realized that it really doesn't matter. And that the best thing for me to do is just to forget altogether that I got into it innocently.'[11] Is this then the implied depressing message of playwrights East and West: that it is easier, or safer, or indeed unavoidable to accept a change of identity required (as means of defence) or imposed (by force) by the outside world?

At first sight it might seem so indeed. Western playwrights have been just as conscious of the destructive moulding-power of certain kinds of role-playing in society. Albee attacks the 'good daddy, good husband, good citizen's-role' in *The Zoo Story*. Genet tests is psychological and social explosiveness in *The Maids* and in *The Blacks*; Osborne and Wesker use the idea of social roles for their attacks on the British class system; Max Frisch explores the pernicious rigidity of thought that goes with social roles. Other examples are numerous and have given rise to ample critical discussion.

Drastically different though all these plays are, they have one thing in common: they are not very funny. Many of them, in fact, exude a combination of earnestness and sentimentality on the one hand, and of brutality on the other. It is in this sense that they are extremely different from the Czech plays which are, with few exceptions, extremely funny. Many Western plays with socially critical content seem to be inspired by an obliquely moralistic attitude: we must show people what reality is *really* like (though I would explicitly exclude Tom Stoppard here).

The Czech playwrights' attitude is completely unburdened by pedagogic intent. Perhaps constant exposure to doctrinaire teachings by the 'gloomy priests' (Milan Kundera's expression) of political institutions – whether they really are gloomy priests or only play their roles is a moot point and therefore a good illustration for this discussion – has made writers aware that laughter is the only weapon against mental violation. 'We are too grave about our lives,' writes Antonín J. Liehm in his remarkable *The Politics of Culture*,' what we need, above all, is the courage to laugh at our existence and through laughter clear the way for understanding. And in this way we earn the right to laugh at cowards, at those who refuse to understand. We desperately need laughter – evil, ironic, malicious, heartless, mocking laughter.'[12]

And so the Czech playwrights have taken the Shen Te situation and led it ad absurdum: if you want to play the hero, Shen Te, go ahead and survey the consequences! Take the Archivist of Klíma's *The Jury*, who refuses to don the mask society requires of him. His courageous stand is not only futile but achieves the exact opposite of what he had intended to achieve. A system, consisting largely of hierarchical roles and the power structure that goes with them, has openings for all kinds of roles. By rejecting the role that the false system of justice requires of him, the gallant Archivist only supports that system. In his case, the role of the opponent, the conscientious objector, has been legalized to work in favour of the system. Similarly, the young man of Klíma's *Café Myriam* wants to reveal the official secret of the poisoned cakes. His idealism is used as proof that freedom still exists.

He who refuses to play the role assigned to him and instead shows his real face is readily integrated into the systematized role-playing, cast in the useful role of the idealist opponent. The joke is on the man who thought he was going to behave like a hero. There is the anything but heroic example of Kundera's Principal in *The Blunder* who has adopted a role in total contradiction to his bon vivant character – that of a severe, rigorously disciplinarian pedagogue. In fact, he plays it so well that he begins to fear 'that my original face, well, let's call it my better one, is gradually disappearing behind the other face.' Besides, there is another danger: 'If they all regard me as one of them, won't I really be one of them? ... and ... what if I suddenly forget that I am only playing a comedy and begin to take it as seriously as everyone else.'[13] Here Kundera defines a man's submission to a double-faced morality in its most subtle and pernicious form.

Now we can attempt to draw another perhaps tenuous but nevertheless recognizable line of distinction between what, for simplicity's sake, we have come to call East and West. In Western plays the victim of a system or a society is permitted to remain the victim. Arthur Miller's Willie Loman is the victim of the false illusions of American society; O'Neill's boarding-house characters in *The Iceman Cometh* are victims of their pipe-dreams in a grim and hopeless reality; Andri in Max Frisch's *Andorra* is a victim and martyr of a totalitarian system; Albee's Jerry is a victim of the loneliness and alienation of modern mass society; Dürrenmatt's Ill is the victim of common greed and the desire to live comfortably, and so on. But neither Klíma's Archivist in *The Jury* nor the young husband in *Café Myriam* is allowed to wear the laurel wreath of victimization which Western literature has so warmly adopted. The young lovers of Klíma's *The Double Room* have learned to use the technique that was used on them and their victimization takes on a sinister air. They will be the ones who victimize next.

In Havel's plays, the hero/victims – from Hugo Pludek to MacHeath – are busy carrying on the system that has subdued them. There can be no victims in a merry-go-round situation. Kohout's pyjama-clad clerk Bláha, who dies on the third floor in a two-man battle with the wine merchant from Saarbrücken, and the naked young couple who lose all their savings to the efficient fire fighters project a kind of mouse-versus-tiger image. The relationship between oppressor and victim is out of proportion – it becomes 'absurd.' If people are constantly forced to lie, they ultimately forget what their real faces were. Those 'better' faces, as Kundera's Principal puts it, distintegrate and disappear. The role becomes the man, frighteningly interchangeable, as Havel implies in *Audience*, devoid of ethical concepts, as Klíma shows in *Games*, mechanically taken on and shed, as Landovský demonstrates in *Closed for Disinfection* – and life becomes a chase for the 'right roles' which might be the wrong ones tomorrow in a society which herds men into Sheep and Goats, into Bald Ones and Hairy Ones, according to patterns which have lost all connection with ethical values.

And so we return to our initial Kafka/Hašek theme. In Kafka's world the hero struggles at all costs to comprehend the absurd situation, fails to understand it, and dies wondering whether it is not all his fault. In Hašek's world the hero assesses the absurd situation, realizes that he cannot grasp it rationally, but goes along with it and survives. With Kafka survival and morality exclude each other; for Hašek morality is survival. Kafka's hero is unable to use a 'second face'; Hašek's hero readily uses as many faces as are needed by any situation. These two dialectical opposites, symbolized by the two great literary figures from Prague, appear under different guises again and again in the Czech theatre of today. It is as if the writers had set themselves the monumental task of achieving in their work a synthesis of these opposing forces. If such a reconciliation is their aim, then their approach to the problem of man in society has a clearly defined ethical basis. Their approach is, to my mind, less conceptual than the approach of Western writers, for whom such concepts as 'equality of opportunity,' 'racism,' 'bias,' 'anti-militarism,' 'poverty,' and 'social alienation,' to name just a few, have built-in value judgments which predetermine the viewpoint of the playwright.

The contemporary writers of Czechoslovakia start from a different premise and have, to use Havel's words, 'a different way of posing questions ... [They] start from reality as it exists at the moment: they form general concepts on the basis of this reality and disregard categories ... I personally don't care a bit about such questions as what is the nature of politics ... Instead I am deeply concerned with the question of whether a particular concrete event or act is in itself, on the basis of my experience, good or bad.'[14] The Czech writers have no solutions to the problems which they expose, but the initial thrust of their writings comes from a clear idea – if not a clear idea of absolute justice and intellectual freedom, yet a clear idea of what happens to a man in a society where justice and freedom do not exist.

II

We all know the sad story of the spoken word in the theatre. We have become familiar with descriptions of the dwindling force of the once all-powerful medium of dramatic language: without surprise we read critical essays about 'playwrights of silence,' 'the impotence of the word,' 'non-sense dialogue,' 'oblique conversations.' Occasionally a critic of culture, such as George Steiner, reacts against the devaluation of language; or a man of the theatre, such as Robert Corrigan, feels that the audience will not much longer 'be content to listen to representations of their own inarticu-lacy,' that we 'come to the theatre to hear what we cannot express for ourselves.'[15] But despite the insistent slogans and catchwords of a variety of voluble political, social, and other movements, the crisis of the word in artistic expression is upon us.

On the whole, playwrights from Sophocles to Shaw have created charac-ters who speak more clearly and fully on stage than they would have spoken in real life. These playwrights trusted the logic of language and believed in its informative power. Only in the late nineteenth century, particularly with Chekhov, Ibsen, and Wedekind, did the stage begin to show the defective-ness of communication between people. Not only did a character's words no longer express what he was really trying to say, but they could be used to conceal the real meaning of his statement. The tool for the discovery of truth had become the mask of truth. Instead of providing clarity, words were beginning to add to man's general confusion about people, the world, and human life.

A future scholar might find it worth while to discover why the most original and outstanding proponents of the inefficacy of language have come from the same part of middle Europe, namely Austria. There is, for example, the Viennese Wittgenstein, the initiator – for better or for worse – of modern linguistic philosophy. There is, of course, Sigmund Freud, after whose discoveries concerning the unconscious content of speech, people's attitude to language changed drastically. Hofmannsthal, the Austrian poet and playwright who became Richard Strauss's librettist, allowed his mag-nificent texts to be dominated by music because he doubted the validity of words. Peter Handke, also from Austria, has made a strong impact on contemporary theatre by putting on stage examples of our perennial verbal confusion and subsequent victimization by language. They all helped create the perfect context for the plays of Václav Havel, who has made language the hero or rather the tyrant of his plays.

Of course, this does not mean to say that the language crisis in the theatre is limited to the region of Austria and Bohemia. Indeed, the recent drama of our whole Western society has in some way or another become in several ways a critique of language. It would be easy to give numerous examples of plays which explore what man has done with language, as well as – and here we have arrived at the most significant and frightening aspect of the problem – what language has done to man, particularly since the Second World War.

In 1950 Ionesco wrote the tautological nonsense-dialogues of *The Bald Soprano* that made him famous. In 1952 Beckett stunned the literary world with the inane monosyllabic conversations of Didi and Gogo, and the outburst of the numb creature Lucky, who breaks down as words get the better of him. In a different way from Ionesco's cackle, language here becomes independent of its user – the whole speech is a flow of vaguely connected words no longer related to their original meaning. The current lively interest in Harold Pinter's plays, which rarely make use of language for the purpose of communication between characters, shows our continual fascination with the problem. Pinter reduces the conceptual content of his characters' speech to a point where it becomes quite unimportant and the language used serves merely as an instrument to explore another character. It does not matter whether they discuss life, the weather, or a late train. In German-speaking countries this tendency is reflected in the tremendous theatrical, critical, and scholarly interest lately shown in the playwright Ödön von Horvath, another Austrian, whose plays explore in a unique way the power of the hollow phrase and the ensuing destruction of people's natural reactions.

Czech playwrights have always been particularly aware of language as a moulder of intellect. It bears repeating that the preservation of their language in the face of other dominating languages (particularly German) had been for a long time a matter of national survival. It is hardly overstating things to say that from its inception their whole literature was written with the idea of national identity in mind. More recently Czech playwrights have discovered, as other playwrights have, that it is possible to lose a language even while keeping it. Mechanization is the villain who imperceptibly steals it. The fixed expressions and values of any system, from the professional jargon of an insurance agency to the platform of a women's liberation movement or to the premises of a political ideology, can lead to the mechanistic use of language and a process of evaluation according to the values of that system. Certain words have taken on an automatically evaluating meaning. They are used mechanically, i.e. with disregard for the original meaning. It is interesting that no important English-speaking playwright has risen to the challenge of making the automatization of language itself the hero of his plays. Beckett and Pinter, although their work consists in an evaluation of language, are basically interested in other things: Beckett in philosophy, Pinter in psychology.

We must therefore, for the purpose of a comparison, turn to Peter Handke whose work has lately become well known in English translation. On 11 May 1967, two German theatres staged premières of Handke's *Kaspar*, a play which the author has said shows 'how by means of talking someone can be made to talk.'[16] The topic is a strange event which actually took place in nineteenth-century Germany, when a young man, Kaspar Hauser, was found wandering through the streets of Nuremberg, and was able to speak only a single sentence. Later he died under mysterious circumstances. Several writers, including Verlaine, Hofmannsthal, and Georg Trakl, were inspired by the story. Kaspar for them represented the true outsider of society, unable to adapt to the ways of the world.

Handke's interest in the figure lies in the opposite direction. If other writers had been fascinated by Kaspar, the stranger, Handke was interested in showing how this stranger could be made known; how he could be moulded into something familiar. That moulding was to be done by means of language. When Kaspar starts out in the play, his face covered – according to stage instructions – with a mask of astonishment, he is able to speak only a single sentence. The whole play is his learning process. Prompters, well-versed in the ways of society, teach him to speak a sentence 'with which to make yourself noticeable,' assure him that a sentence will make him aware of himself, and point out the advantages of language which will help him 'to remove any obstacles.'[17] Slowly, intensely, they demonstrate the power of language as an ordering element, as essential to the perception of time and place as it is to social identity. In actual fact, however, they deprive Kaspar of his original identity, as he becomes incapable of using his own linguistic property, his original sentence. Once he has been made to forget his own words, Kaspar is ready to receive training in the proper use of language which eventually will make him 'completely adjusted' to his environment.

In the first act of Václav Havel's *The Garden Party*, Hugo Pludek does not say much. In fact his comments are limited to about half a dozen monosyllabic comments on his chess play. Three times 'Yes Daddy,' three times 'No Daddy,' three times 'Fine Mum,' plus some trivial bits of information form the total of his oral communication. However, toward the end of the first act, he gives a demonstration of his eagerness to learn. Soon he begins to show his remarkable ability to imitate by quoting his father's topsy-turvy proverbs. Soon his talent for rapid linguistic adjustment to situations becomes obvious. During the second act Hugo's learning and integration process accelerates. At the elitist Garden Party, during which he rises rapidly to social and political success, he starts out by keeping his ears open. After a cautious beginning with the help of one of his father's proverbs, he quickly learns to use the 'right' vocabulary. Soon he is able to impress a high official with this pertinent commentary on the situation of the Office: 'When the new activization of all the positive forces inside the Liquidation Office once more in the forefront of our work as a firm and mighty stronghold of our unity, it was unfortunately precisely the Inauguration Service which succumbed – ... Insinuating themselves by means of effective arguments taken from the arsenal of abstract humanistic cant – which however in reality did not span the confines of the generally conventionalized types of work ... Of the pseudo-familiar inaugurational phraseology hiding behind the routine of professional humanism a profound dilution of opinions.'[18]

Like Handke's Kaspar, Havel's Hugo has learned to use a certain language. The only difference, though an important one, is that Kaspar is carefully emptied of the old language and trained to speak the new one – he is brainwashed and 'normalized,' we might say today – while Hugo is ready to receive the new language without outside pressure. In other words, Kaspar is a passive victim, while Hugo is a volunteer. To be in command of the new language means to him the possibility of attaining stature and fame. When the play starts, Hugo, like Kaspar, seems to be a blank page, but soon we detect in him the eager pupil, ready to memorize the clichés, phrases, and catchwords which have become totally independent of the reality they pretend to reflect. The alienation of the word from reality is complete. But man is the accomplice to this alienation. This is why Havel's vision is a shade darker than Handke's. By denying us the possibility of developing an attitude of sympathy for the victim, Havel deprives us of the reassuring distinction between villain and victim and thus throws the problem back into our laps.

Another difference should be pointed out. Handke's play is an exploration of how a man can be created and destroyed by language, yet the play is an artifact and its reality is and remains in the theatre. The playwright has told us that he does not intend to give a picture of the world outside but proposes to explore the possibilities of the stage in relation to an audience.[19] In the context of his society (and not only his), Havel's play strikes a much more realistic note. In fact, Jan Grossman, who, as a director, knows Havel's work better than anyone else, tells us that Havel shows us 'a hypothetical and therefore possible world.'[20]

One more example: The brainwashing scene in Pinter's *The Birthday Party* and Klíma's *A Bridegroom for Marcela*. In the former (as Martin Esslin first pointed out)[21] language becomes the medium through which a contest of wills is fought out. Starting out rooted in reality with minor reproachful questions about behavior – 'Why are you wasting everybody's time, Webber? ... What would your old mum say, Webber?' – the accusers become more and more rhetorical as they move further away from the real situation. The accusations themselves have no longer anything to do with Stanley Webber's actual life – 'Why did you kill your wife? ... Where is your lechery leading you?' – but the way in which the cross-examination is conducted, the clear separation between the accusers and the accused is established. Stanley is guilty and deserves punishment, no matter what the specific nature of his crimes. His very life becomes an act of guilt. The last insoluble sphinx-like question – 'Which came first? Chicken? Egg?' – is hurled at him, and his inability to answer it becomes the final proof of the offensiveness of his very being: 'You betray your breed ... You're nothing but an odour.'[22] Stanley has been reduced to a howling, inarticulate creature by the sheer weight of language. His feelings of guilt and worthlessness are not the result of a reasoned accusation of his faults or crimes but of an irrational torrent of language used to blunt his intellect.

As we know, Klíma's brainwashing scene is also constructed around an unreal accusation: Kliment supposedly seduced a girl whom in reality he hardly knew. However, the accusation is followed by a demand for a certain action which would erase the initial crime. As in Stanley Webber's case, the subjugation and reduction of Kliment takes place on the level of language. But while Pinter uses language as an irrational force which could destroy by the very weight of its proliferating images and pseudo-legalistic vocabulary, Klíma uses language as a force which can invert and consequently pervert reason.

His investigating officials never use a non sequitur, the way Pinter's characters do. They merely switch the meaning of what Kliment has said to suit their own purposes. For example, when asked whether he will marry the girl whom the official powers have decided he must marry, Kliment is puzzled: 'Marry? But that's ... That must surely be a mistake. I ... We don't even know each other.' The official seems to accept the information: 'Oh, you don't even know her ... (laughs, then suddenly) Are you trying to tell me that we are making mistakes here?' An indifferent phrase has been interpreted as an attack and thus turned into a new form of accusation. Another example: when Kliment tries to explain his situation: 'But, as I told you, I am already engaged,' the two investigators heave sighs of relief: 'There you are, you see?' and 'Finally! I knew that we'd be able to convince him in the end.' And when Kliment with waning strength struggles to straighten out the renewed misunderstanding and explain that he is engaged to another girl, not the girl they are trying to saddle him with, the officials nod in mock sympathy: 'You see, Kliment, that's exactly the point. You don't understand yourself. You are confused about your own feelings.[23] Soon afterwards one of them starts playing with a pistol.

Again we have come up against a distinction that we have noticed before. What seems in Western plays to be a product of irrationality is revealed in Czech plays as the product of a single-minded purpose. In a closed society where one official political language dominates all aspects of the public media, writers are bound to be more acutely aware of the power of one rigidified system of communication. Perhaps we may even speculate that in the West the – greater or lesser – knowledge of the existence in Eastern Europe of such a language has had some oblique positive effect. By helping to create an awareness of how language can obfuscate and dissolve the structure of meaning, such knowledge helps to clarify the boundaries of linguistic stratification. But perhaps this is too sanguine a point of view. Nevertheless, one thing is obvious: In a totalitarian society the imposition of an 'official language' in all walks of public life has paradoxically had a beneficial influence on the best writers in that society by providing them with one grand example of language totally failing to record and order human experience.

III

Much of the recent sociological literary criticism written in the West, particularly the brand coming out of Germany – East *and* West – uses a terminology with implicit value judgments. Writers from Goethe to Genet, from Molière to Kafka, are subjected to critical analysis and interpretations in which concepts like 'ahistorical pessimism,' 'middle class humanism,' 'alienation from the political perspective,' and so forth, multiply. It would be very interesting to ask some of the eager adherents to that philosophy of literature to analyse and interpret some of the plays which have emerged from a society that calls itself classless and officially claims to have achieved the 'Revolution.'

If we recall the mood of the plays we have been discussing, we will quickly realize that nearly all of them explore in some way contemporary man's bewilderment about his own contradictions. Some interesting East German writers, such as Heiner Müller in his play *Mauser* (1974), present the image of a utopian society at the end of an extended social process – an image absent in Czech theatre. The promise of the ultimate perfect society that beckons on the horizon of Brecht's plays (if we read him with less irony than he had himself) goes in the Czech plays not only unmentioned but is made to seem strangely irrelevant. For the Czech writers the big questions are related to the social consciousness of the average man so obliquely that they do not fit any preconceived dialectic or historically deterministic pattern.

I am not saying, however, that Czech plays radiate an air of resignation or pessimism. On the contrary. Despite their closeness in spirit to contemporary theatre in the West, their vision of life is considerably lighter than that of, say, Jack Gelber's *The Connection* or Peter Shaffer's *Equus*. But here we must become a little more explicit.

Even in those Czech plays which deal more or less openly with apparently recognizable social situations (for example, Uhde's *King Vávra*, Klíma's *The Jury*, Kohout's *Fire in the Basement*, Kundera's *The Blunder*) we frequently feel that we are treading in Samuel Beckett's territory: somewhere in the limbo between the Cartesian *cogito* and that outdated rational equipment which is of no more use to Hamm than it is to Didi or the Unnameable. It is perhaps in such moments that the Western reader will most readily respond to what the Czech playwrights have to say.

Samuel Beckett's limbo – to enjoy an amusingly paradoxical image – has become familiar ground for the Western reader. After all, the most formidable poet-playwright of contemporary Western culture has centred all his creative energies on the subject of man's ignorance about who, where, and when he is. Scholars and critics have analysed his writings almost word by word. The student of contemporary Western theatre enters this area of Czech drama well-equipped and ready to analyse. But what he finds is a different kind of existentialism, if we must use that overworked word. It is strangely pure, non-derivative. As I said before, the Czech and Slovak reaction to Beckett was centred around their admiration for his analytical intellect on the one hand, and his histrionic humour on the other. This reaction can aid our approach to the existential dimension of Czech theatre.

There is one aspect of that dimension which is not readily available to the Western theatre-goer or scholar's mind. It is the political explosiveness of the most unpolitical of human attitudes in a society where daily life is politicized. To question the value of human existence, to dwell on the meaninglessness of man's endeavours, to describe the aimlessness of his activities and question his perception of reality – all attitudes which make up one of the chief components of contemporary Western literature – means to take a stand against the chief values of a communist society. To question this means making a political pronouncement precisely by attempting an apolitical assessment of human life, whether in Havel's *The Memorandum* or Klíma's *The Jury* (which have become politically undesirable works), or in Topol's *An Hour of Love*, Vostrá's *Eeny, Meeny, Miney, Mo*, and Smoček's *Cosmic Spring*, which are about as political as Beckett's *Happy Days* or Pinter's *The Lover*. The area is vast and could be approached from many points of view. I will again suggest some kind of pattern at the usual price of oversimplification.

Broadly speaking, there are three ways in which an 'existential' realization enters into the plays of the contemporary Czech theatre. There is, first of all, the time-honoured theme of life being a dream; secondly, the more modern idea of death in life, or – to put it in a more popular way – living versus 'vegetating'; thirdly, the moment of existential shock when a process of alienation takes place and a man realizes that at heart he does not really know why he is alive.

I will first examine their treatment of life as a dream. In the program to his *A Dream Play* Strindberg tells us 'anything can happen; everything is possible and probable. Time and space do not exist. On an insignificant background of reality, imagination designs and embroiders novel patterns, free fancies, absurdities and improvisations.'[24] Josef Topol calls one of his plays 'A Dream in a Play' and another 'A Play in a Dream.' He also stresses that the 'average' family – a little greedy, a little treacherous, a little selfish – who murder the gentle visitor Nightingale, never dreams. On the whole Czech playwrights place a positive value on certain types of dreams – be they day-dreams or dreams in sleep. O'Neill's sharp attack on alcoholic pipe-dreams in *The Iceman Cometh*, and Tennessee Williams contempt for day-dreams of a gracious past, are likely to meet with fresh reactions when exposed to an audience in Czechoslovakia which would. not share the playwright's anger.

Why this fascination in Czechoslovakia with the irrational forces in a man's psyche? Is it 'Slavic Romanticism'? Not quite. Topol's Véna defines his attitude to life by saying 'anything I can't come to grips with causes me difficulties. Big difficulties'; he simultaneously admits that his inability to free himself from what he considers 'real' has made him a mere shadow of a man: 'I'm nothing, I'm wiped out.'[25] Karvaš's wigmaker, the only character in the play who does not enter the general power struggle, feeds his imagination by dreaming of the day when he need not be afraid. Landovský's Hanzl is sustained in his shabby, joyless existence by a dream about an afternoon in his youth when he galloped through a snowy countryside and wanted to die because he was completely happy and there was nothing else to be wished for.

Dürrenmatt has told us that 'reality corrects our ideas.'[26] Czech playwrights suggest the opposite: 'our daydreams correct reality.' Their delight in the freedom of fancy and imagination – and if we go a step further we can call it freedom of thought – occurs again and again in the plays we have considered. The Freudian dream in sleep – a sturdy war-horse from Strindberg to Pinter – with its stress on cause and effect, is largely absent. This kind of dream is, after all, a document for man's slavery to his senses rather than for his freedom of spirit.

The second 'existentialist' theme in Czech theatre could be called that of 'death in life.' Among the sardonic aphorisms of the Polish humourist Stanisław Jerzy Lec we find the following: 'The fact that he has died does not mean that he has ever lived.'[27] This aphorism expresses in a nutshell the dire concern of much of contemporary literature. Automatic reactions and programmed living patterns have become the nightmare of the contemporary playwright. 'What makes you think that you exist?' is the climax of the verbal attack on Stanley Webber in Pinter's *The Birthday Party*. 'You're dead, You're dead. You can't live, you can't think, you can't love. You're dead.'[28] The attack is justified: Stanley Webber knows it. The crime of lovelessness and thoughtlessness is widespread in modern drama from Chekhov's Trigorin to Peter Shaffer's psychiatrist, Dr Martin. The example of Josef Topol best illustrates the appearance of this 'existential' theme in Czech theatre.

Smrt'ak, the village barber in *The End of the Carnival*, is a manipulator whose moral shortcomings are hard to detect because they are effectively concealed. His chief vice is the vicarious enjoyment of harm done to others – although his sober mind, riddled with purely pragmatic conclusions, cannot even fully understand the nature of this harm. Alienated from real human contact, closed to the wonder of the human spirit, he uses his caution and apparently perfect behavior like a protective shield, concealing his own hollowness and emotional brutality. In this intriguing character, on the surface apparently no more than a scoundrel – half annoying, half amusing, but basically harmless – Topol has created a powerful image of evil. Smrt'ak embodies that concealed unobtrusive form of evil of Goethe's Mephisto, that 'spirit of negation' which C.S. Lewis has tried to define in

The Screwtape Letters. In the third chapter we saw how Topol varies and analyses this figure again and again, as it gets less explicitly harmful and becomes more average. His plays show how it becomes less and less possible for the audience to moralize and judge when they see the qualities of this archetypal figure become both more and more abstract and more and more a part of human nature. The luckier ones have less of it, the unluckier ones more.

Life, as lived by the average man, with its repetitive pattern of eating and sleeping and fathering children, has somehow (in the eyes of the Western as well as the East European writer) lost its claim to be called life. The demands of uniformity imposed by a modern society have reduced him to a test case of individualistic behaviour (Havel); an officially filed number (Mahler); the contents of a jar mailed 'this side up' for chemical analysis (Vostrá); a member of 'the people of both sexes' (Uhde); an arbitrarily chosen representative of the people's spirit (Kohout); a sample of youthful idealism (Klíma).

Each of these examples could easily be matched by similar characters from Western plays. From Ionesco's Mr and Mrs Martin (*The Bald Soprano*) to Peter Shaffer's psychiatrist (*Equus*), from Frisch's state prosecutor turned murderer (*Count Öderland*) to Albee's 'good' citizen Peter (*The Zoo Story*), we find characters who seem to be conceived to fit Lec's dictum that dying is no proof of ever having lived.

However, there is a subtle difference between the two cultures. Western playwrights seem to imply that their characters lack some sort of passionate commitment to life; Eastern European playwrights tend to be more ironic, hence less emotional. The Westerners (particularly some American playwrights) seem to combine a lesser sense of humour and irony with a somewhat moralistic attitude. To explore this interesting contrast would take a book in itself. I will only point out that the following comment on Albee's *The Zoo Story* by an American critic, which may be quite acceptable to an American audience, would cause amusement among Czech playwrights and critics alike: 'It is about the maddening effect that the enforced loneliness of the human condition has on the person who is cursed (for in our society it undoubtedly *is* a curse) with an infinite capacity for love.'[29] However, despite the difference in reasoning and mood, playwrights East and West spend much of their creative energy in shaking loose the frozen habits of the average individual's life.

The third area of our exploration, the theme of alienation, is very complex and only a few suggestions about its nature must suffice. It is that little explored area of occasional inexplicable shifts in perspective in man's awareness, when, for example, an average day suddenly for some intangible reason changes its nature, and a man is startled to discover that well-known objects, familiar through daily use, have suddenly become alien and threatening. At this moment he is confronted by the realization that his perceptions are as fragile as the order he has established around and within himself. Whether or not everyone actually experiences such moments of 'existential anxiety,' modern authors wrote about them, and playwrights of the Absurd have attempted to elicit such moments and put them on stage in metaphorical form. How else could we understand such diverse plays as Pinter's *The Dumb Waiter*, Mrożek's *Strip Tease*, and Michelsen's *Drei Akte*?

In the Czech plays these moments of existential recognition are scattered here and there, often in a humorous context, often half concealed. One finds them, for example, at the moment when a character realizes that 'at the end a man stands there alone and without a face – he does not even know what he is – .'[30] Or one suddenly hears an old man's reminiscences which reveal his ignorance about his own life because 'until today I actually didn't know what it was all about. Well, I knew it but I couldn't swear on it.'[31] Or one witnesses such a moment in the conversation between lovers, when the man claims that 'I want to know what I'm doing. In broad daylight. And face to face'; but later bitterly admits a new realization: 'Everyone just pretends that he knows.'[32] Does this imply that an active, rational attitude to life is portrayed as a senseless game of self-deception, a modern version of the Emperor's new clothes? Not really.

These subdued reminders of the frailty of human reason and of the recurring uncertainty about whether the business of living bears ordering take a strangely dynamic turn in Eastern European writing. In the West we have for some time been accustomed to literature and art undercutting reliance on intellect by assessing it as incompatible with reality. Existential anguish has become a commodity. Perhaps we have read too much Beckett.

But if a character in a Czech play suddenly raises her eyes in inexplicable fear and speaks of 'the desert in her soul,'[33] or another character defines life as 'constant waiting from one day to the next, for tomorrow, for better times and then all at once it's the end,'[34] this moment of recognition has an electrifying effect. The instant of 'existential anxiety' becomes, paradoxically, a protest against a society which tries to force social meaning on each individual life and imposes a dutiful optimism. Those fearful moments when man suddenly confronts his own profound uncertainties are the safeguards against being completely possessed by the imposed social system. Paradoxically, then, moments of fear, shock, and awareness of alienation are thus transformed into concealed magical weapons of resistance against a system which, though consistently using a language expressing man's worthiest thoughts, his noblest attitudes, and his finest visions, has in reality converted them into the opposite, into anti-humanism.

I do not doubt the honesty of the Western dramatist who puts on stage semi-brutal reconstructions of how throttled decency turns into viciousness, how shattered hopes exude hatred, how spiritual isolation can turn into a hardened shell. Nonetheless he follows a general trend in which the salutary influence on ticket sales – emotional lacerations draw interest as much as physical brutality – perhaps plays a certain part. (The reader may decide whether the Canadian playwright Michel Tremblay is a case in point; the Austrian playwright Wolfgang Bauer almost certainly is). But be that as it may, the fact is that the writer who does something similar in Eastern Europe performs a hopeful act of courage.

IV

Western theatre critics are a worried breed. Self-conscious American critics worry that the failure to produce 'great theatre' is a measure of the 'failure of American culture.'[35] German critics, mostly philosophically minded, ponder the question whether the theatre still has any justification as a purifying or activating art form.[36] French critics, reacting impatiently against the anti-intellectualism of modern times, regret that the new middle-class theatre audience, 'la grande consommatrice des spectacles populaires,'[37] is depoliticized and incapable of the exaltation of shared revolutionary spirit.

Such problems have not occupied much time in the minds of theatre critics in Czechoslovakia. They are not prone to judge theatre by whether it is 'great' – a short-sighted, even fallacious judgment anyhow – but by whether it works on stage, holds the audience's attention, and tells something about life in some new way. Czech and Slovak critics were (regrettably I must draw the reader's attention to the past tense, since practically all of these critics have been now silenced) rarely concerned with theatre in terms of abstractions and socio-literary theory. As we have seen, the theatre for them is a way of life and they have always – or at least for as long as political vicissitudes would permit – been used to finding their social problems reflected in their literature. Living at the embattled centre of Europe and having experienced several half tragic, half absurd political changes in the past, the Czechoslovaks have developed an instinctive resistance to sweeping idealistic phrases whether on aesthetic, political, or other levels. Moreover, Czechoslovak theatres are subsidized by the state, and actors draw a regular salary, so that box-office worries are eliminated.[38]

When one considers the incredibly lively theatre scene throughout the country – about seven hundred productions are staged each season, with Shakespeare, for example, being staged more often in Czechoslovakia than in England – the setting seems to be ideal in every way for theatre to flourish. However, of course, we know the problem. Today Czech and Slovak playwrights must submit their work to censors who approve only intellectually entirely innocuous material and hence nothing truly creative can emerge. Many playwrights who were part of the extraordinary flowering of Czech dramatic writing during the sixties have now officially been silenced, although in recent years their works have been circulating underground in typescript,[39] which is encouraging proof that the creative spirit still continues to simmer or rather burn under the surface.

I began this book by placing the two figures of Franz Kafka and Jaroslav Hašek at the gates of the recent creative outburst of Czech theatre. And indeed during the discussion of the plays, the tension between these two attitudes to life has emerged again and again from the core of each playwright's thought. Putting it in simplified terms, the tension lies between the urgent desire of man to understand the world in which he lives, and the necessity of accepting it for what it is, without feeling the need to justify this acceptance; or more generally, between man's flaw – his failure to understand why he lives, and his glory – his indomitable spirit which cannot be subdued by the realization of his limitations.

While we may realize that in one way or another all literature ever written is about this theme, we might also remind ourselves that much of Western literature has somehow withdrawn from this awareness. On the one hand Western writers have seemed to question the very adequacy of traditional genres as art forms, and on the other they have tended to become moralistic. Think of Edward Bond's *Bingo* in which he considers Shakespeare, the none too moral man, unworthy of Shakespeare, the moral artist. Or listen to George E. Wellwarth, whose book *The Theatre of Protest and Paradox* has gone through several printings: 'Like most modern playwrights – like most modern thinkers of any kind – Kopit has a distinct tendency to view the rotting underside of life from below.'[40] Czech playwrights would have little sympathy for this description of a modern writer's endeavours. It seems that, in all humility, they have made it their task to explore that void between Pascal's severe statement and his magnificent modification – between man the reed, and man the thinking reed. But they do not find it simple to put Kafka's man, who is painfully aware of his ignorance and dies 'like a dog,' into one category, and Hašek's Švejk, who claims to be 'a genuine idiot' and yet lives to the full, into the other.

This 'system,' this form of order which Kafka's K. questions and Hašek's Švejk takes for granted, appears in many forms in recent Czech theatre, in a manner both more specific and much more varied than its equivalent in Western plays. When Western critics talk about the 'enforced loneliness of the human condition,' or 'man's inability to communicate,' or a playwright's 'wordless demonstration of absolute alienation,'[41] they appeal less to the reader's analytical powers than to his general complaints about twentieth-century life. We would leaf in vain through the pages of Czech and Slovak theatre criticism to find similar statements. The alienation, the lack of communication, the loneliness of man are demonstrated with definite reference to a social situation.

We have seen this alienation take the form of a literal-minded bureaucratic establishment (Havel); a dictatorship setting up ridiculously arbitrary distinctions between friend and foe (Karvaš); a mad merry-go-round of manufactured illusions (Mahler); a group of officials programmed to carry out their official duty at any cost (Klíma). We have recognized it in a microcosmic power struggle of a school (Kundera); in a theme from Greek mythology (Uhde); in a metaphor portraying the balance between free will and force (Smoček). Every time, however – and this is an important distinction – the supra-personal force which suppresses the single man is shown quite clearly to consist of men who are made of the same stuff as he is. They are revealed in all their small likes and dislikes, their wish to close office at five and go home, their fondness for a good dinner, their interest in a secretary's legs, their desire to do well in their jobs. The implication is deflating and terrifying at the same time. The 'system' consists of people who work efficiently and dependably in a group no matter whether it means running a school, a concentration camp, a government, or a public entertainment. When stripped of their official function, they tend to deflate like punctured balloons and become frightened little nobodys just like their 'victims.'

This point is not as simplistic as it might seem to a reader who is used to the much more obvious explorations of power by a writer in a democratic society. But when a ruling system is so towering in its ideological and bureaucratic complexity, the voicing of the realization that the system consists of particles as insignificant as the ruled ones is staggering as well as exhilarating. Kafka's haunting vision of the vast line of ever more powerful doorkeepers who guard the entrance to the law would lose much of its frightening impact if each doorkeeper were described as a cog in a wheel, a small bureaucrat who does the duty assigned to him. But Kafka's Man from the Country who is informed about the doorkeepers is never told this. On the contrary, he is assured of their terrible magnaminity and dies with the sense of his own ridiculous presumptuousness and insignificance.

This unkafkaesque deflation process has been undertaken in one way or another by almost all the playwrights discussed in this book. Although these writers never explicitly describe this process, they constantly imply its effectiveness and in this way they convince us of man's 'mouldability' and the possibility of reducing him to a mechanical functionary who can work and exert power only in one particular set of circumstances. The alarming reality of this process is stressed again and again.

A brilliant example of 'dekafkaizing' is Havel's *Audience* (1975) (companion piece to *Vernissage*, examined in chapter 2), a one-act play with two actors, which is set up in circular form, so that it ends exactly the way it started, only in a reversed situation. The implication, as in Beckett's *Waiting for Godot*, is that it could go on infinitely. A writer, Vaněk, who has been 'normalized,' i.e. assigned to the lowest job in a brewery in order to prevent him from subversive writing – the autobiographical element is obvious – has been called into plant manager Sládek's office.[42] For quite a long time he is offered beer (the sight of which he hates) and 'relaxing' conversation punctuated regularly by the manager's disappearance into the adjoining washroom. As the manager gets progressively more drunk and subsequently more honest, the real reason for the 'audience' emerges like a snake from a flower bed.

After a lengthy, embarrassing display of suspiciously ostentatious joviality, Sládek finally gets to the point, namely, that under certain circumstances Vaněk could be promoted to become store-keeper, an infinitely more attractive job than rolling around heavy barrels in rain and snow. Vaněk's initial delight at this generous offer turns to dismay when he finds out the price to be paid for the softer job. Sládek has been under increasing pressure from the authorities to produce political evidence against Vaněk, and since he has been unable to discover anything incriminating – Vaněk is not only the most punctual and diligent but also the quietest worker in the brewery – he has decided to offer him a deal. After all, for God's sake, what can he tell them every week when they come and want information about subversive activities? And one of those guys who comes for information did Sládek a favour once, and it would be nice if he could repay him now with some assistance. And Vaněk could help if he wanted to: 'You're an intellectual, aren't you? You've got a broad political horizon? You write, don't you? Who else should figure out what they really want to know but a guy like you?'[43]

When, understandably, the deal falls through, Sládek bursts out into a furious attack: 'You with your principles! You'd be willing to take a warm spot in the storage room, sure, that you would accept from me, but to accept also a piece of that swinishness I've got to wade through every day, that you refuse! ... I'm just good enough to make the manure where your principles grow ... one of these days you'll go back among your actresses ... and then you'll be the hero – but what about me? Where can I go back to? Who'll notice me? Who'll value my actions? What have I got out of life? What awaits me? What?'[44] Then he collapses in tears pleading no longer for incriminating evidence, but for a visit from one of Vaněk's actress friends. When his sobs have changed to loud snoring, Vaněk tiptoes out of the room.

A short while later a knock is heard. Sládek recovers momentarily and is as sober as in the first scene. Vaněk walks in buttoning his trousers á la Sládek, sits down, and immediately drains the beer that Sládek has poured. The play has turned full circle, only the roles have been shifted. At the beginning of the play Vaněk responded with a polite phrase to Sládek's greeting. Now the curtain falls on a four-letter word with which he comments on things in general.

Apart from the quality of the play (its mechanistic repetitiveness, its circular shape, the use of completely hollow automatic language, the dead-pan humour) the play most clearly reveals that the authority that wields power consists of little men, more frightened and greedy for their scrap of living than those who suffer under them. And as the final seesaw movement of the plot reverses the situation, the irrational and mechanistically arbitrary element of the power struggle becomes evident.[45]

We are reminded of another Eastern European writer's humourous comment on the arbitrary seesaw of power. In Mrożek's fable *The Lion*, the conscientious lion-prodder Gaius is worried when he notices that one lion, instead of diligently tearing up Christians for the emperor's entertainment, is sitting calmly in a corner, chewing a carrot. In a discussion during which Gaius tries to convince the lion of his assigned duty, the lion teaches him a lesson in Realpolitik about the alibis and ways of behaviour necessary should the present government change. 'Has it never crossed your mind,' the worldly lion enquiries, 'that the Christians could come to power?' Gaius, the dutiful civil servant of the Roman regime, is quick to grasp the wisdom of political foresight, and asks the lion, whether, if the Christians should take over some day, 'will you then testify that I didn't force you to do anything?'[46] With a quote from Cicero, the wise lion serenely returns to his carrot. The author leaves us to imagine with what mixed feelings the formerly so conscientious and single-minded servant of authority will carry out his social duty in the future. The seat on the seesaw of power is none too comfortable.

Milan Uhde's *A Play about the Dove* (1976) is a very different approach to the same problem. Havel's *Audience* treats with the author's particular logic and clarity the topic of the functionary as victim enmeshed in the web of the system he is serving almost as if he were giving us a blueprint of the process. Uhde's play expresses similar thoughts in a very different, cryptic, and poetic form. Where Havel deals with a contemporary, concrete situation, Uhde prevents sharp focussing. The action of his play, as he tells us on the title page, takes place 'in the country and the times of Andrey Biely's novel *The Silver Dove.*' This comment opens up a vast area of speculation. Biely, a prolific symbolist writer of strange, still unrecognized genius, sometimes called a sort of Russian James Joyce, has lately received increasing critical attention in the West, and the novel on which Uhde based his play appeared in English translation in 1974.[47] It is a haunting work about a period of intellectual and emotional upheaval in Russia at the turn of the century, when 'god-seekers' of all sorts – from the intellectually-oriented theosophy of Mme Blavatsky and the anthroposophy of Rudolf Steiner, to more primitive movements like occultism and all kinds of black magic – were part of the vast currents of thought trying to grapple with final questions and answers.

It is significant in our context that Biely's novel, which appeared serially in 1909, was to form the first volume of a trilogy entitled *Vostok ili Zapad?* (East or West?). It is indeed a work about vast opposites and its entire structure reflects schemes of antipodal characters, settings, and situations – each relating to its metaphysical counterpart, light or darkness, cosmos or chaos. The hero, Daryalsky, an educated member of the Russian intelligentsia, engaged to a beautiful young woman, an ideal of purity à la Turgenev, gets involved with a religious group called the 'Doves,' one of the many sects which flourished in the remote vastness of the Russian countryside and which were crushed neither by the church nor by the police of either the Tsar or the Bolsheviks. Attracted and somehow mesmerized by the sensual, earthy power of a woman in the sect, Daryalsky enters the inner circle of the group, and is finally killed when trying to escape and regain his freedom from the irrational bondage.

In his dramatic adaptation Milan Uhde has selected from the exceedingly complex canvas of the novel one thread and woven it into a closely integrated theatrical work. Despite its dramatic tension, it has a distinctly lyrical quality which emerges partly from the very sparseness and simplicity of the language, and partly from the strong symbolic structure which represents the elementary forces of water, fire, and earth, all pervaded by the spirit, be it God's or man's, be it good or evil.

Five acts, named after the events of the holy or unholy rites of the 'Doves' – Enticement, Inspection, Annunciation and Consecration, Play about the Dove, and The Wrath of God – are separated into nineteen scenes which take place alternatively inside and outside the cottage of Andrey, one of the sect's members. A young man from town, Vitalij, a medical student, gets initiated into the dark world of the 'Doves,' falls in love with Andrey's daughter, Marja, gets trapped by the zealots and finally dies together with Marja in the burning house, set aflame by the torches of members of the 'Dove' community, of whom Vitalij himself says that they do not know what they are doing and why. At the end Pavel, the epileptic leader of the sect, who spins a hypnotic web around his followers, writhes on the floor outside the house where are dying the only two people able to distinguish lies from the truth, and thoughts from imaginings. The curtain falls as Pavel, rising to his knees, calls hoarsely into the audience, 'You. You have seen it. You know it. How we need him. Give him to us. Give us the Christ.'[48]

Apart from its other philosophic qualities, Biely's cosmic novel was deeply concerned with the problem of recognition and perception, in other words – more familiar to this context – the distinction between the mask and the face, or the play and reality. Uhde grasped this basic artistic urge of the Russian writer and transferred it into his play with surprising poetic instinct. Here, in a roundabout way, we have come back to the essential argument of these pages. The dark and passionate *A Play about the Dove* is like a luminous poetic symbol of the most important themes and qualities we have encountered in the dramatic output of this small nation which, since the late nineteen thirties, has been striving to distinguish spiritual values outside a totalitarian ideology which claims to help them overcome their human weaknesses but basically uses these same weaknesses to exert power.

In the commmunity of the 'Doves' no-one is really himself. Everyone has Kundera's 'second face'; the spiritual leader speaks a version of Havel's Ptydepe which no-one understands, and which only the sceptical newcomer identifies as Homer's Greek – the shipwrecked Ulysses' words to

Nausicaä, the fearless Princess. The other members of the Dove-ideology take his words to be the voice of God manifesting itself through his servant. As in Klíma's *Games*, the characters do not know who pretends or 'plays'; moreover they do not realize when they 'play' themselves. They are involved in the spiritual confines of the sect, and although it is obvious that their leader's epileptic fits occur at well-timed moments and that the messages of God which he receives are precariously close to his own wishes (which include sleeping with Marja whom he promises to help conceive a new Christ, whom she can proudly carry around in her bulging womb before he will save the world).

Every member of the sect has some inside information about everyone else which gives him a tool for blackmail and power. The web of concealed wrongdoings and crimes thickens with hints of dark deeds of the past, which emerge more and more clearly as events press to the inevitably tragic end. The interplay between real and invented facts (the audience rarely knows what is really true) runs through the play like a counterpoint of intangible forces of good and evil. The interplay is visual (the illuminated room contrasts with the darkness outside; the homey and reassuring flame of the candles changes into the destructive blaze of the torches at the end); sensual (the love scenes between Marja and Vitalij on the one hand and the constant, seemingly religious but actually lecherous and – worse – at times completely cynical references of the other villagers to the act of procreation which is to give them the new Saviour); and spiritual (the words of truth exchanged between the lovers contrast with the shady insinuations about debts and guilt, forbidden pleasures and concealed killings which emerge from the talks of the other characters).

Have we strayed far from the mundane discussion in the office of Havel's brewery manager? Not at all. Basically Uhde's play is about the same two tendencies: man's desire to formulate some kind of moral pattern, and his need to assess the reality around him in order to preserve or attain what he takes to be his safety. The lion in Mrożek's parable, unburdened by ethics, is only concerned about the latter – his safety. Less intelligent and not as secure in his amorality, the manager in Havel's ironic model of reality in a totalitarian state tries, when alcohol has weakened his suppressing mechanism, to figure out what is wrong with his position as boss and what is right about the position of his employee and/or victim. Marja's case is more complex. As a child she had been brought into the settlement of the 'Doves' by her father who in turn had joined it only because of the entreaties and promises of another member of the sect, who in his turn was in love with Marja's mother and used this means to have her closer. The doll within a doll – or lie within a lie – situation is obvious. Marja recognizes only one thing: that there is no escape for her. 'I wanted ... It just didn't work out,' she tells her lover before the house goes up in flames. She had wanted indeed, and tried to sell herself, physically as well as spiritually, in order to assure some form of safety, of being left in peace; she would even have consented to play the Mother of God and bear the new Christ for the village – a sullen, promiscuous Virgin Mary to a dubious Saviour. In the end she only wants Vitalij's child, but by then it is too late. 'Isn't it all the same?'[49] she asks, sipping her home-made liquor. She no longer knows what is good or bad. Perhaps she never knew.

With *A Play about the Dove* Milan Uhde has written a poetic parable of social man's ethical confusion under a spiritual dictatorship – an eloquent plea from a writer who has little hope of being published in his own country. The 'Doves' had God and his language on their side. And he who has language can formulate ideas and ideals and hence gain power over others. Milan Kundera once pointed out the danger of an ideology which began as the advocate of virtues and ideals and gradually converted them into the opposite: 'When one sees how a great humanist movement can be subverted into something entirely different and how all human qualities are destroyed in the process, one begins to realize the fragility of human values altogether.'[50]

In the background lurks a larger question, which can be put in two different ways, depending on who asks it. A conscientious citizen, conscious of living in what is still called the 'free world,' might ask: *Is there* a basic difference between the writers in his own society, and the playwrights writing in a totalitarian society where values are fixed, good and bad are officially determined, and people are told what is good for them rather than being asked what they think is good for them? Another equally conscientious citizen, worried by the chaos of values, outbursts of violence, and various forms of corruption in a modern democracy, would start his question with *What is* the difference between ...?

The answer is again given in full awareness of over-simplification. Czech playwrights have a strong Western cultural tradition. They know their Shakespeare, Voltaire, Ibsen, and Pirandello, as well as they know their Gogol and Chekhov. Thus they have been influenced by the same great shapers of modern consciousness as playwrights in the West. Certain developments in modern society – pure science, technology, what Matthew Arnold called 'instrument knowledge,' medicine, ecology – work largely outside political systems. Problems and questions that they raise are filtered past the ideologies down to the individual. The discovery of the computer affects the office worker in New York, Paris, or Prague in similar ways. The invention of a new drug will raise certain hearts in Eastern Europe as well as on the Pacific coast. The Czechoslovak writer has a particular resilience to political pressures, partly due to his awareness that most of his creative ancestors have had to do their writing under unfavourable conditions of one kind or another.

A playwright needs strong, clearly defined problems that will capture his audience's imagination and stir their minds in two brief hours. In Czechoslovakia the writer lives in a society where the ancient, truly dramatic problems facing man – his idea of freedom, his sense of justice, his hunger for knowledge, his fear of death – have been systematically and definitively solved for him by his society, and have, as it were, been taken away from him as a subject for discussion. He will therefore seek to reintroduce these questions into his work in a changed and masked form, and when he succeeds, they will be even more exciting and exhilarating than in the West.

The writers and intellectuals ostracized by this system of government have given up any claim on the needs of an average member of society. They only live for their cause. In the moving words of the writer Alexandr Kliment: 'The damned ones carry on. Why shouldn't they! In sleepless nights they have thought it all out: "We have pondered, read and written enough about existential border situations; now we are experiencing them!" The intellectuals are engaged in a battle which may appear dramatic and tragic and which takes place silently, secretly, in isolation. They try to overcome and to outwit forces which are stronger than they. Who will succeed in doing it? ... Who will retain his own level under these entirely abnormal, absurd, and inhuman conditions? Who will manage to raise his two or three children and in addition create a significant work, not merely a fragment, a few marginal notes to his own person and his times?'[51]

As I attempted these sketchy comparisons between some of the playwrights of a small country, located in the proverbial heart of Europe which, through the vicissitudes of political change, has now become part of 'Eastern Europe,' I began to realize with increasing clarity that, despite the different social system under which they live, and in spite of which they try to write, the Czech writers' consciousness is very much part of the consciousness of the West. The fact that they have been deprived of a voice in their own country has not prevented them from grasping, on a truly international scale, the complex problem of assessing artistically man's situation today. Moreover – a hopeful conclusion for man's creativity in general – we find in their work and their courage proof that the stultifying grip of a rigid political system cannot permanently smother the artistic imagination. Carried forward by their own deep convictions about forms of freedom and justice, and their uncompromising urge to speak the truth, they continue working and creating in spite of all obstacles – paradoxically may even be spiritually strengthened by these obstacles – to bear witness in our perplexing modern world to the endurance of man's reason and the resilience of his spirit.

Notes

Translations into English are by the author except for quotations from well-known translations of certain authors (e.g. of Strindberg, Ionesco, Camus, Mrożek), where the notes refer to the English versions, and in the case of Czech plays which have already been published in English (e.g. Vera Blackwell's translations of several of Václav Havel's plays). Where a Czech play has been translated into English but is not yet published in English, the author has made use of the translation and noted it, but has referred to the Czech original in the notes (e.g. in the case of George and Christina Voskovec's translation of Josef Topol's *Cat on the Rails*).

INTRODUCTION

1 For example, Jan Kadár and Elmar Klos's film *Shop on Main Street*, based on Ladislav Grosman's novel of the same name, won the Academy Award for best foreign-language film of 1965; Jiří Menzel's film *Closely Watched Trains*, based on Bohumil Hrabal's text, won the same award for 1967; in 1976 Miloš Forman won the Academy Award for best director for his film *One Flew Over the Cuckoo's Nest*, based on Ken Kesey's novel. For an informative, as well as entertaining study of Czech cinema see Josef Škvorecký *All the Bright Young Men and Women – A Personal History of the Czech Cinema* tr Michael Schonberg (Toronto 1971).

2 For an extensive treatment of the history of Czech threatre to the end of the eighteenth century, see the Czechoslovak Academy of Sciences *Dějiny českého divadla* Chief Editor František Černý (Prague 1968). For an English study see Arne Novák *Czech Literature* tr Peter Kussi, with a Supplement by William E. Harkins (Ann Arbor 1976).

3 Jakub Arbes *Z českého jeviště* (Prague 1964) 33

4 Otakar Fencl, Introduction to *The Czechoslovak Theatre Today* (Prague 1963) 9

5 Arbes *Z českého jeviště* 33–77

6 The New York world première production ran for 111 performances. For more detail about the London production see *The London Times* 7 May, 7 June, and 11 June 1923.

7 For a thorough discussion of Czech amateur theatre culture see František Černý 'La signification de l'amateurisme pour la culture théâtrale tchèque' *Acta Universitatis Carolinae –philosophica et historica* 5 83–99.

8 Jan Grossman 'Kafkova divadelnost' *Divadlo* (Nov. 1964) 1

9 The recent careful and resourceful translation of *The Good Soldier Švejk* by Cecil Parrot (Harmondsworth 1974) is a vast improvement on the older translation by Paul Selver (Garden City 1930).

10 Kate Flores 'Biographical Note' *The Kafka Problem* ed Angel Flores (New York 1946) 6

11 Albert Camus *The Myth of Sysiphus* tr Justin O'Brien (New York 1959) 100

12 Edmund Wilson *Classics and Commercials* (New York 1950) 392

13 Franz Kafka *Tagebücher 1910–1923* ed Max Brod (New York 1948 and 1949) 418; English translation: *The Diaries of Franz Kafka* I 1910–1913 tr Joseph Kresh (New York 1948), II 1914–1923 tr Martin Greenberg with Hannah Arendt (New York 1949)

14 *Narodní Listy* 6 June 1924 5; quoted in Josef Čermák 'Česká kultura a Franz Kafka' *Česká literatura* roč. 16 (1958) 465. Kafka's *Briefe an Milena* (New York 1952) have become almost as famous as his literary works; English translation: *Letters to Milena* tr Tania and James Stern (London 1953).

15 Kafka's friend, literary executor, and later chief editor, Max Brod, immediately objected to this categorization.

16 Pavel Eisner 'Franz Kafka a Praha' *Kritický měsíčník* 9 (1948) 82

17 The first Czech edition of *To the Lighthouse* appeared in the mid-sixties but went largely unnoticed.

18 Despite the fact that it was the Kafka Conference of 1963 which started the Kafka-wave in Czechoslovakia, Czech readers had had an earlier introduction to Kafka. His novella *Der Bau* (*The Burrow*) appeared in *Světová literatura* ed Josef Škvorecký 3 (1957) 132, together with an illuminating essay on Kafka by his outstanding Czech translator, Pavel Eisner. For this occasion Škvorecký's editor-in-chief Jan Řezáč commissioned the Czech painter František Tichý to draw a portrait of Kafka. It is that same portrait (nicknamed 'big-eared Kafka') which has been reprinted in most pictorial volumes on Kafka and Kafka's Prague, often with no credits given to the eminent painter.

19 Jan Kott 'Podivné myšlenky o Kafkovi' *Divadlo* (Nov. 1964) 66

20 Antonín J. Liehm 'Franz Kafka and Eastern Europe' *Telos* 23 (1975) 58

21 Joachim Fontheim, who had also directed Pavel Kohout's *August August, august*

22 Cf Jochen Schmidt 'Heisst Kafka August? – Die "Amerika" – Dramatisierung von Kohout/Klíma in Krefeld' *Theater heute* 19. Jg. N.4 (April 1978) 58.

23 Antonín Liehm 'Franz Kafka dix ans après' *Les temps modernes* 29 no 323 (1973) 2295

24 Friedrich Dürrenmatt *Die Physiker* in *Komödien II und frühe Stücke* (Zürich 1963) 350

25 Angel Flores 'Introduction' *The Kafka Problem* ix

26 Erich Heller 'The World of Franz Kafka' *The Disinherited Mind* (New York 1959) 201

27 Grossman 'Kafkova divadelnost' 1–17

28 *Ibid* 4; see also my chapter 4, introduction.

29 Grossman 'Kafkova divadelnost' 8

30 For a brief discussion of the reception of the novel in Prague see Milada Součková *A Literary Satellite, Czechoslovak-Russian Literary Relations* (Chicago and London 1970) 27ff.

31 Karel Kosík 'Hašek and Kafka' *Telos* 23 (1975) 88

32 Applying Northrop Frye's archetypes we could, for example, claim that Hašek's work represents the central pattern of the comic vision of man – a hero who copes with the order around him as if it were an easily manageable flock of sheep and who thus represents the reader's wish-fulfilment – while Kafka's works reveal the central pattern of the tragic vision – a deserted, helpless, betrayed hero, dominated by some form of tyranny. Cf Frye 'Archetypes of Literature' *Fables of Identity* (New York 1963) 7–20.

I RESPONSES: EAST AND WEST

1 Július Pašteka 'Súčasné divadlo absurdity' *Slovenské divadlo* roč. 13 (1965) 192

2 Martin Esslin 'Preface to the Second Edition' *The Theatre of the Absurd* revised ed (New York 1969) x

3 Sergej Machonin untitled article *Literární noviny* č. 3 16 Jan. 1965 3 (hereafter Machonin 16 Jan. 1965)

4 'Eugène Ionesco ouvre le feu,' textual report of Ionesco's opening address to the Eighth Congress of the International Theatre Institute, Helsinki, June 1959, in 'Théâtre dans le Monde' 8 (autumn 1959) 171

5 Ivan Klíma *Theaterstücke mit begleitenden Reflexionen des Autors* 'Reflexion I' tr Gerhard and Alexandra Baumrucker (Lucerne and Frankfurt/Main 1971) I/7. The Baumruckers are resourceful translators of a large number of Czech

works (prose and drama) into German. Their names will appear frequently in these notes.

6 Machonin 16 Jan. 1965
7 Werner Mittenzwei *Gestaltung und Gestalten im modernen Drama* (Berlin 1965) 98, 99
8 Machonin 16 Jan. 1965
9 Oleg Sus 'Theorie absurda' *Divadlo* (May 1963) 5
10 Kenneth Tynan 'Ionesco, Man of Destiny?' *Observer* London 22 June 1958
11 Tynan 'The Theatre Abroad: Prague,' *The New Yorker* (April 1967) 118
12 Machonin 16 Jan. 1965
13 Zdeněk Hořínek 'Zastavení na Zábradlí' *Divadlo* (Oct. 1965) 15
14 Ionesco *Notes et contre-notes* (Paris 1966) 252
15 Geneviève Serreau *Histoire du 'nouveau théâtre'* (Paris 1966) 41
16 Ionesco *Notes* 290
17 Ibid 289
18 Ibid 288
19 Ibid 289
20 Hořínek 'Berenger a nosorožci' *Divadlo* (April 1969) 33
21 Ibid
22 Esslin *Theatre* 151, 152
23 Hořínek 'Berenger a nosorožci' 34
24 Ionesco *Notes* 143
25 Ibid 142–3
26 Serreau *Histoire* 125
27 Hořínek 'Obrazy a obrady' *Divadlo* (Dec. 1967) 61
28 Esslin *Theatre* 175
29 George E. Wellwarth *The Theatre of Protest and Paradox* (New York 1964) 116
30 Werner Kliess *Genet* (Velber bei Hannover 1967) 32
31 Hořínek 'Úděl zavržence' *Host do domu* roč. 15 č. 6 (1968) 61
32 Kenneth Tynan is aware of this phenomenon ('The Theatre Abroad: Prague' 103).
33 Introduction to the Slovak translation of *Krapp's Last Tape* signed 'J.K.' *Slovenské divadlo* roč. 11 č. 3 (1963) 402–3
34 Josef Kaustitz 'Beckettovy hry o štěstí a neštěstí žít' *Divadlo* (Dec. 1963) 28
35 Hořínek 'Ionesco a ti druzí' *Divadlo* (April 1965) 76
36 Petr Pujman, Introduction to a selection of Beckett's plays in Czech translation, quoted in Zdeněk Hořínek 'Absurdní výběr z Becketta' *Divadlo* (Sept. 1965) 75
37 Ibid 74
38 Zdeněk Kozmím 'Dvojí balanc mezi komikou a úzkostí' *Plamen* roč. 9 č. 8 (August 1967) 85
39 Vladimír Štefko 'Sám sobě Godotem' *Divadlo* (Dec. 1969 double number) 79

277 Notes / Responses: East and West

40 Hořínek 'Absurdní výběr z Becketta' 75
41 Grossman 'Současný Brecht' *Divadlo* (Sept. 1958) 410
42 *The Good Woman of Setzuan*, staged in Belgrade 19 Oct. 1954
43 For more information on Brecht in Poland see Andrzej Wirth 'Brecht in Polen' *Akzente* 12 (1965) 394–403.
44 The Berlin Ensemble presented *Mother Courage, Terror and Misery of the Third Reich*, and *Galileo* at the J.K. Tyl Theatre in Prague between 15 and 20 April 1958. They took the same plays to Bratislava.
45 Grossman 'Theorie a tvorba' *Divadlo* (June 1957) 455
46 'Brechtovské okouzlení' unsigned editorial *Divadlo* (April 1962) 6
47 The collected plays of Voskovec and Werich appeared under the title *V + W Hry osvobozeného divadla* 2 vols (Prague 1956).
48 Cf Bertolt Brecht *Schriften zum Theater* (Frankfurt/Main 1960) 31, 262.
49 The exchange of comments between Jitka Bodláková and Josef Kopecký appeared in *Divadlo* in the spring issues of 1963.
50 Dušan Pokorný 'Fysikové a roboti' *Literární noviny* roč. 12 č. 47 23 Nov. 1963 8; Zdeněk Herman 'Piškot na váš účet' *Divadlo* (Dec. 1965) 39–41
51 Hořínek 'Cesta k lidovému divadlu' *Divadlo* (May 1964) 34
52 Signed 'Sm' 'Devět otázek pro Friedricha Dürrenmatta' *Literární noviny* roč. 13 č. 27 4 August 1964 1 and 8
53 Jitka Bodláková 'Fysikové a Dürrenmatt' *Divadlo* (Jan. 1963) 57
54 Hořínek 'Dürrenmattovy historie' *Divadlo* (Sept. 1969) 28
55 Machonin 'Dramatik a doba' *Literární noviny* roč. 14 č. 43 23 Oct. 1965 3
56 Esslin *The Peopled Wound: The Work of Harold Pinter* (New York 1970) 161
57 Vladimír Štefko 'Divadlo ironie a relativity' *Divadlo* (Feb. 1969) 78
58 Jindřich Černý 'Dlouhá cesta O'Neilla k nám' *Divadlo* (Sept. 1966) 56–7; Milan Lukeš 'Millerův člověk mezi lidmi' *Divadlo* (Jan. 1961) 30–3; review by 'pat' of Tennessee Williams' *Vytetovaná růže (The Rose Tattoo)* in *Divadlo* (Feb. 1964) 20–2; Jiří Konůpek 'Dramatická setba Paula Claudela' *Divadlo* (June 1968) 32; Lukeš 'Kdopak by se Bonda bál?' *Divadelní noviny* roč. 8 č. 3 8 Oct. 1969 7
59 Eric Bentley 'Sartre's Struggle for Existenz' in *Sartre – A Collection of Critical Essays* (Englewood Cliffs, NJ 1965) 73–9, reprinted from *Kenyon Review* 10 (1948); R.-M. Albérès *Jean-Paul Sartre* 7th ed (Paris 1964) (see especially ch. 5, section 3 'Le philosophe du neomarxisme *La Critique de la Raison dialectique*' 106–11); Maurice Cranston *Sartre* (Edinburgh and London 1962) 11
60 Article by 'pat' 'Jak hrát Sartra?' *Divadlo* (Dec. 1964) 74
61 Hořínek 'Absurdní výběr z Becketta' 74
62 Jana Patočková 'Hra na téma století' *Divadlo* (Jan. 1969) 51, 55
63 Alena Urbanová 'Svoboda člověka mezi lidmi' *Divadelní noviny* roč. 7 č. 7 8 Dec. 1968 3
64 Machonin 23 Oct. 1965

65 Jindřich Černý 'Camusova moderní tragedie' *Divadelní noviny* roč. 12 č. 18
7 May 1969

66 Thomas Hanna *The Thought and Art of Albert Camus* (Chicago 1958) 71

67 Sus 'Theorie absurda' 2–3

68 Sigmund Freud *Gesammelte Werke* 6 (4th ed London 1969) 209–10

69 Ionesco *Notes* 138

70 Georges Schlocker 'Unberechenbarer Beifall' *Theater heute* (June 1970) 62

71 Machonin 23 Oct. 1965

72 Jindřich Černý in *Lidová Demokracie*, quoted in Andreas Razumovsky
'Der Mechanismus von Feigheit und Macht' *Frankfurter Allgemeine Zeitung*
8 August 1965

73 Ibid

74 Esslin 'Politisches Theater – absurd' *Theater heute* (Jan. 1966) 8

75 Esslin *Theatre* 271

76 Tynan 'The Theatre Abroad: Prague' 102

77 George Bernard Shaw *Saint Joan* in *The Collected Works* 17 (New York 1930)
162

78 Max Lerner in *The New York Post*, quoted in the cover text of the Pocket Book
edition of Edward Albee *A Delicate Balance* (New York 1970)

79 The other two plays were Molière's *Tartuffe* and the Czech writer Oldřich
Daněk's *Vrátím se do Prahy* (I shall return to Prague).

80 Broadcast on Radio Prague, 2 Feb. 1970

81 Edward Albee *A Delicate Balance* 122

82 Esslin 'Politisches Theater – absurd' 11; Vera Blackwell 'The New Czech
Drama' *The Listener* 5 Jan. 1967 10 (Ms Blackwell has translated several of
Havel's plays into English); E.J. Czerwinski 'Jesters and Executioners: The
Future of East European Theatre and Drama' *Comparative Drama* 5 No. 3
(1971) 123; Jarka M. Burian 'Post-War Drama in Czechoslovakia' *Educational
Theatre Journal* 25 (1973) 311

83 An excellent introduction to an analysis of Havel's use of language, without
more far-reaching conclusions, is Paul I. Trensky 'Václav Havel and the
Language of the Absurd' *The Slavic and East European Journal* 13 (1969)
42–65.

84 See, for example, the entry on Klíma in the German reference guide to modern
international drama, Siegfried Kienzle *Modernes Welttheater* (Stuttgart 1966);
English translation, *Modern World Theatre* (New York 1970).

85 Pavel Landovský *Wegen Desinfektion geschlossen* première 8 Sept. 1978,
at the Werkstattbühne, Theater der Stadt Bonn; (see also ch. 7, notes 45
and 47).

86 Dieter Gerber 'Ein Stück aus einer anderen Welt' *General-Anzeiger* 12 Sept.

1978; Marieluise Müller 'Der Autor durfte sein Stück nicht sehen' *Nürnberger Zeitung* 11 Sept. 1978; Siegfried Schmidt 'Triste Szenen aus dem Prager Alltag' *Bonner Rundschau* 11 Sept. 1978

87 Jochen Schmidt 'Mit den besten Grüssen von Schwejk' *Frankfurter Allgemeine Zeitung* 14 Sept. 1978; Hannes Schmidt 'Katz und Maus im Staatsrestaurant' *Neue Ruhrzeitung* 14 Sept. 1978; Harry Lerch 'Prag: Wegen Desinfektion geschlossen' *Rhein Zeitung* 22 Sept. 1978

88 Havel 'Politics and the Theatre' *The Times Literary Supplement* 28 Sept. 1967 870

89 Ibid 880

90 For an admirable and well-documented illustrated study of Svoboda see Jarka M. Burian *The Scenography of Josef Svoboda* (Middletown, Conn. 1971).

91 For a full length study in Czech on Krejča see Jindřich Černý *Otomar Krejča* (Prague 1964); in French see *Otomar Krejca et le théâtre za branou de Prague* Supplément à *Travail Théâtral* (Lausanne 1972); in English see Jarka M. Burian 'Art and Relevance: The Small Theatres of Prague' *Educational Theatre Journal* 23 (1971) 246–56.

92 Oscar G. Brockett and Robert F. Findlay *A History of European and American Theatre and Drama since 1870* (London 1973) 647

2 VÁCLAV HAVEL

1 Tom Stoppard *Jumpers* (London 1972)

2 Charter 77, signed by over 300 Czech and Slovak writers and intellectuals, has become a symbol of the struggle for human rights and freedom of expression; the Charter urged the Czechoslovak government to carry out the promises it made at Helsinki in 1975, and pointed out that anyone who tried to claim these rights was persecuted.

3 Stoppard, Introduction to *Every Good Boy Deserves Favour & Professional Foul* (London 1978) 8. More recently Stoppard has written *Dogg's Hamlet*, *Cahoot's Macbeth*, the second part about the production of *Macbeth* put on in a Prague apartment by Pavel Kohout and his friends, some of them banned from the Czech stage (see illustration).

4 *Every Good Boy & Professional Foul* 93

5 Ibid, Introduction 9

6 For a lively discussion of the surprising parallel between the two playwrights see Kenneth Tynan 'Profiles' *The New Yorker* (19 Dec. 1977) 41ff.

7 Václav Havel 'Politics and the Theatre'

8 Havel 'Dovětek autora' *Hry 1970–1976* (Toronto 1977) 306. This is the first publication in Czech of five of Havel's plays which were not allowed to be published in Czechoslovakia.

9 This idea is formulated in Hořínek 'Člověk systematizovaný' *Divadlo* (Oct./Nov. 1968) 4–10.

10 Another way of revealing the absurdity of language on stage is reflected in the experiments in silence of Samuel Beckett and the Austrian writer Peter Handke.

11 Grossman 'Předmluva' in Havel *Protokoly* (Prague 1966) 12–13. Jan Grossman, who worked very closely with Havel and directed both *The Garden Party* and *The Memorandum* at the Theatre On the Balustrade in Prague, informs us that Havel's world 'consists of real components, existing everywhere, even banal in their daily occurrence'; and that the playwright's method in presenting them is 'exactly as real, we might even say "logical."' The fact that these considerations caused Grossman doubts as to whether Havel could be counted among the 'absurd' playwrights merely shows how vague the term itself has remained even in the minds of people who have given it some thought.

12 Ionesco *The Bald Soprano* in *Four Plays* tr Donald M. Allen (New York 1969) 23

13 Beckett *Waiting for Godot* (New York 1954) 12

14 Esslin, Introduction to *Three East European Plays* (Harmondsworth 1970) 16. For a more detailed discussion of the relation between Hašek and Kafka see Kosík 'Hašek and Kafka' 84–8.

15 *Vernissage* in *Hry 1970–1976* 276

16 Andreas Razumovsky 'Der Mechanismus von Feigheit und Macht' *Frankfurter Allgemeine Zeitung* 5 August 1965

17 Havel *The Memorandum* tr Vera Blackwell (London 1967) 11; original publication: *Vyrozumění* in *Protokoly*

18 Cf *Spiklenci* in *Hry 1970–1976* scenes i and xv.

19 Havel *The Increased Difficulty of Concentration* tr Vera Blackwell (London 1972) 16; original publication: *Ztížená možnost soustředěni* in *Divadlo* (May 1968)

20 Dürrenmatt *Ein Engel kommt nach Babylon* in *Komödien I* (Zürich 1963) 244

21 Havel *The Garden Party* tr Vera Blackwell (London 1969) 21; original publication: *Zahradní slavnost* in *Protokoly*

22 Ibid 16

23 Ibid 19, 36

24 Ibid 73–4

25 The play won the 1968 *Village Voice* award for the best foreign play of the Off Broadway season.

26 Machonin 'Vyrozumění' *Literární noviny* roč. 14 č. 40 2 Oct. 1965 5

27 Jan Grossman's contribution to a discussion on theatre, 'Politisches Theater in Ost und West' *Theater 1965* 53

28 *The Memorandum* 45

29 Havel 'Anatomie gagu' *Protokoly* pp. 126, 127, 129. (Havel has found a fortui-

tous way of rendering the Brechtian expression 'Verfremdung.' 'Ozvláštnění'
carries the implication of both 'alien, distant' and 'strange.' The English
'estrangement' is no happier a translation than the French 'distantiation.')

30 Kafka *Der Prozess* (Frankfurt/Main 1946) 255–7
31 *The Memorandum* 88
32 An American publication, for example, regards the broader vision of the play as
reducing rather than increasing its appeal: 'The satire is less sharp, for its only
object is the absurdity of scientific attempts to analyze man in the name of
humanistic goals'; Jarka M. Burian, 'Postwar Drama in Czechoslovakia'
Educational Theatre Journal 25 (1973) 311. A German critic, commenting on the
poor quality of the Berlin production of the play, reveals his own lack of
understanding by arguing approximately as follows: Since German producers,
unlike Czech ones, need not camouflage their sociological opinions, this Czech
'revival of absurd theatre' inspires them less for its concealed political implications than for its comical scenes that can be played straightforwardly for good
laughs; Peter Iden 'Spiele mit der Zeit oder: Schwierigkeiten mit der Verstän-
digung' *Theater heute* 10 Jg. Nr. 1 (Jan. 1969) 42–3. However, in his recent
article on Tom Stoppard, Kenneth Tynan has drawn attention to the importance
of Havel's play (cf ch. 2 note 6).
33 Hořínek 'Člověk systematizovaný 7
34 *Concentration* 60
35 It is this particular aspect of the play which anticipated Tom Stoppard's Professor Moore in *Jumpers* by four years.
36 *Concentration* 29
37 Ibid 74
38 Havel 'Nachbemerkung' to *Erschwerte Möglichkeit der Konzentration* tr Franz
Peter Künzel *Theater heute* 10. Jg. Nr. 1 (Jan. 1969) 56
39 Unlike the other quotations from *The Conspirators*, this quotation refers to the
German translation of an amended version of the play, *Die Retter* tr Franz Peter
Künzel (Reinbek 1972) 95. Because of the great difficulty in communicating with
these writers in Czechoslovakia, Sixty Eight Publishers in Toronto, who produced the attractive volume of *Hry*, included an earlier version of *The Conspirators* in which the above quotation reads: 'You are the only one who is able
to breathe life into me' (60).
40 Ibid 101
41 Havel 'Dovětek autora' 307
42 Ibid 308
43 Ibid
44 To date it has been staged in Italy, Germany, and Canada.
45 Havel 'Dovětek autora' 308

46 John Gay *The Beggar's Opera and Polly* from the original editions of 1728 and 1729 (London 1923) 82

47 Ibid 83

48 *Žebrácká opera* in *Hry 1970–1976* 121

49 Ibid 184

50 Ibid 149

51 See William Eben Schultz *Gay's Beggar's Opera, its Content, History and Influence* (New Haven 1923) ch. 21.

52 C.F. Burgess ed *The Letters of John Gay* (Oxford 1966) 72; Lotte Lenya-Weill 'Threepenny Opera' *Brecht as They Knew Him* (Berlin 1974) 62

53 Havel 'Dovětek autora' 309

54 Ibid

55 The internationally acclaimed Czech novelist Milan Kundera commented humorously on what he calls everyone's urge to write the 'obituary of the novel ... though this is possibly the least dead of all art forms'; 'Comedy is everywhere' *Index on Censorship* 6 no. 6 (Nov./Dec. 1977) 6.

56 Havel 'Dovětek autora' 309

57 *Vernissage* 292

58 Ibid 296

59 Havel 'Dovětek autora' 310

60 Gabriel Laub is a writer, critic, and pamphleteer who has been living in Hamburg since 1968. He is the author of several collections of satirical writings in German. *Double Barrelled Attack* (*Doppelfinten*), a collection of ironic essays, with Hans-Georg Rauch's illustrations appeared in Charles Scribner jr's English translation (New York 1977).

61 *Protest* tr Gabriel Laub (Hamburg 1978) 14. The Czech original is circulating in Czechoslovakia in typescript as a publication of *Edice Petlice*.

62 Ibid 10, 11, 14, 15, 25

63 Havel 'Dovětek autora' 310

64 Paul I. Trensky 'Václav Havel and the Language of the Absurd' *The Slavic and East European Journal* 13 (1969) 44. This article contains perceptive comments on Havel's language.

65 Ödön von Horvath *Geschichten aus dem Wiener Wald* (Frankfurt/Main 1970) 43

66 Ionesco *Jack or the Submission* in *Four Plays* 109

67 Harold Pinter *The Caretaker* and *The Dumb Waiter* (New York 1961) 51–2

68 *The Garden Party* 32, 38; *The Memorandum* 109

69 *The Garden Party* 53

70 *Concentration* 32

71 *Žebrácká opera* 158

72 *The Garden Party* 14

73 In the original Czech, the author has here achieved a double comic effect. The

teacher's name is Peřina, which sounds as synthetic as any piece of Ptydepe vocabulary, but a Czech audience is bound to think of its similarity to 'peřina,' meaning feather bed. Vera Blackwell's choice of the name 'Lear' for this character in her English translation of the play does not seem particularly fortunate.

74 *The Memorandum* 72–3
75 Ibid 40
76 *Concentration* 49–50, 55
77 *The Memorandum* 58–9
78 *Concentration* 42–3
79 Ibid 57
80 Havel 'Politics and the Theatre' 879
81 *The Garden Party* 63
82 Ibid
83 Ibid 64
84 *The Memorandum* 107–8
85 Ibid 109
86 *Concentration* 70
87 Ibid 71–2
88 *Žebrácká opera* 138–9
89 Gay *Opera* 51
90 Czech has different forms for singular and plural of nouns and verbs, and this renders the speech even more amusing. Some of the effect gets lost in English.
91 *Žebrácká opera* 160–1
92 One of the section headings in ch. 3 of Peter Farb's *Word Play: What Happens When People Talk* (New York 1974), a full exploration of this topic
93 *Žebrácká opera* 182
94 *Protest* 51
95 Ibid 43, 45–6
96 Ibid 46–7
97 Ibid 49–50
98 Ibid 51
99 Havel 'Politics and the Theatre' 879
100 Havel 'An Open Letter' *Encounter* 45 (Sept. 1975) 24

3 PAVEL KOHOUT

Six of Kohout's plays discussed here did not appear in Czechoslovakia but were published in German translation in Germany and Switzerland. In the latter cases, references are to the German publications.

1 Jan Císař 'Složitý případ' Afterword to Pavel Kohout *August August, august* (Prague 1968) 79
2 Alena Urbanová, Introduction to Kohout *Taková Láska* (Prague 1967) 25
3 It should be added here that these observers, too, have realized that since the Soviet occupation Kohout has endured various forms of persecution and harrassment with a steadfast courage and no sign of bending to pressure. Tom Stoppard's recent *Cahoot's Macbeth* is a tribute to the courage of Kohout and his friends (see ch. 2 n. 3, and illustration).
4 Also published in book form: Günter Grass/Pavel Kohout *Briefe über die Grenze. Versuch eines Ost-West-Dialogs* (Hamburg 1968)
5 *Weissbuch in Sachen Adam Juraček, Professor für Leibeserziehung und Zeichnen an der Pädagogischen Lehranstalt in K. kontra Sir Isaac Newton, Professor für Physik an der Universität Cambridge, nach zeitgenössischen Unterlagen rekonstruiert und mit höchst interessanten Dokumenten ergänzt von Pavel Kohout* tr Gerhard and Alexandra Baumrucker (Frankfurt/Main 1973); Kohout *Aus dem Tagebuch eines Konterrevolutionärs* tr Gustav Solar and Felix R. Bossonet (München 1969)
6 'Erstes Intermezzo' 5 in Kohout *3 Theaterstücke: So eine Liebe, Reise um die Erde in 80 Tagen, August August, August; mit Prolog, Epilog und Intermezzi;* the plays tr Lucie Taubová; the Prologue, Epilogue, and Intermezzi tr Magda Štitná and Felix R. Bossonet 2nd ed (Lucerne and Frankfurt/Main 1971)
7 *Taková láska* 34
8 Cf Kohout 'Erstes Intermezzo' 24.
9 In his comments to a German edition of his selected plays the playwright himself gives us a description of the stage set. 'On either side of the stage there were five chairs from where the actors were called either front stage to be cross-examined or onto a pyramid consisting of seven steps in order to reconstruct scenes from the past. Above were two dozen of various lights, living-room lamps, white round balls of light suggesting university lecture halls, street lights and gas lanterns. My friend and steady stage set designer, Zybyněk Kolář, used the barest means to create a stage that would provide precise orientation for the audience in addition to having a suggestive impact on its imagination. By means of lights and sounds people were led to imagine furnished apartments, noisy street-corners, fields at night, crammed lecture halls, nervous railway stations and even a roaring train' (Kohout 'Erstes Intermezzo' 9–10).
10 Kohout 'Zweites Intermezzo' 3
11 Kohout 'Erstes Intermezzo' 12. (The friend was Václav Lohniský, the director of the Vinohrady Theatre.)
12 Ibid 13
13 Ibid 14

14 The reference here is to the German translation of the play, *3 Theaterstücke: Reise um die Erde in 80 Tagen* 96. The Czech version, *Cesta kolem světa za 80 dní* in *Divadlo* (Feb. 1962) enclosure 25, shows a slight variation in the last sentence. Rather than introducing himself with the combined astronauts' names, the young man says only: 'It wouldn't mean anything to you, Sir,' and is about to walk off stage as three young men crossing the stage greet him with the refrain of a 1961 hit song: 'Good morning, Major Gagarin ... !' The older man, obviously puzzled, shakes his head. By the time the German translation appeared eight years later, the astronaut-profession had expanded and the playwright – once again seizing a good opportunity – changed the ending and achieved two things: the play was not only updated but also gained political respectability.

15 Karel Čapek *Válka s Mloky* (Prague 1972) 213

16 Kohout 'Zweites Intermezzo' 4

17 Součková *A Literary Satellite* 48

18 After the Communist take-over in 1948 Čapek had been declared a bourgeois writer whose only (and ideologically minor) claim to acceptance was that he was an anti-fascist. His literary image was saved by an enthusiastic dissertation of a young Russian student of literature. Since his dissertation was Russian, it was, of course, auctoritas, and Čapek's reputation was re-established.

19 For a fuller discussion of the political aspects of Čapek's novel, see William E. Harkins *Karel Čapek* (New York and London 1962) ch. 10. An additional insight into the see-saw of literary censorship is that various parts of the original text of *War with the Newts* were omitted in the post-1948 editions of the novel: most notably the 'Molokoff Manifesto,' a spoof on the grandiloquent statements of Soviet statesmen, containing a pun on the name of the Soviet Minister of Foreign Affairs V. Molotov, a name which is etymologically close to the Czech word 'Mlok,' meaning a newt. (I owe this inside story to Josef Škvorecký who at the time worked in the publishing house which brought out the 'censored' version of Čapek's novel.)

20 Kohout 'Comment' dated Sept. 1962 to Karel Čapek/Pavel Kohout *Válka s Mloky* in *Divadlo* (Feb. 1963)

21 Ibid 26

22 Jaroslav Hašek's *Osudy dobrého vojáka Švejka za světové války* was written between 1921 and the author's death in 1923, at which time he had completed only four of the planned six volumes. This discussion will keep the Czech spelling of Švejk's name, since there seems no reason to use the generally accepted German spelling 'Schweik.'

23 Erwin Piscator staged the work in his proletarian theatre in Berlin where it ran in 1929, with the great actor Max Pallenberg in the title (and only) role. The other

roles were filled with puppets and film strips conceived by Georg Grosz.

24 Kohout 'Zweites Intermezzo' 5
25 Ibid 7–8
26 Ibid 7
27 Klaus Watner 'Hamburger Revuen' *Theater heute* (Nov. 1968) 31
28 Cf Kohout 'Zweites Intermezzo' 11.
29 Ibid 12–13
30 Enid Welsford *The Fool* (Garden City, NY 1961) 318
31 *August August, august* 13
32 Santayana 'The Comic Mask' 135–6
33 *August* 16
34 Ibid 72. This is a reference to the poem *Balada o snu* (Ballad on Dreams) by the Czech poet Jiří Wolker (1900–24) whom the Manager is paraphrasing. The reference becomes even more ironic if we remind ourselves that Jiří Wolker was an idealistic socialist poet.
35 Ibid 77–8
36 Ibid 72
37 Ibid 'Epilog' 4
38 Kohout, a letter of 30 Jan. 1974, reprinted in the program of the double bill performance of *Pech unterm Dach* and *Brand im Souterrain* at the Stadttheater Ingolstadt in the spring of 1974, 2. The program contained the entire text of both plays in German translation by Gerhard and Alexandra Baumrucker. The original Czech titles are *Pech pod strechou* and *Požár v suterénu*.
39 *Krieg im dritten Stock/Evol* (Lucerne and Frankfurt/Main 1970) 22
40 Ibid 31, 32
41 *Pech unterm Dach* 9
42 Kohout, letter of 30 Jan. 1974
43 *Brand im Souterrain* 33
44 Kohout, letter of 30 Jan. 1974
45 In October 1976 *Poor Murderer* (translated, from the Czech original and the German version of Gerhard and Alexandra Baumrucker, by Herbert Berghof and Laurence Luckinbill) was staged at the Ethel Barrymore Theatre in New York with Laurence Luckinbill and Maria Schell in the main parts. The author himself was denied permission by the Czechoslovak authorities to attend the première of his play. In a letter of 30 September 1976, which was reprinted in the playbill, we find the moving lines: 'You're about to see a play created five years ago. Since then it has appeared on tens of stages, in hundreds of performances, and has been seen by thousands of people. I don't know who all the people are who have seen it but I know one person who never saw it: me.'

46 The Academy of Medicine in St Petersburg devoted an entire meeting to an analysis of Kerzhentsev's character; as a result a paper was published, dealing with the psychiatric analysis of Andreyev's story. Cf James B. Woodward *Leonid Andreyev* (London 1969) 77–8.

47 Kohout *Poor Murderer* (New York 1977) 98

48 Ibid

49 Ibid 100

50 Dieter Stér 'Gespräch mit Peter Weiss, Frühjahr 1964' in Karlheinz Braun ed *Materialien zu Peter Weiss' 'Marat/Sade'* (Frankfurt/Main 1967) 95

51 Kohout *Roulette* tr Gerhard and Alexandra Baumrucker (Lucerne 1975)

52 James B. Woodward *Leonid Andreyev* 178; see also 177–84 for a lucid discussion of *Darkness* and its background.

53 *Poor Murderer* 20, 21, 23

54 Hans Peter Riese 'Kohouts *Roulett* in Luzern – Ein Revoluntionär und ein Mädchen' *Frankfurter Allgemeine Zeitung* 22 August 1975 26

55 Pavel Kohout and Ivan Klíma *Amerika* (*nach Franz Kafka*) typescript (1974); see also ch. 4.

56 For example, Jan Císař 'Složitý případ' 79

57 'Zu Hause bleiben, nicht nachgeben – ein Interview mit dem Prager Dramatiker Pavel Kohout' *Frankfurter Allgemeine Zeitung* 1 Jan. 1976 10

4 IVAN KLÍMA

Seven of Klíma's plays discussed here did not appear in Czechoslovakia but were published in Germany and Switzerland in German translations, which are referred to in the following notes. (*Hromobití* in *Hry* was published for performance only in mimeographed form.)

1 Grossman 'Kafkova divadelnost' 3

2 Cf Zdeněk Hořínek 'Poznámky k procesu' *Divadlo* (Jan. 1967) 61–6.

3 Grossman 'Kafkova divadelnost' 11

4 Klíma *Zámek* (Prague 1965) 7

5 Klíma *Theaterstücke* (Lucerne and Frankfurt/Main 1971) II/7

6 Ibid II/2

7 Hans Schwab-Felisch 'Das sozialisierte Schloss' *Theater heute* (March 1966) 46

8 Alena Urbanová 'Pohodlí zámku' Afterword to Ivan Klíma *Zámek* 68

9 Zdeněk Hořínek 'Úděl zavržence' 61

10 Jiří Jirásek *Kamení* (Brno 1967) 18

11 Grossman 'Kafkova divadelnost' 17

12 See Christian Gneuss 'Wandlungen in Prag, die tschechische Theaterstruktur und das Unbehagen an der Spielerei' *Theater heute* (Nov. 1966) 4.
13 Kafka *Das Schloss* (Frankfurt/Main 1958) 13
14 Jochen Schmidt 'Heisst Kafka August?' 58
15 Kohout and Klíma *Amerika*
16 Kafka *Amerika* (New York 1953) 9
17 Jochen Schmidt 'Heisst Kafka August?' 58
18 The production opened on 22 Sept. 1978 under the direction of Maxi Tschunko.
19 Kafka *Amerika* 195–6
20 Dürrenmatt *Die Panne* (Zürich 1959)
21 Klíma *Theaterstücke* I/8
22 Klíma *Mistr* (Prague 1967) 59
23 Klíma *Porota* in *Divadlo* (Sept. 1968) 85
24 Ibid 97
25 Ibid 92
26 Ionesco *Rhinoceros* tr Derek Prouse in *Rhinoceros, The Chairs, The Lesson* (Harmondsworth 1967) 97, 103
27 Eva Šormová 'Porota' *Divadlo* (Sept. 1969) 57–8. The same idea, though modified, is expressed in Paul Kruntorad, 'Das Wechselspiel zwischen Drama und Bühne' *Theater heute* (Jan. 1969) 37.
28 Klíma *Porota* 97
29 Dürrenmatt 'Theaterprobleme' *Theater-Schriften und Reden* (Zürich 1966) 120
30 Klíma *Theaterstücke* IV/7
31 Ibid I/8
32 Ibid IV/8
33 Ibid I/6
34 *Klara und zwei Herren* in Klíma *Theaterstücke* 3; (Czech title: *Klára a dva páni*)
35 In the play Klara uses this phrase in variations more than twenty times.
36 Nikos Kazantzakis *Zorba the Greek* (London 1961)
37 *Klara und zewi Herren* 3
38 Ibid 19–21
39 Ibid 7, 17, 27
40 Klíma *Theaterstücke* III/5
41 The play opened (under the title *The Sweetshoppe Myriam*) as a double bill with *Klara and Two Men* (under the title *Klara*) at the Cubicolo Theatre in New York in February 1971. It closed after ten performances.
42 Klíma *Theaterstücke* III/7
43 *Konditorei Myriam* in Klíma *Theaterstücke* 31, 35 (Czech title: *Kavárna Myriam*)
44 Klíma *Theaterstücke* IV/5

45 Ibid IV/1

46 Ibid

47 *Ein Bräutigam für Marcella* in Klíma *Theaterstücke* 15, 25, 29; (Czech title: *Ženích pro Marcelu*)

48 *Konditorei Myriam* 16

49 *Ein Bräutigam* 21, 26

50 Klíma *Theaterstücke* IV/5

51 Ibid IV/7

52 Klíma *Blitz und Donner* tr Gerhard and Alexandra Baumrucker (Bärenreiter-Verlag Schauspielvertrieb, mimeographed; Kassel n.d.)

53 Klíma *Spiele* tr Gerhard and Alexandra Baumrucker (Bärenreiter-Verlag Schauspielvertrieb, mimeographed; Kassel n.d.)

54 Ibid 57

55 Ibid 7

56 Ibid 132–3, 134

57 Ibid 142

58 Ibid 96, 115, 144. (The German translation varies from the Czech original, which has been followed here.)

59 Ibid 57, 108, 112, 139

60 The anagram Kamil/Klíma implies that the author identified here with his character.

61 *Games* 144

62 Grossman 'Kafkova divadelnost' 9

5 JOSEF TOPOL

1 Otakar Blanda 'The Revolt of Youth' Afterword to Josef Topol *Jejich den* (Prague 1962) 97

2 *Jejich den* 57, 60, 62

3 Jindřich Černý 'Krejča: Schnitzler, Topol' *Divadelní noviny* roč. 12 č. 11 12 Jan. 1969 3

4 Ibid

5 Karel Kraus ' "Fin du carnaval" de Josef Topol, Etude précédée d'un aperçu de la dramaturgie tcheque depuis 1945' in Jean Jacquot ed *Le Théâtre Moderne II: Depuis la deuxième guerre mondiale* (Paris 1967) 305–6

6 Topol *Zwei Nächte mit einem Mädchen* tr Lydia Tschakert (Universal Edition Schauspiel, mimeographed, Vienna 1972) 227; (original Czech title: *Dvě noci s dívkou*)

7 Topol *Kočka na kolejích* in *Divadlo* (Feb. 1965) 93

8 Otomar Krejča 'Director's Note' *Jejich den* 4

9 Topol was the youngest Czech author ever to have a play performed at the National Theatre in Prague (see Krejča 'Note' 1).

10 Ibid 5

11 Topol *Konec masopustu* in *Divadlo* (May 1963) 14

12 Michael Anderson et al *Crowell's Handbook of Contemporary Drama* (New York 1971) 105

13 Kraus ' "Fin du carnaval" ' 297–314

14 *Konec masopustu* 14

15 Karel Kraus, Program Note to the opening performance of *The End of the Carnival* on 14 Nov. 1964 at the National Theatre in Prague, reprinted in *Svědectví* 7 No. 25 (1965) 127

16 Ionesco *Notes* 143

17 Sergej Machonin 'Kočka na kolejích' *Literární noviny* roč. 14 č. 50 11 Dec. 1965 6

18 Rolf Michaelis 'Einsame Masken' *Theatre heute* Jg. 7 Nr. 7 (1966) 18–19

19 See Burian 'Drama in Czechoslovakia' 307; Tynan 'Theatre abroad' 112.

20 *Kočka* 91

21 Ibid 87

22 Ibid 89, 92, 96

23 Ibid 94

24 Topol *Slavík k večeři* in *Divadlo* (March 1967) 81

25 Ibid 84

26 Ibid 19, 82, 85

27 Jan Císař 'Čas lásky a smrti' *Divadlo* (Feb. 1969) 37

28 *Slavík* 90, 91

29 Císař 'Láska a smrt' 38

30 *Slavík* 91

31 Topol *Hodina lásky* in *Divadlo* (Oct./Nov. 1968) 60

32 Ibid 62

33 Ibid 65

34 *Zwei Nächte* 213–14

35 *Hodina lásky* 61

36 Krejča 'Director's Note' 7

37 Machonin 11 Dec. 1965

38 The main actors, Marie Tomášová and Jan Tříska, have been widely acclaimed for their meticulous performance. They also acted the leading roles in *An Hour of Love* and in Krejča's internationally famous staging of *Romeo and Juliet* in Josef Topol's innovative and outstanding translation.

39 Cf Leoš Suchařípa 'Člověk je stejně sám' *Divadlo* (March 1966) 7–8.

40 These two plays, together with Chekhov's *Three Sisters* and Zdeněk Mahler's adaptation of Nestroy, *The Rope with Only One End*, were all performed by Krejča's ensemble of The Theatre Behind the Gate as the Czech entry at the annual International Theatre Festival in London, England, in the spring of 1969.
41 *Hodina lásky* 68
42 *Slavík* 90
43 Kraus 'Masopustní tragedie' *Divadlo* (Feb. 1965) 22
44 Beckett *Waiting for Godot* (New York 1954) 14
45 George Santayana 'The Comic Mask' *Soliloquies in England* (New York 1923) 137
46 *Jejich den* 62
47 *Konec masopustu* 12
48 Ibid 7, 12, 50
49 *Kočka* 89, 91, 93, 94
50 Ibid 89
51 *Hodina lásky* 68
52 Ibid
53 Santayana 'The Comic Mask' 139
54 August Strindberg, Author's Note to *A Dream Play* in *Six Plays of Strindberg* tr Elizabeth Sprigge (Garden City, NY 1955) 193
55 It is unfortunate that at the time of the completion of this book I had not had the opportunity to read Topol's most recent full-length play *Sbohem Sokrate* (Goodbye Socrates) which was written in 1976 and is circulating in typescript in Czechoslovakia as an item of *Edice Petlice*.
56 *Zwei Nächte* 213

6 LADISLAV SMOČEK

1 Aside from the obvious meaning of the word 'Semafor' is an abbreviation of 'sedm malych forem' (seven small forms). It had been hoped that the theatre would develop seven areas.
2 Jiří Suchý, Jiří Šlitr, and Ivan Vyskočil had actually founded the Theatre On the Balustrade which they opened in Dec. 1958 with the performance of *Kdyby tisíc klarinetů* (If a Thousand Clarinets).
3 Miroslav Horníček's untitled essay in Jiří Suchý *Semafor* (Prague 1965) 208
4 Ibid 207–8
5 Cf Jarka M. Burian 'Art and Relevance' esp. 239–46.
6 Jaroslav Vostrý 'Doslov' (Afterword) to Smoček *Piknik, Podivné odpoledne dr. Zvonka Burkeho, Bludiště* (Prague 1967) 122 (hereafter, Smoček *Piknik*)

7 Smoček *Piknik* 93
8 Ibid 58
9 Ibid 59
10 Vostrý 'Doslov' 124. Vostrý also mentions that Norman Mailer's *The Naked and the Dead* may well have been a source of inspiration for Smoček's *Picnic* but he also feels that traces of this attitude are to be found in Smoček's earlier short plays, written at a time when he could not yet have read Mailer.
11 Smoček *Piknik* 61. It may be pointed out here that Smoček himself told a friend that the idea for this black farce had been suggested to him by a Grand Guignol performance he saw in Paris.
12 Ibid 69
13 Ibid 92
14 Ibid 70
15 Ibid 92
16 Hořínek 'Činoherní klub 1965–66' *Divadlo* (Sept. 1966) 14
17 Bentley *The Life of the Drama* (New York 1967) 241
18 Smoček *Piknik* 97
19 Ibid 109
20 Ibid 98, 100, 102
21 Ibid 109, 110
22 Ibid 118, 119, 120
23 Kafka *Der Prozess* (Frankfurt/Main 1946) 257
24 Smoček *Piknik* 101
25 The idea of a different type of maze, a maze of mirrors, was not foreign to the Czech audience. There is a mirror-maze in Prague, on the Petřín Mountain. Moreover they had at that time the opportunity to see Orson Welles's film *The Lady from Shanghai* with its famous scene in the maze of mirrors.
26 Beckett *Waiting for Godot* (New York 1954) 17–18
27 Smoček *Kosmické jaro* typescript No. 6105/70 published by Dilia (Prague 1970) 63

7 LIFE IN A GROUP

1 Bentley *The Life of the Drama* 58–9
2 Jan Rozner in *Kultúrny život* 14 June 1958; reprinted in František Hrubín *Srpnová neděle* (Prague 1967) 116
3 Vratislav Blažek *Třetí přání* (Prague 1967) 85–111
4 Cf George Steiner *The Death of Tragedy* (London 1961), and Dürrenmatt 'Theaterprobleme' esp. 120–4.

5 Cf Pirandello *L'Umorismo* 2nd ed (Florence 1920).
6 Esslin *Theatre* 11–65; Frederick J. Hoffman *Samuel Beckett, The Language of the Self* (New York 1964)
7 *Ibsen's Collected Works* tr and ed James Walter McFarlane 6 (London 1960) 58
8 Milan Uhde *Král Vávra* (Prague 1965). The Czech audience is sure to think here of Karel Havlíček Borovský (1821–56) and his anti-Austrian satirical poem *Král Lávra*, set in mythical Ireland, but in fact based on the ancient legend of King Midas. This literary association, of course, greatly increases the impact of Uhde's play, since its title establishes it a priori as an anti-government satire.
9 This expression is used in the list of characters as well as in the text.
10 Uhde *Vávra* 29
11 Ibid 33
12 Ibid 23. The sentence is another quotation from Jiří Wolker's poem, *Ballad of Dreams*. Although the poem is deeply serious, Uhde introduces it in an amusing manner by making the quotation part of a hilarious argument on the 'dialectics' of objectivity and subjectivity, and secondly by attributing it in the text to 'George' Wolker. Though 'George' is English for 'Jiří,' this translation of the poet's first name has an alienating and hence amusing effect: perhaps somewhat like 'Wilhelm Shakespeare.'
13 Ibid 24, 30
14 Ibid 59, 73
15 Peter Karvaš *Velká paruka* tr from Slovak by Vladimír Reis (Prague 1965) 8, 10
16 Ibid 24
17 Ibid 92
18 Dürrenmatt 'Theaterprobleme' 120
19 Uhde *Děvka z města Théby* in *Divadlo* (May 1967) 87, 91
20 Ibid 86, 90, 91, 94
21 Ibid 94
22 Quoted in David Magarshack *Chekhov the Dramatist* (London 1952) 118
23 Anton Chekhov *The Cherry Orchard* tr and ed Ronald Hingley *The Oxford Chekhov* 3 (London 1964) 198
24 Alena Vostrá *Na ostří nože* in *Divadlo* (Jan. 1969) 90, 98
25 Milan Kundera *Ptákovina* in *Divadlo* (Jan. 1969) 90
26 Jan Císař 'Lidská přirozená bytost' *Divadlo* (March 1967) 7
27 Milan Kundera's novel *Žert* (The Joke) appeared in English translation by David Hamblyn and Oliver Stallybrass (London 1969).
28 *Ptákovina* 87
29 Pavel Landovský *Hodinový hotelier* in *Divadlo* (Feb. 1969) 92, 95
30 Ibid 84, 87
31 Ibid 96, 97

32 Zdeněk Mahler *Mlýn, Šaškárna o deseti obrazech* vol. 2, Dilia duplicated typescript, series Malá řada (Prague 1965); a somewhat different version of the play appeared earlier under the title *U zdi* (At the Wall) in *Divadlo* (June 1962). Page references will refer to the later typescript edition.

33 Written originally for the National Theatre in Prague in constant collaboration with Karel Kraus and Otomar Krejča, *The Mill* was finally rejected by the theatre on ideological grounds. The affair resulted in Krejča's finally severing his ties with the National Theatre and founding his own theatre 'Behind the Gate.' Prior to this break he took the play to the Slovak National Theatre in Bratislava where it was staged in a Slovak translation.

34 This does not mean that I am suggesting Mahler was influenced by Weiss's play. He had been working on *The Mill* for at least four years and done a lot of research on German concentration camps. Even when he completed the final version of *The Mill*, he probably did not know *Marat/Sade*, which appeared in Ludvík Kundera's Czech translation only in 1966.

35 Jindřich Černý 'Ztraceni v soukolí mlýna' *Divadlo* (Sept. 1965) 62

36 This is another instance which proves how deeply certain aspects of the 'absurdity' of Czech theatre are anchored in reality: for instance, at the mass execution of the male inhabitants of the town of Lidice, following the shooting of Reichsprotektor Heydrich by partisans, one of the men exeucted was in fact a Nazi agent provocateur, who, after having performed his part in the bloody event, was thus simply and effectively silenced.

37 Mahler *Mlýn* 173

38 Karel Kraus and Zdeněk Mahler *Provaz o jednom konci* published by Dilia (Prague 1967)

39 This is Karl Kraus (1874–1936), the Viennese writer, critic, and editor of the famous journal *Die Fackel*. The similarity of names with the Czech writer Karel Kraus is purely coincidental.

40 Jindřich Černý 'Nestroy před bránami' *Divadlo* (Feb. 1968) 67

41 Alena Vostrá *Na koho to slovo padne* in *Divadlo* (Jan. 1967) 81

42 Ibid 82–3

43 Ibid 100

44 In his note to *The Blacks* Jean Genet stresses the fact that the play 'écrite par un Blanc est destinée a un public de Blancs'; should it ever be played to an entirely black audience, it would be necessary to invite a white person to each performance, welcome him in a special way and make him sit in the first row: 'On jouera pour lui. Sur ce Blanc symbolique un projecteur sera dirigé durant tout le spectacle.' Should no white person be available, the black audience should be supplied with white masks at the door. In case they refused, a mannequin would have to be used; Genet *Les Nègres* (Paris 1963) Author's Note 13.

45 Pavel Landovský *Sanitární noc* typescript (1976); reference made to German translation by Gerhard and Alexandra Baumrucker *Wegen Desinfektion geschlossen* (Bärenreiterverlag Schauspielvertrieb, mimeographed; Kassel n.d.). My own English rendering of Landovský's title is a direct translation from the Baumruckers' felicitous German translation.

46 *Wegen Desinfektion geschlossen* 5

47 The first production of the play (see ch. 1, note 85), directed by Günter P. Fieber who had also directed Pavel Kohout's one act plays *Bad Luck under the Roof* and *Fire in the Basement* at the Stadttheater Ingolstadt in 1974, had to eliminate for reasons of space the apartment above, which obviously lessened the histrionic tensions of the play.

48 Vostrá *Na koho to slovo padne* Author's Comment 81

49 From a comment 'Was soll's?' by Egon Kochanowski, published in the program to the Bonn production

50 Ota Filip 'Ein Theaterstück aus einer anderen Welt' published in the program to the Bonn production. Ota Filip now lives in Munich. His numerous publications include *The Road to the Cemetery* (1967), *The Ascension of Lojsek Lapaček from Silesian Ostrava* (1970), and *The Maculate Conception* (1976).

8 ASPECTS OF HISTORY

1 Josef Škvorecký's *Zbabělci* (The Cowards) was written in 1948, published in 1958, but soon withdrawn from the market by the censors; *The Cowards* tr Jeanne Němcová (New York 1970).

2 The film (1967) based on Hrabal's *Ostře sledované vlaky* (Closely Watched Trains) received the Grand Prix at the international festival in Mannheim in 1967, and the Academy Award for best foreign-language film of 1967.

3 František Hrubín 'Autor, divadlo a diváci' *Rudé pravo* 28 Nov. 1968

4 'Otázky autorovi' in *Majitelé klíčů* (Prague 1964) 14

5 Ibid 11, 12

6 It should be noted here that not all 'occupation plays' are poor. Apart from Mahler's *The Mill* (discussed in chapter 7) and Ludvík Kundera's *The Total Cock-Crow*, two occupation plays of more than passing interest have been written by the Slovak writer Peter Karvaš. *Polnocná omsa* (Midnight Mass) was first performed at the Slovak National Theatre in Bratislava in May 1958, and a few months later in Czech translation at the Playhouse of the National Theatre in Prague. The play's setting is a Slovak town during the German occupation just before its liberation by the forces of the Slovak resistance. By analysing a conflict between the members of one family, each with different sets of values,

the playwright openly discusses and attacks the selfishness, greed, and opportunism of collaborators, and stresses the need for solidarity and idealism.

Karvaš's *Antigona a ti druzi* (Antigone and the Others), first produced in 1962, is set in a Nazi concentration camp. The leader of a small group of resistance fighters has been shot while escaping. A young woman prisoner 'Anti' realizes that he must be given proper burial in order to prove to the other prisoners that they are not alone, and thus counter their fear and deteriorating morale. The new angle on the Greek Antigone story is that Karvaš's 'Anti' cannot perform her task alone. She needs others to help her. The process of gaining a certain moral consciousness takes place no longer within the single individual but is expanded to a whole group. Anti's example shows the prisoners that there is hope in their forming one group with unified ideas and beliefs.

Ludvík Kundera's *Totální kuropění* (The Total Cock-Crow), produced in 1961, although it too deals with life in a wartime camp, is a very different type of play. It is set in a work camp outside Berlin. The author calls it 'A piece with many scenes, many persons and one jazz band.' The characters, including Frenchmen, Russians, Czechs, Poles, Spaniards, and many others, are a motley group of civilians of all ages and professions.

7 Milan Kundera, Afterword to *Majitelé klíčů* (Prague 1962; rpt 1964) 109–10
8 Ibid 110, 111–12
9 Michel Cournot 'Les propriétaires des clés' *Le Monde* 12 April 1974
10 The volume was Matěj Kopecký (1775–1847), *Komedie a hry*, as Hrubín writes in a program note to the performance of *Oldřich and Božena* at the Vinohrady Theatre, quoted in František Červínka 'O Hrubínův model historie' *Divadlo* (Jan. 1969) 38–9.
11 Two well-known examples are Friedrich Hebbel's *Agnes Bernauer* (1851) and Franz Grillparzer's *Die Jüdin von Toledo* (The Jewess of Toledo) (1836).
12 František Hrubín *Oldřich a Božena* in *Divadlo* (Oct./Nov. 1968) 113
13 František Pavlíček *Nanebevstoupení Sašky Krista* (Prague 1968). (This was Pavlíček's fifth play, not including seven plays for children.)
14 Isaac Babel (1894–1941) who had been declared an 'unperson' during the period of Stalinism and eliminated from all official records, was among the writers rehabilitated in 1956 and in 1957. A one-volume edition of his works was published in Moscow. For more information see George Gibian *Interval of Freedom, Soviet Literature during the Thaw 1954–57* (Minneapolis 1960) 10–11n.
15 Pavlíček *Saška Krist* 94
16 Ibid 12, 104
17 Ibid 12, 42
18 Ibid 87–8

19 Oldřich Daněk *Čtyřicet zlosynů a jedno neviňátko* (Prague 1966). (It should be pointed out here that Daněk and Smoček are the only playwrights in this book some of whose plays – not including the one discussed here – are performed on the Czechoslovak stage.)

20 Ibid 12–13, 44. (In Daněk's handling of songs we recognize the influence of Brecht, whose *Caucasian Chalk Circle* he had directed while in charge of the F.X. Šalda Theatre in Liberec from 1953 to 1956.)

21 Ibid 39

22 Ibid 39, 47

23 Peter Weiss *Pronásledování a zavraždění Jana Paula Marata předvedené divadelním souborem blázince v Charentonu za řízení Markýze de Sade* tr Ludvík Kundera (Prague 1966)

24 Helena Šimácková 'Člověk – to je ustavičné tvoření sebe sama' in Daněk *Čtyřicet zlosynů* 78

25 Zdeněk Hořínek 'Paradoxy paraboly' *Divadlo* (April 1966) 56

26 Leszek Kołakowski *Klucz niebieski* (Warsaw 1964) 68. For the English edition, see *The Key to Heaven* tr Salvator Attanasio (New York 1972) 51–2 (also available in French and German translations).

27 Pavlíček *Saška Krist* 102

28 Ibid

29 Daněk *Čtyřicet zlosynů* e.g. 69, 74

30 Milan Kundera, Afterword to *Majitele klíčů* 111

31 Daněk *Čtyřicet zlosynů* 29

32 Dante *The Inferno* tr John Ciardi (New York 1964) 42

9 EAST MEETS WEST

1 Ibsen *Peer Gynt* tr and ed Michael Meyer (New York 1963) 139

2 Cf Max Frisch *Biedermann und die Brandstifter Stücke 2* (Frantfurt/Main 1964) 87–156.

3 Jack Richardson *The Prodigal* (New York 1960) 113; Ionesco *Rhinoceros* 123–4; Havel *Žebrácká opera* 182–3

4 Richardson *The Prodigal* 108, 109

5 Havel *Žebrácká opera* 182

6 Ionesco *Rhinoceros* 93, 98, 99

7 Robert W. Corrigan 'The Disavowal of Identity in the Contemporary Theatre' *The New Theatre of Europe* 2nd ed (New York 1964) 14–15

8 Pirandello *Cosi è (se vi pare)* (Verona 1975) 214; Havel *Žebrácká opera* 175

9 Brecht *Der gute Mensch von Sezuan, Stücke VIII* (Frankfurt/Main 1962) 406

10 Klíma *Ein Bräutigam für Marcella* 27–8
11 Milan Kundera *Ptákovina* 90
12 Antonín J. Liehm *The Politics of Culture* tr Peter Kussi (New York 1973) 131
13 Milan Kundera *Ptákovina* 87
14 Liehm *Politics of Culture* 390
15 Corrigan, Introduction to *The New Theatre of Europe* 27
16 Peter Handke *Stücke I* (Frankfurt/Main 1972) 103
17 Ibid 112, 113
18 Havel *The Garden Party* 50–1
19 Peter Handke *Ich bin ein Bewohner des Elfenbeinturms* (Frankfurt 1972) 54
20 Jan Grossman 'Předmluva' in Havel *Protokoly* 13
21 Esslin *The Peopled Wound* 230
22 Pinter *The Birthday Party* 47–52
23 Klíma *Ein Bräutigam für Marcella* 9, 24, 25
24 Strindberg, Author's Note to *A Dream Play* 193
25 Topol *Kočka* 88, 89
26 Dürrenmatt *Romulus der Grosse* in *Komödien I* (Zürich 1958) 83
27 Stanisław Jerzy Lec *Mysli nieuczesane* (Krakow 1960)
28 Pinter *The Birthday Party* 52
29 Wellwarth *Protest and Paradox* 276
30 Mahler *Mlýn* 99
31 Landovský *Hodinový hotelier* 86
32 Topol *Kočka* 93
33 Ibid 96
34 Smoček *Kosmické jaro* 25
35 Alvin B. Kernan, Introduction to *The Modern American Theatre* (Englewood Cliffs 1967) 2–3
36 See, in the last ten years of *Theater heute* for example, the numerous discussions about the possible moral impact of political or documentary theatre.
37 Serreau *Histoire*
38 This is, of course, a very salutary feature of Eastern European theatre. As one Czech writer put it, literature can be killed by censorship but it can also be killed by commercialism.
39 See note to preface for a comment on *Edice Petlice*.
40 Wellwarth *Protest and Paradox* 291
41 Ibid 276; Raymond Williams *Modern Tragedy* (London 1966) 153; Ernst Wendt *Moderne Dramaturgie* (Frankfurt/Main 1974) 115
42 Although Sládek is a common Czech name, it is used in this case in its original meaning of chief maltster.
43 Havel *Audience* in *Hry 1970–1976* 263

44 Ibid 265–6
45 In an article which appeared simultaneously with my completion of this book
   Pavel J. Trenský expresses the theory that the theme of *Audience*, which had
   been conceived primarily as Havel's personal variation on the theme *odi pro-
   fanum vulgus*, had undergone a change due to the political circumstances in the
   author's society: 'The meaning of this thought had shifted from a principally
   aesthetic area to an ethical one: the moral responsibility of the author is more
   important than his creative effort' ('České drama v exilu' *Proměny* roč. 3 c. 50
   July 1978 38). To this interesting idea I would like to say that Havel is basically
   an ethical writer – almost a moral philosopher – and consistently explores the
   ethical core of any situation about which he writes; and I believe that Havel's
   interest in the play was centered on the character of Sládek rather than the
   autobiographical figure of Vaněk. I find support for this theory in the striking
   analysis of the 'ethics' of Staněk in *Protest* which was written three years after
   Audience.
46 Slawomir Mrożek *The Lion* in *The Elephant* tr Konrad Syrop (New York 1962)
   44, 45
47 Andrey Biely *The Silver Dove* tr George Reavey (New York 1974)
48 Milan Uhde *Hra na holuba* typescript (1976) 85
49 Ibid 68, 83
50 Quoted in Liehm *The Politics of Culture* 141
51 Alexandr Kliment 'Intellektuelle' in *Stunde namens Hoffnung, Almanach
   tschechischer Literatur 1968–1978* (Frankfurt/Main 1978) 166 and 167. The
   volume was collected and edited in Czechoslovakia under the Czech title
   Hodina naděje by the poet and prose writer Jiří Gruša, the playwright Milan
   Uhde, and the prose writer Ludvík Vaculík; it also contains collages by the
   well-known Czech artist and poet Jiří Kolář. The translation into German of
   Kliment's essay is by Pavel Peter.

Playwrights and plays

The plays are listed alphabetically by author: English title (in italics), Czech title, details of première, original publication (book form, followed by journal), and translations. An asterisk signifies an *Edice Petlice* edition.

BLAŽEK, Vratislav (1925–)
   The Third Wish Třetí přání *Première* June 1959, Divadlo Komedie, Prague; *Orig. Pub.* Prague 1960; also in *Divadlo* (Sept. 1960)

DANĚK, Oldřich (1927–)
   Forty Scoundrels and One Innocent Babe Čtyřicet zlosynů a jedno neviňátko *Première* Jan. 1966, Divadlo E.F. Buriana, Prague; *Orig. Pub.* Prague 1966; also in *Divadlo* (March 1966)

HAVEL, Václav (1936–)
   Audience Audience* *Première* (in German) Oct. 1976, double bill with *Vernissage*, Akademietheater des Burgtheaters, Vienna; *Orig. Pub.* in Václav Havel *Hry*; also in *Svědectví* 51 (1976); *Translations* English: *Conversation* tr George Theiner in *Index on Censorship* (autumn 1976); *Audience* tr Vera Blackwell in Václav Havel *Sorry* London 1978; German: *Audienz* tr Gabriel Laub in Václav Havel *Drei Stücke* Reinbek bei Hamburg 1977
   The Beggar's Opera Žebrácká opera* *Première* (Amateur actors; one performance only) Nov. 1975, Horní Počernice, Czechoslovakia; in English March 1976, Teatro Stabile, Trieste; *Orig. Pub.* in Havel *Hry*; *Translation* German: *Die Gauneroper* tr Franz Peter Künzel, duplicated by Rowohlt Theater Verlag, Reinbek bei Hamburg 1974

The Conspirators Spiklenci *Première* (in German) 1974, Theater der Stadt, Baden-Baden; *Orig. Pub.* in Václav Havel *Hry 1970–1976* Toronto 1977; *Translation* German: *Die Retter* tr Franz Peter Künzel, duplicated by Rowohlt Theater Verlag, Reinbek bei Hamburg 1972

The Garden Party Zahradní slavnost *Première* Dec. 1963, Divadlo Na zábradlí, Prague; *Orig. Pub.* in Václav Havel *Protokoly* Prague 1966; also in *Divadlo* (Sept. 1963); *Translations* English: *The Garden Party* tr Vera Blackwell, London 1969; German: *Das Gartenfest* tr August Scholtis in Václav Havel *Zwei Dramen, Essays, Antikoden* Reinbek bei Hamburg 1967

The Increased Difficulty of Concentration Ztížená možnost soustředění *Première* April 1969, Divadlo Na zábradlí, Prague; *Orig. Pub.* Prague 1969; also in *Divadlo* (May 1968); *Translations* English: *The Increased Difficulty of Concentration* tr Vera Blackwell, London 1972; German: *Erschwerte Möglichkeit der Konzentration* tr Franz Peter Künzel in *Theater Heute* 10 Jg. Nr. 1 (Jan. 1969)

The Memorandum Vyrozumění *Première* July 1965, Divadlo Na zábradlí, Prague; *Orig. Pub.* in Václav Havel *Protokoly*; *Translations* English: *The Memorandum* tr Vera Blackwell, London 1967; German: *Die Benachrichtigung* tr Eva Berkmann in Václav Havel *Zwei Dramen*

The Mountain Resort Horský hotel* *Orig. Pub.* in Havel *Hry*; *Translation* German: *Das Berghotel* tr Gabriel Laub, duplicated by Rowohlt Theater Verlag, Reinbek bei Hamburg 1974

Protest Protest *Première* (in German) planned for Nov. 1979, double bill with Pavel Kohout's *Attest*, Burgtheater, Vienna; *Orig. Pub.* (in German) *Protest* tr Gabriel Laub, duplicated by Rowohlt Theater Verlag, Reinbek bei Hamburg 1978

Vernissage Vernisáž *Première* (in German) Oct. 1976, double bill with *Audienz*, Akademietheater des Burgtheaters, Vienna; *Orig. Pub.* in Václav Havel *Hry*; *Translations* English: *Private View* tr Vera Blackwell in Václav Havel *Sorry*; German: *Vernissage* tr Gabriel Laub in Václav Havel *Drei Stücke*

HRUBÍN, František (1910–)

August Sunday Srpnová neděle *Première* April 1958, Činohra Národního divadla v budově Tylova divadla, Prague; *Orig. Pub.* Prague 1958

Oldřich and Božena Oldřich a Božena *Première* Sept. 1968, Divadlo na Vinohradech; *Orig. Pub.* Prague 1969; also in *Divadlo* (Oct./Nov. 1968)

KARVAŠ, Peter (1920–)

Antigone and the Others Antigona a druhí *Première* 1962, Národné divadlo, Bratislava; *Pub.* (in Czech) *Antigona a ti druzí* tr Sergej Machonin, Prague 1962

The Great Wig Velká parochňa *Première* 1964, Slovenské Národné divadlo,

Bratislava; *Pub.* (in Czech) *Velká paruka* tr Vladimír Reis, Prague 1965; also in *Divadlo* (Nov. 1964)

KLÍMA, Ivan (1931–)

(with Pavel Kohout) *America (after Franz Kafka)* Amerika (nach Franz Kafka) *Première* (in German) March 1978, Theater Krefeld; *Orig. Pub.* (in German) *Amerika*, duplicated by Bärenreiter-Verlag Karl Vötterle, Kassel n.d.

A Bridegroom for Marcela Ženich pro Marcelu *Première* (in German) Oct. 1979, Kleines Theater in der Josefstadt, Vienna; *Orig. Pub.* (in German) *Ein Bräutigam für Marcella* in Klíma *Theaterstücke*

Café Myriam Cukrárna Myriam *Première* (in German) Oct. 1969, Kleines Theater in der Josefstadt, Vienna; *Orig. Pub.* Prague 1969; *Translation* German: *Konditorei Myriam* in Klíma *Theaterstücke*

The Castle Zámek *Première* Oct. 1964, Divadlo na Vinohradech, Prague; *Orig. Pub.* Prague 1965; also in *Divadlo* (Sept. 1964); *Translation* German: *Das Schloss* tr Ehrenfried Pospisil in Ivan Klíma *Theaterstücke* Lucerne 1971

The Double Room Pokoj pro dva* *Orig. Pub.* (in German) *Doppelzimmer* in Klíma *Theaterstücke*

Games Hry* *Première* (in German) *Spiele* Oct. 1975, Kleines Theater in der Josefstadt, Vienna; *Orig. Pub.* (in German) *Spiele* tr Gerhard and Alexandra Baumrucker, duplicated by Bärenreiter-Verlag Karl Vötterle, Kassel n.d.

The Jury Porota *Première* April 1969, Komorní divadlo, Prague; *Orig. Pub.* in *Divadlo* (Sept. 1968)

Klara and Two Men Klára a dva páni *Première* (in German) *Klara und zwei Herren* 1971, Akademietheater des Burgtheaters, Vienna; *Orig. Pub.* Prague 1968; *Translation* German: in Klíma *Theaterstücke*, all except *Das Schloss*, tr Gerhard and Alexandra Baumrucker

The Master Mistr *Orig. Pub.* Prague 1967

Thunder and Lightning Hromobití *Orig. Pub.* (in German) *Blitz und Donner* tr Gerhard and Alexandra Baumrucker, duplicated by Bärenreiter-Verlag Karl Vötterle, Kassel n.d.

KOHOUT, Pavel (1928–)

Around the World in Eighty Days Cesta kolem světa za 80 dní *Première* March 1962, Divadlo S.K. Neumanna, Prague; *Orig. Pub.* Prague 1962; *Translation* German: *Reise um die Erde in 80 Tagen* in Kohout *3 Theaterstücke*

August August, august August August, august *Première* May 1967, Divadlo na Vinohradech; *Orig. Pub.* Prague 1968; *Translation* German: *August August, August* in Kohout *3 Theaterstücke*

Bad Luck under the Roof Pech pod střechou* *Première* (in German) double bill with *Fire in the Basement*, Feb. 1974, Stadttheater, Ingolstadt; *Orig. Pub.* (in

German) *Pech unterm Dach* tr Gerhard and Alexandra Baumrucker, theatre program of Stadttheater, Ingolstadt, for première of 15 Feb. 1974
Fire in the Basement Požár v suterénu* *Première* (in German) double bill with *Bad Luck under the Roof*, Feb. 1974, Stadttheater, Ingolstadt; *Orig. Pub.* (in German) *Brand im Souterrain* tr Gerhard and Alexandra Baumrucker, printed theatre program of Stadttheater, Ingolstadt, for première of 15 Feb. 1974
The Good Song Dobrá píseň *Première* March 1952, Divadlo na Vinohradech, Prague; *Orig. Pub.* Prague 1952
Josef Švejk Josef Švejk (based on Hašek's novel) *Première* Dec. 1963, Divadlo na Vinohradech, Prague; *Orig. Pub.* Prague 1966
Poor Murderer Ubohý vrah* *Première* Sept. 1974, Volkstheater, Vienna; *Orig. Pub.* (in English) *Poor Murderer* tr Herbert Berghof and Laurence Luckinbill, Harmondsworth and New York 1977; *Translation* German: *Armer Mörder* tr Gerhard and Alexandra Baumrucker, Lucerne and Frankfurt/Main 1972
Roulette Ruleta* *Première* (in German) August 1975, Stadttheater Luzern; *Orig. Pub.* (in German) *Roulette* tr Gerhard and Alexandra Baumrucker, Lucerne 1975
Such a Love Taková láska *Première* Oct. 1957, Realistické Divadlo, Prague; *Orig. Pub.* in Pavel Kohout *Tři hry* Prague 1958; also Kohout *Taková láska* Prague 1967; *Translation* German: *So eine Liebe* in Kohout *3 Theaterstücke: So eine Liebe, Reise um die Erde in 80 Tagen, August August, August; mit Prolog, Epilog und Intermezzi* plays tr Lucie Taubová, Prologue, Epilogue, and Intermezzi tr Magda Štítná and Felix R. Bossonet, 2nd ed, Lucerne and Frankfurt/Main 1971
The Third Sister Třetí sestra *Première* March 1960, Realistické divadlo, Prague; *Orig. Pub.* Prague 1960; also Prague 1961
War on the Third Floor Válka ve třetím poschodí* *Première* (in German) March 1971, Akademietheater des Burgtheaters, Vienna; *Orig. Pub.* (in German) *Krieg im dritten Stock* tr Gerhard and Alexandra Baumrucker in Kohout *Krieg im dritten Stock, Evol* Lucerne and Frankfurt/Main 1971
War with the Newts Válka s mloky *Première* Jan. 1963, Divadlo na Vinohradech; *Orig. Pub.* in *Divadlo* (Feb. 1963)

KUNDERA, Ludvík (1920–)
Totální kuropění The Total Cock-Crow *Première* June 1961, Mahenovo Divadlo, Brno; *Orig. Pub.* Prague 1962; also in *Divadlo* (Sept. 1961)

KUNDERA, Milan (1928–)
The Blunder Ptákovina *Première* Jan. 1969, Divadlo F.X. Šaldy, Liberec; *Orig. Pub.* in *Divadlo* (Jan. 1969)

The Owners of the Keys Majitelé klíčů *Première* April 1962, Činohra Národního divadla v budově Tylova divadla, Prague; *Orig. Pub.* Prague 1964; also in *Divadlo* (Nov. 1961)

LANDOVSKÝ, Pavel (1936–)
Closed for Disinfection Sanitární noc *Première* (in German) Sept. 1978, Werkstattbühne des Theaters der Stadt, Bonn; *Orig. Pub.* (in German) *Wegen Desinfektion geschlossen* tr Gerhard and Alexandra Baumrucker, duplicated by Bärenreiter-Verlag Karl Vötterle, Kassel n.d.
Rooms by the Hour Hodinový hotelier *Première* May 1969, Činoherní klub, Prague; *Orig. Pub.* in *Divadlo* (Feb. 1969)

MAHLER, Zdeněk (1928–)
The Mill Mlýn *Première* May 1965, Slovenské Narodné divadlo, Bratislava; *Orig. Pub.* Prague 1965; original title *At the Wall* (U zdi), published in *Divadlo* (June 1962)
(with Karel Kraus) *The Rope with Only One End* Provaz o jednom konci (based on Nestroy) *Première* Nov. 1967, Divadlo za bránou, Prague; *Orig. Pub.* Prague 1967

PAVLÍČEK, František (1923–)
The Heavenly Ascension of Saška Krist Nanebevstoupení Sašky Krista *Première* Nov. 1967, Divadlo na Vinohradech, Prague; *Orig. Pub.* Prague 1968; also in *Divadlo* (Nov. 1967)

SMOČEK, Ladislav (1932–)
Cosmic Spring Kosmické jaro *Première* March 1970, Činoherní klub, Prague; *Orig. Pub.* Duplicated by Dilia, Prague 1970
Dr. Bell Burke's Strange Afternoon Podivné odpoledne dr. Zvonka Burkeho *Première* March 1966, Činoherní klub, Prague; *Orig. Pub.* in Smoček *Piknik*; also in *Divadlo* (May 1966)
The Maze Bludiště *Première* March 1966, Činoherní klub, Prague; *Orig. Pub.* in Smoček *Piknik*
Picnic Piknik *Première* March 1965, Činoherní klub, Prague; *Orig. Pub.* in Smoček *Piknik, Podiviné odpoledne dr. Zvonka Burkeho, Bludiště* Prague 1967; also in *Divadlo* (Jan. 1964)

TOPOL, Josef (1935–)
Cat on the Rails Kočka na kolejích *Première* Nov. 1965, Divadlo Za bránou, Prague; *Orig. Pub.* in *Divadlo* (Oct./Nov. 1968)

The End of the Carnival Konec masopustu *Première* Nov. 1964, Národní divadlo, Prague; *Orig. Pub.* Prague 1963; also in *Divadlo* (May 1963)

Goodbye, Socrates Sbohem, Sokrate *Orig. Pub.* (in German) *Auf Wiedersehen, Sokrates* tr Peter Künzel, Frankfurt/Main 1978

An Hour of Love Hodina lásky *Première* Dec. 1968, Divadlo Za bránou, Prague; *Orig. Pub.* in *Divadlo* (Oct./Nov. 1968)

Nightingale for Dinner Slavík k večeři *Première* March 1967, Divadlo Za bránou, Prague; *Orig. Pub.* in *Divadlo* (March 1967)

Their Day Jejich den *Première* Oct. 1959, Činohra Národního divadla v budově Tylova divadla, Prague; *Orig. Pub.* Prague 1962

Two Nights with a Girl Dvě noci s dívkou* *Orig. Pub.* (in German) *Zwei Nächte mit einem Mädchen oder wie man Diebe bestiehlt* tr Lydia Tschakert, duplicated by Universal Edition, Vienna 1972

Wind at Midnight Půlnoční vítr *Première* March 1955, Armádní divadlo, Prague; *Orig. Pub.* Prague 1956

UHDE, Milan (1936–)

King Vávra Král Vávra *Première* (with music by Ladislav Štancl) Feb. 1964, Večerní Brno, Brno; *Orig. Pub.* Prague 1965; also in *Divadlo* (Dec. 1964)

The Whore of the City of Thebes Děvka z města Theby *Première* April 1967, Tylovo divadlo; *Orig. Pub.* in *Divadlo* (May 1967)

A Play about the Dove Hra na holuba*

VOSTRÁ, Alena (1938–)

Eeny, Meeney, Miney, Mo Na koho to slovo padne *Première* Dec. 1966, Činoherní klub, Prague; *Orig. Pub.* in *Divadlo* (Jan. 1967)

On the Knife's Edge Na ostří nože *Première* Dec. 1968, Činoherní klub, Prague; *Orig. Pub.* in *Divadlo* (Dec. 1968)

Index